CW01540533

HEARTSHAPER PRIMARY 2ND EDITION
Published by David C Cook, 4050 Lee Vance Drive Colorado Springs, CO 80918, U.S.A.
Integrity Music Ltd., a division of David C Cook, Brighton, BN1 2RE, United Kingdom.

The graphic circle C logo is a registered trademark of David C Cook. All rights reserved.

Except for brief excerpts for review purposes, no part of this book may be reproduced or used in any form without written permission from the publisher with the exception of the activity pages on which permission is expressly given.

ISBN 978-0-8307-7910-9

© 2019 David C Cook

Scripture quotations (marked NIV) taken from the Holy Bible, New International Version Anglicised Copyright © 1979, 1984, 2011 Biblica. Used by permission of Hodder & Stoughton Ltd, an Hachette UK company. All rights reserved. 'NIV' is a registered trademark of Biblica UK trademark number 1448790.

The David C Cook Team: Ian Matthews, Lynne Humphreys, Mark Prentice, Mary Prentice, Abbie Robson, Judy Gillispie, Lu Ann J. Nickelson, Katie Wetherbee.

Cover Design: beatroot.media   Cover image: Adobe stock

First Edition 2019

0 1 2 3 4 5 6 7 8 9 10

Contents

How to Use HeartShaper®

Welcome to HeartShaper Children's Curriculum!

With HeartShaper Children's Curriculum, children will be engaged in Bible stories through multisensory learning, Bible skill-building, and focused life application.

Here's how to start
- Pray for God's help to guide children to a relationship with Jesus Christ.
- Read these introductory pages and the pages for each session. The leaders' pages will guide you through the session step-by-step.

How the sessions are organised

1 Focus In: Children are introduced to the lesson theme and focus.

2 Explore His Word: Children will interact with the Scripture passage and develop Bible skills.

3 Make It Real: Children will discover how the Scripture applies to their lives.

4 Live It Out: Children will plan and begin to practise the principles of what they've learned.

Downloadable Activity Pages

All of the activity pages in this resource are available to download and print free-of-charge as needed from **www.heartshaper.co.uk**. These are available as both black & white and colour pages.

Important things to know

Scripture lists the passage children will learn in each session.

Focus is the main thought that children will learn and remember in each session.

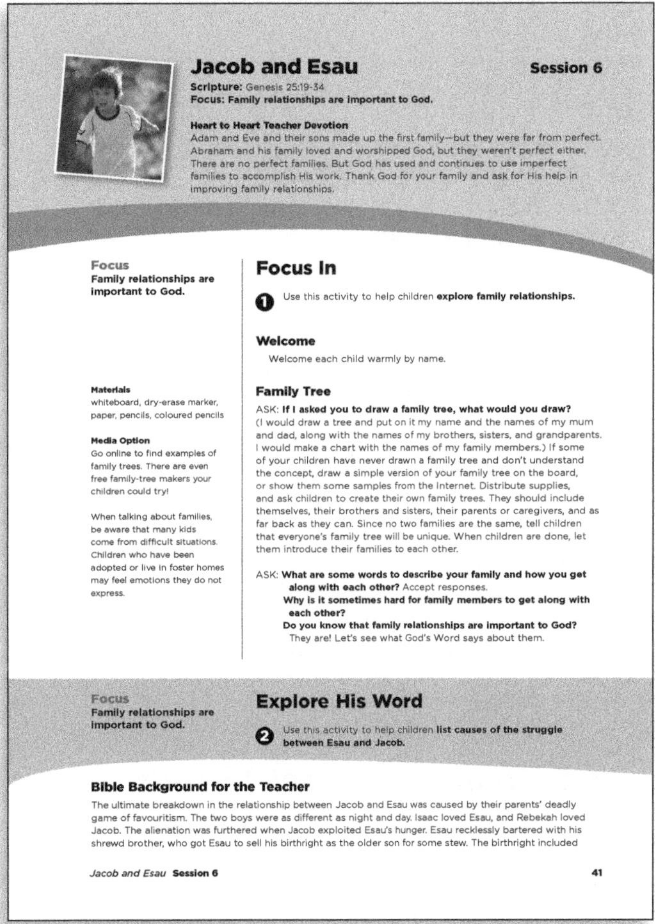

Activities are easy to prepare and teach. Everything you need is contained within this book and activities are included in every step. YOU choose what works best for you and the different kinds of learners in your class. You can do any or all of the photocopiable Activity pages provided for each session.

Teaching Primary Aged Children

With HeartShaper, Primary aged children will grow spiritually

They can know these important facts:
- Only God and Jesus deserve their worship
- Jesus is God's Son; Jesus is their Saviour and friend
- God expects them to obey Him and His Word
- The Bible tells them all they need to know about God and Jesus

They can show these godly attitudes:
- Love God, feel He is special and want to worship Him
- Love Jesus and want to follow His example
- Feel confident and willing to talk about Jesus

They will learn how to:
- Worship God in a variety of ways
- Follow Jesus' example of being a good friend
- Tell others about Jesus
- Pray sentence prayers, asking God for help or forgiveness and thanking Him

With HeartShaper, Primary aged children will develop Bible skills

They will build on these Bible skills:
- Know the Bible is God's special book that tells about God and Jesus
- Know there are two parts of the Bible, an Old Testament and New Testament
- Retell basic facts about main Bible characters
- Begin to sequence events in main Bible stories

They will develop these new Bible skills:
- Begin to understand the major emphasis of the Old and New Testaments
- Know how to find Bible verses
- Begin to read Bible verses
- Develop Bible-reading comprehension skills

Reach children with special needs

HeartShaper gives the resources you need to train teachers and adapt lesson activities so you can include children with special needs in your Sunday school sessions.

Look for this symbol throughout the teacher guide to identify activities that work well for everyone, including those with special needs.

Example

<table>
<tr>
<td>

Speak Up! Prayer Reminders 

SAY: **We can pray and ask for God's help so that we can live boldly for Jesus. Let's make prayer reminders. Then we'll pray to God.** Distribute the Activity page and other supplies. Read the directions and let children make their prayer reminders. Be prepared to provide additional help as needed with fine-motor activities such as cutting and applying tape.

</td>
<td>

Materials
markers, scissors, tape

Craft

</td>
</tr>
</table>

When you see this symbol, it means the activity will work well for all children, including those with special needs, or it may give you a helpful tip on how you can tweak the activity to make it better for those with special needs.

Are you Short on Time?
If you only have a shorter session then you can still use HeartShaper in your Sunday school class. Simply start the session at section 2 (Explore His Word) and jump to section 4 (Live It Out).

Take a Break
If you want to hand out a drink or a snack then the ideal time is between section 3 (Make It Real) and section 4 (Live It Out).

Plan to Be Safe
Know your church's security guidelines and safeguarding policies and follow them. Know the location of first-aid supplies. Before serving snacks, be aware of any allergies children may have. Know where each child's parents or guardians are during the time children are in the session.

Plan to Include All Children
Be sensitive to each child's family situation. If you have a child with disabilities, learn about their special needs. Plan to include the child in all activities and show him or her the unconditional love of Jesus.

Group Management

Preventing Problems
* Develop an atmosphere of love and acceptance.
* Set realistic standards that can be enforced.
* Recognise accomplishments and good behaviour.

Working with a Child with ADD or ADHD
* Give special love and attention.
* Enlist additional helpers.
* Involve the child in primarily quiet activities.
* Minimise distractions, close window blinds or curtains, and move chairs so they are not facing open doors.

Individual Discipline Problems
* Be positive.
* Talk in private.
* Focus on the child's strong points.
* Be flexible.
* Remain calm and overlook unimportant matters.

Working with a Child Who Is Bored
* Challenge the child with a special task.
* Provide choices in things to do and ways to do them.
* Incorporate activities that are of interest.
* Accept the child's feelings.

Working with a Child with Aggressive Behaviours
* Affirm positive behaviour.
* Show them your acceptance.
* Remove them if aggressive behaviour can become harmful to others. Explain the behaviour necessary to return.

Icebreakers

Forming Groups

- Have the children pick numbers when they come into the session. Everyone with the same number sits together that day.

- Give everyone part of a Scripture. They have to find the people with the other parts of the Scripture to form a team.

- Cut old greeting cards into quarters or sixths. Have children find their group by piecing their card back together.

Question of the Day

- Each week post the 'Question of the Day' on a large piece of paper or a whiteboard. Questions could be about favourite foods, activities, books, films, animals, Bible stories, or Bible verses. Encourage children to share their responses with partners or in small groups.

Find a Person

- Prepare a list of 10 to 20 statements describing something about a person. Give the children the list when they come into the session. Give them a certain amount of time to find a person that fits each description and have that person sign their name next to the statement. A person can sign their name only once on a list. Whoever has the most signatures at the end of the set time is the winner. Examples of statements to use: Find someone who likes spinach. Find someone who is wearing jewellery. Find someone who has a younger sister.

The Bible Is God's Word
Session 1

Scripture: Deuteronomy 8:3; 2 Samuel 22:31; Psalm 119:9-16, 89, 105; Isaiah 40:8; 2 Timothy 3:16-17
Focus: The Bible is God's Word.

Heart to Heart Teacher Devotion

A steady light, a nourishing rain, a skillful sword—the Bible uses a wide variety of images to portray its purpose and its use. First Peter 1:25 says, 'The word of the Lord endures forever.' Whatever else changes in our lives, our nation, or our world, we know that the Bible is God's Word—and it will stand forever.

Focus
The Bible is God's Word.

Materials

Activity pages *How Did We Get The Bible* pages 14-15, watch (or stopwatch), whiteboard, dry-erase marker

Teaching Tip
Display the Timeline poster from the back of the book and the teaching posters. The teaching posters can be downloaded from **www.heartshaper.co.uk**
It will help children think about the main focus of each lesson this quarter. Pair up strong readers or older children with younger children so that all can take part in activities which require looking at text.

Focus In

1 Use this activity to help children **explore the Bible.**

Welcome

Welcome each child warmly by name.

How Did We Get the Bible? 

Greet any guests and find out one interesting thing about each child. Distribute the leaflets, and have children turn to the How Did We Get the Bible? activity. Ask children to listen carefully as volunteers read. Then divide the session into two (or more) teams, and have the teams huddle up. SAY: **Let's play the 10-Second Game. When I ask you a question, your team has 10 seconds to answer. You get 100 points for correct answers. If your team doesn't answer correctly in 10 seconds, the other team gets 10 seconds to answer.** Ask questions from How Did We Get the Bible? and keep score on the board. Or instead of making the activity a competition, state facts and have children identify whether the statements are true or false.

ASK: **What do you find surprising about the Bible?** Accept responses. **What questions do you have about the Bible?** If children ask any questions you're not sure about, tell them that you'll research and bring back some answers next week. Tell them to do the same.

SAY: **The Bible is such an amazing book! Did you know that the Bible is the best-selling book of all time?**

Focus
The Bible is God's Word.

Explore His Word

2 Use the activity to help children **discover at least three things God teaches us through the Bible.**

Bible Background for the Teacher

Since God created us, He knows what we need and what is best for us. Through His Word He provides guidelines for a life that will bless us and bring glory to Him. If we follow its directions, which are described as flawless and eternal, God's Word will keep us from stumbling and falling and will always point us in the right direction.

The Bible speaks of itself throughout as the Word of God. It uses such phrases as 'and God said,' 'my word,' and 'the word of the Lord came to me.' Psalm 119 elevates God's Word and helps us remember the place it should have in our lives. The Bible isn't just a good book—the Bible is God's Word!

Bible Exploration

Deuteronomy 8:3; 2 Samuel 22:31; Psalm 119:9-16, 89, 105; Isaiah 40:8; 2 Timothy 3:16-17

Materials

Bibles, Activity page 16 *Dig Deeper* activity, pencils

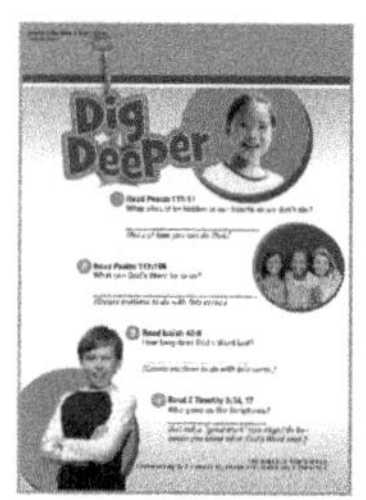

Media Option

Record children acting and doing motions. Let them watch the video before leaving.

SAY: **Today we'll look at some verses from several books in the Bible—some in the Old Testament and some in the New Testament.**

ASK: **How can we find out where books are in the Bible?** (For a printed Bible, look at the contents page in the front of a Bible to find the books. For a Bible on a computer, phone, or e-reader, open the Bible to the contents page.) Have children turn to the contents page in their Bibles.

What's the difference between the Old and New Testaments? (Lots of possible responses: The Old Testament tells about God making the world; tells about people like Noah, Moses, and Abraham; tells about things that happened before Jesus was born; tells how God prepared for salvation. The New Testament tells about Jesus coming to earth and dying on the cross; tells how Christians such as Peter and Paul told about Jesus; helps us know how God wants us to live; tells how God sent and offers salvation.)

SAY: **Let's dig deeper and discover more about God's Word.** Have children turn to the *Dig Deeper* activity. Ask them to form four groups. Two groups will do some acting; the other two groups will create actions. Assign each group a Scripture to read and question to answer. Groups should work together to create actions or do some acting. (If you have a small session, work through the Scriptures as one group.) Circulate among the groups, helping them as needed.

When everyone is ready, ask the first group to read its question and answer it. Ask all children to write in the correct answer. Then have the first group do its acting. The rest of the children can guess what they're doing. Continue in the same manner with the other groups. The groups that created actions can first do their actions while reading the Scripture. Then they can lead the rest of the children in doing the motions. (Answers: 1=God's Word; 2=lamp for our feet and a light on our path; 3=forever; 4=God)

ASK: **How can you either start or continue to hide God's Word in your heart?** (read God's Word, study God's Word by myself and with others, memorise some verses, think about God's Word and what I should do about it, listen to Scripture that is set to music)

Light helps us keep going on the right path. It also helps us so we don't stumble and fall. How can God's Word be a light for you? (It can help me not to do wrong things. It can help me to do right things.)

SAY: **God chose to communicate to us through His Word. Let's remember that the Bible is God's Word and is useful for us every day.**

Make It Real

3 Use this activity to help children to know that the Bible guides our way in life.

Materials
Hidden phone or music player, scarf as a blindfold

The Good Guide

During a break hide a mobile phone or music player somewhere in your room that children won't see easily. Set it to play music but so quietly that everyone would have to be silent to hear it. Ask for two volunteers to be 'guides' and whisper to them the location of the phone playing the music. Ask for a third volunteer to be blindfolded. One guide will tell the blindfolded child carefully and correctly how to reach the music but the other guide will give wrong instructions and distractions.

SAY: **Everyone needs to be very quiet and listen really carefully. Can you hear some music coming from somewhere in our room? These two guides are going to give directions to help <name of child> to find their way to the music. One will be helpful and one isn't.**

Repeat so that others can take turns finding and guiding to the music.

SAY: **As God's Word, the Bible is like a good and helpful guide in our lives. It can point us in the right way on life's journey as we grow. But we need to listen carefully to what God tells us.**

Live It Out

4 Use this activity to help children **make a commitment to read the Bible and learn from it**.

Materials
chocolate chip cookies, toothpicks, napkins, paper plates, Bible

Teaching Tip
Be sure to check about food allergies before using this activity.

Note
This object talk is adapted from *Super Fun Science Multisensory Object Talks from the Psalms* by Heno Head. Copyright © 2011 by Heno Head, Jr. Used by permission.

Strike It Rich!

ASK: **When we really believe something, it causes us to act. If you believe that the Bible is God's Word, what are you going to do about it?** Accept responses.

SAY: **In the old West, people searched for gold. They wanted to strike it rich!** Put a chocolate chip cookie on a plate. **Let's see if we can strike it rich in this mine that's just full of nuggets! Before we do, let's see what Psalm 119:72 says about the value of gold.** Read Psalm 119:72 aloud. **David said that God's Word is more precious, more valuable, than gold or silver.** Use a toothpick to dig out chocolate chips. **Looks like I am striking it rich with some chocolate chips! But you can dig deep and strike it rich every day by reading God's Word.** Let children enjoy some cookies.

SAY: **Think about it—the God of the universe wrote just *one book* for you and me. It's the most important book we can ever read. Let's make a commitment to God that we'll read His Word and learn from it. Let's talk to God about that right now.** Tell children that you'll read some verses from Psalm 119. When you pause, they should silently say those same words to God as a prayer. PRAY: **Dear God, 'I seek you with all my heart.'** Pause. **'Do not let me stray from your commands.'** Pause. **'I have hidden your word in my heart, (pause) that I might not sin against you.'** Pause. **'Your word is a lamp for my feet, a light on my path.'** Pause. **In Jesus' name, amen.**

How Did We Get

1 The Bible was written by about 40 men. They learned about the things they wrote from prophets and angels or dreams and visions from God. They also wrote about things they saw or that other people saw. God told the men what to write. The Holy Spirit also helped them (2 Peter 1:21).

6 Johannes Gutenberg invented the printing press in 1454. For the first time, Bibles were not so expensive. Many were printed in Latin. Now many people could own a Bible. Before the printing press, a Bible cost about a year's salary.

7 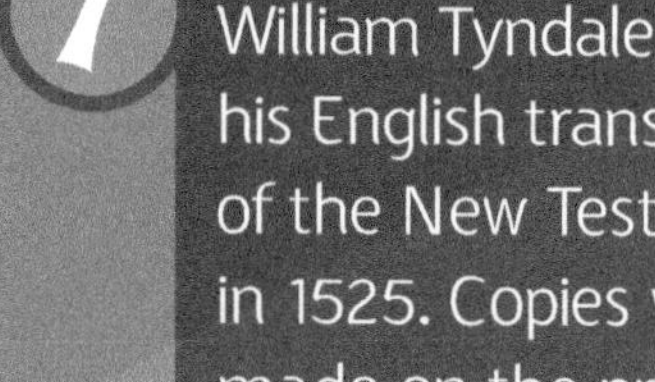
William Tyndale finished his English translation of the New Testament in 1525. Copies were made on the printing press. Some wicked people did not want the Bible translated into English. Tyndale was arrested and killed in 1536 because of his translation.

8 Miles Coverdale finished his English translation of the Bible in 1535. He mainly used Tyndale's work to complete his own. He dedicated the Bible to King Henry VIII. The king allowed the Bible to be sold in England. This was the first *complete* Bible to be printed in the English language.

he **BIBLE?**

2 The 39 Old Testament books were written between 1500 and 400 BC. They tell us how God created the earth and about the history of God's people. Most of the Old Testament was written in Hebrew. Parts were written in Aramaic. These are the books that Jesus called 'the Scriptures' and 'the word of God.'

3 The 27 New Testament books were written in Greek. They were written after Jesus went to Heaven. The last ones were finished before AD 100. They tell about Jesus' life on earth and the beginning of the church.

n Wycliffe translated Bible into English n the Latin translation. finished this in 1382. and his assistants to handwrite the ies they made.

4 The good news of Jesus spread to other countries. People wanted the Bible in their own languages. The Bible was translated into Latin in AD 400.

9 The best-known Bible is the *King James Version*. King James **I** told 54 Bible scholars to work on a new English translation. They finished in 1611.

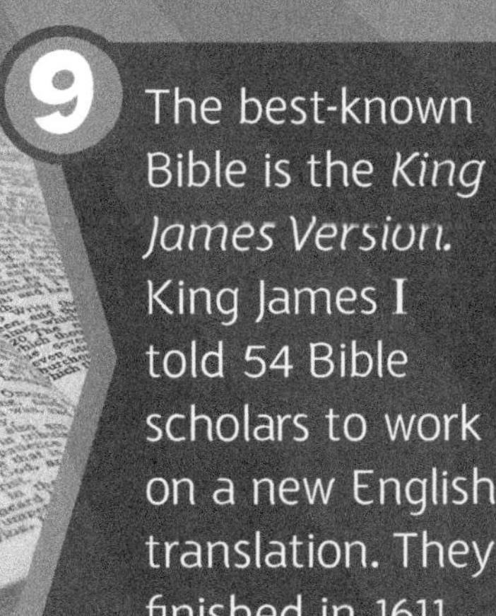

10 Today there are many versions of the Bible in the English language. The entire Bible has also been translated into over 500 other languages.

Dig Deeper

1 **Read Psalm 119:11**
What should be hidden in our hearts so we don't sin?

____

(Act out how you can do that.)

2 **Read Psalm 119:105**
What can God's Word be to us?

____

(Create motions to do with this verse.)

3 **Read Isaiah 40:8**
How long does God's Word last?

____

(Create motions to do with this verse.)

4 **Read 2 Timothy 3:16, 17**
Who gives us the Scriptures?

____

*(Act out a 'good work' you might do
because you know what God's Word says.)*

The Earth Is God's Work

Scripture: Genesis 1:1, 27; 2:1; Psalm 104:5, 10-12, 19, 24-25
Focus: God shows His power through His creation.

Heart to Heart Teacher Devotion

'LORD my God, you are very great; you are clothed with splendor and majesty.' These words from Psalm 104:1 introduce a hymn to the creator. Sometimes we repeat the story of creation so often that we fail to realise God's awesome power, that everything we know and see and touch comes from Him. Let's offer praise and worship to our powerful God!

Focus
God shows His power through His creation.

Materials
modelling dough, paper plates, timer (optional: foil)

 Art

Teaching Tip
If modelling dough is not available, provide sheets of foil to be crumpled and shaped into creations.

 Provide support to children who might struggle with creating a sculpture, and reassure everyone that this is just for fun; no one will be graded!

Focus In

1 Use this activity to help children **experience the vastness of God's creation.**

Welcome

Welcome each child warmly by name.

Clay Creations

Give each child a clump of dough on a paper plate. SAY: **Think about everything God created. Now think about something you really like that God created. You have one minute to form that with your dough. Remember, it must be something that God created.** Set the timer. When one minute is up, have children pair up and guess what each other made. Ask how many were successful in guessing what their partners made. If time permits, let children form something else from God's creation, and have partners guess what was created.

ASK: **Why do you think God created so many different things?** Accept responses.
What do you think is the biggest thing God created?
What do you think is the best thing God created?

SAY: **God's creation is amazing! Let's find out what the Bible says about God the creator and how God shows His power through His creation.**

Focus
God shows His power through His creation.

Explore His Word

2 Use this activity to help children **discover what the Scriptures say about God the creator.**

Bible Background for the Teacher

Creation did not happen by accident or by chance. It was a deliberate act of God. He spoke, and the heavens and the earth came into existence. Not only was everything created by Him (Colossians 1:16), but everything continues to exist by His power (Colossians 1:17; Hebrews 1:3).

God created the earth as a flourishing place to meet all the needs of people and animals. God declared that everything He created was 'good.' But when God crowned His creative acts by making people in His own image and likeness, He said it was 'very good.'

The God who reveals himself in the Bible is the all-powerful creator. His creation is also evidence of His love for us. He alone is worthy of our worship.

Bible Exploration   Genesis 1:1, 27; 2:1; Psalm 104:5, 10-12, 19, 24-25

Before session, write these Scripture references, spaced out, on roll paper: Psalm 104:5; Psalm 104:10-11; Psalm 104:12; Psalm 104:19; Psalm 104:24; Psalm 104:25; Genesis 1:27.

Ask children to open their Bibles to Genesis, the first book of the Bible. SAY: **The book of Genesis tells about the beginning of all things.** Ask children to look at Genesis 1:1, and have a volunteer read that verse aloud. **Our history begins with God making the world and everything in it.**

Ask children to open their Bibles to the contents page. SAY: **Look in the Old Testament listing of books. Find the book of Psalms; then turn to Psalm 104. Let's read more about God's work of creation.** Have volunteers read verses 5, 10-12, 19, 24, and 25 aloud.

SAY: **Look at what God did. He put the earth in place on its foundations. He made the water for animals and birds. He made all the creatures that live in the sea. He made the moon and the sun. These verses aren't a complete list of what God made. But they help us remember how God shows His power through His creation.**

Ask children to turn to Genesis 1:27, and have a volunteer read it aloud. Then have children turn to Genesis 2:1, and have a volunteer read it aloud. Stand by the Bible time line and point to the first icon. SAY: **History—*His* story—began with God's powerful act of creation. He created the sky and everything in it, plants, fish, birds, animals—then He made people. After He made people, His work of creation was done. Only our powerful, awesome God could do what He did.**

Let children illustrate God's creation. Place the prepared roll paper on a table or floor. Assign individual children or pairs of children to illustrate each of the Scripture passages on the paper. When children are done, display the roll paper and let children talk about what they drew.

Have children look at the activity page *Did You Know?* and ask a volunteer to read how God shows His power through creation.

ASK: **Why is God the only one who could create the world?** (God alone has the knowledge and power to create out of nothing.)
What do you think is the most awesome part of God's creation? Accept responses.

SAY: **God's work of creating is beyond our understanding or imagination. But it's clear that God shows His power through His creation. Let's think about ways God's power is seen in our world.**

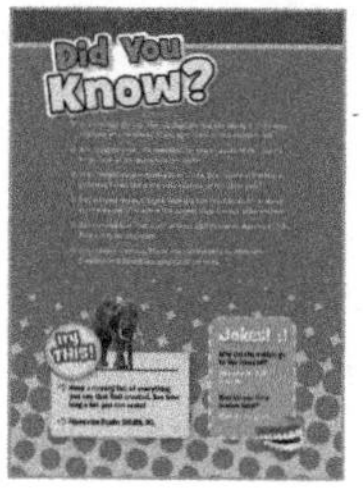

Make It Real

3 Use this activity to help children **explore ways God's power is seen
in our world.**

Materials

Activity pages *God's
Power* page 20-21, pencils 

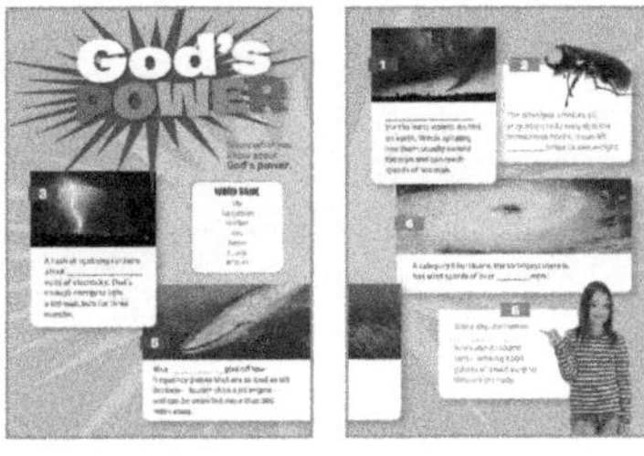

Interesting Facts

Tigers can weigh 225kg or more
and run at speeds of 35–45
mph. Whales can weigh over
90 tonnes. Cheetahs can run
up to 70 mph. Mosquitoes that
carry malaria can kill more than 1
million people each year. Eagles
can dive at 150 mph. Bears can
weigh up to 362kg and run 35
mph.

Media Option

Go online to find photos and
videos of some ways God's
power is seen in our world.

God's Power

SAY: **Let's play a game called What's More Powerful?** Ask children
to stand in a line. **I'll name a pair of things God created. If you think
the first one is the most powerful, take a step forward. If you think the
second one is the most powerful, take a step backward. 1. Tiger; whale.**
After children take a step either way, have them defend their answers.
Use the information from the narrow column to give a factual answer.
Then have children step back to the original line. Do the same with each
of these pairs: 2. **Cheetah; mosquito.** 3. **Eagle; bear.** Add more pairs
if you'd like. **It's hard to know which of these is the most powerful;
they're all powerful in their own ways. But one thing is clear—God
shows His power through His creation in many ways.**

Distribute the activity leaflets *God's Power*. Do the page together as
a session. (Answers: 1=Tornadoes; 2=850; 3=1 billion; 4=13,000; 5=155;
6=whales; 7=heart)

ASK: **What are some other ways God's power is seen in our world?**
    Accept responses.

SAY: **God's power is really amazing! When we stop to think about how
God shows His power through His creation, it should help us want to
worship and praise Him.**

Live It Out

4 Use this activity to help children **worship God the creator.**

Materials

Bibles, paper, pencils,
coloured pencils 

Write

Psalms of Praise 

SAY: **God shows His power through His creation.** Have children turn
in their Bibles to Psalm 104. **The writer of this psalm praised and
worshipped God for being the creator. Look at how the writer started—
by praising the Lord. Look at Psalm 103.** Pause for children to do so. **It
starts the same way. Many of the psalms start by praising God. Now
it's your turn to write a psalm to praise and worship God the creator.**
Distribute supplies. Tell children they can work alone, with a partner, or
in a small group. Encourage them to name some things God created. Tell
them that, if needed, they can get ideas by reading a few psalms in their
Bibles. When children are finished, encourage them to also illustrate
their psalms of praise.

Ask children to silently say their psalms as prayers to God. After a short
time of silence, close in prayer.

God's POWER

Show what you
know about
God's power.

3

A flash of lightning contains
about ___________________
volts of electricity. That's
enough energy to light
a 100-watt bulb for three
months.

WORD BANK

155
Tornadoes
1 billion
850
heart
13,000
whales

5

Blue _____________ give off low-
frequency pulses that are as loud as 188
decibels—louder than a jet engine—
and can be detected more than 500
miles away.

1

_______________________ are the most violent storms on earth. Winds spiraling into them usually exceed 100 mph and can reach speeds of 300 mph.

2

The strongest creature (in proportion to its weight) is the rhinocerous beetle. It can lift _________ times its own weight.

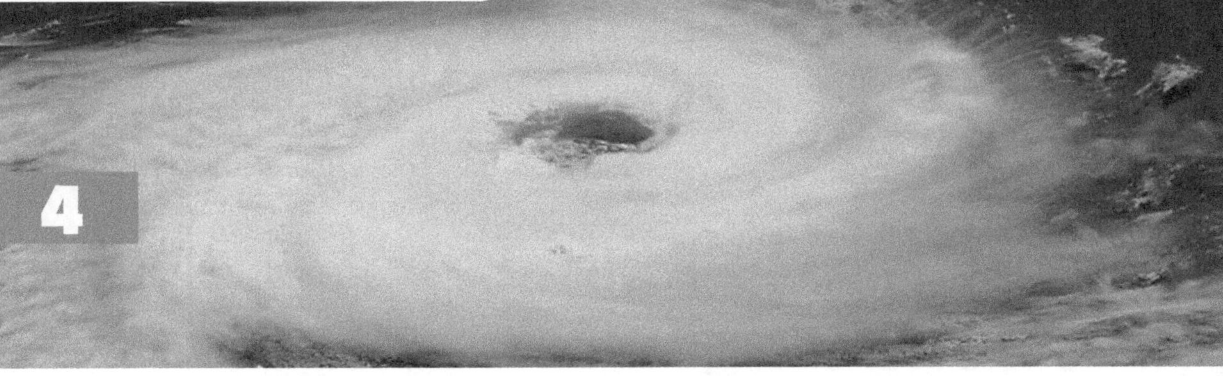

4

A category 5 hurricane, the strongest there is, has wind speeds of over _________ mph.

6

Every day, the human

_______________ beats about 100,000 times, sending 2,000 gallons of blood surging through the body.

Did You Know?

○ God created the sky. During daylight, the sky appears to be blue because air scatters blue sunlight more than it scatters red.

○ God created water. It's essential for life on earth. Water covers 70 percent of the surface of the earth.

○ God created trees—hundreds of kinds. Ever heard of the black gum tree? How about the bald cypress or the plum yew?

○ God created the sun. Light from the sun reaches earth in about eight minutes. The sun is the largest object in our solar system.

○ God created fish. There are at least 20,000 known species of fish. There may be lots more.

○ God created animals. There are estimated to be between 3 million and 30 million species of animals.

try THIS!

⇨ Keep a running list of everything you see that God created. See how long a list you can make!

⇨ Memorise Psalm 119:89, 90.

Jokes! :)

Why did the cookie go to the hospital?

Because he felt crummy!

How do you fix a broken tuba?

With a tuba glue!

The Tower of Babel

Session 3

Scripture: Genesis 11:1-9
Focus: God wants to be first in our lives.

Heart to Heart Teacher Devotion
How you spend your time and your money is also a good indicator of what's important to you. The people who built the Tower of Babel obviously spent their time and money on something that displaced God from being first in their lives—and God was displeased. Resolve to learn from their mistake and keep God first in your life.

Focus
God wants to be first in our lives.

Materials 
2 small glass jars, white rice (enough to fill each *Object Lesson* jar to the top), 2 walnuts in their shells (or 2 golf balls)

Teaching Tips
Continue to display the Timelines and teaching posters. Putting God first is difficult for every human being. Reassure children that God understands this and He always loves us.

Focus In

❶ Use this activity to help children **discover some things that people put first in their lives.**

Welcome

Welcome each child warmly by name.

Room for God 

Begin by placing one walnut into one of the empty jars. SAY: **The walnut represents God's being put first in our lives.** Add the rice. **The rice represents all the other things in our life, important and not so important.** Ask children to notice that when the walnut is placed into the jar first, the rice fills in all around the walnut. **When we put God first, other things can come after that.** Take the second jar and pour the rice in first. Then try to put the walnut into the rice. The walnut will not go entirely into the jar. **When we don't put God first in our lives, it may mean that we won't have much, if any, room for God.**

ASK: **How can you put God first in your life when you're choosing what to watch on TV or what video game to play?** (I wouldn't watch or play something that has bad language in it. I wouldn't watch or play something that my parents don't want me to.)
How can you put God first in your life when you're deciding what to spend your money on? (I could give some of my money to God. I could give some of my money to help those who are in need.)
What's another way you can put God first in your life?

SAY: **When we love God and realise that God wants to be first in our lives, that's right where we'll put Him.**

Focus
God wants to be first in our lives.

Explore His Word

❷ Use this activity to help children **explain the events that occurred at the Tower of Babel.** 

Bible Background for the Teacher

Several generations of Noah's three sons—Shem, Ham, and Japheth—had lived since the flood. But prideful people once again met with God's displeasure. They had not obeyed His command to 'fill the earth' (Genesis 9:1); they were content to go no farther than Shinar. Being of one speech, all humankind egotistically conspired to build a city with a tower. They planned for it to reach to the heavens.

Since stone was scarce in Mesopotamia, mud bricks were baked, and tar was used for mortar. The people's proud intent was to urbanize and make a name for themselves by this titanic enterprise.

Knowing their motives, however, God confounded their efforts by confusing their language so they could not understand one another, thus frustrating and making impossible a united effort. The result was the scattering of people over all the earth, thus fulfilling God's plan. We should honour, worship, and put Him first in our lives if we are to receive the blessings He desires for us to enjoy.

Bible Exploration   Genesis 11:1-9

Ask children to turn in their Bibles to Genesis 11:1-9. SAY: **Let's listen to find out what the people who lived in a place called Shinar were doing.** Ask volunteers to read the verses aloud. **The people were building what's called a ziggurat. A ziggurat is a type of temple-tower. It's square at the bottom and has sloping sides, with steps that lead to a small shrine, or worship area, at the top.**

SAY: **One reason God was displeased was because the people had not obeyed His command to 'fill the earth'** Have a volunteer read Genesis 9:1. **The people at Shinar were content to go no farther than Shinar. Let's see if we can discover what happened.** Ask the session to gather in an open area in your room. Give them the building materials you've brought, and challenge them to pretend to be the people of Shinar, working together to make the tallest ziggurat possible. Encourage them to talk together to plan how to build it and then work together. Remind them that their goal is to build a tower that reaches to the heavens. After a few minutes, call time, and inspect the tower. Then read Genesis 11:3, 4 aloud.

SAY: **Nice tower! But the people of Shinar were trying to reach the heavens. They wanted to be in charge, not God. They wanted to trust in their own skills and abilities, not God. They wanted to put themselves first, not God. God saw what they were doing, that the people were rebelling against Him and His authority. They forgot that God wants to be first in our lives.** Read Genesis 11:5-7 aloud. **God needed to stop man's rebellion against Him. People began speaking different languages.** Tell children that if they know another language, even a couple of words, they should start speaking it and keep it up until you stay to stop. For children who don't know another language, tell them to make one up and start talking. After a short time, tell children to stop talking.

Read verse 8 aloud. Have children get into groups based on the language they were speaking. All those that made up a language can get together in one group. Ask the groups to go to different areas in the room. Read verse 9 aloud. SAY: **Because the people rebelled against God and forgot that God wants to be first in our lives, God confused their language and scattered them over the whole earth.**

SAY: **The people of Shinar found out in a very dramatic way that God wants to be first in our lives. Let's think how we can make sure that God is first in our lives.**

Make It Real

3 Use this activity so that children **discover some ways to put God first in their lives.**

Materials

Activity pages *God Wants to be #1* on pages 26-27, pencils

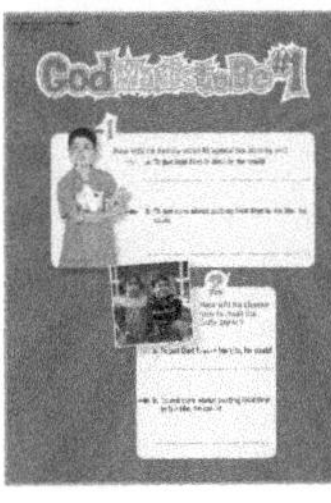
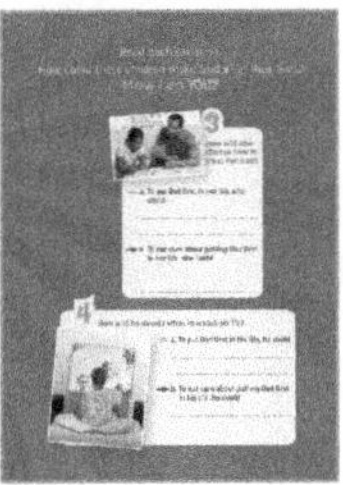

God Wants to Be Number 1

Divide the session into small groups (or have children find partners). Ask each group to form a line, letting groups decide which member will be first, second, and so forth. Don't give any other instructions. After the groups are lined up, ask groups how they decided who would be first. SAY: **Let's think about how we can put God first in our lives.** Have children sit down and turn in their activity leaflets to God Wants to Be #1. Ask children to look at the first situation. Read the question aloud.

ASK: **What is something he could do to put God first in his life?** (He could give some of his money to God. He could give some of his money to help those who are in need.)

What is something he could do if he didn't care about putting God first in his life? (He could spend all the money on himself. He could use his money for something that his parents and God wouldn't be very happy about.)

Have children get into their small groups again, and assign each group one of the situations to work on. Tell the groups that they can either tell how they would finish the two sentences or act out ways to finish them. When the groups are done, let each group either report how they finished the sentences or do their acting. Encourage all the children to finish the sentences as they're talked about. SAY: **When we love God and realise that God wants to be first in our lives, that's right where we'll put Him.**

Focus
God wants to be first in our lives.

Live It Out

4 Use this activity to help children **choose to put God first in their lives.**

Materials

Activity page *Take the Challenge* on page 28, pencils (optional: audio player and praise music from your collection)

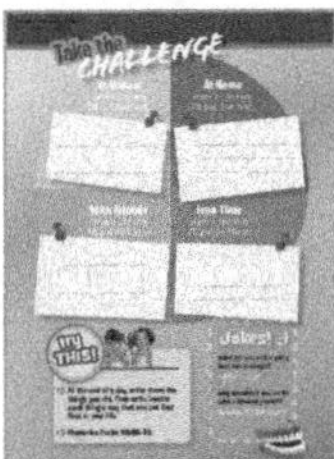

Take the Challenge

SAY: **The people of Shinar chose to put themselves first, not God. What's your choice?** Have children turn in their activity leaflets to *Take the Challenge*. **Here's your challenge: put God first at school, at home, when you're with friends, and when you have free time. In other words, I hope you take the challenge to put God first *all* the time.** Encourage children to write on the lines how they plan on putting God first in their lives in each situation. If you like, play some praise music while children work.

When children are done, ask them to bring their activity leaflets with them to the closing prayer circle. SAY: **Look at what you just wrote. God wants to be first in our lives. A great way to keep God first in our lives is to pray and talk to Him often.** After a short time of silent prayer, close in prayer.

God Wants to Be #1

1

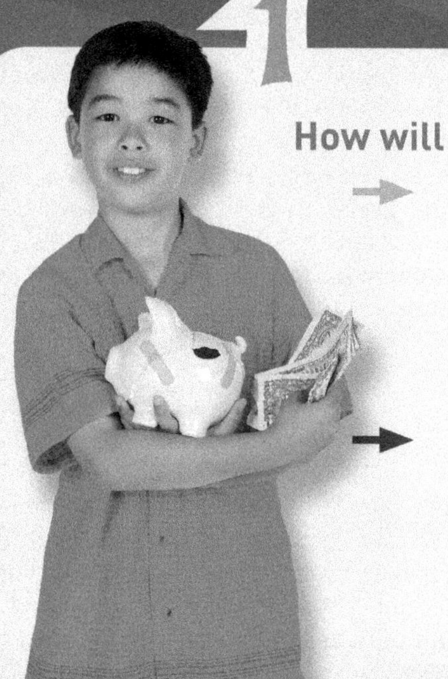

How will he decide what to spend his money on?

➡ a. To put God first in his life, he could

____

____

➡ b. To not care about putting God first in his life, he could

____

____

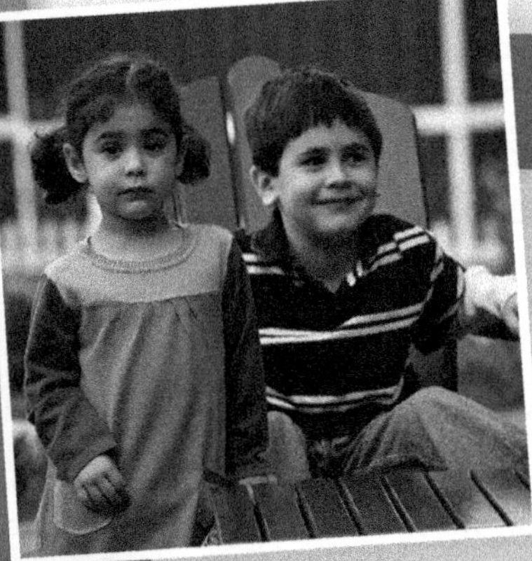

2

How will he choose how to treat his little sister?

➡ a. To put God first in his life, he could

____

____

➡ b. To not care about putting God first in his life, he could

____

____

Read each situation.
How could these children make God #1 in their lives?
How can YOU?

3

How will she choose how to treat her dad?

→ a. To put God first in her life, she could

____

____

➤ b. To not care about putting God first in her life, she could

____

____

4

How will he decide what to watch on TV?

→ a. To put God first in his life, he could

____

____

➤ b. To not care about putting God first in his life, he could

____

____

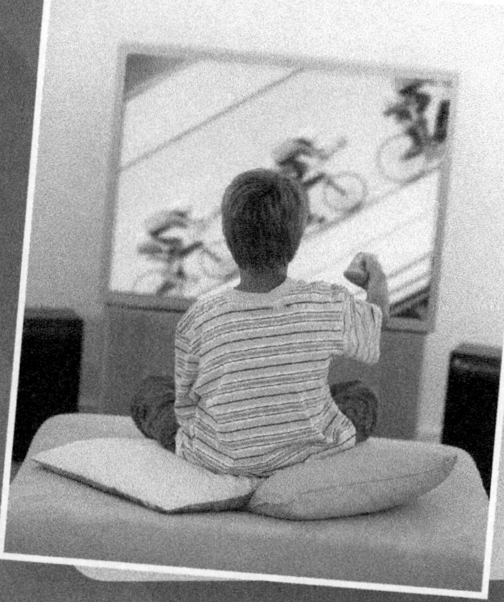

HeartShaper Preschool Yellow Edition, Activity page
Permission is granted to reproduce this page for ministry purposes only—not for resale.

Take the CHALLENGE

At School
Here's one way
I'll put God first:

____

____

At Home
Here's one way
I'll put God first:

____

____

With Friends
Here's one way
I'll put God first:

____

____

Free Time
Here's one way
I'll put God first:

____

____

try THIS!

➡ At the end of a day, write down the things you did. Then write beside each thing a way that you put God first in your life.

➡ Memorise Psalm 119:89-90.

Jokes! :)

What do you call a pony that has a cough?

A little hoarse!

Why shouldn't you write with a broken pencil?

Because it's pointless!

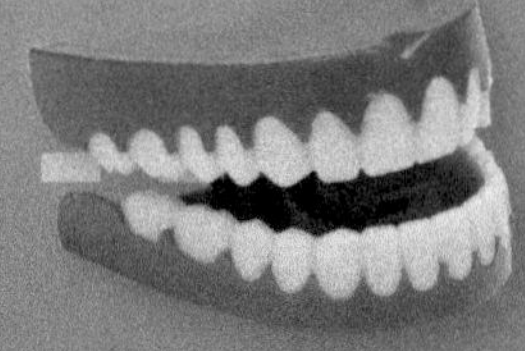

The Birth of Isaac

Session 4

Scripture: Genesis 17:1-9, 15-16; 18:1-14; 21:1-3
Focus: God keeps His promises.

Heart to Heart Teacher Devotion
An assurance, pledge, vow, guarantee, commitment, contract, covenant—all synonyms of the word *promise*. It's great when businesses honour their guarantees and we love it when friends keep their assurances to us. But our ability to keep promises can't stand up against God's. He's the greatest promise keeper of all! God keeps His promises—always has, always will.

Focus In

(1) Use this activity to help children **explore the importance of keeping promises.**

Welcome

Welcome each child warmly by name.

I Promise

Have children sit in a circle while you stand in the middle. SAY: Today we are going to learn about promises. Let's try to keep a promise. Please say this promise with me: 'I promise that I won't laugh.' Allow the children to respond, and then explain that you are going to try to get them to break their promise. Show silly pictures or read jokes aloud. When a child laughs, ask him to help you make the others laugh. Allow the child to choose from the prepared pictures and joke cards. Emphasise that promises can be hard to keep. Point out that God never breaks one of His promises to us.

SAY: **Although these were silly promises for a game, real promises are important to keep.**

ASK: **What happens when someone makes a promise but doesn't keep it?** Accept responses.

SAY: **Let's find out whether or not God kept a promise that He made long ago to a man and his wife.**

Materials
Pictures of people or animals doing silly things, jokes printed on index cards

Game

Explore His Word

(2) Use this activity to help children **tell about the promises God made to Abraham and Sarah.**

Bible Background for the Teacher

When Abram was 75 years old, God made him a promise that he would be the father of a great nation through which all people on earth would be blessed. As time passed, Abram got older and Sarai remained childless. Abram and Sarai wrongly thought they could fulfill God's promise of a child through a surrogate mother, Hagar, Sarai's maidservant.

The Lord reiterated the promise through three men who appeared at Abraham's tent. Abraham urged them to accept his hospitality. Because it was hot and dusty, he provided them with water so they could wash their feet. He then served them a lavish meal. At that time, God revealed that by the same time next year Sarah would have a son. Sarah was eavesdropping. When she heard the announcement, she laughed because she was well past the age of childbearing. But Abraham and Sarah were to learn that nothing was impossible for God. Sarah, at the age of 90, gave birth to a son. She named him Isaac.

Bible Exploration   Genesis 17:1-9, 15-16; 18:1-14; 21:1-3

Ask a volunteer to stand by the Bible time line and tell what the first four icons stand for. SAY: **Sometime after the building of the Tower of Babel, God called Abram to leave his home and travel to where God wanted him to go. Abram obeyed God. This is where we pick up God's story.** Ask children to turn in their Bibles to Genesis 17:1. Ask a volunteer to read the verse aloud. SAY: **Let's find out about the promise God made to Abraham and his wife Sarah.** Choose two children to write on the board the promises they hear God make. Divide the rest of the session into three groups, and have the groups huddle up. One group is to listen for times when God speaks. Whenever they hear something that God is going to say, they should say, 'God promised.' The second group should listen for times Abraham speaks or is referred to. When they hear Abraham's name or Sarah's name, they should say, 'I'm trusting You, God.'

Read Genesis 17:1-9 and 15-16. Be sure to pause after *God, Abraham,* and *Sarah* so that the groups can respond. Make sure that the volunteers write all God's promises on the board. Then read Genesis 18:1-14 and Genesis 21:1-3. When finished, thank everyone for participating. Then direct children' attention to the board. SAY: **Look at all the promises God made to Abraham and Sarah.**

ASK: **What do you think are the biggest promises God made to Abraham and Sarah?** (that Abraham would be the father of many nations; that they would have a son even though they were old)

Have children turn to Activity page *God's Promises.* Let them pair up to complete the four questions. When children are done, have volunteers read the sentences and fill in the blanks. (Answers: 1=father; 2=son; 3=kings; 4=Sarah)

ASK: **How do you know that God kept His promise that Abraham and Sarah would have a son?** (Isaac was born to them.)

SAY: **Abraham and Sarah found out that nothing is too hard for the Lord and that God keeps His promises—every one of them!**

Materials
Timeline poster on page 32, Bibles, whiteboard, dry-erase markers, Activity page *God's Promises* on page 33, pencils

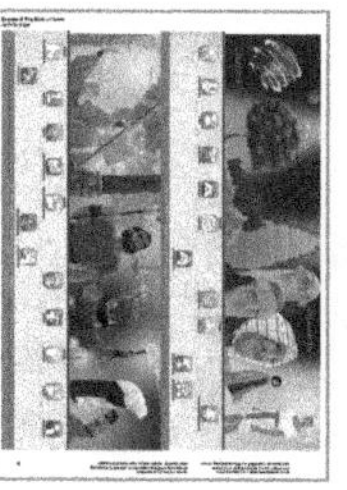
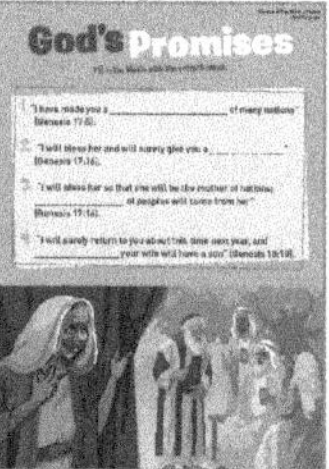

Teaching Tip
If you have a small session, listening assignments can be given to individuals or pairs of children.

Make It Real

3 Use this activity to help children **discover promises that God has kept.**

Focus
God keeps His promises.

More of God's Promises

SAY to a child: **I promise to give you ____** (name something you have available). Give that item to the child. Say to another child: **I promise to give you ____** (name something else you have available). Then give it to the child. Say to another child: **I promise to give you ____** (name something else you have available). Then give it to the child.

Materials
Activity page *More of God's Promises* on page 34, pencils, items in your room, Bibles

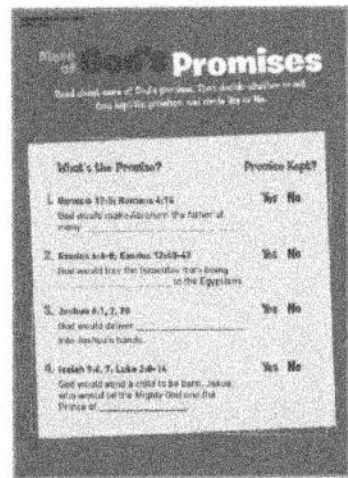

Teaching Tip

If you have a small session, have children work in pairs or do this activity as one group.

 You may want to assign roles within the groups: Scripture readers, listeners who will complete the open-ended sentences, decision makers for Promises Kept? choices. Work through the first set of Scriptures and be sure each person understands what he or she is to do.

ASK: **If I were to keep on making promises, would you believe my promises? Why or why not?** (Yes, because you kept your promises so far.)

SAY: **Let's think about the promises God has made and discover whether or not He has kept His promises.** Have children turn in their activity leaflets to More of God's Promises. Divide the session into four small groups, and assign each group one of the Scripture passages to read, fill in the blank, and then decide whether or not God kept His promise. When groups are ready, ask each group to read its completed sentence and tell whether or not God kept that promise. (Answers: 1=nations; 2=slaves; 3=Jericho; 4=Peace; God has kept all His promises!)

SAY: **Because of God's faithfulness in keeping promises in the past, we can believe that God keeps His promises—both now and forever!**

Live It Out

4 Use this activity to help children to **thank God for keeping His promises**.

Materials

whiteboard, dry-erase marker, Bibles, 4 lengths of roll paper, markers  Art

Promise Posters

Write the following Scripture references on the board: Genesis 9:11-16; Exodus 6:6-8; Joshua 6:1-2; Isaiah 9:6-7. SAY: **Each of these Scripture passages tells about a promise that God made to someone or about someone.** Divide the session into four groups (or have children work with partners), and assign each group one of the Scripture passages. Each group should look up their Scripture passage, read it, and make a poster about the promise of God they read about. Their challenge is to use only five words or less to summarise God's promise and draw only one or two symbols or simple drawings to represent God's promise. The groups should also be prepared to tell whether or not God kept that promise. Encourage all children to participate in their groups in some way.

When groups are done, ask the members of the Genesis 9 group to show their poster and tell about it. Ask them whether or not God kept that promise, and how they know whether He did or not. Have the other groups do the same.

Let's thank God right now for His promises and for keeping them. PRAY: **Dear God, thank You for the promise of hearing us when we pray. And thank You for always keeping Your promises. In Jesus' name, amen.**

CREATION
THE FALL
PATRIARCHS
ISRAELITES IN EGYPT
Creation
Garden of Eden
Noah
Tower of Babel
Abram's call
2067 BC
Isaac born
Abraham tested
Jacob & Esau
1899 BC
Joseph sold
Joseph in Egypt
Joseph forgives
Slavery in Egypt 400 years
GOD PREPARES FOR SALVATION
Art by Gustavo Mazali
Sheet 2, Fall, Middle Elementary Resources, HeartShaper® Curriculum
THE EXODUS
CONQUEST
JUDGES
1446 BC
Moses' birth & call
Moses & Aaron
Passover
Exodus
Ten Commandments
Joshua succeeds Moses
1406 BC
Crossing the Jordan
Joshua & Jericho
Deborah
Gideon
Ruth & Boaz
1100 BC
Samuel
Saul anointed
GOD PREPARES FOR SALVATION
Art by Gustavo Mazali
Sheet 2, Fall, Middle Elementary Resources, HeartShaper® Curriculum

God's Promises

Fill in the blanks with the correct words.

1. 'I have made you a _________________________ of many nations' (Genesis 17:5).

2. 'I will bless her and will surely give you a _______________' (Genesis 17:16).

3. 'I will bless her so that she will be the mother of nations; _________________ of peoples will come from her' (Genesis 17:16).

4. 'I will surely return to you about this time next year, and _______________ your wife will have a son' (Genesis 18:10).

HeartShaper Preschool Yellow Edition, Activity page
Permission is granted to reproduce this page for ministry purposes only—not for resale.

More of God's Promises

Read about more of God's promises. Then decide whether or not God kept His promises, and circle Yes or No.

What's the Promise?	Promise Kept?

1. Genesis 17:5; Romans 4:18   Yes   No

God would make Abraham the father of many ________________________________.

2. Exodus 6:6-8; Exodus 12:40-42   Yes   No

God would free the Israelites from being ________________________ to the Egyptians.

3. Joshua 6:1, 2, 20   Yes   No

God would deliver ________________________ into Joshua's hands.

4. Isaiah 9:6, 7; Luke 2:8-14   Yes   No

God would send a child to be born, Jesus, who would be the Mighty God and the Prince of ____________________.

Abraham Is Tested

Session 5

Scripture: Genesis 22:1-19
Focus: God can be trusted.

Heart to Heart Teacher Devotion
Abraham discovered that God's tests are not always predictable. You'll probably discover that too. Abraham's faith and trust in God pulled him through one of the biggest challenges he would ever face. The same kind of faith and trust in God will pull you through life's challenges. We serve a God who is worthy of our trust.

Focus
God can be trusted.

Materials
Activity page *It Takes Trust* on page 40, paper, pencils

Discuss

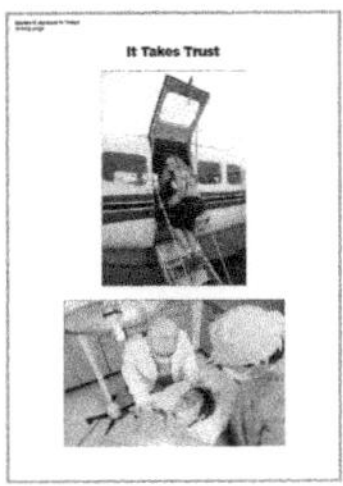

Before starting this activity, define *trust* and give a few concrete examples that clarify the concept.

Focus In

❶ Use this activity to help children **explore the concept of trust.**

Welcome

Welcome each child warmly by name.

It Takes Trust

Divide the session into two groups. Give each group one of the pictures from the activity page, along with paper and pencils. SAY: **Look at your picture. Think together about all the aspects of trust that might be needed by the person involved in your situation. Make the biggest list of things that you can.** After several minutes, let each group show its picture and name all the aspects of trust that they came up with. (Possible responses: The girl getting on the plane would trust that the airplane would fly; trust that the pilot could safely fly the plane, etc. The person in the operating room would trust that the doctors know what they're doing; that the instruments used on her would be sterile; that she would come through the operation, etc.)

ASK: **What is a situation you've been in when you had to have trust?**
Accept responses.
What do you mean when you say that you trust someone? (I believe that person will tell the truth; I know that person will do what she says she will do.)

SAY: **Let's keep thinking about trust as we discover what the Bible says about it.**

Focus
God can be trusted.

Explore His Word

❷ Use these activities to help children **examine how Abraham trusted God.**

Bible Background for the Teacher

After Abraham's lengthy stay in the land of the Philistines, the true nature of his faith was tested by God (Hebrews 11:17-18). By now Isaac was probably a teenager. God's instruction to Abraham was to take his much-loved son and sacrifice him as a burnt offering. The location of the site of the sacrifice would eventually become the site of the temple in Jerusalem, Mt. Moriah (2 Chronicles 3:1).

Isaac's submissiveness to his father is noted by the fact that he permitted himself to be bound and laid on the altar. But Abraham's hand was stopped by God, and in place of his son, Abraham offered up a ram, which had been caught by its horns in a nearby thicket. So Abraham's faith stood the test as proved by his obedience (James 2:21-22). God renewed His promise to Abraham as to the numerous descendants he would have and that through them all nations would be blessed. Here allusion is made to Jesus, who would come as the Saviour of the world (Acts 3:25; Galatians 3:8).

Bible Exploration   Genesis 22:1-19

ASK: **What have we been learning about *history*?** (It's *His* story. It's God's story.)

Ask a volunteer to stand beside the Bible time line and tell about the first six icons. Then SAY: **Though Abraham and Sarah were very old, God blessed them with a son named Isaac. This is where we pick up God's story.** Ask children to turn in their Bibles to Genesis 22:1. Have a volunteer read that verse aloud. Direct children's attention to the map. Have a volunteer find Mt. Moriah and Beersheba on the map. **These places are mentioned in today's Bible story.**

Divide the session into two groups; one group will be the Abraham group, the other group will be the Isaac group. Have the children in each group sit together. **The Scripture we're studying today tells about the time when Abraham was asked to do something hard—very hard. When I pause from reading the Scripture verses, the Abraham group or the Isaac group or both groups should show on your faces what Abraham or Isaac might have been feeling, and/or pantomime what they were doing.**

Read Genesis 22:1-19, pausing frequently for children to show on their faces what Abraham and Isaac might have been feeling and/or pantomime what they were doing. As needed, prompt the groups to respond appropriately. When finished, thank everyone for their participation.

Distribute the activity leaflets and pencils, and have children look at Abraham Is Tested. Read the directions aloud, and do the page together. (Answers: 1=Isaac; 2=lamb; 3=God; 4=trusted; 5=ram; 6=bless)

ASK: **How did Abraham trust God?** (He trusted that God would provide a ram for the offering.)
Because Abraham trusted and obeyed God, what did God promise him? (to bless him, to make his descendants as numerous as the stars in the sky and sand on the seashore, through his offspring all nations would be blessed)
How would all nations, all people, be blessed through the descendants of Abraham? (Jesus would come as the Saviour of the world.)

SAY: **God told Abraham to do a hard thing—maybe the hardest thing a person could do. But Abraham trusted God so much that he did exactly as God had told him to. Abraham knew that God can be trusted, even though Abraham didn't know how things would turn out. That can be true in our lives too. God may ask us to do a hard thing or something that we don't quite understand. That's when we need to remember that God can be trusted. Let's think more about that.**

Materials

Activity page *Abraham is Tested* on page 38, Bibles, *Old Testament Map* on page 325, pencils

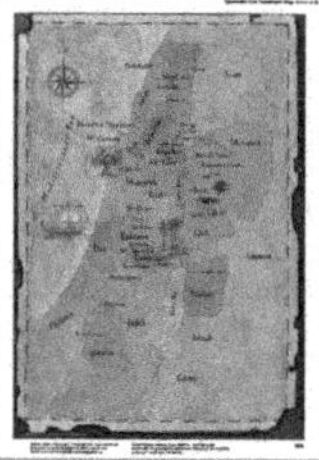

Media Option

Go to www.biblegateway.com and play a dramatised reading of the Bible verses.

Make It Real

3 Use this activity to help children **realise that they can trust God**.

Materials
Activity page *Trusting God* on page 39

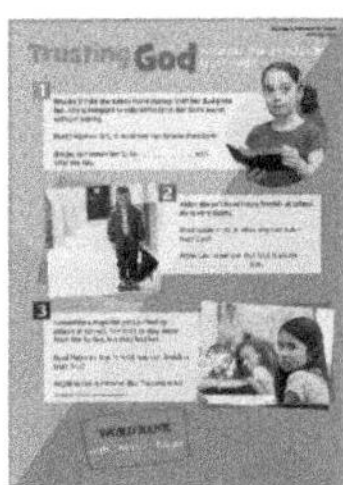

Trusting God

SAY: **Even though most of us could probably be trusted a lot of the time, there's only one person who can be trusted *all* the time.** Have children turn to Activity leaflets *Trusting God*. Get children into small groups (or find partners), and assign one of the situations to each group. Tell groups to read their situations, look up the Scriptures, and finish the sentences. When groups are finished, let them read their situations and Scriptures aloud and finish their sentences. Encourage everyone to finish their sentences. (Answers: 1=God; 2=content; 3=helper; 4=fears; 5=with)

SAY: **These are ways that you and I can also trust God. No matter the situation we find ourselves in, it's so great to know that God can be trusted!**

Focus
God can be trusted.

Live It Out

4 Use this activity to help children **choose to put their trust in God**.

Materials
masking tape, paper, blindfolds, Bibles, whiteboard, dry-erase marker

Game

Teaching Tip
Make sure children know that *anxiety* means 'a fearful concern.'

Trust Walk is good for engaging children, but the activity may be difficult for a child with sensory challenges. Allow children to choose whether they will participate in the activity or observe as the actions are performed by others in the session.

Trust Walk

Use tape to mark off a large square on the floor, and put several sheets of paper inside the square.

Have children pair up, and invite two or three pairs of children to stand along one side of the square. Help one child in each pair to put on a blindfold. The partners without blindfolds can stand anywhere they want to outside the square. SAY: **The object of this game is for the person who is not blindfolded to direct his or her blindfolded partner to reach the other side without stepping on any paper. If a blindfolded partner steps on paper, that pair is out. The blindfolded partners must listen to and trust whatever their partners say to do. Ready, go!** Repeat until all the pairs have had a turn. Then have children sit down. **There are a lot of people we can trust, but there's no one but God we can trust all the time.**

Ask children to turn in their Bibles to Psalm 56:3-4, and have volunteers read those verses aloud. Ask children to tell when we can trust God (when afraid). Write 'afraid' on the board. Continue in the same manner with these verses: Philippians 4:19 (write 'needs' on the board); Hebrews 13:5b (write 'when feeling alone' on the board); 1 Peter 5:7 (write 'anxiety' on the board). SAY: **When you're afraid, feel alone, have needs, or are anxious, remember to trust God. Only God can be trusted all the time.**

SAY: **Let's finish our time with a moment to be silent.**
After a short time of silence, close with prayer, thanking God for the example of Abraham and asking for His help in trusting Him in every situation.

✓Abraham is Tested.

Fill in the blanks and show what you know! For help, see the Word Bank.

1 God told Abraham to take _______________ to the region of Moriah and offer him as a sacrifice.

2 Abraham said, '_______________ will provide the lamb.'

3 Abraham _______________ and obeyed God.

4 God provided a _______________ for the sacrifice.

5 God said to Abraham, 'I will _______________ you, and through your offspring all nations on earth will be blessed.'

WORD BANK

trusted	bless
Isaac	God
ram	

Trusting God

How can these children trust God?

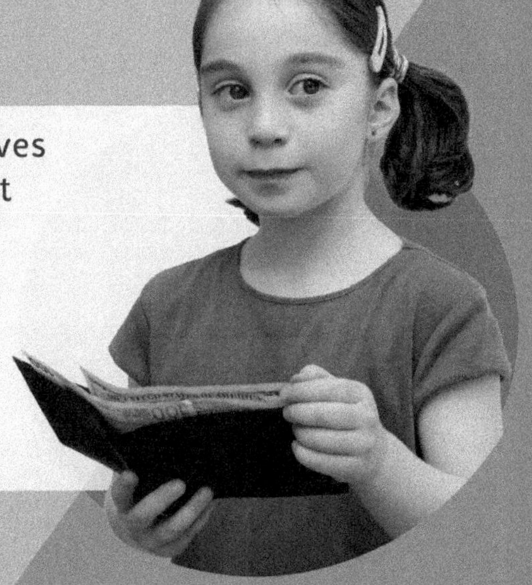

1

Brooke thinks she needs more money than her dad gives her. She is tempted to take some from her dad's wallet without asking.

Read Hebrews 13:5. In what way can Brooke trust God?

Brooke can remember to be _______________ with what she has.

2

Aiden doesn't have many friends at school. He is very lonely.

Read Isaiah 41:10. In what way can Aiden trust God?

Aiden can remember that God is always _______________ him.

3

Sometimes Angelina gets bullied by others at school. She tries to stay away from the bullies, but they find her.

Read Hebrews 13:6. In what way can Angelina trust God?

Angelina can remember that the Lord is her _______________.

WORD BANK

with   helper   happy

It Takes Trust

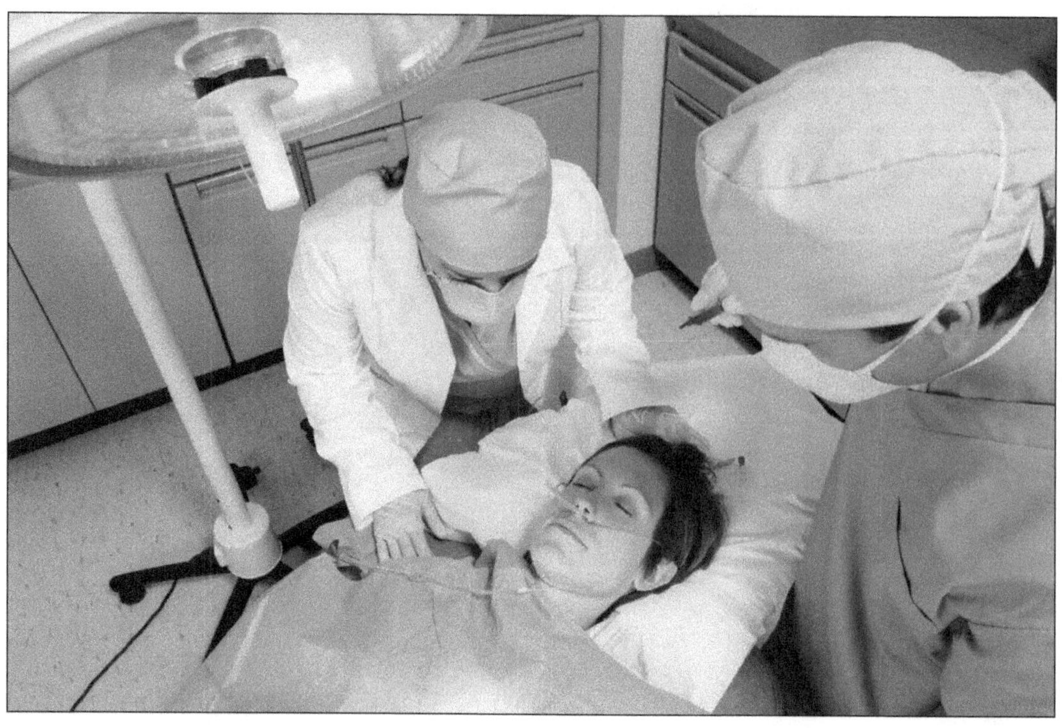

HeartShaper Preschool Yellow Edition, Activity page
Permission is granted to reproduce this page for ministry
purposes only—not for resale.

Rather than photocopy this page you can download
and print all activity pages in both colour and
black & white from **www.heartshaper.co.uk**

Jacob and Esau

Scripture: Genesis 25:19-34
Focus: Family relationships are important to God.

Heart to Heart Teacher Devotion
Adam and Eve and their sons made up the first family—but they were far from perfect. Abraham and his family loved and worshipped God, but they weren't perfect either. There are no perfect families. But God has used and continues to use imperfect families to accomplish His work. Thank God for your family and ask for His help in improving family relationships.

Focus
Family relationships are important to God.

Materials
whiteboard, dry-erase marker, paper, pencils, coloured pencils

Media Option
Go online to find examples of family trees. There are even free family-tree makers your children could try!

When talking about families, be aware that many kids come from difficult situations. Children who have been adopted or live in foster homes may feel emotions they do not express.

Focus In

 Use this activity to help children **explore family relationships.**

Welcome
Welcome each child warmly by name.

Family Tree
ASK: **If I asked you to draw a family tree, what would you draw?**
(I would draw a tree and put on it my name and the names of my mum and dad, along with the names of my brothers, sisters, and grandparents. I would make a chart with the names of my family members.) If some of your children have never drawn a family tree and don't understand the concept, draw a simple version of your family tree on the board, or show them some samples from the Internet. Distribute supplies, and ask children to create their own family trees. They should include themselves, their brothers and sisters, their parents or caregivers, and as far back as they can. Since no two families are the same, tell children that everyone's family tree will be unique. When children are done, let them introduce their families to each other.

ASK: **What are some words to describe your family and how you get along with each other?** Accept responses.
Why is it sometimes hard for family members to get along with each other?
Do you know that family relationships are important to God?
They are! Let's see what God's Word says about them.

Focus
Family relationships are important to God.

Explore His Word

2 Use this activity to help children **list causes of the struggle between Esau and Jacob.**

Bible Background for the Teacher

The ultimate breakdown in the relationship between Jacob and Esau was caused by their parents' deadly game of favouritism. The two boys were as different as night and day. Isaac loved Esau, and Rebekah loved Jacob. The alienation was furthered when Jacob exploited Esau's hunger. Esau recklessly bartered with his shrewd brother, who got Esau to sell his birthright as the older son for some stew. The birthright included the inheritance rights of the firstborn and, more importantly, the covenant promises that God had made to Abraham and Isaac.

But God's purpose was not frustrated by the evil schemes of people. In His power He used them to accomplish His eternal plan.

Bible Exploration   Genesis 25:19-34

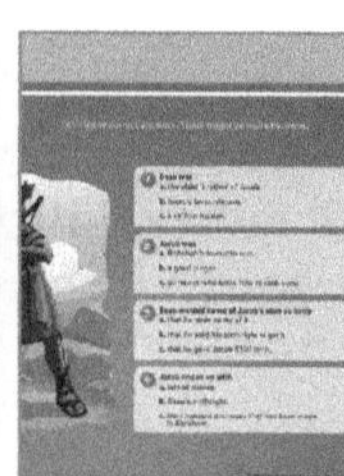

Ask children to open their Bibles to Genesis, the first book of the Bible. Ask them to explain what the book of Genesis is about (the beginning of all things, the history of how the world began). Ask a volunteer or two to stand by the Bible time line and tell about the first seven icons.
SAY: **This is where we pick up God's story.** Have children turn to Genesis 25, and have a volunteer read verse 19 aloud. Write 'Abraham' on the board. Write 'Isaac' below 'Abraham,' drawing an arrow from Abraham to Isaac. Have another volunteer read verse 20 aloud. Ask children to name the woman who became Isaac's wife. Write 'Rebekah' beside 'Isaac.'

Read the first sentence of verse 21. SAY: **Raise your hand if you think the Lord answered Isaac's prayer.** Pause for children to do so; then read the rest of verse 21, along with verses 22 and 23. **Rebekah was going to have twins! But what God said about her babies was very strange. Back in Isaac and Rebekah's time, whoever was younger served the one who was older. But God said that the older would serve the younger.** Read verses 24-26.

ASK: **What did Isaac and Rebekah name their twins, and which boy was born first?** (Esau and Jacob; Esau)

SAY: **Let's find out what happened to Esau and Jacob after they were older.** Read verses 26-34. Choose two children to pretend to be Jacob and Esau and act out what they hear. When finished, thank the children for their participation. **Oh my! There were a lot of problems in Isaac's family.** Distribute the activity leaflets, and ask children to look at *A Struggle Between Brothers*. Let children do the page alone or pair up to complete the activity. When children are finished, ask volunteers to read each sentence and give their answers. (Answers: 1=a, b, c; 2=a, c; 3=b; 4=b, c)

ASK: **What were some of the causes of the struggle between Esau and Jacob?** (Isaac loved Esau, while Rebekah loved Jacob. Esau was foolish in thinking he had to have food right then and selling his birthright to Jacob. Jacob took advantage of Esau's hunger to get the birthright.)

SAY: **Later in life, Jacob tricked Esau and got the special blessings that should have gone to Esau. After that, Jacob had to leave in order to be safe from Esau's anger. Many years later Jacob and Esau were reunited. When they met, they hugged each other and showed by their actions that they had forgiven each other. We can learn a lot from Jacob and Esau. While none of our families are perfect, let's remember that since family relationships are important to God, we should plan to improve them every day.**

Jacob and Esau **Session 6**

Make It Real

3 Use this activity to help children **discover ways to improve family relationships**.

Materials
apples (enough for each
child to have a couple
of slices), paper plate, knife,
bowl with some lemon juice (or
orange juice), napkins, Bibles,
whiteboard, dry-erase marker

Science

Protection for Families

Slice an apple, and put a slice on the paper plate. Dip another slice into lemon juice, and put that slice on the plate also.

ASK: **What's going to happen to these apple slices?** (The slice dipped in lemon juice will not turn brown; the other one will.)
Why will the slice dipped in lemon juice not turn brown? (The lemon juice binds with oxygen, which keeps that oxygen away from the apple. It's oxygen that makes the slice not dipped in lemon juice turn brown.)

As you talk, slice the apples so that each child gets a few slices.

SAY: **Similar to how lemon juice protects the apple from turning brown, following God's Word can protect our families from bad things, such as mean words, unkind behaviour, lies, and impatience.**

ASK: **What's a way that you can be patient with your family? be kind to your family? do good for your family?**

SAY: **Family relationships are important to God! Let's follow God and improve relationships with our families.**

Live It Out

4 Use this activity to help children **plan to improve family relationships**.

Materials
paper, marker, reusable
adhesive

Action

Something More!
Encourage children to do
Spotlight on Families, found
in Activity page *Spotlight on
Families* on page 46, during a
quiet time this week.

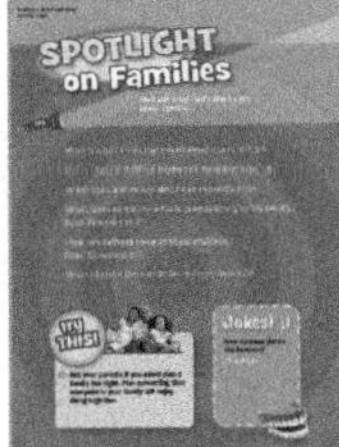

Turn It Around

Draw a happy face on one sheet of paper and a sad face on another sheet of paper. Display the papers on opposite walls. Draw children's attention to the happy and sad faces. SAY: **Since family relationships are important to God, I hope that you want to follow God's Word and have good relationships with *your* family. Doing so must make God happy. *Not* doing that must make God sad.** Ask children to line up in the middle of the room. **Here's something that might happen to you— your brother tries to start an argument with you.** Tell children that since that would not improve family relationships, they should turn toward the sad face and take one step forward.

ASK: **What could you do that would turn the situation around, to turn the bad situation into a good one?**

Once a child has suggested a possible solution, tell all the children to turn around and take two steps toward the happy face. SAY: **Your sister won't help you with the jobs your mum asked both of you to do.** Continue with similar situations until all the children have reached the wall with the happy face on it. PRAY: **Dear God, thank You for our families. Help us to realise the role we can play in turning around bad family situations. Give us the help we need to improve our family relationships. In Jesus' name, amen.**

A Struggle Between Brothers

1 **Esau was**
a. the older brother of Jacob.

b. Isaac's favourite son.

c. a skillful hunter.

2 **Jacob was**
a. Rebekah's favourite son.

b. a good singer.

c. someone who knew how to cook stew.

3 **Esau wanted some of Jacob's stew so badly**
a. that he stole some of it.

b. that he sold his birthright to get it.

c. that he gave Jacob £100 for it.

4 **Jacob ended up with**
a. lots of money.

b. Esau's birthright.

c. the covenant promises that had been made to Abraham.

SPOTLIGHT on Families

Find out what God's Word says about families.

Who is a gift from the Lord? Read Psalm 127:3-5.

What should children listen to? Read Proverbs 1:8.

What does a wise son do? Read Proverbs 15:20.

What does someone who is greedy bring to his family? Read Proverbs 15:27.

How are fathers to raise their children? Read Ephesians 6:4.

What pleases the Lord? Read Colossians 3:20.

➩ **Ask your parents if you could plan a family fun night. Plan something that everyone in your family will enjoy doing together.**

Deborah and Barak

Session 7

Scripture: Judges 4:1-10, 12-16, 23-24; 5:31c
Focus: God wants us to follow His commands.

Heart to Heart Teacher Devotion

Deborah told Barak about God's command: Barak was to lead a battle against an enemy. God commands those who follow Him to love Him more than anything and to love our neighbours as we love ourselves. Those are very big commands to follow. Our desire to follow and obey His commands comes from our love for Him: 'This is love for God: to keep his commands. And his commands are not burdensome' (1 John 5:3).

Focus
God wants us to follow His commands.

Materials
football, board game, cookbook, paper, pencils

Discuss

Before Session
Place the football, board game, and cookbook in different parts of your room. Place a sheet of paper and a pencil by each item.

Focus In

1 Use this activity to help children **discover the importance of following commands.**

Welcome

Welcome each child warmly by name.

List of Instructions

Draw childrens' attention to the items you've placed in the room. Tell them to form small groups by gathering beside the item that interests them the most.

SAY: **To use your item in the best way, there are certain instructions to follow. Your challenge is to come up with a big list of instructions, rules, and commands that you need to follow when using your item.** After several minutes, call time. Let the groups quickly read the lists they came up with.

ASK: **What happens when someone doesn't follow the rules or commands while playing football? playing a board game? following a recipe?**
Why is it important for *us* to follow the instructions or commands of people we trust? (They want the team to do well. They don't want others to get hurt.)

SAY: **Today we'll discover how two Old Testament people chose to follow God's command. Let's find out what happened.**

Explore His Word

② Use these activities to help children **tell how Deborah and Barak followed God's command.**

Bible Background for the Teacher

Today's text tells about the cycle of sin, oppression, deliverance, peace, and sin again—a cycle repeated throughout the book of Judges.

Deborah's role as judge included settling disputes as judges do today. She also held the roles of prophet and wife, and acted as a mother to Israel. Deborah's direct participation in military service was due only to Barak's refusal to go into battle without her. After assembling an army as God had commanded, Barak and his 10,000 men camped at Mt. Tabor. The Lord lured the Canaanite army with its 900 chariots of iron to the flood plains of the Kishon River. From Deborah's victory song, it is learned that God caused the Kishon River to overflow its banks, bogging down the Canaanite chariots—causing Sisera, the Canaanite commander, to flee on foot (Judges 5:4, 20-21). As was prophesied in 4:9, God handed Sisera over to another woman named Jael. She slyly lured Sisera into a trap and then drove a tent peg through the temple of his head (vv. 17-21). The victory was won, and the land had peace for 40 years. Unfortunately, that peace would dissolve when Israel's failure to obey God reoccurred—starting the destructive cycle all over again (6:1).

Bible Exploration   Judges 4:1-10, 12-16, 23-24; 5:31c

Show children the map. Have volunteers point out these places: Hazor, Harosheth Haggoyim, Ramah, Bethel, Kedesh, Mt. Tabor, and the Kishon River. Tell children that all these places are a part of today's Bible story. SAY: **Look in the Old Testament section and find the book of Judges. Turn to Judges 4:1-2.** Have a volunteer read those verses aloud.

SAY: **The Bible story today has some high points—meaning that something good happened. When you hear a high point, raise your hands up high.** Have the children do this. **The story also has some low points—meaning that something not so good happened. When you hear a low point, put your hands down low.** Have the children do this. **When you hear about a so-so time, meaning that something not really good or bad happened, put your hands in-between.** Have the children do this.

Ask for a volunteer or two to stand in front and lead everyone in doing the motions. Read Judges 4:1-10, 12-16, 23-24, and 5:31c aloud. Pause where needed so children can do the motions. Emphasise and explain any parts that the children seem confused about.

ASK: **How did Deborah follow God's command?** (She told Barak that God wanted him to fight against Sisera, the leader of Jabin's army.)
How did Barak follow God's command? (Barak led the Israelite army against Sisera and his army.)

Hand out the Activity page *Who Said It?* Ask volunteers to read each sentence and tell who said it. (Answers: 1=God gave the command and Deborah told it to Barak; 2=Barak; 3=Deborah; 4=Deborah) SAY: **The command that God communicated to Barak through Deborah was not an easy command to follow. Sisera's army had 900 armoured chariots—the most fearsome battle machines of the ancient world. But Deborah and Barak knew that God wants us to follow His commands. They chose to follow God's command because they believed what God said—that He would give Sisera and his army into their hands. And that's exactly what happened.**

Materials

Activity page *Map* on page 52, Bibles, Activity page *Who Said It?* on page 50, pencils

Action

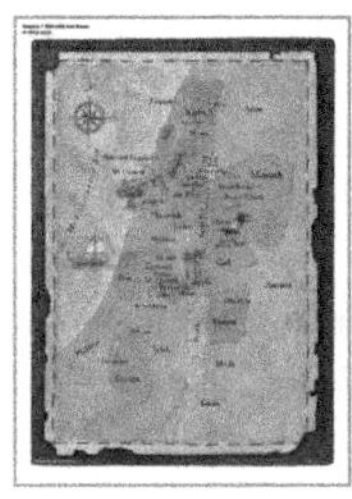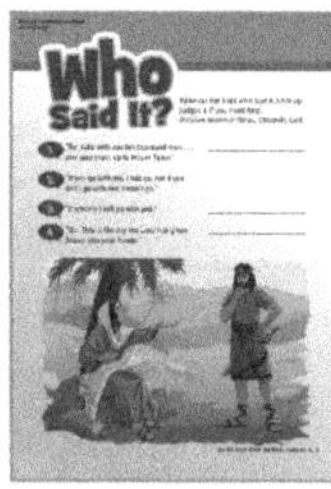

Deborah and Barak **Session 7**

Make It Real

3 Use this activity to help children **identify some of God's commands He wants them to follow.**

Materials
Activity page *Sum It Up!* on page 51, pencils, Bibles

 Consider modifying this activity by having pairs of children work together to create small posters, rather than doing a writing activity.

Sum It Up!

Ask a volunteer hold a Bible and stand beside you. SAY: **Our friend is going to open the Bible and point. Wherever his finger lands, that's a command of God we need to obey.** Have the volunteer open the Bible, point to something, and read it. It most likely will not be one of God's commands, and therefore, it won't make much sense. Have another volunteer do the same. Ask children if this is a good way to find out about God's commands and what *is* a good way to find out about God's commands and how to follow them (read and study the Bible). Have children turn in their activity leaflets to *Sum It Up!* Have children pair up, and assign each pair one of the Scriptures to look up and finish the sentence. Let each pair share its answer. (Answers: 1=Lord, neighbour; 2=lie; 3=Forgive; 4=Share)

ASK: **Why do you think God wants us to follow His commands, such as sharing, showing love, obeying parents, not lying, and not worrying?** (He loves us and knows what's best for us. He wants us to have good lives that honour Him.)

Live It Out

4 Use this activity to help children **decide to follow God's commands.**

Materials
plates, bowls, marbles (1 per small group of children), battery-operated tealight

It's Your Turn

Help children get into small groups (or find partners). Give each group a plate and a marble. SAY: **Work together. Place the marble on the plate and rotate the plate in a circular manner, slowly increasing the speed. Your goal is to keep the marble on your plate.** After the marbles have fallen off, ASK: **Why did the marbles fall off?** (The sides of the plates weren't high enough.)

Give each group a bowl. Tell them to try the same thing again, but this time they are to use the bowl. Groups should have more success. When children are done experimenting, SAY: **The sides of the bowls acted as protection and a guide to keep the marbles from flying out into the room. God's commandments are kind of like that. Some of His commands help guide our thoughts and actions. Some of His commands help protect us. All His commands are worth following.**

Place the tealight in a central location and turn it on. SAY: **Silently talk to God about His commands that are hard for you to follow, and ask for His help.** After a short time of silence, close in prayer.

Who Said It?

Write on the lines who said it. Look up Judges 4 if you need help.
Possible answers: Barak, Deborah, God.

1 'Go, take with you ten thousand men . . . and lead them up to Mount Tabor.' _______________________

2 'If you go with me, I will go; but if you don't go with me, I won't go.' _______________________

3 'Certainly I will go with you.' _______________________

4 'Go! This is the day the LORD has given Sisera into your hands.' _______________________

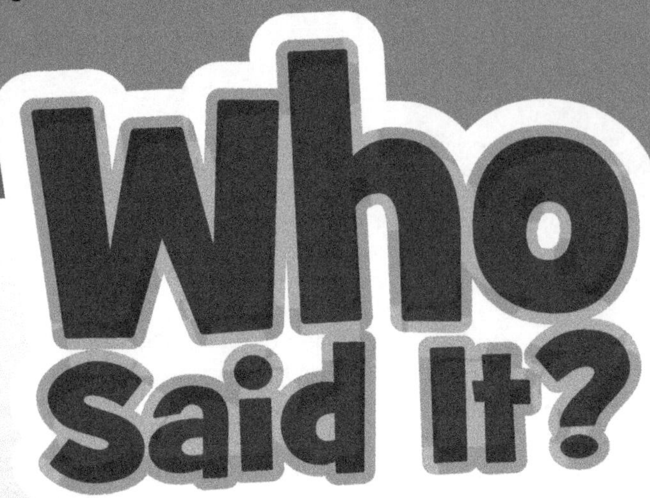

Sum it UP!

Discover some of God's commands He wants us to follow.

1

Matthew 22:37-39 Sum it UP!

'Love the _____________ your God. . . .

Love your _____________________.'

2

Colossians 3:9 Sum it UP!

'Do not _____________ to each other.'

3

Matthew 6:14 Sum it UP!

_____________________ others and

God will forgive you.

4

Romans 12:13 Sum it UP!

'_____________________ with the Lord's

people who are in need.'

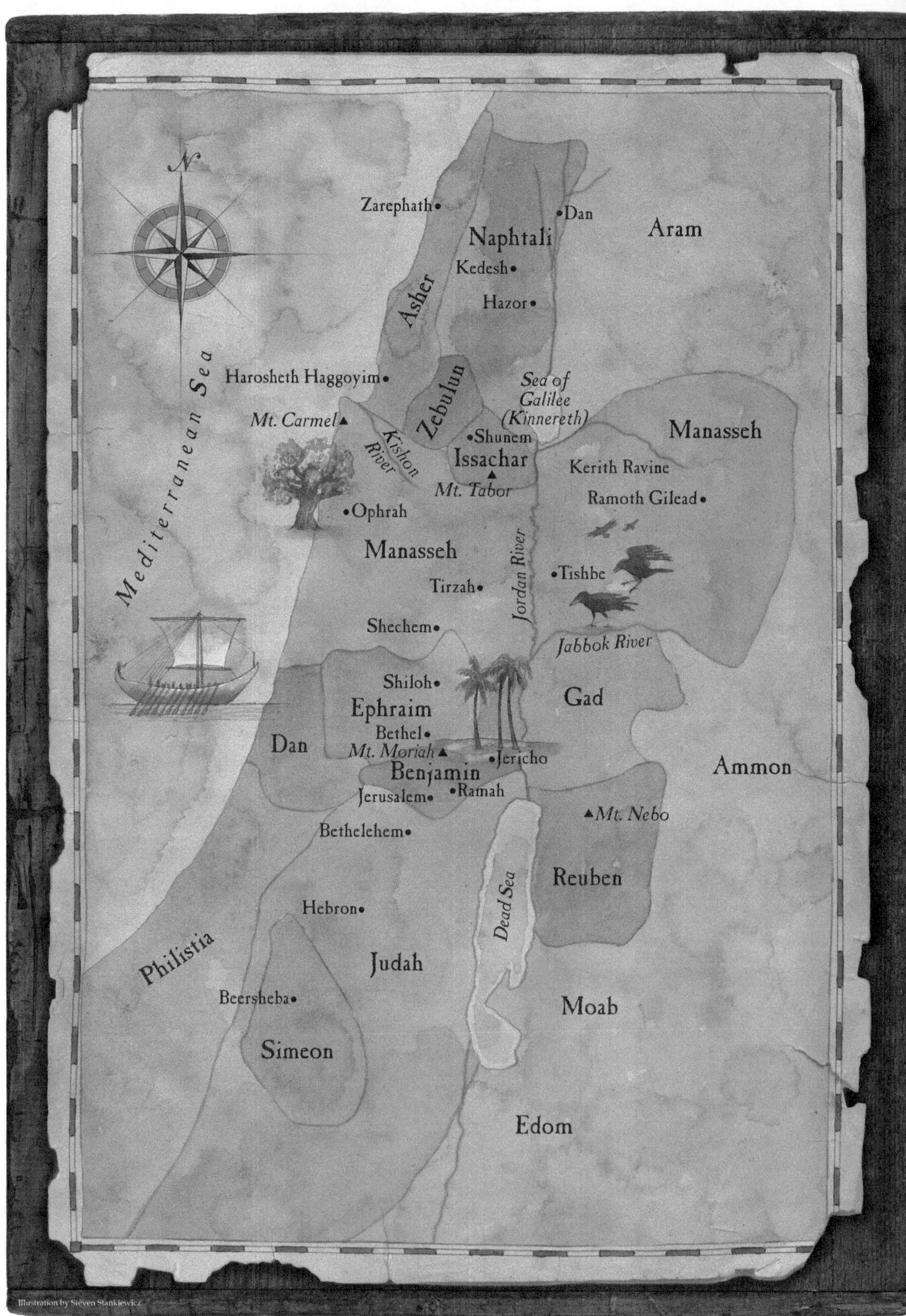
N
Mediterranean Sea
Zarephath•
•Dan
Aram
Naphtali
Kedesh•
Hazor•
Asher
Harosheth Haggoyim•
Zebulun
Sea of Galilee (Kinnereth)
Manasseh
Mt. Carmel▲
Kishon River
•Shunem
Issachar
Kerith Ravine
Ramoth Gilead•
Mt. Tabor▲
•Ophrah
Manasseh
Jordan River
•Tishbe
Tirzah•
Shechem•
Jabbok River
Shiloh•
Gad
Ephraim
Bethel•
Mt. Moriah▲
•Jericho
Dan
Benjamin
Ammon
Jerusalem•
•Ramah
▲Mt. Nebo
Bethelehem•
Reuben
Hebron•
Dead Sea
Philistia
Judah
Beersheba•
Moab
Simeon
Edom
Illustration by Steven Stankiewicz

Saul Becomes King

Session 8

Scripture: 1 Samuel 8:4-10, 18-22a; 9:15-17; 10:1, 20-24
Focus: Pray for God's will to be done.

Heart to Heart Teacher Devotion

'Be careful what you ask for—you might just get it!' No doubt you've heard this and maybe even said it a few times. Unfortunately, the Israelites got what they asked for. The Israelites decided to take things into their own hands, asking for a king but in doing so they rejected God as their king. Huge mistake. Let's learn from the Israelites and be careful what we ask for. May our every request be in line with God's will.

Focus
Pray for God's will to be done.

Materials
none

Action

Remind children to stay in their own space. Consider using carpet squares or some other 'boundary' to help children who need a more visual cue.

Teaching Tips
You could let children take turns calling out things they ask for.

Continue to display the Bible Timelines.

Focus In

1 Use this activity to help children **explore what kinds of things they ask for.**

Welcome

Welcome each child warmly by name.

Take a Step

Have children stand in a line, one behind the other. Make sure you leave some space to the right of the line. SAY: **Let's think about what kinds of things you ask for. If you've ever asked a parent for money, take a step to the right. If you've ever asked a teacher for help, take a step to the right. If you've ever asked a brother, sister, or cousin to stop bothering you, take a step to the right. If you've ever asked a friend to play a game with you, take a step to the right. If you've ever asked God to help you feel better, take a step to the right. If you've ever asked a parent to buy you something, take a step to the right. If you've ever asked a friend to keep a secret, take a step to the right.** Continue, as time permits, with other things children might ask for. Then have them sit down. **Based on how far some of you moved to the right, you ask for lots of things!**

ASK: **What are some other things you ask for?** Accept responses.

SAY: **In today's Bible story, God's people asked for something. Let's find out what that was and what happened.**

Focus
Pray for God's will to be done.

Explore His Word

2 Use these activities to help children **tell what God did when His people asked for a king.**

Bible Background for the Teacher

Israel's problem was peer pressure! The only nation on earth to be chosen as God's 'treasured possession' (Deuteronomy 7:6) wanted an earthly king to fight its battles, just as 'all the other nations' had (1 Samuel 8:5, 20). Israel chose to reject God as their king; therefore, their request to Samuel for a king was considered treason (10:19).

Israel was warned about the hardships an earthly king would impose (1 Samuel 8:11-18). No longer would Israel merely cry out to God for deliverance from a foreign oppressor, but its cries would be for relief from its own oppressive king (v. 18). Despite the warnings, 'the people refused to listen to Samuel' (v. 19). Saul was chosen by God to be Israel's first king (9:15-17). God had already established regulations for a king many years earlier in the Old Testament law (Deuteronomy 17:14-20). Israel's king was not to be sovereign but to submit to the sovereignty of God (1 Samuel 12:14, 15).

Samuel revealed to Saul that he was God's choice for king by anointing him with oil (10:1). In verses 20-24, God revealed His choice publicly. The 12 tribes of Israel were presented, and the tribe of Benjamin was chosen. The clans of Benjamin were presented, and Matri's clan was chosen. From this clan, Saul, son of Kish, was revealed as king. Unexpectedly, Saul was nowhere in sight but was later found hiding among the supplies (v. 22)! Though perhaps reluctant and apprehensive about his new role as king, Saul's calling was confirmed by God in a victory over the Ammonites (11:11-13). Following this great event Saul was officially inaugurated as Israel's first human king (vv. 14, 15).

Bible Exploration 1 Samuel 8:4-10, 18-22a; 9:15-17; 10:1, 20-24

Write on the board '1 Samuel 8:4-10, 18-22a; 9:15-17; 10:1, 20-24.' Ask volunteers to stand by the Bible time line and tell about Deborah. SAY: **Samuel was the last judge of the Israelites. This is where we pick up God's story.**

Ask children to turn in their Bibles to 1 Samuel 8:4. SAY: **I'm going to read God's Word today as you listen. The Scriptures are written on the board so you can follow along. Listen for what the Israelites asked for and what happened.** Ask a volunteer to find Ramah and Benjamin on the Bible map. Tell children that these places are mentioned in today's Scripture. Read the Scripture passage.

ASK: **What did the Israelites ask for?** (an earthly king)
    What happened? (God gave them a king.)
    Why did the Israelites want a king? (The other nations had kings.)
    What was wrong with asking for a king? (It meant that the people had rejected God as their king.)

Distribute the activity leaflets and pencils, and have children turn to *Saul Becomes King*. Give children a minute to work on the page. Then have volunteers read the sentences, changing each sentence to make it true. (Answers: 1=cross out 'governor,' write 'king'; 2=cross out 'Samuel,' write 'God'; 3=cross out 'speak,' write 'listen'; 4=cross out 'Solomon,' write 'Saul'; 5=cross out 'The elders,' write 'God')

SAY: **The Israelites forgot that familiar saying: be careful what you ask for! The Israelites were not careful what they asked for at all! They were God's chosen people. *He* was their king! But they rejected God as their king and asked instead for an imperfect, earthly king to rule them. They forgot to pray for God's will to be done. Because of their request, God gave them King Saul. But it wasn't long until Saul disobeyed God and God rejected Saul as king. Unfortunately, the people got what they asked for.**

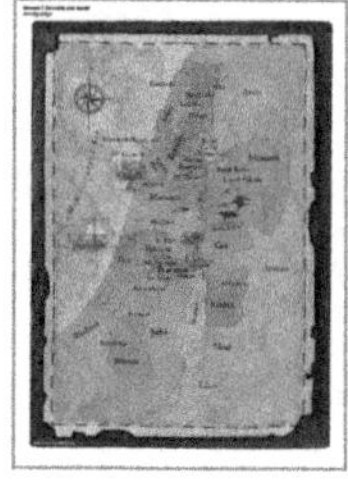
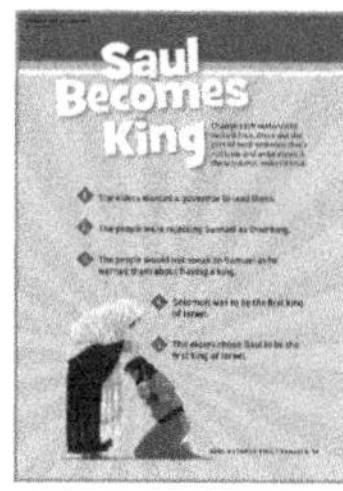

Make It Real

3 Use this activity to help children **discover what the Bible teaches we should ask God for.**

Materials
timer, Activity pages *You Decide!* on pages 56-57, pencils, Bibles

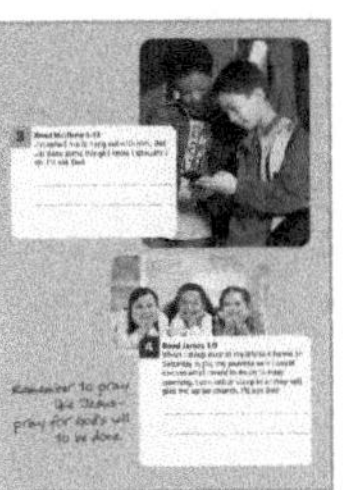

Teaching Tip
Display the *Prayer Poster*. The poster can be downloaded from **www.heartshaper.co.uk/resources**

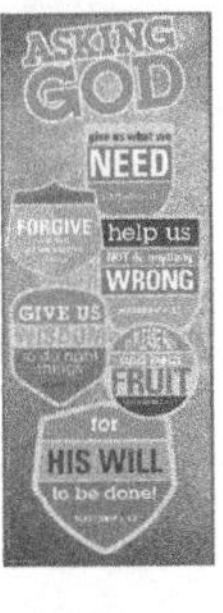

You Decide!

Have children pair up. SAY: **Ask your partner to give you something you think he or she can give you right now, such as money, a smile, or a joke. Keep asking until your partner gives it to you or time is called.** Gives children a minute, then call time. SAY: **I wonder if that is how we sometimes talk to God; asking God to 'give me, give me, give me' without really thinking about** *what* **we should be asking God for or praying for God's will to be done.**

Ask children to turn in their Bibles to Matthew 6:9-10, and have volunteers read those verses aloud. SAY: **Jesus' prayer helps us know how to pray.** Hand out Activity page *You Decide!* **Let's discover some things that the Bible teaches we should ask God for.** Have a volunteer read Matthew 6:11. Have another volunteer read the first situation.

ASK: **What should the girl ask God for?** (to give her family what they need)

Ask children to write that on the lines. Do the same with the other three situations. (Possible answers: 2=to forgive me and for help to forgive my little brother; 3=to help me not to go someplace where I'll be tempted to do wrong; 4=for wisdom to do the right thing) SAY: **Jesus prayed for God's will to be done. We need to always pray for God's will to be done too.**

Live It Out

4 Use this activity to help children **decide to ask God for the right things.**

Materials
Reusable adhesive, large sheets of blank paper, colouring pens

Make sure posters are placed at eye level for anyone who uses wheelchair. You may want to allow children to do the walk as partners, or pair older ones with younger ones or those who need help with reading or understanding the instructions.

Prayer Walk Posters

Put children into pairs or threes. Give each group one of the blank papers and coloured pencils or pens. SAY: **Draw a picture and write some words about some things you can ask God for.** Give examples to help get ideas going: food/homes for people in need, healing when people are sick, forgiveness, help when we are scared or sad.

When children have finished, display the Prayer Walk posters in different parts of your room.

SAY: **When you pray, I hope you'll decide to pray as Jesus prayed. Pray for God's will to be done, and ask God for things that Jesus taught us to ask Him for.** Tell children that they're going to take a prayer walk. They can start the prayer walk at any poster. They should silently pray the prayer that's on that poster and then pray their own prayer about that topic. When children finish praying at one poster, they should move to the right to the next poster. Encourage children to not talk or bother anyone so everyone can pray.

1 **Read Matthew 6:11**

I overheard my mum say that we don't have much money. I'll ask God

____

____

____

You Decide!

How will these stories end? Look up the Scriptures.
Write on the lines what these children should ask God for.

2 **Read Matthew 6:12**

My big sister is cross with me again just because I used something that belongs to her. That's nothing! My little brother got something sticky on my computer! But he did tell me he was sorry. I'll ask God

____

____

____

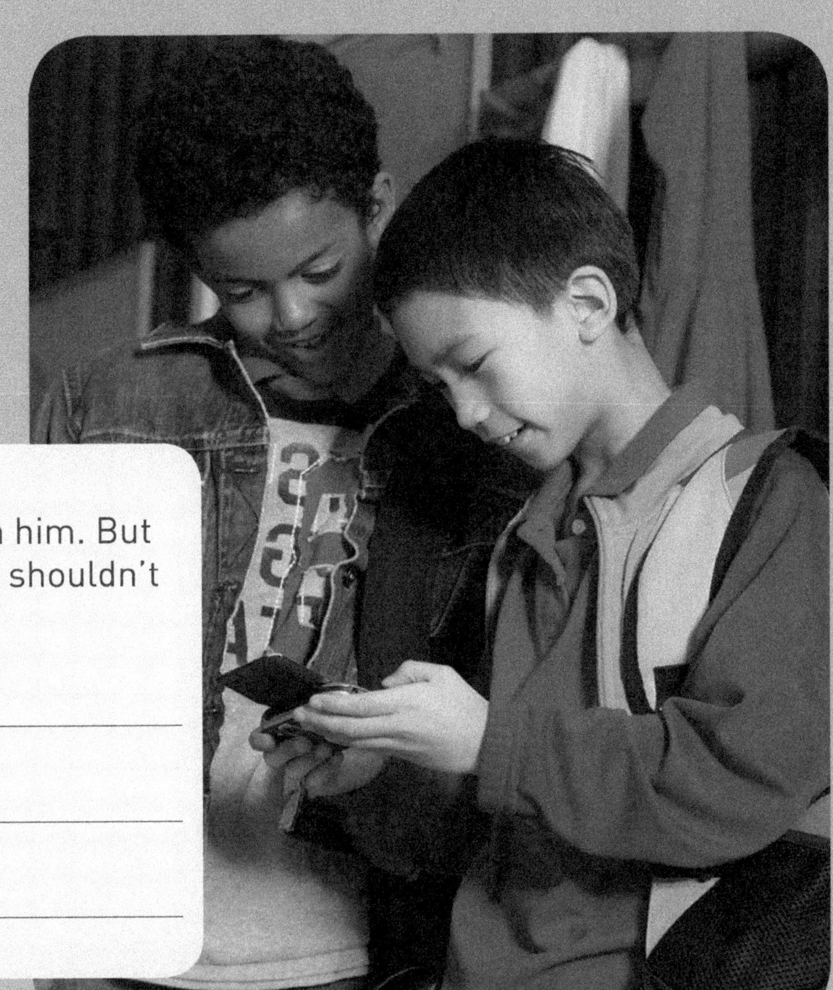

3 Read Matthew 6:13

Jin asked me to hang out with him. But Jin does some things I know I shouldn't do. I'll ask God

____

____

____

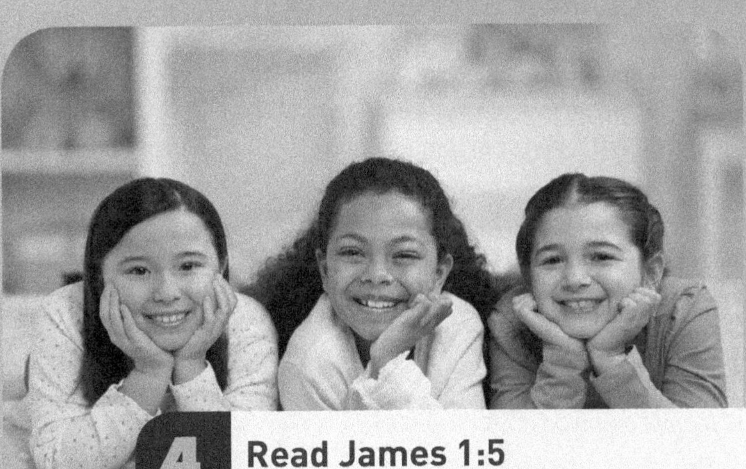

Remember to pray
like Jesus—
pray for God's will
to be done.

4 Read James 1:5

When I sleep over at my friend's home on Saturday night, my parents said I could choose what I want to do on Sunday morning. I can either sleep in or they will pick me up for church. I'll ask God

____

____

____

Saul Becomes King

Change each sentence to make it true. Cross out the part of each sentence that's not true, and write above it the word that makes it true.

1. The elders wanted a governor to lead them.

2. The people were rejecting Samuel as their king.

3. The people would not speak to Samuel as he warned them about having a king.

4. Solomon was to be the first king of Israel.

5. The elders chose Saul to be the first king of Israel.

Samuel Serves God

Session 9

Scripture: 1 Samuel 12:1-25
Focus: Serve God with all your heart.

Heart to Heart Teacher Devotion
Your faithful service becomes a thank-you note sent straight to God's heart. Faithful service puts you in the same company as Deborah, Barak, Gideon, and Samuel, to name a few. But you don't need to lead a battle or crown a king to be one of God's faithful servants. Just follow Ephesians 6:7: 'Serve wholeheartedly, as if you were serving the Lord, not people.'

Focus In

1 Use this activity to help children **explore ways they can serve God.**

Welcome

Welcome each child warmly by name.

Noughts and Crosses Serve

Draw a noughts and crosses grid on the board. Divide the session into two teams, and assign which team will be *X* and which will be *O*. Ask the teams to huddle up. SAY: **Start thinking of ways that someone your age can serve God. It could be serving at home, at school, in your neighbourhood, or other places. It could be serving your family, friends, neighbors, or people you don't know. When it's your team's turn, you'll have 20 seconds to give an answer. You cannot give an answer that someone has already said.** Select a spokesperson for each team. The entire team should be involved with thinking of ways they can serve God. Let teams place their *X*s and *O*s after each good answer they give. Play as many games as you have time for.

ASK: **What's a favourite way that you like to serve God?** Accept responses.

SAY: **There are a lot of ways we can serve God. Sometimes serving God is fun and easy. Other times it can be hard work. No matter how you serve God, you should serve God with all your heart. Let's see what the Bible says about that.**

Focus
Serve God with all your heart.

Materials
whiteboard, dry-erase markers

Game

Teaching Tip
Mix up the teams so that younger children and older children are in a team together.

Explore His Word

Focus
Serve God with all your heart.

2 Use these activities to help children **tell about Samuel's message to the Israelites.**

Bible Background for the Teacher

Israel had gathered at Gilgal for the inauguration ceremony of King Saul (1 Samuel 11:14-15). Samuel, now 'old and grey' (12:2), was retiring as Israel's leader, but would still function as its prophet. Samuel began his farewell address with a reminder that it was at Israel's request that God had instructed him to set a king over them. Though Samuel himself had not been king, no one could deny that he had been a leader of integrity. Samuel recounted their nation's history to prove how God had always functioned as Israel's king. By asking for a human king, Israel had rejected God, its true king.

Samuel stated that if God were to bless their new government, both the subjects and the king had to remain loyal to the Lord and faithfully serve Him. Blessings for obedience and curses for disobedience are spelled out in Deuteronomy 28. To make this point clear, the Lord brought about a powerful thunderstorm during the wheat harvest—normally a dry season. Such a miracle served not only to literally put the fear of God into the people (see a similar incident at Mt. Sinai in Exodus 19:16) but also led them to repent, and it confirmed that everything Samuel had said was true.

Bible Exploration   1 Samuel 12:1-25

SAY: **God always had a plan and that plan was to send salvation. Starting with creation through the prophet Samuel and until Jesus was born, God prepared for salvation. God sent salvation when He sent Jesus to earth.** Ask volunteers to tell who Samuel and Saul were. (Samuel was one of God's prophets; Saul was the first king of Israel.)

Ask children to turn in their Bibles to 1 Samuel 12:1-2. Have volunteers read those verses aloud. Ask for three volunteers who are willing to read special words during the Bible story. The first volunteer will read all of verse 4, except 'they replied.' The second volunteer will read the last sentence of verse 5, except 'they said.' The third volunteer will read verse 19, except 'The people all said to Samuel.' Tell the volunteers to be ready and you will cue them when it's their turn. When you read the words, 'The people replied' or 'The people said,' pause, as a cue for the readers. You need to pause reading to allow the children to read their words.

Tell the rest of the children that they are going to do hand gestures during the Bible story for three words they will hear: *serve, obey,* and *heart. Serve:* Both hands are held in front of the body with the palms facing up; they are moved alternatingly back and forth. *Obey:* The hands start at the head and are pulled down in a gesture of obedience. *Heart:* The middle finger taps the chest over the area of the heart. Have children practice the signs.

SAY: **Let's pretend that we're in the crowd of Israelites who have gathered at Gilgal to confirm Saul as king. Look! Samuel is standing! He wants to speak. Everyone is getting very quiet to hear what this prophet of God has to tell us. He has served God and us for a long time!** Cue the readers at the appropriate times and pause. Also remember to lead the children in doing the gestures.

ASK: **If you had to sum up what Samuel told the people, what would you say?** (obey God and serve Him with all your heart) Ask children to say this phrase with you and do the hand gestures.

Hand out the Activity page *Samuel's Farewell Speech.* Let children work on the page by themselves. Then have volunteers read the sentences and fill in the blanks. (Answers: 1=Aaron; 2=Barak; 3=serve; 4=evil; 5=heart, great.)

SAY: **Samuel reminded the Israelites about all the great things God had done for them, so that they would *want* to obey and serve God. The same is true for you too. When you think about all the great things God has done, I hope it leads you to want to obey and serve God with all your heart.**

Materials

Resources sheet 2, Bibles, Activity pages *Samuel's Farewell Speech* on pages 62-63, pencils

Listen

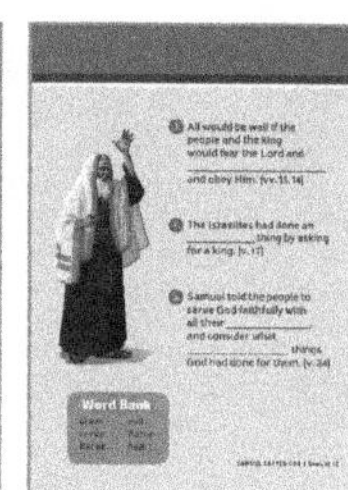

Make It Real

3 Use this activity to help children **desire to serve God with all their hearts.**

Materials
large coffee filters, scissors, black washable markers, small paper plates, water in small cups, newspapers (or plastic) to cover tables

Science

Note
A rainbow of colours (or at least a few colours) will appear and spread because black ink is made of coloured pigments and water. When water is added, the pigments dissolve and spread through the filter, revealing the colours that mix to create black.

Service That Spreads

Tell children to get up and interview each other. SAY: **Ask two people this question: What is something you do with all your heart? Then ask two others this question: What is something you do halfheartedly?** When the interviews are done, let children report what their friends said they did with all their hearts and halfheartedly. **You seem to know the difference between doing something with all your hearts and doing something halfheartedly. As we do a science experiment, think about this question: Why should you want to serve God with all your heart?**

Cover the tables with newspapers. Give each child a coffee filter. Instruct them to cut a circle out of the coffee filter and then draw a solid heart in black pen about the size of a 50 pence piece in the center of the circle. Have children guess what will happen when they add water on top of the heart. Then children should place their circles on a paper plate and add a few drops of water. SAY: **When you serve God with all your heart, it's kind of like what's happening in your experiments. God can take your wholehearted service and not only make it beautiful, but make it spread to touch the lives of many people. When you serve God with all your heart, it spreads joy to many others and to yourself. And most importantly, it brings joy to God. God wants you to serve Him with *all* your heart, not halfheartedly. You can do that when you remember all the great things God has done and how much He loves you.**

Focus
Serve God with all
your heart.

Live It Out

4 Use this activity to help children **serve God.**

Materials
Activity page *Serving Challenge* on page 64, pencils

Service Project

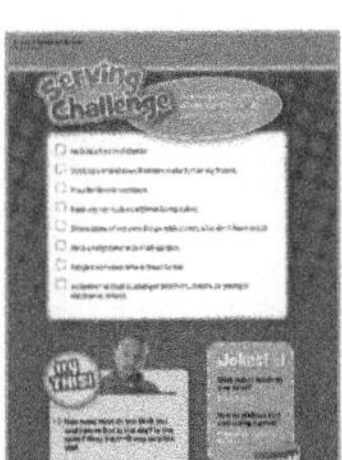

Serving Challenge

Hand out Activity page *Serving Challenge*. Read the directions and give children time to put ticks by the ways they'd like to try serving God. Let volunteers share a few things they've ticked. SAY: **I noticed that for most of these you don't even need to go anywhere different from where you already go. I noticed that these are all things children your age can do. I noticed that some of you already do some of these things! I noticed that all of these need your time. And of course, I noticed that when you do any of these things, you should serve God with all your heart!**

Ask children to gather for prayer. Have several volunteers pray aloud, asking for God's help as they serve Him. Encourage all children to pray silently with those who are praying aloud. Encourage children to follow through on their plans of serving God. SAY: **However you serve God, remember to serve God with all your heart!**

Samuel's Farewell Speech

Finish the sentences to find out some things Samuel told the Israelites. Use the Word Bank or your Bible (1 Samuel 12) for help.

1. God helped the Israelites when He sent Moses and _______________________ to lead the people out of Egypt. (v. 6)

2. When the people cried to the Lord for help, He sent them Jerub-Baal, _______________________, Jephthah, and Samuel. (v. 11)

Word Bank

great	evil
serve	Aaron
Barak	heart

3. All would be well if the people and the king would fear the Lord and ________________________ and obey Him. (vv. 13, 14)

4. The Israelites had done an _______________ thing by asking for a king. (v. 17)

5. Samuel told the people to serve God faithfully with all their _______________, and consider what _______________ things God had done for them. (v. 24)

Word Bank

great	evil
serve	Aaron
Barak	heart

Serving Challenge

How will you serve God with all your heart? Put a ✔ by the ones you want to try.

- [ ] Help at an animal shelter.
- [ ] Stick by a friend even if others make fun of my friend.
- [ ] Pray for family members.
- [ ] Keep my room clean without being asked.
- [ ] Share some of my own things with others who don't have much.
- [ ] Help a neighbour with their garden.
- [ ] Forgive someone who is mean to me.
- [ ] Volunteer to read to younger brothers, sisters, or younger children at school.

try THIS!

➡ **How many ways do you think you could serve God in one day? in one week? Keep track—it may surprise you!**

Jokes! :)

What makes music on your head?
A headband!

How do athletes stay cool during a game?
They stand near the fans!

Solomon Asks God for Wisdom

Scripture: 1 Kings 3:4-14; 4:29-34
Focus: God hears us and can help us know right from wrong.

Heart to Heart Teacher Devotion
Reflect about the prayers you offer to God. Do you thank God and praise Him often in your prayers? Do you tell God you love Him? Do you pray for others? Do you ask for forgiveness? Prayer is simple, yet very powerful. Prayer can draw and keep you close to God. Pray for God's help in making right choices. He will answer!

Focus
God hears us and can help us know right from wrong.

Materials
Activity page *Wise Words* on page 69, pencils

Activity Page

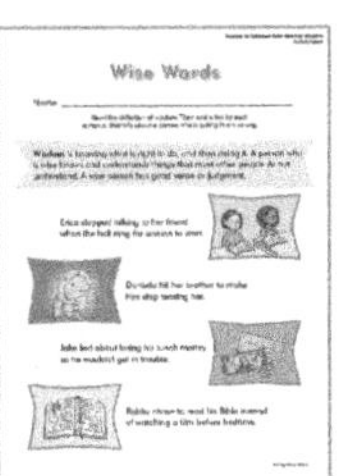

Focus In

1 Use this activity to help children **define *wisdom*.**

Welcome

Welcome each child by name.

Wise Words

Have the children gather at tables. SAY: **Today we are going to talk about wisdom. Let's discover what that word means.** Distribute the activity page. Read the directions and do the page together.

ASK: **How were some of these children acting in wise ways?** (obeyed rules; showed respect; put God first)
What could the children who were not acting wisely have done differently? (acted kindly; told the truth)

SAY: **One way we can grow wiser is by praying to God. God hears us and can help us know right from wrong.**

Focus
God hears us and can help us know right from wrong.

Explore His Word

2 Use these activities to help children **tell what Solomon asked God for and how God answered.**

Bible Background for the Teacher

During the early part of his reign, King Solomon, son and successor of King David, went to Gibeon, a city northwest of Jerusalem. At Gibeon, Solomon earnestly sought the Lord's favour by sacrificing 1,000 burnt offerings. Solomon was probably about 20 years old at the time. His conversation with God indicates an enormous amount of maturity. God not only gave Solomon what he asked but also many good things for which he didn't ask. This illustrates the principle that Jesus later spoke of in Matthew 6:33 and Luke 12:31 regarding the rewards of seeking God's kingdom before personal gain.

Bible Exploration   1 Kings 3:4-14; 4:29-34

SAY: **Today's Bible story comes from the Old Testament book of 1 Kings.**
Write '1 Kings 3:4' on the board. Help the children find 1 Kings 3:4 in their
Bibles. Ask a volunteer to read the verse. SAY: **The king referred to in
this verse is King Solomon. He was the son of David, and like his father,
Solomon loved God. Listen for what Solomon prayed for and how God
answered his prayer.**

**King Solomon went to the city of Gibeon to worship God. The king
offered 1,000 offerings to God.** Show 10a. **The offerings showed that
Solomon wanted to give his best to God. He wanted to follow God and
please God. One night God came to Solomon in a dream. God said,
'Ask for whatever you want. I will give it to you.'** Show 10b.

Hmmm. **Anything?**

ASK: **What do you think Solomon would ask for?**
What would you ask for if God said you could have anything?
Pause from telling the story and let the children respond.

First, Solomon thought of his father, King David. Show 10c. **Solomon
said, 'God, You have been very kind to my father and me. Now I sit on
my father's throne. But I am only young, and there are many people in
Your kingdom.** Show 10d. **I can't even count the number of people! But
I want to rule them well. I ask for a heart that will know the difference
between right and wrong.'** Show 10e.

**Solomon's request pleased God. God said, 'You did not ask to be rich.
And you did not ask for a long life. Since you asked to be able to
choose right and make wise decisions, I will give you what you asked.
I will give you wisdom to help you do right and make right choices.**
Show 10f. **You will be wiser than anyone. But I will give you more than
that. I will also give you riches. People will honour you. And you will
live a long life too.' King Solomon was known everywhere for being
wise. God gave Solomon the ability to make good decisions and right
choices. Solomon wrote 3,000 wise sayings. He wrote 1,005 songs. He
knew and taught about plants, animals, birds, reptiles, and fish. People
came from all over the world to hear Solomon talk about these things.**

**Solomon thought of God and others first. He asked God to help him
know right from wrong. God heard and answered Solomon's prayer.
God made Solomon very wise. And God gave Solomon even more than
he asked for. God also gave Solomon riches, honour, and a long life.**

Bible Review Activity

ASK: **How did God answer Solomon's prayer?** (God made Solomon wiser
than anyone; God gave Solomon riches, honour, and a long life.)

Distribute the activity page *Solomon's Prayer* and pencils. Read the
directions aloud and do the page together. (Statements 1, 2, 4, 5 are
true; 3 and 6 are false.)
Place the story cards in a bag. Have the children sit in a circle. As you
play some music, children can pass the bag. When you pause the music,
the child holding the bag should choose a card from the bag and tell
how the picture on the card relates to the Bible story.

whiteboard, dry-erase
marker, Bibles,
Activity Page *Solomon's
Wisdom Story Cards* on page
68, sticky tape

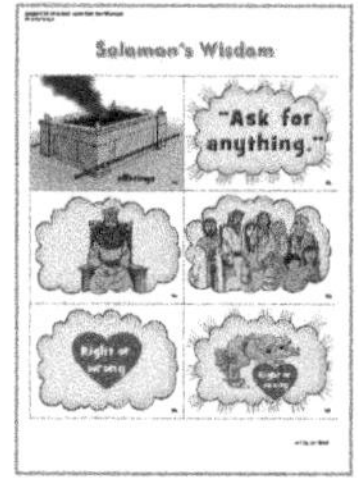

Before the Session
Photocopy and cut up Activity
page *Solomon's Wisdom* into
six story-cards. Decide how you
will display the story cards. The
cards can be displayed on a
wall near your Bible story area,
or you can use tack magnets to
display them on a whiteboard.

Materials

Activity page *Solomon's
Prayer* on page 70,
pencils, paper bag

Make It Real

3 Use this activity to help children **understand that they need God's help to know right from wrong.**

Materials

money, canned food item, toy (or game)

Object Lesson

Note

Using a larger denomination of money, such as a £10 note, will prompt the children to expand their thinking. A favourite food item or toy will challenge them too.

Choices, Choices

SAY: **Solomon made the right choice when he asked God for wisdom. Let's think about why we need to pray and ask God to help us make right choices.** Show and talk about each item, one at a time.

ASK: **What are some ways you could use this money?** (buy something for myself; give part or all of it to others)
What could you do with this food item? (eat it; give it to a food bank; share it with someone)
You've wanted this toy for a long time. What could you do to get the toy or game? (take the toy from someone else, ask someone to buy one for you, earn money to purchase the toy)
How could praying to God help you make the right choice with each item we looked at?

SAY: **It's not always easy to make a wise choice. We need God's help. When we pray to God, God hears us and can help us know right from wrong.**

Live It Out

4 Use this activity to help children **ask God to help them know right from wrong.**

Materials

objects used for Make It Real Option activity (money, canned food item, toy or game), 3 sheets of paper, marker

Pray

Wise Choices Prayer Walk

Before the session, write the following sentence prayers on separate sheets of paper: (money) God, help us know how to use money and other things we have in the right way; (food item) God, help us choose to do right and share with others; (toy) God, help us choose to put You first—always! After you have finished Choices, Choices in Make It Real, place the objects and prepared papers in three different places around the room.

SAY: **Just as God heard and answered Solomon's prayer, God hears us and can help us know right from wrong. Let's take a prayer walk and ask God to help us know right from wrong.** Lead children to the first prayer stop. Ask one volunteer to hold the object. Another volunteer could read the prayer. Move to the other two stops and do the same. Close the prayer time by thanking God for His help in making the right choices.

Solomon's Wisdom

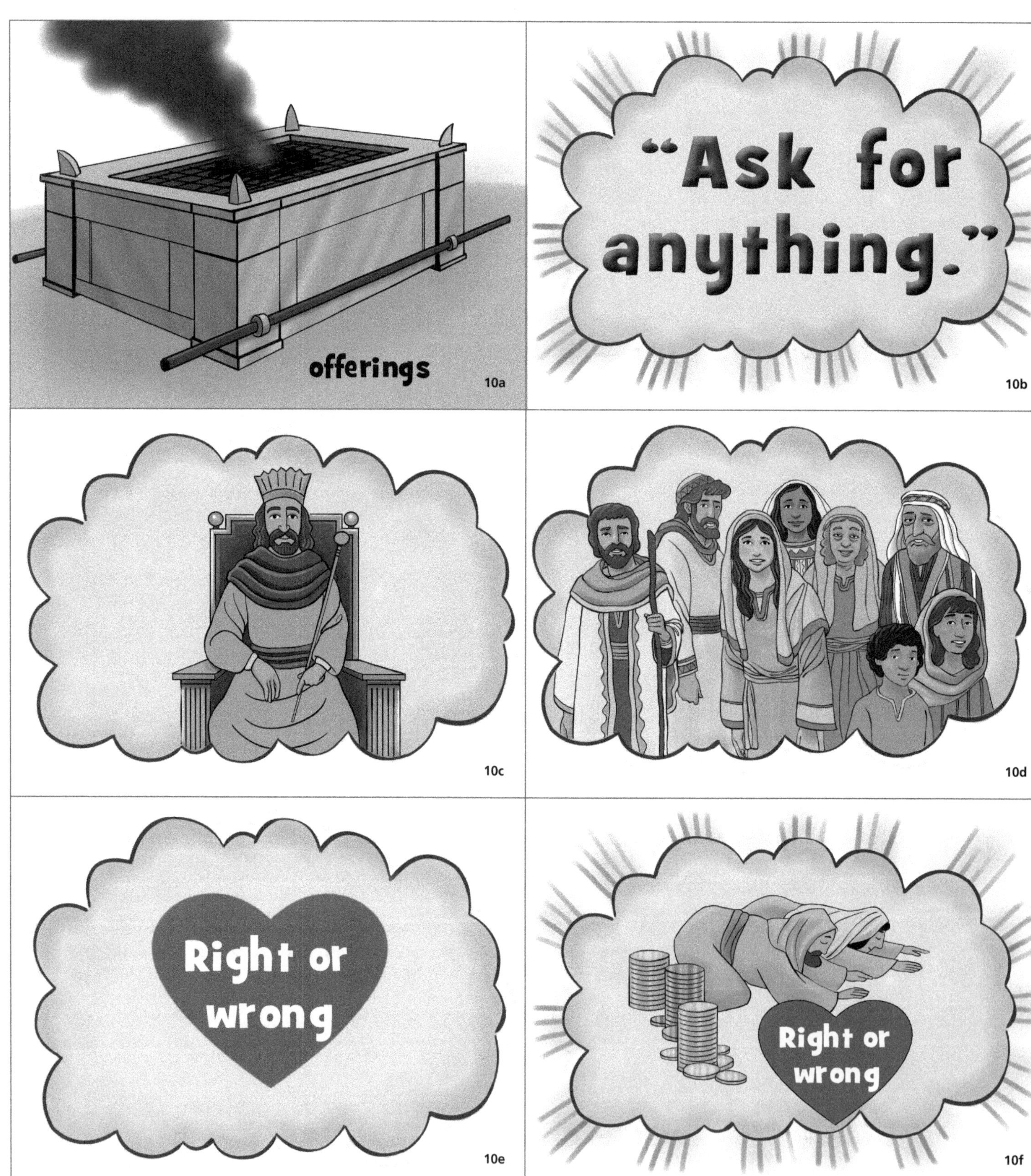

Art by Len Ebert

HeartShaper Preschool Yellow Edition, Activity page
Permission is granted to reproduce this page for ministry
purposes only—not for resale.

Rather than photocopy this page you can download
and print all activity pages in both colour and
black & white from **www.heartshaper.co.uk**

Wise Words

Name ____

Read the definition of *wisdom*. Then add a tick by each
sentence that tells about a person who is acting in a wise way.

Wisdom is knowing what is right to do, and then doing it. A person who is wise knows and understands things that most other people do not understand. A wise person has good sense or judgment.

Erica stopped talking to her friend
when the bell rang for session to start.

Danielle hit her brother to make
him stop teasing her.

Jake lied about losing his lunch money
so he wouldn't get in trouble.

Robby chose to read his Bible instead
of watching a film before bedtime.

Art by Mary Rojas

Solomon's Prayer

Read each sentence. If a sentence is true, circle
the *T.* If a sentence is false, circle the *F.*

1. **Solomon wanted to be a good leader.** T   F

2. **God came to Solomon in a dream.** T   F

3. **Solomon asked God for money.** T   F

4. **God gave Solomon wisdom.** T   F

5. **God also gave Solomon riches.** T   F

6. **No one listened to Solomon.** T   F

Bible Fun Facts

The Bible says that King Solomon spoke
3,000 wise sayings and he wrote 1,005
songs. Solomon knew about plant life and
about animals and birds, reptiles and fish.
Solomon wrote three books of the Bible:
Song of Songs, Proverbs, and Ecclesiastes.

Art by Len Ebert and Margeaux Lucas

Hezekiah Asks for God's Help   Session 11

Scripture: 2 Kings 19:14-19; 20:1-7; 2 Chronicles 29-30
Focus: God has the power to answer our prayers.

Heart to Heart Teacher Devotion
Just as Hezekiah believed, we know God hears and answers prayers for healing. Think about the prayers you offer up to God. Be sure to pray for those who are sick, but remember that there are many other aspects of life to talk to God about too.

Focus
God has the power to answer our prayers.

Materials
Activity page *A Bad Day* on page 74 (optional: puppets)

Discuss

Something More!
Have volunteers act out some of the bad day situations. Or provide puppets and let the children use the puppets to tell about a really bad day.

 Some children become anxious when talking about life situations. Consider showing a picture of a person, rather than having an actual child act out having a bad day.

Focus In

❶ Use this activity to help children **explore having a bad day.**

Welcome
Welcome each child by name.

A *Really* Bad Day
Have the children gather in a circle. SAY: **Let's talk about having a bad day—a *really* bad day! I'll ask some questions and you can tell how you feel when certain things happen.** Use the pictures from Activity page, *A Bad Day* to help children understand.

ASK: **How do you feel when . . .**
    your best friend is sick?
    someone makes fun of you?
    you have bad news to tell to someone?
    What other things make a day really bad for you?

SAY: **We are going to learn about a king who was having a bad day. The king prayed to God. God has the power to answer our prayers. He has the power to help us through our bad days.**

Focus
God has the power to answer our prayers.

Explore His Word

❷ Use these activities to help children **tell what Hezekiah did when he received bad news.**

Bible Background for the Teacher

Hezekiah was one of Judah's good kings. Hezekiah faithfully served God by restoring the temple worship that had been abandoned during the reign of his father, King Ahaz (see 2 Chronicles 28:24; 29:1-4, 35). God answered Hezekiah's prayer and healed him by using the medicines of the time (2 Kings 20:7). God also graciously extended Hezekiah's life by 15 years. When Hezekiah asked for a sign, he was given the choice of whether a shadow should go back or forward 10 steps. It happened just as he requested.

Bible Exploration 2 Kings 19:14-19; 20:1-7; 2 Chronicles 29-30

Write '2 Kings 19:14' on the board. SAY: **In the Old Testament books of 1 and 2 Kings, we learn about men who were kings. Today we are going to learn about King Hezekiah.** Help the children find 2 Kings 19:14 in their Bibles. Ask a volunteer to read the verse. Ask two volunteers to play the parts of King Hezekiah and Isaiah. Give each a name sign to wear and have the volunteers sit beside you. Ask the children to listen for what happened to King Hezekiah. **Whenever I say 'That was a . . . ,' you can complete the sentence by saying 'good day' or 'bad day.'**

King Hezekiah had bad days and good days. When Hezekiah became king, he saw that God's house had not been taken care of. It needed many repairs. That was a <u>bad day</u>. The king asked the people to fix the temple. When all the repairs had been made, King Hezekiah went to the temple. He invited all the people to come and thank God. That was a <u>good day</u>!

But soon a mean king from another country said he was going to take over God's people. That was a <u>bad day</u>. Hezekiah prayed and asked for God's help. Have Hezekiah kneel and pretend to pray. **God had the power to answer the king's prayer. God answered and helped His people.** Have King Hezekiah stand. **That was a <u>good day</u>.**

One day King Hezekiah became very sick. That was a <u>bad day</u>. Have Hezekiah lie on a mat. **While Hezekiah was sick, the prophet Isaiah came to visit him.** Have Isaiah kneel beside Hezekiah. **Isaiah told Hezekiah, 'The Lord God says you are going to die. You should put everything in order.' That was a *really* <u>bad day</u>! King Hezekiah knew he needed help. He turned his face to the wall.** Have Hezekiah turn over. Show the 'God's First Aid' bag and pull the praying hands card from the bag. **The king prayed to God. Hezekiah said, 'Lord, please remember that I have been faithful to You. I have done what You say is good.' Then Hezekiah cried. He did not want to die.** Show *Teaching Picture* 11. Hezekiah can pretend to pray and cry. Hand Hezekiah a tissue from the bag.

Prompt Isaiah to get up and start to walk away. **Before Isaiah left the king's palace, God spoke to Isaiah.** Isaiah stops. **God said, 'Go back and tell Hezekiah that I have heard his prayer. I will heal him. In three days, Hezekiah should go to the temple. I will add 15 years to his life. I will save his city too.'** Isaiah goes back to Hezekiah. **Isaiah then had Hezekiah's servants make a paste from figs and put it on Hezekiah.** Remove cream from bag and pretend to apply it to a place on Hezekiah's arm. **Soon King Hezekiah got well. That was a <u>good day</u>! God had heard Hezekiah's prayer. God had the power to answer the king's prayer. God healed King Hezekiah, and Hezekiah lived 15 more years.**

Bible Review Activity

ASK: **What did Hezekiah pray for, and how did God answer his prayers?**
(Hezekiah prayed for God's help against a mean king; God helped His people. Hezekiah prayed that he would get better and not die; God gave him another 15 years to live.)

Have the session form two groups. Give one group the King Hezekiah name card; the second group can hold the Isaiah name card. The groups should stand when they hear a statement that describes their person.
SAY: **I had the people repair God's temple.** (King Hezekiah)
I told the king God's message that the king was going to die. (Isaiah)
I told the king that God was going to heal him. (Isaiah)

whiteboard, dry-erase marker, Bibles, Activity page *Bible Story Cards* page 75, string or wool, scissors, tape, paper bag, antibiotic cream, tissue, mat (or pillow)

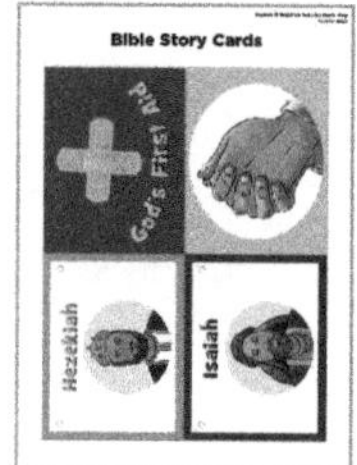
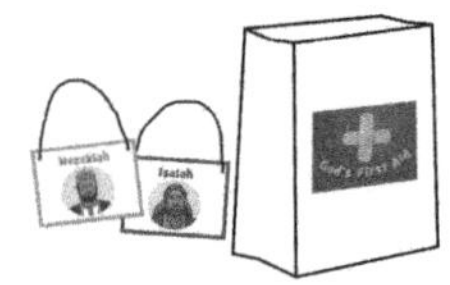

Before the Session
Attach strings to the Hezekiah and Isaiah name cards. Tape the God's First Aid card to the front of a paper lunch bag. Place the praying hands picture card inside the bag, along with a tissue and tube of antibiotic cream.

Materials
Activity page *Bible Story Cards* page 75

SAY: **God heard and answered King Hezekiah's prayers. God has the power to answer our prayers too.**

Focus
God has the power to answer our prayers.

Make It Real

3 Use this activity to help children **name times when they need to pray and ask for God's help.**

Materials
whiteboard, dry-erase colouring pens

Game

 This activity can work well for children who have difficulty drawing, if they can choose a picture that is predrawn (or from a magazine) that shows someone in a situation where prayer is needed.

Guess a Time

SAY: **King Hezekiah prayed and asked God to help His people against an enemy king. Hezekiah also prayed to God when he was sick. Let's take turns drawing pictures of times when we need to pray to God. We'll see whether we can guess what is being drawn.**

Let the children take turns drawing pictures of times when they might need to pray for others or themselves. (Examples: Someone is sick in bed; someone is afraid of a lightning storm.) If children are having trouble drawing something, offer to assist or draw for them. Or they can give verbal clues about the situation they are thinking of. Have the other children try to guess what is being drawn (or described). Talk about what they could pray for in the situation. Remind children that we should pray for real needs, not just wants.

SAY: **We can pray to God when others need His help and when we need His help. God has the power to answer our prayers.**

Focus
God has the power to answer our prayers.

Live It Out

4 Use this activity to help children **pray to God about a hard situation.**

Materials
Activity page _Prayer Pockets_ on page 76, scissors, tape, pencils (or markers)

Craft

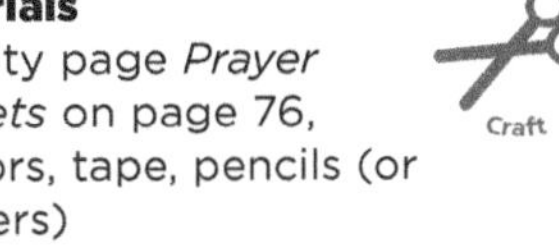

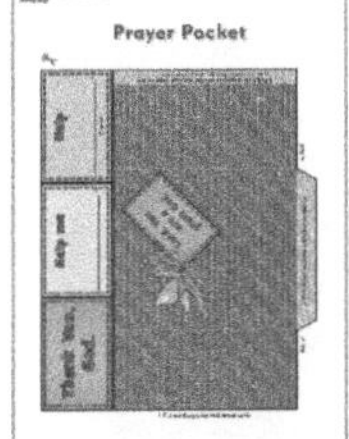

Before the Session
Prepare a sample of the prayer pocket.

Teaching Tip
Use these prayer activities to remind children of the needs of missionaries that your church supports or to share about people in your congregation who are sick or elderly.

Prayer Pockets

SAY: **We can pray to God about hard situations that we face. And we can pray for others who are having hard times. God has the power to answer our prayers. Let's make prayer pockets and then pray to God.** Distribute the activity pages and supplies. Show how to cut, fold, and tape the pockets. Encourage children to write on one card something that they want God to help them with. On another card they can write the name of someone they know who needs God's help. Provide assistance as needed.

Have children bring their completed crafts to a closing prayer circle.
SAY: **The insect on the front of this pocket is called a praying mantis. The mantis has large front legs that are bent and held at an angle and make it look as though it is praying. When we pray, we often sit or kneel or fold our hands. Decide how you would like to pray now. Then use the cards in your prayer pockets and pray to God.** Allow time for children to pray. Close the prayer time. PRAY: **Dear God, thank You for listening to us. We believe You have the power to answer our prayers. In Jesus' name we pray, amen.**

A Bad Day

Bible Story Cards

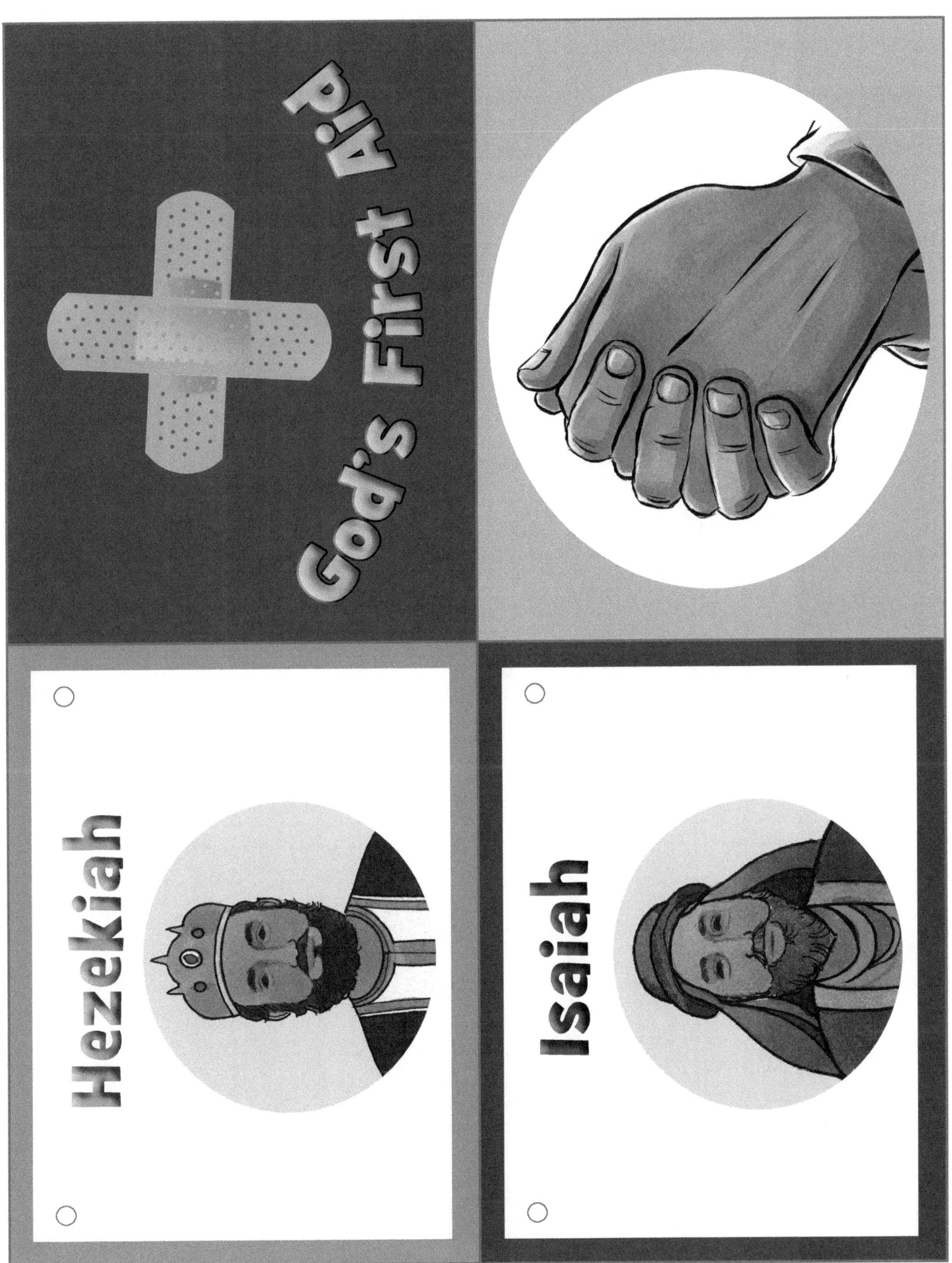

Prayer Pocket

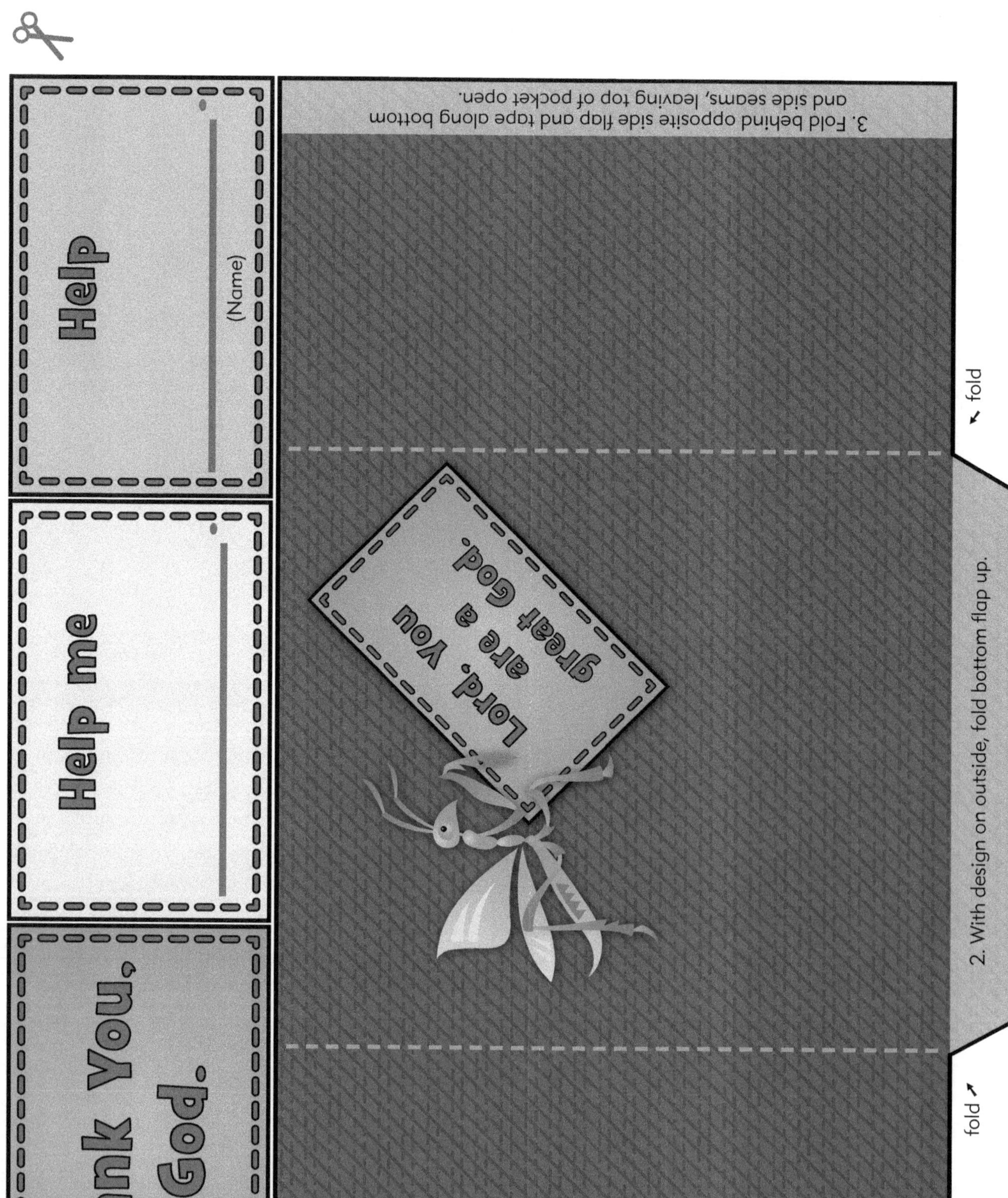

1. Cut out the pocket and prayer cards.

Jehoshaphat and God's People Pray and Worship God

Scripture: 2 Chronicles 20:1-30
Focus: God hears our praise and worship.

Heart to Heart Teacher Devotion

What's the first thing you do when trouble comes? Do you panic, cry or ask friends for help? Do you try to fix it yourself? Jehoshaphat's first action was to call a praise and worship meeting. And after God brought victory to His people, Jehoshaphat gathered the people to praise and worship God more! The next time you face a challenge, be a Jehoshaphat—stop, pray, and worship.

Focus
God hears our praise and worship.

Before Session
Write the words 'praise' and 'worship' on the board. Then in a vertical column, write the letters G_R_E_A_T on the board.

Discuss

Materials
whiteboard, dry-erase marker

Action

Focus In

1 Use this activity to help children **explore what it means to praise and worship God.**

Welcome

Welcome each child by name.

How Do You Say 'Great!'?

Have children gather near the board. SAY: **We all love to hear someone say to us, 'That's great!' We like it when others are excited for us. Let's think of other words we might use to describe something great.** Point to the letters on the board. Have children brainstorm words or phrases beginning with each letter that express the idea of *great.* (Examples: G—grand, R—remarkable, E—excellent, A—awesome, T—totally cool!) Review the list. SAY: **I'm going to count to three. When I say 'three,' everyone should jump up and shout 'Great!' in some way. One, two, three!** Let children respond.

ASK: **How do you think God feels when we say 'God, You are great!'? How do you think God feels when we show love to Him?**

SAY: **God hears our praise and worship. He sees what we do to honour Him. Let's learn about a time when a king and God's people praised and worshipped God.**

Focus
God hears our praise and worship.

Explore His Word

2 Use these activities to help children **tell how Jehoshaphat and God's people showed their trust in God.**

Bible Background for the Teacher

The response of King Jehoshaphat of Judah to the news that a vast army of enemies was headed his way was not the expected response of a king. Jehoshaphat led his country in fasting and prayer. He acknowledged God and he admitted their dependence on God. On the morning of the battle, Jehoshaphat appointed men to sing to the Lord. In the end, the army of Judah did not even have to raise a hand against the enemy. God himself defeated Judah's enemy. The battle was won with prayer and praise.

Bible Exploration   2 Chronicles 20:1-30

Write '2 Chronicles 20:1' on the board. SAY: **Second Chronicles tells about men who were kings. Today we will learn about King Jehoshaphat.** Choose two volunteers to stand beside you and wear the name cards for Jehoshaphat and Jahaziel. The rest of the children will be Israelites who lived in Judah. Tell the children that they should mimic any actions you do as you tell the story.

Jehoshaphat was the king in Judah. He lived in the city of Jerusalem. King Jehoshaphat loved God. Cross hands over heart; prompt children to mimic the action. **He wanted the people of Judah to love God too. One day, some of the king's friends came to warn him.** Wag pointer finger. **They said, 'A huge army is coming! They are already close by.' King Jehoshaphat was alarmed.** Open eyes wide. **But the king did not panic.** Shake head no. **Instead, he told everyone in Judah that they would have a special time of prayer.** Clasp hands, as though praying. **No one was to eat during that time so they could spend all their time praying and thinking about God.**

Raise arms and look upward. **'O Lord,' King Jehoshaphat prayed, 'You rule over all the kingdoms on earth. You are powerful and strong.** Flex muscles. **Our friends and family, who lived here before us, told us that whenever times of trouble came, we should tell You all our problems. They said You would hear our prayers and save us. Lord, now an enemy is coming.** March in place. **They want to drive us from this land.** Push hands outward. **We can't go to war against them.** Shake head no. **We would surely lose.** Show thumbs-down. **We are looking to You for help.'** Look upward.

God told Jahaziel, a Levite teacher, to speak to the people. Have Jahaziel step forward. Jahaziel said, **'Listen!** Cup hand around ear. **The Lord says, 'Don't be afraid or discouraged. This is not your battle; it's God's.** Point upward. **Tomorrow, get up** (stand) **and go** (march in place) **to the place where the enemy is. You won't have to fight.** Punch air with closed fists. **Just go out and watch what God does.** Place hand over eyes; look around. **The Lord will be with you.''**
Then King Jehoshaphat and all the people bowed down and worshipped God. Kneel and bow at waist. **They thanked God for hearing their prayers. Some of the people stood up and praised God with loud voices.** Stand; raise arms and look upward.

The next morning, Jehoshaphat's army got up early to go to the place of God's battle. Stretch, as though waking up. **King Jehoshaphat chose some men to sing and praise God while leading the army to the battleground.** Have king point to a few children to join him. **The singers marched in front of the army.** March in place. **They sang, 'Give thanks to the Lord. For His love endures forever.'** Repeat phrases.

Then an amazing thing happened! God caused the enemy armies to fight against each other. Punch fists in air. **By the time Jehoshaphat's army got to the battleground, the enemies were all dead. God had won the battle for His people!** Cheer. **King Jehoshaphat led his army back to Jerusalem.** March in place. **They went to the temple. They played harps and lyres and trumpets.** Pretend to play instruments. **The people had trusted and worshipped God. God heard their praise and worship, and He answered their prayers.**

Materials
whiteboard, dry-erase marker, Bibles, Activity page *Bible Story Name Cards* on page 80, string or wool, scissors

Before Session
Attach strings to the King Jehoshaphat and Jahaziel name cards.

Bible Review Activity

ASK: **How did Jehoshaphat and God's people show that they trusted God?** (They did not panic at bad news. They had a special time of prayer and remembered what God had done for them. They sang as they went to battle. They praised God after the battle.)

SAY: **God heard the praise and worship of His people. God hears our praise and worship too.**

Focus
God hears our praise and worship.

Make It Real

3 Use this activity to help children **identify times when they can praise and worship God.**

Materials
Activity page *Don't Stop Praying game cards* on page 81, paper bag

Before Session
Cut out and fold the game cards and place them in the paper bag.

Don't Stop Praying Game

SAY: **King Jehoshaphat and God's people praised and worshipped God when they were facing a problem. They praised and worshipped God after He helped them too. Let's name times or ways we can praise and worship God.** Have the children form two teams. Let team players take turns pulling cards from the bag. Read each card aloud. If the player who selected the card can give an answer, the team is awarded 2 points. If the player is not sure how to answer, he can ask for help from his teammates. Award the team 1 point. Give bonus points whenever you hear an answer that you think is especially insightful. Play as time allows.
SAY: **We should never stop praising and worshipping God. God hears our praise and worship. He will be with us.**

Focus
God hears our praise and worship.

Live It Out

4 Use this activity to help children **praise and worship God.**

Materials
Activity page *Praise & Worship Pyramid* on page 82, pencils (or colouring pens), scissors, glue sticks

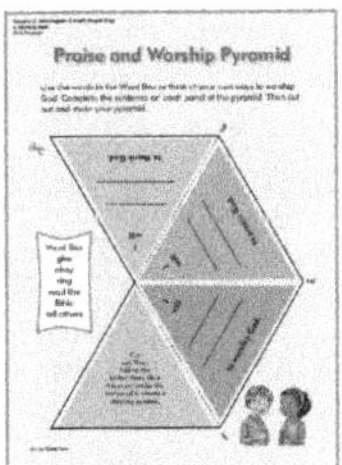

Praise and Worship Pyramid

SAY: **We know God hears our praise and worship. Let's make pyramids that will help us remember to praise and worship God. Then we'll praise and worship Him.** Distribute the activity page and supplies. Read the instructions and let the children make their pyramids. Be sure to offer assistance as needed in cutting and assembling the pyramids.

When everyone has finished, ask the children to gather in a closing prayer circle. Ask volunteers to share specific prayer needs they are concerned about. Maybe they know someone who is sick, or maybe there is a problem at home or school. Lead in prayer after the children have shared. PRAY: **Dear God, we praise You because You are great. We remember what you did to help King Jehoshaphat and Your people. We will obey and honour You. In Jesus' name, amen.**

Encourage the children to take their pyramids home. Every day they can turn the pyramid and praise or worship God in one of the ways written on the pyramid. Close the session in prayer.

Bible Story Name Cards

HeartShaper Primary Blue Edition, Activity page
Permission is granted to reproduce this page for ministry
purposes only—not for resale.

Rather than photocopy this page you can download
and print all activity pages in both colour and
black & white from **www.heartshaper.co.uk**

Don't Stop Praying Game Cards

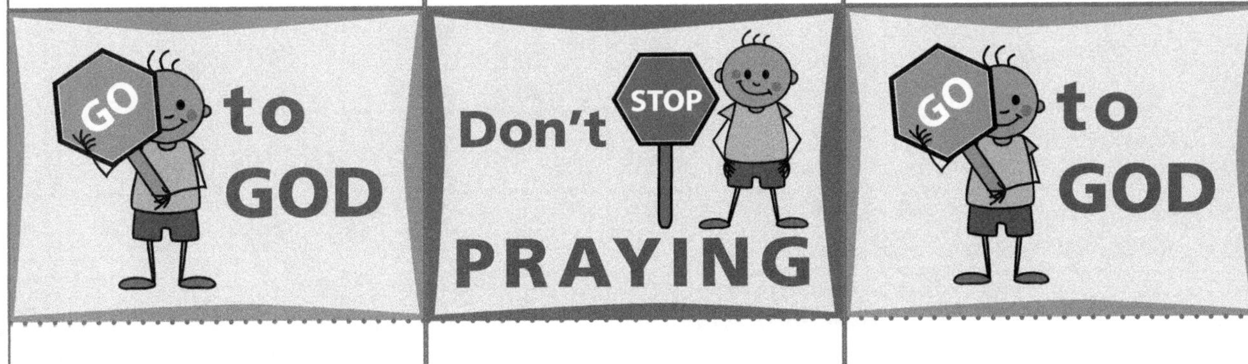

fold ↗

fold ↗

fold ↗

Your mum is sick. You know God has power to help in hard times. What can you do?

Name a time you can trust and ask God to help you.

You remember a time when God helped your family. What can you do?

Name a time you can trust and ask God to help you.

You are afraid of standing up to some bullies at school. What can you do?

Name a time you can praise and worship God.

You are nervous about being in the school play, even though you know your part. What can you do?

Name a time you can trust and ask God to help you.

God helped you remember the maths facts you studied. What should you do?

Use with Session 12

Praise and Worship Pyramid

Use the words in the Word Box or think of your own ways to worship God. Complete the sentence on each panel of the pyramid. Then cut out and make your pyramid.

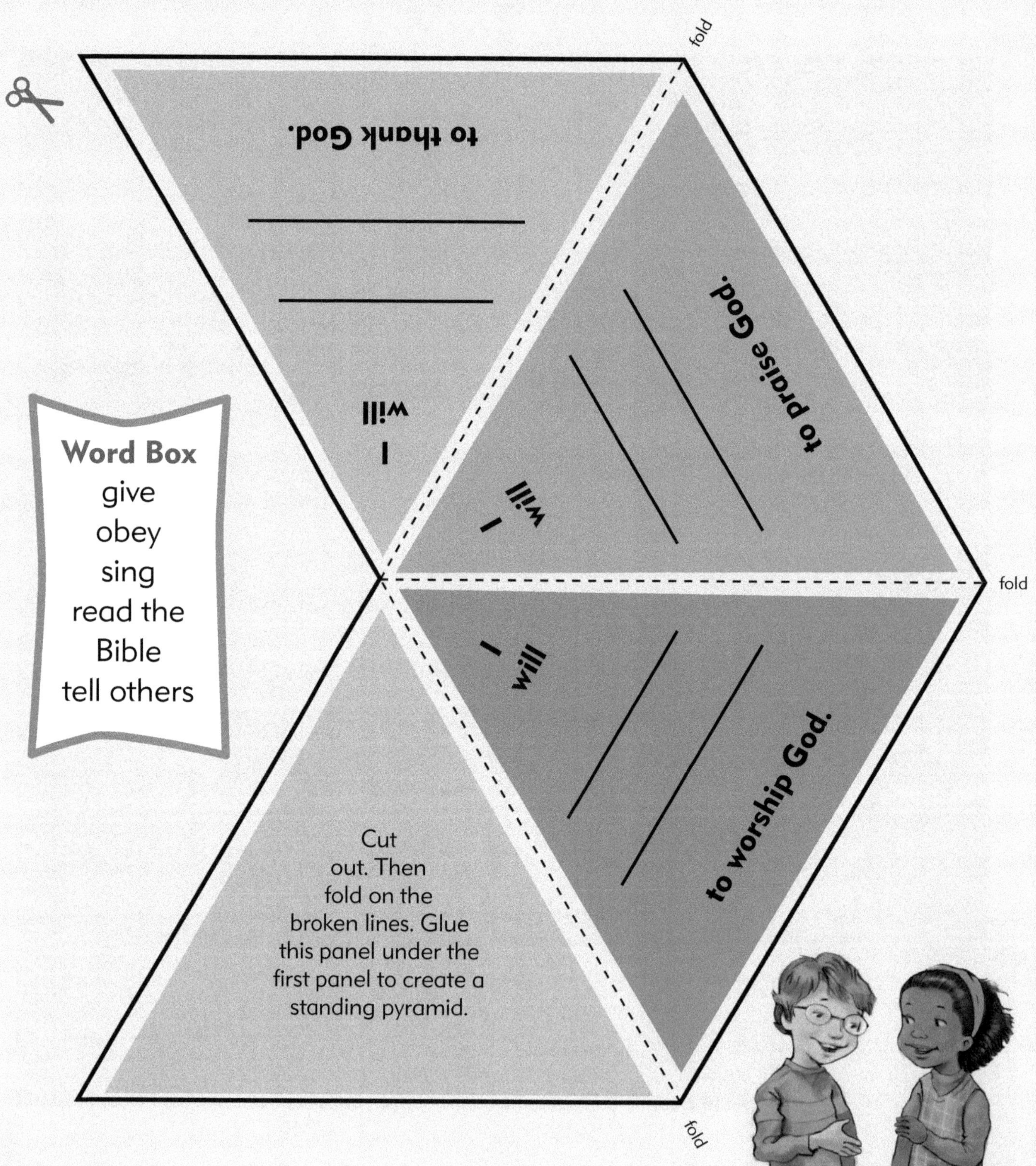

Art by Karen Lee

Manasseh Asks God for Forgiveness

Scripture: 2 Chronicles 33:1-20
Focus: God hears our prayers for forgiveness.

Heart to Heart Teacher Devotion

God is truly a forgiving and merciful God! God not only forgave King Manasseh of all his evil doings, but God blessed him beyond measure. Let the story of Manasseh and God's forgiveness give you hope. God will forgive a sincere and truly repentant heart. Let go of any pride you may have and ask God for His forgiveness.

Focus
God hears our prayers for forgiveness.

Materials
none

Action

Something More!
Let the children make up situations to say to the rest of the session.

Focus In

① Use this activity to help children **tell what *forgiveness* means**. Use the Bible Memory activity to introduce the memory verse.

Welcome

Welcome each child by name.

Is That Forgiveness?

Have children gather and sit in a circle. Explain that you are going to read some situations in which something wrong was done. If someone in the situation is giving forgiveness, the children can show thumbs-up. If forgiveness is not being shown, they can show thumbs-down.

SAY: **Joshua's mom broke a promise to him. She asked him to forgive her. Joshua gave his mum a hug.** (thumbs-up)
Ethan's sister said something unkind to him. She said she was sorry. Ethan is still angry and plans to do something unkind to his sister. (thumbs-down)
Aisha was angry and pushed Allie; Allie cried. Aisha said she was sorry. Allie said it was OK. (thumbs-up)

SAY: **We have been shown forgiveness when we do not have to pay a punishment for something we have done wrong. We're going to learn that God hears our prayers for forgiveness.**

Focus
God hears our prayers for forgiveness.

Explore His Word

② Use these activities to help children **tell how God answered Manasseh's prayer for forgiveness.**

Bible Background for the Teacher

Manasseh, Judah's longest reigning king, assumed the throne at age 12 and reigned for 55 years. Unfortunately, for most of those years, Manasseh was possibly Judah's most wicked king (see 2 Chronicles 33:9). His sins included reestablishing the worship places devoted to Baal and participating in practices of the occult. He killed his own sons in child sacrifice to the false god Molech.

God permitted Manasseh to be taken captive by the Assyrians to the city of Babylon, where Manasseh finally repented and humbly cried out to God for forgiveness. And true to His nature, God forgave Manasseh, allowing him to return to Jerusalem to continue his reign as king. The fruits of Manasseh's repentance are seen in the fact that he removed the objects of Judah's idolatrous worship and restored the worship of the one true God.

Bible Exploration   2 Chronicles 33:1-20

Review what the various kings prayed for. (Solomon prayed for wisdom. Hezekiah prayed for God's help. Jehoshaphat led the people to praise and worship God.) Write '2 Chronicles 33:1' on the board. **Second Chronicles tells us about one more king, King Manasseh.** Help children find 2 Chronicles 33:1 in their Bibles. Ask a volunteer to read the verse. SAY: **Listen for what Manasseh prayed and how God answered Manasseh's prayer.**

Point to the beginning of the line on the board. **Manasseh was only 12 years old when his father, King Hezekiah, died. Manasseh became the king of Judah, but he forgot how kind God had been to his father. As King Manasseh grew older, he began to do more and more bad things that hurt God.** Attach 13a to the board. Do the same with the other cards as the story is told. **Instead of worshipping God, Manasseh began to build idols for the people to worship. He forgot that God made the stars, and he worshipped the stars instead of God. Manasseh even had some of his own sons killed.**

Display 13b. **God tried to speak to King Manasseh and the people of Judah, but no one paid any attention to God. They just wanted to do things their own way. So God allowed some enemies of Judah to enter Jerusalem. The enemy army made King Manasseh a prisoner.** Display 13c. **The soldiers put heavy chains on the king's legs and wrists. Then they led the king away to a country far from his home.**

King Manasseh knew there was not one person in all of Judah who could save him—not his best fighting men, not his whole army, not a surprise attack, not a big war. Then King Manasseh thought about God. Manasseh probably thought about all the times God had saved His people from their enemies. Manasseh knew that only God had the power to save him too.

But Manasseh had not loved and served God as he should have. King Manasseh knew he needed to ask for God's forgiveness. Display 13d. **The king began to pray and tell God how very sorry he was for all the bad things he had done in Judah—things that had hurt God.**

God heard the king's prayer and offered forgiveness to Manasseh. God allowed Manasseh to go back to Jerusalem to be king once more. Manasseh had changed! Manasseh wanted to please God instead of hurt Him. Display 13e. **King Manasseh tore down the idols and rebuilt a stronger wall around God's city, Jerusalem. Manasseh and his people began to worship and serve the one true God once again.**

Display 13f. **Manasseh was king of Judah for 55 years. He was king in Judah longer than any other king. Manasseh made wrong choices and sinned, but then he told God he was sorry. God heard and answered Manasseh's prayer for forgiveness.**

Bible Review Activity

ASK: **What did Manasseh pray for, and how did God answer his prayer?**
(He prayed for forgiveness. God forgave Manasseh and let him return to Jerusalem to be the king again.)

Materials
whiteboard, dry-erase marker, Bibles, Activity page *Bible Story Cards* on page 86, tack magnets, (optional: clothes line and 6 pegs)

Before the Session
Draw a long horizontal line across the board. At left end of the line, write '12 years old.' At the right end of the line, write '55 years.'

Something More!
Have two volunteers stand at opposite sides of your storytelling area, holding a clothesline between them. As you tell the story, ask other children to come up and clip the Bible story cards to the line.

Materials

Activity page *Manasseh Prays* on page 87, pencils, Bible Story Cards 13a–13f, paper lunch bag

Activity Page

Distribute the activity pages and pencils. Do the page together. Remove the Bible story cards from the board (or clothesline) and place them in a paper bag. Let volunteers take turns choosing cards from the bag. Then they can tell about the parts of the Bible story pictured on their cards.

SAY: **Manasseh prayed for forgiveness, and God forgave him. God hears our prayers for forgiveness too.**

Focus

God hears our prayers for forgiveness.

Make It Real

3 Use this activity to help children **name things for which they need to ask forgiveness.**

Materials

Activity page *Please Forgive* on page 88, pencils, whiteboard, dry-erase marker

Activity Page

Note

Children will finish off the Please Forgive activity during Live It Out.

Please Forgive

SAY: **God answered King Manasseh's prayer for forgiveness. Let's think about wrong choices we make that we need to ask forgiveness for.** Distribute the activity pages and pencils. Read the directions aloud. Talk about the pictured situations.

ASK: **Why did these children need to ask God for forgiveness?** (cheated on a test; did not obey rules; forgot to be thankful to God)
What are some other things you might need to ask forgiveness for doing or not doing? (lie; disobey parents or teachers; treat others badly; steal; use God's name in a wrong way; be angry with others; break a promise; put other things before God) Make a list on the board as children name them.

SAY: **It is important to remember to ask for God's forgiveness when we sin and make wrong choices. Remember, God hears our prayers for forgiveness.**

Focus

God hears our prayers for forgiveness.

Live It Out

4 Use this activity to help children **pray for forgiveness.**

Materials

Activity page *Please Forgive* on page 88, pencils, list of things to be forgiven compiled in Make It Real

Pray

Note

If children did not do the first part of the activity earlier, you can complete it together at this time.

'Please Forgive Me, God'

Be sure the children have their activity pages. Refer to the list on the board. SAY: **We have named things for which we might need God's forgiveness. We love God and want to honour Him. We don't want to go on disobeying God. At the bottom of your activity page, write a prayer, asking God to forgive something you have done wrong or forgotten to do to honour Him. Then we'll pray and ask God to help us obey Him.**

Allow time for children to write their prayers. If children cannot think of something they need to ask forgiveness for, they can write a prayer asking God to help them make right choices. Lead in a closing prayer. PRAY: **Dear God, we know You hear our prayers for forgiveness. We know You offer forgiveness to those who believe in Your Son, Jesus. Forgive the things we have done wrong. Forgive us when we have not honoured You as we should. Help us choose to obey Your Word. In Jesus' name, amen.**

Manasseh Asks God for Forgiveness **Session 13**

Manasseh Bible Story Cards

HeartShaper Primary Blue Edition, Activity page
Permission is granted to reproduce this page for ministry
purposes only—not for resale.

Rather than photocopy this page you can download
and print all activity pages in both colour and
black & white from **www.heartshaper.co.uk**

Manasseh Prays

Name ____

Manasseh was only **TWELVE** years old when he became king.

Manasseh did **THINGS** that were wrong.

God punished **MANASSEH** for the wrong things he did.

Manasseh prayed and asked God to **FORGIVE** him.

God **HEARD** Manasseh's prayer.

Art by Roy Green and Len Ebert

HeartShaper Primary Blue Edition, Activity page

Please Forgive

Using the words in the Word Box, help these children finish their prayers. Then write your own prayer.

Word Box
rules
test
food

Dear God,
Please forgive me for cheating on a
___ ___ ___ ___ .

Dear God,
Please forgive me for not
playing by the
___ ___ ___ ___ ___ .

Dear God,
Please forgive me for not being thankful
for my ___ ___ ___ ___ .

Dear God,
Please forgive me __________________

__________________ .

Art by Mary Rojas

Elijah Obeys God

Scripture: 1 Kings 17:1-16
Focus: God wants us to obey Him.

Heart to Heart Teacher Devotion

If God had made us robot-like creatures, we'd have no trouble obeying Him. But God chose to create us with free will. He gave us the ability to make choices, and the ability to love and obey Him, or not. How pleased God must be when we obey Him; how sad He must be when we don't. May we honour God today by choosing to obey Him.

Focus

God wants us to obey Him.

Materials

none

Game

 As written, this activity may be difficult for a child who has social, language, or motor difficulties. Changing the rules could prompt a meltdown. Consider offering a discussion activity in which you show pictures of times when children would need to follow directions. Then discuss why obeying rules is important.

Focus In

1 Use this activity to help children **explore the consequences of not obeying instructions.**

Welcome

Welcome each child by name.

Red Light, Green Light

Choose a volunteer to be the STOP light. Ask all the other children to form a line at least 5 metres away from the volunteer to play a game of Red Light, Green Light. The 'stoplight' should face away from the children and call out 'Green light!' At this point the children are allowed to move toward the stoplight. At any point, the stoplight should whirl around and say 'Red light!' If the stoplight catches any children moving, they are out. Play resumes when the stoplight turns back around and says 'Green light!'

After all the children reach the stoplight or are out, start a new game with you as the stoplight. This time, change the rules in any way you want to, but don't tell the children. You could call out 'Yellow light' or 'Purple light.' When any children move, they are out. You could call children out for moving on 'Green light.' You get the idea—change the rules without telling the children.

ASK: **When you play a regular game of Red Light, Green Light, how easy is it for you to obey the instructions?** Accept responses. **When are some times it's hard for you to obey instructions? What happens in real life for not obeying instructions?** (get in trouble; get a bad grade; get hurt)

SAY: **Let's keep thinking about obeying instructions as we dig into God's Word.**

Explore His Word

② Use these activities to help children **tell how Elijah obeyed God.**

Bible Background for the Teacher

Israel had seen some wicked rulers, but Ahab and his wife Jezebel were the worst! God's response was to send Elijah to King Ahab with a proclamation stating that it would not rain for three and a half years! (See 1 Kings 18:1; Luke 4:25; James 5:17.)

The Lord commanded Elijah to go to the Kerith Ravine to escape the drought. When the brook dried up, God sent Elijah to Queen Jezebel's native land, Zarephath of Sidon. There, Elijah asked a starving widow with 'only a handful of flour in a jar and a little olive oil in a jug' (1 Kings 17:12) to feed him. The prophet assured her that 'the jar of flour will not be used up and the jug of oil will not run dry until the day the LORD sends rain on the land' (v. 14). Elijah was not merely asking the widow for food, but for faith. The widow 'went away and did as Elijah had told her' (v. 15). The faith and obedience of both Elijah and the widow stand in sharp contrast to the Baal worship that was promoted by King Ahab.

Bible Exploration   1 Kings 17:1-16

Have a volunteer show on the map Tishbe, Kerith Ravine, Jordan River, and Zarephath. Tell children that these places are in today's Bible story. Ask children to turn in their Bibles to the table of contents page. Ask them to locate the book of 1 Kings.

ASK: **What do we call the Old Testament books of Joshua through Esther when we refer to them as a group of books?** (History)

Ask children to turn to 1 Kings 17:1, and have a volunteer read the verse aloud. SAY: **Elijah was a prophet of God who spoke God's words to the people. In this case, Elijah spoke God's words to the evil King Ahab and his wife, Jezebel. The king and his wife had forced on the Israelites the worship of the idol Baal. And Jezebel had tried to kill God's prophets and replace them with the prophets of Baal. Because of this wickedness, God sent Elijah to King Ahab with a message. As I tell you more about this, I'll stop once in a while. When I stop, make the face you think that person might have made at that moment, and freeze your face. Are you ready?**

Read 1 Kings 17:1. SAY: **Show on your face how King Ahab might have looked, and freeze your face!** Look at the children' faces. **You're right; Ahab was not happy!** Read verses 2-6. **Show on your face how Elijah might have looked, and freeze your face!** Look at the children' faces. **What an amazing thing God did! But it only happened because Elijah obeyed God.** Read verses 7-9. SAY: **Show on your face how Elijah might have looked, and freeze your face! God asked Elijah to once again trust and obey Him. Let's find out what Elijah did.** Read verses 10-12. **Show on your face how the widow might have looked as Elijah asked her for bread. The widow was so poor that she was just about out of food.**

Read verses 13-14. SAY: **Show on your face how the widow might have looked, and freeze your face! It all sounded so amazing!** Read verses 15, 16. **Show on your face how Elijah and the woman might have looked, and freeze your face! What an amazing thing God did! But it only happened because Elijah obeyed God and the woman followed Elijah's instructions.**

Bible Review Activity

Hand out Activity page *Elijah and a Widow*. Let children take turns reading the sentences and filling in the blanks. (Answers: 1=Elijah, Ravine, brook,

Materials
map from session 7 on page 52; Bibles; Activity pages *Elijah and a Widow* on pages 92-93; pencils

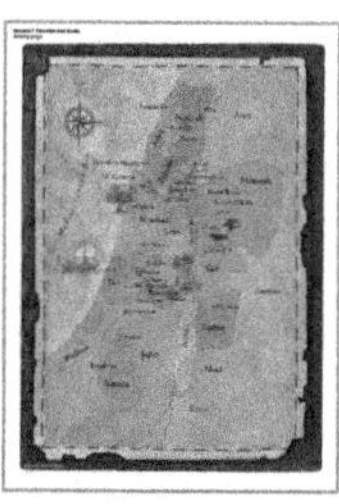

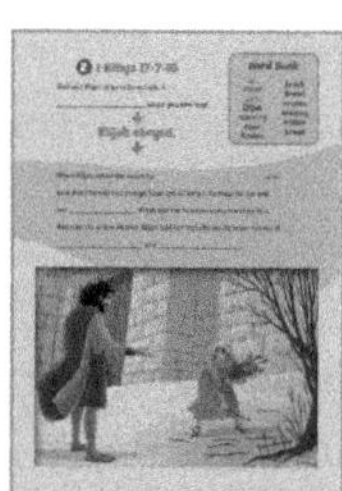

Teaching Tip
Put children in pairs so that stronger readers can help younger children.

ravens, bread, meat, morning, evening; 2=widow, bread, son, flour, oil)

ASK: **Do you think it was easy for Elijah to go to Zarephath so a widow could give him food? Why do you say that?** (No, Elijah probably knew that widows were usually poor.)

Let's be like Elijah, obeying God because we love Him, knowing that it's the best thing to do!

Make It Real

3 Use this activity to help children **discuss reasons to obey God.**

Materials

long length of roll paper, markers, Bibles, pencils, sticky tape

Art

Scriptures

Leviticus 22:31
Psalm 78:7
Isaiah 40:28
Luke 6:47-48
John 14:15, 21
Acts 5:32
2 Thessalonians 1:8
1 John 2:3-5

Banner of Obedience

ASK: **What are some reasons for obeying God?** Accept responses.

Lay the roll paper where it's easy for everyone to work on it. SAY: **Let's make a big banner showing reasons the Bible gives us for obeying God.** Assign each pair of children one of the Scriptures listed in the narrow column. Tell children to illustrate their passage, write it out, or do some illustrating and writing. As children work, help them as needed to mainly focus on the reason to obey God that's in their Scripture. When everyone is finished let volunteers talk about their reasons to obey God.

ASK: **Which reason to obey God is one that you had never really thought about before?** Accept responses.

SAY: **God wants us to obey Him, and I** *want* **to obey Him because of who He is and to show Him how much I love Him. I hope you want to do the same!** Be sure to display the banner in your room.

Live It Out

4 Use this activity to help children **choose to obey God.**

Materials

Activity page *Prayer Prompts* on page 94, pencils

Pray

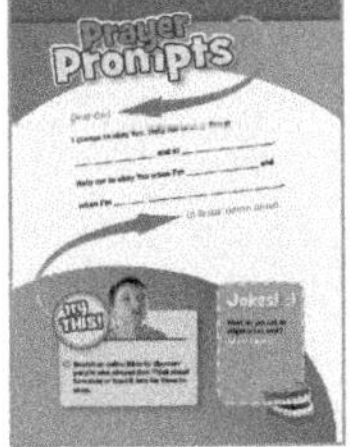

Prayer Prompts

ASK: **Will you choose to obey God? How about when life gets hard, like it did for Elijah—will you still choose to obey God?**

SAY: **I hope you remember that God wants us to obey Him. He doesn't force us; it's our choice. Since obeying God can sometimes be hard, we need to pray and ask God for His help.** Hand out Activity page *Prayer Prompts.* Read the prayer aloud. Give children some ideas as to how they might fill in the blanks. (Ideas: obey God at school, home, with friends; obey God when tempted to not obey, playing sports, etc.) Have children fill in the blanks. Offer support with writing as needed. When they're done, give children time to silently pray their prayers to God.

After a short time of silence, ask for three volunteers to pray. Ask a volunteer to start the prayer by praising and worshipping God for being the creator. Ask the next volunteer to praise God for everything He has done. Ask the last volunteer to ask for God's help in obeying Him.

Elijah and a Widow

Find out what happened when Elijah obeyed God.

1 | 1 Kings 17:1-6

God told ___________________ to go to

the Kerith ___________________.

Elijah would drink from a

___________________________, and

___________________________ would

supply food.

↓

Elijah obeyed.

↓

God sent ravens with ______________

and ___________________ for

Elijah. The ravens came in the

____

and in the ___________________________.

2 **I Kings 17:7-16**

God told Elijah to go to Zarephath. A

_______________________________ would give him food.

⬇

Elijah obeyed.

⬇

When Elijah asked the widow for _______________________________, she

said that she only had enough flour and oil for a little meal for her and

her _______________________. Elijah told her to make some bread for him.

Because the widow obeyed, Elijah told her that she would never run out of

_______________________ and _______________________.

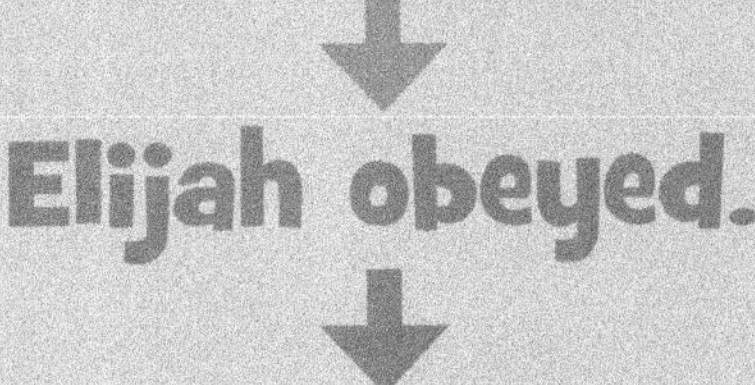

HeartShaper Primary Blue Edition, Activity page

93

Prayer Prompts

Dear God,

I choose to obey You. Help me to obey You at ________________ and at ________________.

Help me to obey You when I'm ________________ and when I'm ________________.

In Jesus' name, amen.

try THIS!

➡ **Search an online Bible to discover people who obeyed God. Think about how easy or hard it was for them to obey.**

Jokes! :)

What do you call an alligator in a vest?

An investigator!

Prophecies About Jesus' Birth

Scripture: Isaiah 7:14; 9:6; Micah 5:2, 4-5a
Focus: God planned to send Jesus.

Heart to Heart Teacher Devotion

We are amazed and awed by God's magnificent plan to save us by sending His Son. We see His faithfulness to the plan and His attention to detail as the plan unfolds. We see new beginnings for Jonah and the people of Nineveh. We see a new beginning foretold in the words of the prophets. And, thank God, we can see that there is a new beginning for us as well!

Focus
God planned to send Jesus.

Materials
paper, pencils

Discuss

Focus In

1 Use this activity to help children **explore the accuracy of modern-day predictions.**

Welcome

Welcome each child by name.

Make Your Predictions

Tell children to listen to these actual predictions that were made for the year 2015. They should raise their hands when they hear something that actually happened. SAY: **Vehicles will drive themselves. There will be a hotel in orbit around the earth. There will be computer-enhanced dreaming. Dolls will come with a personality chip.**

ASK: **How do we know whether these predictions came true?** (Either they saw or heard about the things or they didn't.)

Have children pair up. Distribute pencils and give each pair a sheet of paper. SAY: **Now it's your turn to make a couple of predictions about something that will happen in the coming year. Try to come up with at least two predictions and write them on your paper.** When children are done, have them pass their papers to the right. **Look at what your friends wrote. If you think those predictions will happen this year, put a tick by them.** Then have children pass their papers to the right again. Keep going until the predictions are back to those who wrote them.

SAY: **It will be interesting to see whether your predictions come true. Let's see whether some predictions in the Bible came true.**

Focus
God planned to send Jesus.

Explore His Word

2 Use these activities to help children **talk about Jesus and describe how the prophecies were fulfilled.**

Bible Background for the Teacher

In the time of the prophet Isaiah, God's people lived in two separate kingdoms: the northern kingdom called Israel and the southern kingdom called Judah. In this historical context the prophet gave the Immanuel sign to Ahaz, king of Judah. A young child soon to be born—possibly Isaiah's own son—would bear the figurative name 'God [is] with us.' Before that child grew much beyond infancy, the Syrian and Israelite threat would evaporate (Isaiah 7:14-16). But the Immanuel prophecy held meaning far beyond the immediate situation, for it referred ultimately to God's own Son, born of a virgin and bringing peace to the whole world (Matthew 1:22-23).

At about the same time as Isaiah, Micah prophesied to the southern kingdom. He spoke of Judah's ideal king, born in King David's town of Bethlehem, and ruling God's people in peace in the name of God (Micah 5:2, 4-5). Christians today can thank God for these ancient prophecies that foretold of our Saviour, Jesus Christ.

Bible Exploration   Isaiah 7:14; 9:6; Micah 5:2, 4-5a

SAY: **You've probably had to wait for something you really wanted. Maybe it was a gift or a holiday. The Israelite people also waited for something, but it wasn't either of those things. Let's find out what it was.** Have children turn in their Bibles to the contents page. For Bibles on a tablet computer, phone, or e-reader, children can open to the contents page. Ask them to look in the Old Testament section and find the book of Isaiah.

ASK: **What are the books of Isaiah through Malachi called when referred to as a group of books?** (books of Prophecy)

Have children turn to Isaiah 7:14, and ask a volunteer to read it aloud. Next have children turn to Isaiah 9:6, and ask a volunteer to read it aloud. Then have children turn to Micah 5:2, 4-5a, and ask volunteers to read those verses aloud. SAY: **Isaiah and Micah were two of God's prophets. God would speak to them and tell them what to say to people to help them learn about Him. In the verses we just read, Isaiah and Micah were prophesying, or making predictions, about what would happen *several hundred years in the future*!**
ASK: **Who were Isaiah and Micah prophesying, or making predictions, about?** (Jesus)

Divide the session into two groups. Assign one group the passages from Isaiah; assign the other group the Micah passage. Using a dry-erase marker, make a long mark down the middle of the whiteboard. Label one side 'Isaiah' and the other side 'Micah.' SAY: **In your group, work together to discover what your passage is saying about Jesus and His birth. As soon as you discover something, have someone from your group write it on the board. Try your best to put it in your own words.** Give groups several minutes to do this. Help children as needed to understand the passages. When groups are finished, read aloud what they've written, clarifying anything children seem confused about.

SAY: **God helped Isaiah and Micah know that someone very special was coming—the one people had been waiting for, the Saviour! You see, since before time began, God planned to send Jesus. Isaiah and Micah were able to make some very specific predictions about Jesus and His birth because God gave them the facts. Let's look again at what these two Old Testament prophets predicted about Jesus and His birth.**

Distribute the Activity page *Prophecies About Jesus*. Work together as a large group to finish the sentences. (Answers: 1=Judah; 2=Bethlehem; 3=shepherd; 4=ruler; 5=son)

ASK: **Was Jesus from the clan of Judah and born in Bethlehem?** (yes)
    Is Jesus a shepherd and a ruler? (yes)
    Is Jesus the Son of God who was born of a virgin? (yes)

SAY: **The predictions made by the prophets about Jesus and His birth were 100 percent right! Now let's think about why God planned to send Jesus.**

Materials
Bibles, whiteboard, dry-erase markers, Bible time lines, Activity page *Prophecies About Jesus* on page 100, pencils

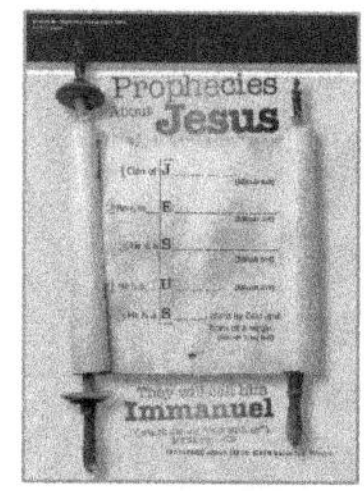

Teaching Tip
Have older children or stronger readers work in pairs or groups with younger children to support them.

Make It Real

3 Use this activity to help children **understand why God planned to send Jesus.**

Materials
Activity pages *It's Impossible* and *It's Possible* on pages 98-99, pencils

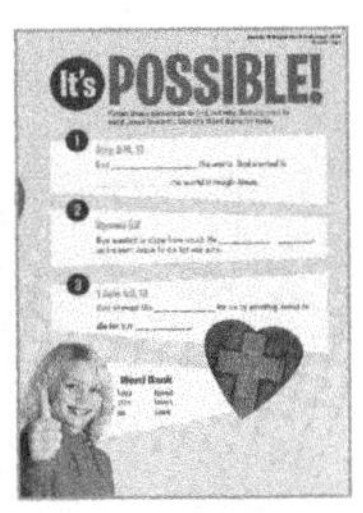

Action

Teaching Tip
If you have any children who wouldn't be able to do this, come up with a contest that's better suited for your group.

It's Possible!

Ask children to stand up and count to 10 while running in place, along with doing arm circles. As soon as children either stop counting or running in place or doing arm circles, they are out. If this is too easy for some children, add something else for them to do. SAY: **I think it would be impossible to keep doing all those things for very long.** Have children sit down and turn in their activity leaflets to It's Impossible! Let children have fun trying to figure out the optical illusions. SAY: **Another thing that seems impossible to understand is *why* God would want to save us from our sins, why He would plan to send Jesus to earth.** Have children look in their activity leaflets at It's Possible! Do the page together. (Answers: 1=loved, save; 2=loves us; 3=love, sins)

ASK: **According to God's Word, why did God plan to send Jesus?**
(because He loves us, to save us from our sins)

Live It Out

4 Use this activity to help children **thank God for His plan to send Jesus.**

Materials
duct tape or masking tape (light coloured so children can write on it), scissors, Bibles, paper, permanent fine-tip markers

Object Lesson

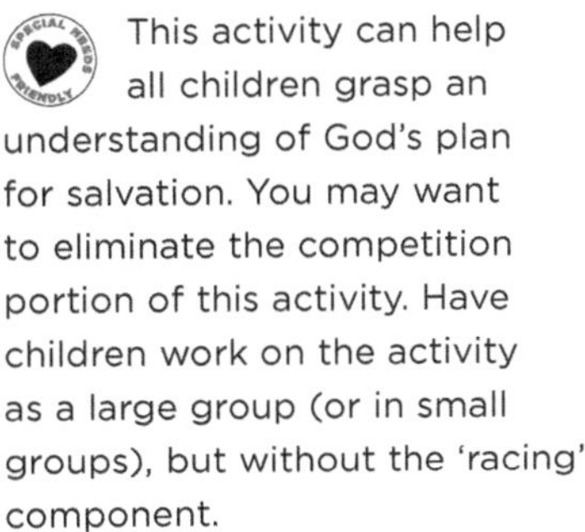

This activity can help all children grasp an understanding of God's plan for salvation. You may want to eliminate the competition portion of this activity. Have children work on the activity as a large group (or in small groups), but without the 'racing' component.

All Tangled Up

Divide the session into two teams. Give each student a long length of duct tape. SAY: **Your goal is to be the first team to make a ball of duct tape. Each of you will add your length of duct tape, rolling and wadding it into the ball. Ready? Go!** When teams are finished, congratulate the winning team. **Now your goal is to be the first team to unroll the ball so the duct tape is usable.** This should be very hard to do, if not impossible. After a short time, SAY: **Pretty impossible, isn't it? Your balls of tape are a messed up, tangled, sticky blob! That's like sin. Sin messes us up, gets us tangled up, and leaves us in sticky situations. Fortunately, God planned to send Jesus to help us out of the mess that sin makes in our lives. But *why*? Why would God plan to send Jesus?** Ask children to turn in their Bibles to John 3:16-17; Romans 5:8; and 1 John 4:9-10. Have volunteers read those verses aloud.

ASK: **Why did God plan to send Jesus?** (because He loves us; to save us from our sins)

Give each child two lengths of duct tape and a sheet of paper. Tell children to use the duct tape to form a cross on the paper. They should write on it why God planned to send Jesus. SAY: **It's amazing that the prophets' predictions about Jesus and His birth were 100 percent right! Even more amazing is *why* God planned to send Jesus. Let's thank God for loving us so much!**

It's IMPOSSIBLE!

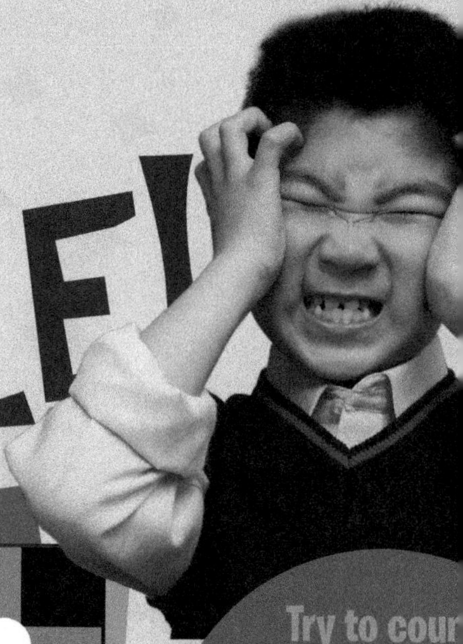

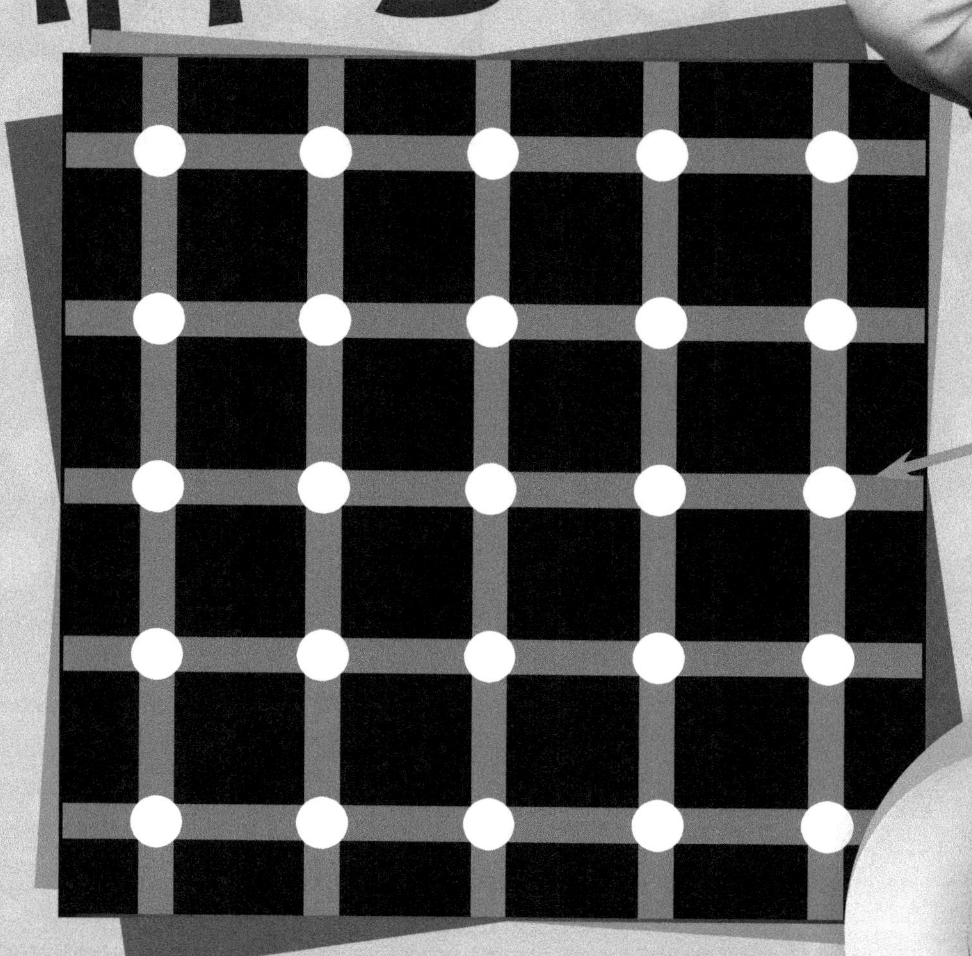

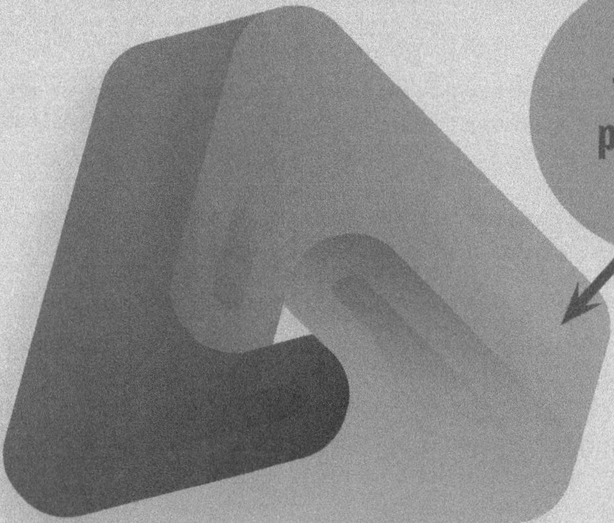

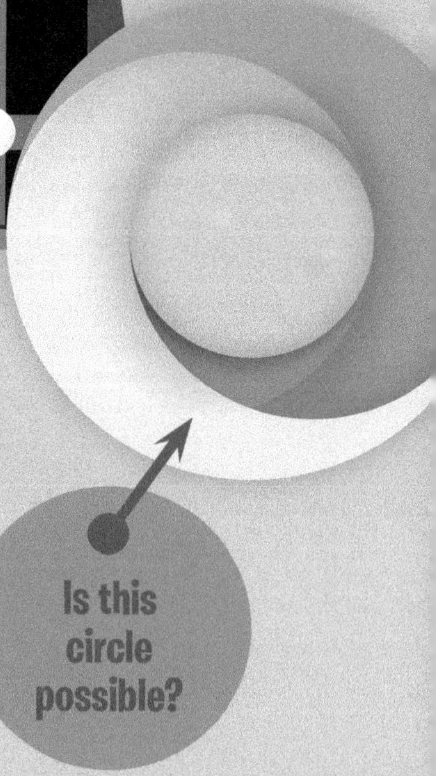

It's POSSIBLE!

Finish these sentences to find out why God planned to send Jesus to earth. Use the Word Bank for help.

1 **John 3:16, 17**

God ___________________ the world. God wanted to

___________________ the world through Jesus.

2 **Romans 5:8**

God wanted to show how much He ___________ ________,
so He sent Jesus to die for our sins.

3 **1 John 4:9, 10**

God showed His _______________ for us by sending Jesus to

die for our _______________.

Word Bank

love	loved
sins	loves
us	save

Prophecies About Jesus

1 Clan of **J** ___ ___ ___ ___ . (Micah 5:2)

2 Born in ___ **E** ___ ___ ___ ___ ___ ___ ___ . (Micah 5:2)

3 He is a **S** ___ ___ ___ ___ ___ ___ ___ . (Micah 5:4)

4 He is a ___ **U** ___ ___ ___ . (Micah 5:2)

5 He is a **S** ___ ___ , given by God and born of a virgin. (Isaiah 7:14; 9:6)

They will call him Immanuel

(which means 'God with us').
Matthew 1:23

Jesus Is Born

Session 16

Scripture: Luke 2:1-20
Focus: Jesus came to us.

Heart to Heart Teacher Devotion
'When the set time had fully come, God sent his Son, born of a woman, born under the law, to redeem those under the law, that we might receive adoption to sonship' (Galatians 4:4-5). This is the gospel in four words—God sent, redeems, adopts. Jesus came to us to redeem us, so that we could be adopted into God's family. Pause right now to praise God for His wondrous plan!

Focus
Jesus came to us.

Materials
whiteboard, dry-erase marker, watch with second hand

Game

Focus In

❶ Use this activity to help children **identify characters in the story of Jesus' birth.**

Welcome

Welcome each child by name.

Strike-A-Pose Charades

List on the board the characters involved in the birth of Jesus: Caesar Augustus, Joseph, Mary, baby Jesus, shepherds, angel, heavenly host.
SAY: **These people were all a part of Jesus' birth.** If you have any children who may not be familiar with the characters involved in the birth of Jesus, review who they are.

Divide the session into two teams. Tell one team to huddle up and choose a character listed on the board. The members of that team should then all strike a pose and hold it, as if each of them were that character. The other team has 20 seconds to huddle up and decide which character the other team has chosen. Then let the other team have a turn, continuing in the same manner. Keep playing until all the characters have been chosen at least once.

ASK: **Which character do you find the most interesting?** Accept responses.

SAY: **Caesar Augustus, Joseph, Mary, the shepherds, the angel, the heavenly host—they all had important roles in the birth of Jesus. It's so amazing that Jesus came to us!**

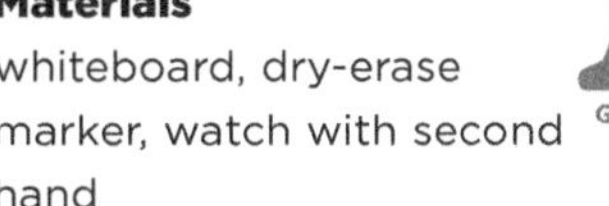

Focus
Jesus came to us.

Explore His Word

❷ Use these activities to help children **retell about Jesus' birth from different points of view.**

Bible Background for the Teacher

The manger where Mary laid Jesus as a newborn could either refer to a feeding box as traditionally depicted or to the whole stable where they stayed. In either case God's Son came into His world in humble circumstances. The first visitors to see the new baby also came from humble circumstances.

Some shepherds sleeping out in the pasture to guard their flocks received the news, along with some confirming signs, from God's angels. In the town of David (Bethlehem), they would find a Saviour, God's anointed deliverer, the Messiah. The traditional translation of Luke 2:14, 'on earth peace, good will toward men,' comes from later manuscripts of Luke's Gospel. Based on earlier and better manuscripts, the *New International Version* refers to people of God's favour; that is, 'those on whom his favour rests.'

The last scene of the passage draws a contrast between the shepherds' joyful public proclamation of what they had seen and Mary's quiet reflection on what her baby's birth might mean. Both are appropriate ways to celebrate that Jesus came to us.

Bible Exploration   Luke 2:1-20

Display the *Bible Map* on activity page 106 and also refer to the Bible Timelines if you have displayed them.

ASK: **When you want to read about Jesus' birth, where would you find it in your Bible?** (New Testament, Gospels, Matthew and Luke)

Ask a volunteer to stand by the Bible map and point out the towns of Nazareth and Bethlehem. Have another volunteer read about these places from the map. Have children turn in their Bibles to Luke 2:1-3, and have volunteers read those verses aloud. SAY: **The stage is set. What happened because of Caesar's decree? What happened in the towns of Nazareth and Bethlehem? Let's listen in as Joseph, Mary, and the shepherds tell us about Jesus' birth from their points of view.** Read the rest of the Bible verses 3-20.

ASK: **Who lived in Nazareth?** (Joseph and Mary)
In what town was Jesus born? (Bethlehem)
Would you like to have been Joseph, Mary, or a shepherd? Why?
Accept responses.
What would you say is the main thing that makes baby Jesus different from other babies? (He's God's Son.)

Read the verses again, this time letting volunteers act out some of the parts. Possible parts would be: Joseph, Mary, shepherd, angels. Be sure to start by reading Luke 2:1-3; someone could also act out the part of Caesar Augustus. Children can just pretend to talk or they may want to say the words from the Bible for their characters. Thank children for their participation.

Distribute the Activity page *Certificate and Record of Birth*. Do this page together as a session, letting different children call out the correct answers. (Answers: Jesus; male; Bethlehem; other; manger; cloths; angel; animals; shepherds; Mary; Joseph; God)

ASK: **What is the good news of great joy?** (Jesus, the Saviour, was born.)
Why do you think people were amazed at what the shepherds told them? (They had never heard of an angel announcing a baby's birth before; all the things that the angel told the shepherds would happen, did happen.)

SAY: **We thank God that Jesus came to us! Let's discover *why* Jesus came.**

Bibles, Activity page *Bible Map* on page 106, Activity pages *Certificate and Record of Birth* on pages 104-105, pencils, sticky tape

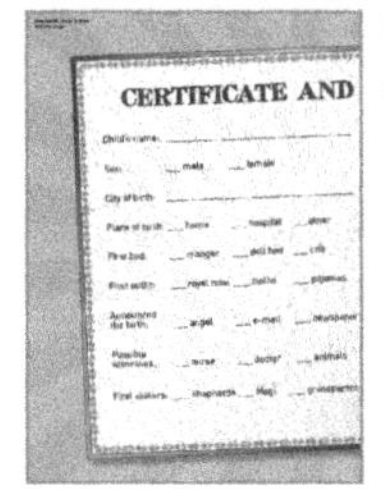

Make It Real

3 Use this activity to help children **remember why Jesus came.**

Materials

craft paper (or craft foam), scissors, markers, string, hole punch (optional: sequins, glitter glue, other items for decorating ornaments, songs about Jesus' birth from your music collection)

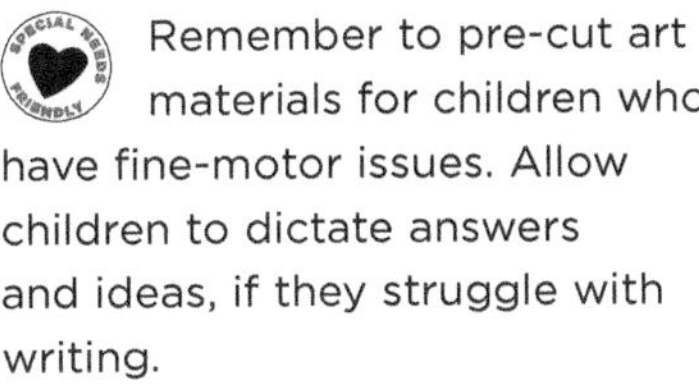

Remember to pre-cut art materials for children who have fine-motor issues. Allow children to dictate answers and ideas, if they struggle with writing.

Ornament Thanks

SAY: **Let's make some ornaments that will remind us to thank Jesus for coming to be our Saviour.** Distribute supplies. Tell children they can design their own ornaments, making them any shape they desire. On the ornaments children should write their thanks to Jesus in their own words for coming to be the Saviour for all people. If desired, play songs about Jesus' birth as children work.

When children are done making the ornaments, close with a time of prayer. SAY: **It is so amazing that Jesus came to us! Jesus came to earth with only one purpose—to be our Saviour. I am so glad He did! As we thank Jesus, let's try something different for our prayer time. Look at your ornament. When I say 'Let's pray,' we all will read at the same time from our ornaments the thanks we wrote to Jesus.**

Encourage children to speak and pray respectfully. **Let's pray.** When the prayer is finished, encourage children to take their ornaments home and put them where they and others will be reminded of why Jesus came to us!

Live It Out

4 Use this activity to help children **thank Jesus for coming as the Saviour.**

Materials

yellow paper, pencils (or pens), nativity set (optional: scissors)

Manger Thanks

Before the session, tear (or cut) yellow paper into strips approximately 4cm wide, one strip per child. Display the nativity set where children can gather around it.

SAY: **Let's take time right now to thank Jesus for coming as the Saviour.** Distribute the strips of paper. **On the strips of paper, write your thanks to Jesus for coming to be the Saviour for all people or write a prayer for someone you care about - a friend or family member.** Encourage children to write using their own words. They might want to use some words or phrases from the Scriptures talked about in the Bible Exploration time.

When children are ready, ask them to put their papers around the manger in the nativity set. As everyone stands around the manger, ask a few volunteers to pray, thanking Jesus that He came to earth to be the Saviour of all people.

CERTIFICATE AND

Child's name: _______________________________

Sex: ___ male ___ female

City of birth: _______________________________

Place of birth: ___ home ___ hospital ___ other

First bed: ___ manger ___ doll bed ___ crib

First outfit: ___ royal robe ___ cloths ___ pyjamas

Announced the birth: ___ angel ___ e-mail ___ newspa

Possible witnesses: ___ nurse ___ doctor ___ animals

First visitors: ___ shepherds ___ Magi ___ grandpar

ECORD OF BIRTH

other's name: _______________________

ather's name: _______________________

eavenly
ather's name: _______________________

First Family Photo

Sites from
Jesus' Early Life
and the
Beginning of His Ministry

Jesus Is Taken to the Temple — Session 17

Scripture: Luke 2:21-40
Focus: Jesus is the promised Messiah.

Heart to Heart Teacher Devotion
The Jewish people waited for a deliverer, the Messiah. When Anna and Simeon saw baby Jesus, they knew right away that Jesus was the long-awaited Messiah. Their response was to praise and thank God. Thank God that you recognise Jesus as the Messiah, your deliverer!

Focus
Jesus is the promised Messiah.

Materials
large sheets of drawing paper, pencils, reusable adhesive, flashlights  Art

 Remember that tracing a silhouette requires a steady hand and a patient mind-set—a difficult set of skills for some children. Consider having extra adult volunteers available to do the silhouette tracings.

Focus In

(1) Use this activity to help children **explore how they recognise people.**

Welcome
Welcome each child by name.

Silhouettes

Have children get into groups of three. Give each group three sheets of paper, a pencil, and a flashlight. Tell children that they're going to draw silhouettes of each other. Use one group to demonstrate this. Have one child sit on a chair against a wall. Another child should attach a sheet of paper on the wall behind the seated child's head. The last child should stand a few feet from the seated volunteer and shine a flashlight on her head. The child who attached the paper to the wall will draw on the paper the outline of the seated child's head. Each student needs to have a silhouette drawn. Ask children to write their names on the backs of their papers; then collect them.

After they've finished, gather everyone back together. SAY: **Let's see how well you recognise each other by seeing their silhouettes.** One at a time, hold up a silhouette. Ask the student closest to you to guess who it is. If that student guesses incorrectly, ask the next student to identify the person. Keep going until someone guesses correctly. Then hold up the next silhouette and do the same, letting all children have a turn guessing.

ASK: **How do you usually recognise people?** (hearing them; seeing them; seeing their uniforms; hearing something about them) **How would you recognise someone you had never met or never heard?** Accept responses.

SAY: **In today's lesson, two people recognise someone they had never met or heard, but they knew about Him. Let's dig into God's Word to find out about it.**

Explore His Word

2 Use these activities to help children **describe what happened when Simeon and Anna met Jesus, the promised Messiah.**

Bible Background for the Teacher

At the temple, Mary and Joseph met two people who recognised Jesus' nature and destiny. Simeon had had a promise from God that he would live to see the Messiah, and he had special instructions to visit the temple that day. After acknowledging that God had kept His promise and Simeon could die content, Simeon prophesied about Jesus' destiny and the sorrow it would bring Mary. The prophetess Anna had lived a long time. The text does not say clearly whether 84 referred to her age or to how long she had lived as a widow. In either case, she showed her devotion to God by constantly worshipping at the temple, fasting, and praying. Like Simeon, she recognised that the redemption of Jerusalem would hinge on this holy child.

At the end of the passage, the Gospel writer emphasises Joseph and Mary's compliance with God's law. Unlike Matthew, Luke does not mention the flight to Egypt (Matthew 2:13-18). Instead he tells how the family moved from their temporary residence in Bethlehem back to their home in Nazareth. The last verse describes Jesus' growth in body and spirit.

Bible Exploration   Luke 2:21-40

Ask children to turn in their Bibles to Luke 2:21-24. Have volunteers read those verses aloud. SAY: **Eight days after Jesus was born, Mary and Joseph took Jesus and traveled to Jerusalem to do what the law of Moses required. Mary, Joseph, and baby Jesus were in the temple courts when some pretty amazing events happened. Let's find out!** Divide the session into groups of four; if possible, have both boys and girls in each group. Tell each group to choose who will portray each person in the Bible story: Mary, Joseph, Simeon, and Anna. Give each group a baby doll. **Listen closely as I read. When I say 'Group pose!' your group is to quickly stage a group pose that shows what was happening right then to Mary, Joseph, Simeon, Anna, and baby Jesus. Hold the pose until I say 'Unpose.'**

Before reading Luke 2:25-28 aloud, tell children that *Messiah* means 'the expected king and deliverer of the Jews', 'the deliverer', or 'the one who saves'. Then read and encourage each group to quickly get into a group pose. Help them as needed to know how to pose. Simeon should be holding the baby doll, and Mary and Joseph should be looking on, wondering what's going on. Anna is not in this scene. After you've looked at all the group poses, say 'Unpose'. Read verses 28-32; then say 'Group pose!' Groups should get into a pose and hold it until you say 'Unpose.'

Read the following verses, stopping after each one for groups to pose, then unpose: verse 33; verses 34 and 35; verses 36-38; verse 39; and verse 40. When finished, thank everyone for their participation and ask children to sit down.

ASK: **What did Joseph and Mary do after Simeon said that Jesus was the promised Messiah?** (wondered)
What do Simeon's and Anna's stories help us know about Jesus? (He's God's Son. He's the promised Messiah. He's the one who brings salvation and redemption [makes us acceptable to God])

SAY: **Simeon and Anna were among the first to know that Jesus is the promised Messiah. But they weren't the last! Praise God that we can also know Jesus as our Messiah and Saviour!**

Materials
Bibles, baby dolls (1 per small group), Activity page *Bible Story Cards* on page 111, pencils

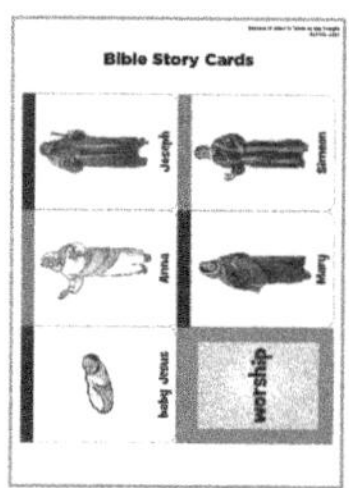

Teaching Tip
If you have a small session, ask for four volunteers who will act out the Bible story and strike various poses that you suggest.

Materials
Cut out the Bible Story card images of Mary, Joseph, Jesus, Simeon, Anna and Worship from activity page 111. Get children to retell the Bible story to one another in small groups using the images.

Make It Real

3 Use this activity to help children **understand their need to accept Jesus as their Messiah.**

Our Need

Materials

Bibles, Activity page *Our Need* on page 110, pencils

Action

Have children stand up. Tell them to stand on one leg and see who can stand that way the longest. If this is taking too long, tell children to also tap their heads while rubbing their tummies. Children are out when their other leg touches the ground or anything else.

After all the children are out, SAY: **I think it would be impossible to stand on one leg forever!** Have children sit down and look at Activity page *Our Need*. Read the directions aloud and do the page together. For #1, ask all children to turn in their Bibles to Romans 3:10, 23, and have volunteers read those verses aloud. Then have a volunteer finish the sentence. (sin)

SAY: **Since sin separates us from God, we need help!** Have a volunteer read Romans 6:23 aloud. Have another volunteer read and finish the sentences. (death, life) Do the same with Acts 2:38 (repent, forgiveness) and Acts 13:38 (Jesus). **Let's be as wise as Simeon and Anna and recognise that Jesus is the promised Messiah. But let's do more than recognise Him. Let's *accept* Him as our Messiah and Saviour and *live* for Him every day!**

Teaching Tips

If you have any children who can't stand on one leg, have children do another contest, such as seeing who can stare at someone the longest without blinking.

Live It Out

4 Use this activity to help children **talk with Jesus about His being their Messiah.**

Praise and Thanks

Materials

Activity page *Praise and Thanks* on page 112, reusable adhesive, battery-operated tealight candle

Pray

SAY: **Simeon recognised Jesus as the promised Messiah and praised God. Anna recognised Jesus as the promised Messiah and thanked God. Now it's your turn to praise and thank God that Jesus is the promised Messiah.** Display on a wall the Praise and Thanks printable file, and have children gather around it. **Let's pray these words to God.** When finished, tell children that they'll pray it again, but this time they should change each 'We' to 'I' and 'our' to 'my'. Lead children in praying the words again.

Then ask children to spread out as much as possible. If possible, dim the lights and turn on the tealight candle. Encourage children to silently talk to Jesus about His being their Messiah. They might want to pray again the words from the printable file. After a short time of silence, close in prayer.

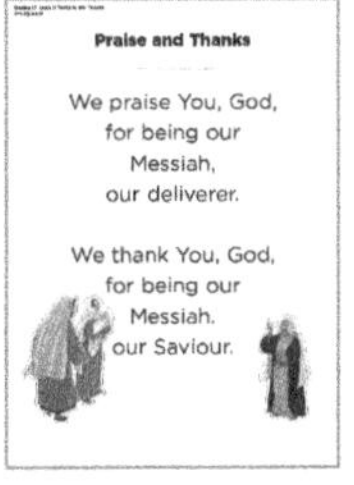

Teaching Tip

If you have a large session, you might want to give each student a copy of the printable file.

our need

Read these Scriptures and finish the sentences.
Why do you need to accept Jesus as your Messiah and Saviour?
Use the Word Bank for help.

1 **Romans 3:10, 23**
It is impossible for people not to _______________.

2 **Romans 6:23**
Sin brings _______________.

Jesus brings eternal _______________ with God.

3 **Acts 2:38**
We are to _______________ and be baptised for the

_______________ of sins.

4 **Acts 13:38**
Through _______________ our sins are forgiven.

Word Bank repent   sin   forgiveness   death   Jesus   life

Bible Story Cards

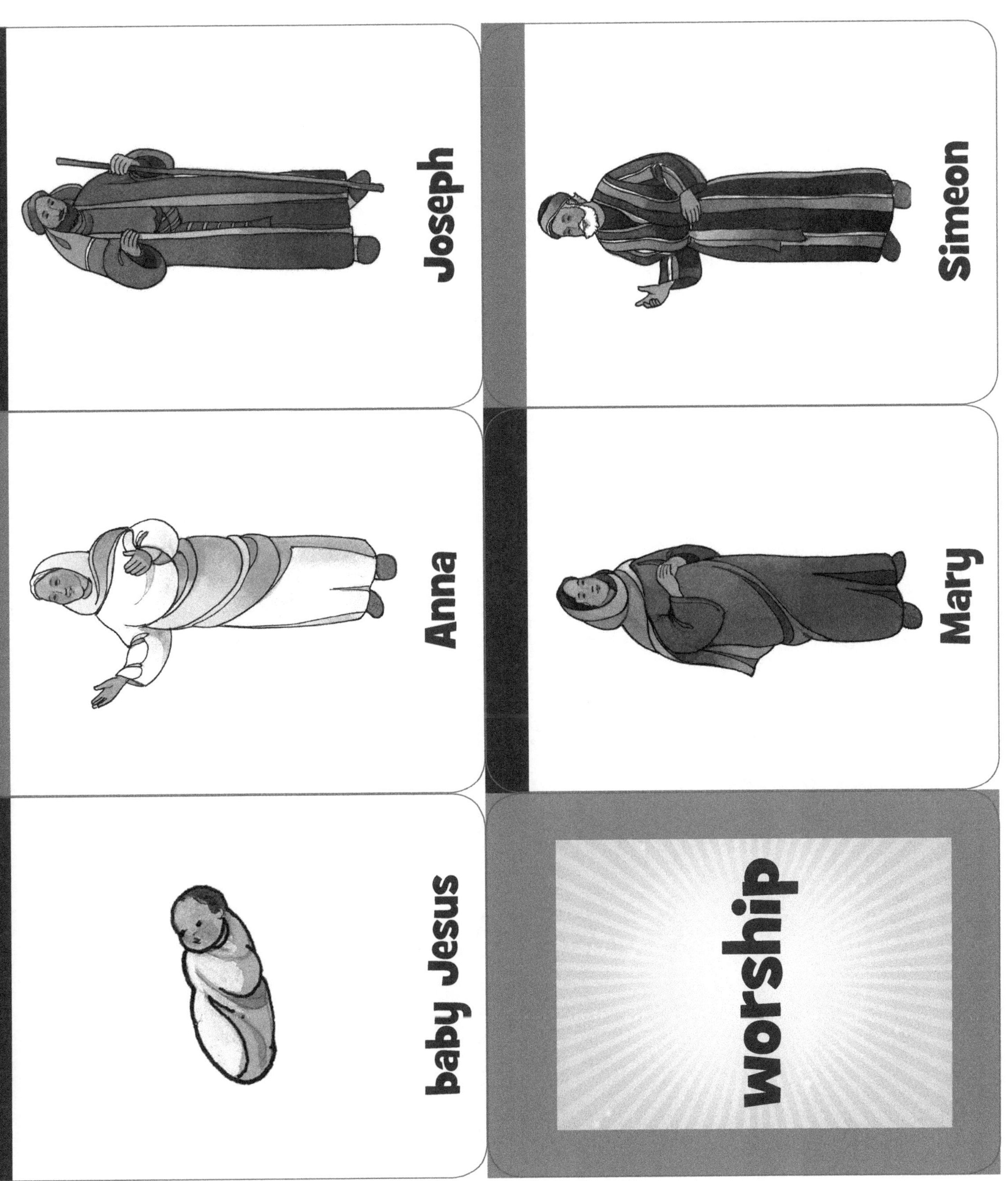

HeartShaper Primary Blue Edition, Activity page

Praise and Thanks

We praise You, God,
for being our
Messiah,
our deliverer.

We thank You, God,
for being our
Messiah,
our Saviour.

Jesus and the Wise Men

Session 18

Scripture: Matthew 2:1-12
Focus: Jesus likes gifts too!

Heart to Heart Teacher Devotion
The Magi worshipped Jesus by presenting Him with priceless gifts. The gifts we give to Jesus are different from theirs, yet more priceless—lives dedicated to Him and acts of service done in His name. As you prepare to teach the children in your session, remember that what you do is a gift to Jesus and an act of worship to Him. Offer King Jesus the best gift that you can!

Focus
Jesus likes gifts too!

Materials
Activity page *Favourite Gifts* on page 117, scissors, watch

Game

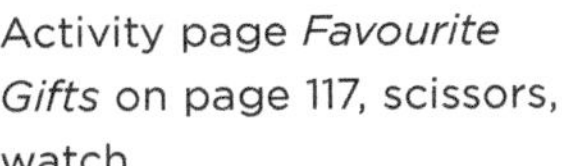

 This activity, as written, might be difficult for children who have trouble taking turns and trading. As an alternative, pass around a pretty wrapped package and tell the children to share their ideas of a perfect gift. Then lead into Explore His Word.
SAY: **Let's dig into the Bible and discover how we can give gifts to Jesus.**

Focus In

1 Use this activity to help children **identify favourite gifts**.

Welcome
Welcome each child by name.

Favourite Gifts
Before the session, make as many copies of the Activity page as needed so each child will have a card. Cut apart the cards.

Give each child one of the gift cards.

SAY: **On these cards are some gifts you might get. If you don't like the gift you have, you can trade with someone. Or if the gift you have isn't your favourite, you can trade to try to get your favourite. You have one minute, and there is no limit to the number of times you can trade. Ready? Go!** When one minute is up, ask children to return to their seats.

ASK: **Who has a gift that you'd love to get?** Let those children share what gift cards they have.
Who has a gift that you wouldn't want at all? Let those children share what gift cards they have.
What are some favourite gifts you like to get? Why? Accept responses.

SAY: **It's fun to get gifts! Did you know that Jesus likes gifts too? Let's dig into the Bible and find out about that!**

Explore His Word

2 Use these activities to help children **describe how the Magi worshipped Jesus.**

Bible Background for the Teacher

The tradition of three Magi comes only from the fact that the writer names three gifts. The picture of them as kings and the traditional names given them come from imagination, not Scripture. But they knew God's Messiah when they saw Him, even if Herod, 'king of the Jews', did not. Herod believed the biblical prophecies, even though he committed murder to protect his throne. The passage his scholars turned to for information on the Messiah's birthplace came from Micah 5:2, where the prophet foretold of a great ruler who would come from the hometown of David, Israel's great king. Many have assigned meaning to the Magi's gifts: gold for a king, incense for a priest, and myrrh for one who would die. All these gifts suited Jesus well. God protected His Son by supernaturally warning the Magi to bypass Herod's court on their way home. Having worshipped God's Son, they left the pages of the Bible as mysteriously as they came.

Bible Exploration   Matthew 2:1-12

Have children turn in their Bibles to Matthew 2:1, and have a volunteer read the verse aloud. SAY: **Matthew, the writer of this Gospel, doesn't tell us how much time has gone by since Jesus was born. As I tell you more about this familiar event, I'll stop once in a while. When I stop, make the face you think that person might have made at that moment, and freeze your face.** Read Matthew 2:1-2. **These men, who studied the stars, came from an unnamed country in the east. We really don't know much about them, but they must have been wealthy to have gone on such a long journey. Show on your face how the Magi might have looked, and freeze your face!** Look at the children's faces. **The Magi were probably excited; they knew their journey was about to be over.** Read verse 3. **Show on your face how King Herod might have looked, and freeze your face!** Look at the children's faces. **You're right. Herod was mad!** *He* **was the king! What were these travelers talking about?** Read verses 4-8. **King Herod found out that a ruler would be born in Bethlehem. Show on your face how King Herod might have looked as he spoke with the Magi.** Look at the children's faces. **Herod came up with an evil plan. The Magi would find this new king and tell Herod. Then Herod would destroy this new king.**

Read verses 9-10. SAY: **Show on your face how the Magi might have looked when the star stopped over the place where the child was.** Look at the children' faces. **Their long journey was over!** Read verse 11. **Show on your face how the Magi might have looked as they worshipped Jesus and gave Him their gifts.** Look at the children's faces. Read verse 12. **Show on your face how the Magi might have looked after having the dream.** Look at the children's faces. **Having worshipped Jesus, the Magi left as mysteriously as they came.**

ASK: **What gifts did the Magi give to Jesus?** (gold, frankincense, myrrh) **What is frankincense?** (a costly incense) **What is myrrh?** (a resin used to make perfume that was used in the preparation of a body for burial)

Besides giving gold, frankincense, and myrrh to Jesus, what else did the Magi give Jesus? (their worship; the time it took to travel to see Him)

Give out Activity page *Wise Men Worship* and do the page together or in small groups. Ask children to call out their answers when everyone has time to finish. Answers: 1 = Jerusalem, 2 = Bethlehem, 3 = star, 4 = worshipped, 5 = gifts.

Materials

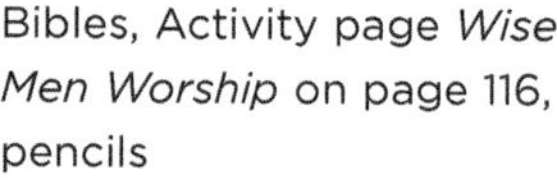

Bibles, Activity page *Wise Men Worship* on page 116, pencils

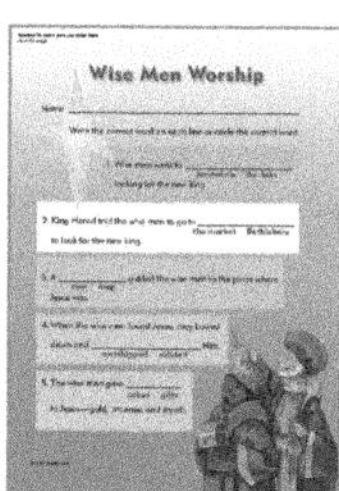

Teaching Tip

For Bibles on a tablet computer, phone, or e-reader, children can open to the contents page. Ask them to look in the New Testament section and find the book of Matthew.

SAY: **Just as we like gifts, Jesus likes gifts too! The gifts the Magi gave to Jesus probably seemed quite unusual to Mary and Joseph. But the Magi knew this was no usual child. Let's be thinking about what _we_ can give to Jesus.**

Make It Real

3 Use this activity to help children **discover what they can give to Jesus.**

Materials

Create guidelines and give some parameters for this activity. Rehearse or model the way children should move around the room, so that they know what to do.

Before the session gather Christmas gift tags or use Christmas cards with a blank reverse side. Write one gift idea on each card and leave some blank. Hide the tags around your room for children to discover.:
• prayers for family
• love and kindness
• prayers for friends
• sharing our money
• prayers for the world
• giving time to help
• saying good things to encourage people
• caring for plants, animals

Worship Gifts for Jesus

SAY: **You have 20 seconds to search the room to find a gift to give to Jesus. Go!** After 20 seconds, let children share the gifts they found. SAY: **That can't be the best way to find gifts to give to Jesus, can it? Let's discover the kinds of gifts Jesus likes to get. Hidden around the room are gift tags for Jesus. Search the room and find one or two and bring them back to decorate them. Write 'from' and your name on the tag. These gift tags show gifts that we can give to Jesus. Some tags are blank for you to write your own gift for Jesus onto it.**

SAY: **Jesus likes gifts too! We don't have to give Him gifts like the Magi gave Him. The gifts He likes from us are when He sees us serving, loving, sharing, and encouraging others. And those are gifts that we all can give to Jesus!**

Live It Out

4 Use this activity to help children **commit to giving their gifts to Jesus.**

Materials

Activity page _Gift Boxes_ on page 118, card stock, scissors, pencils, coloured pencils, clear tape

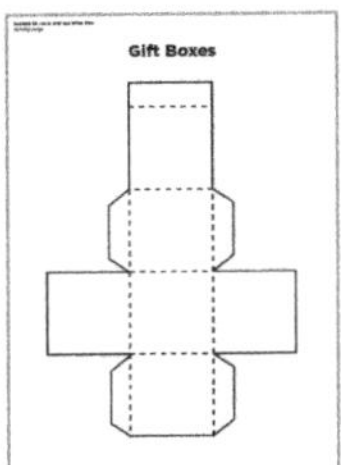

Be sure to offer assistance with fine-motor activities as needed.

Gift Boxes

Before the session, print onto card stock one copy per child of the _Gift Boxes_ Activity page.

SAY: **Take a few minutes and decide what gifts you'll give to Jesus this week. Remember, Jesus likes gifts too! And when we love and serve others, those are gifts to Jesus.** Give children a copy of the gift box pattern and have them cut out the boxes. Challenge children to write either on the inside or outside of their boxes (or both!) which gift or gifts they will commit to giving to Jesus this week. Then they can decorate their boxes before folding and taping the edges together, forming a box.

Have children gather for prayer. SAY: **Put your gift boxes where you'll see them often and be reminded that Jesus likes gifts too! Let's pray and ask for God's help in giving our gifts to Jesus.** Ask volunteers to pray.

Wise Men Worship

Name ____

Write the correct word on each line or circle the correct word.

1. Wise men went to ________________________
   Jerusalem   the lake
   looking for the new king.

2. King Herod told the wise men to go to ________________________
   the market   Bethlehem
   to look for the new king.

3. A _______________ guided the wise men to the place where
   star   map
   Jesus was.

4. When the wise men found Jesus, they bowed
   down and _______________________ Him.
   worshipped   saluted

5. The wise men gave _______________
   cakes   gifts
   to Jesus—gold, incense, and myrrh.

Art by Karen Lee

Favourite Gifts

Cut apart on the dotted lines.

video game	pyjamas	guitar
pencil case	Bible	art set
phone	computer	clothes
chocolate	drum set	socks
football	bicycle	board game
book	game system	trainers

HeartShaper Primary Blue Edition, Activity page
Permission is granted to reproduce this page for ministry purposes only—not for resale.

Gift Boxes

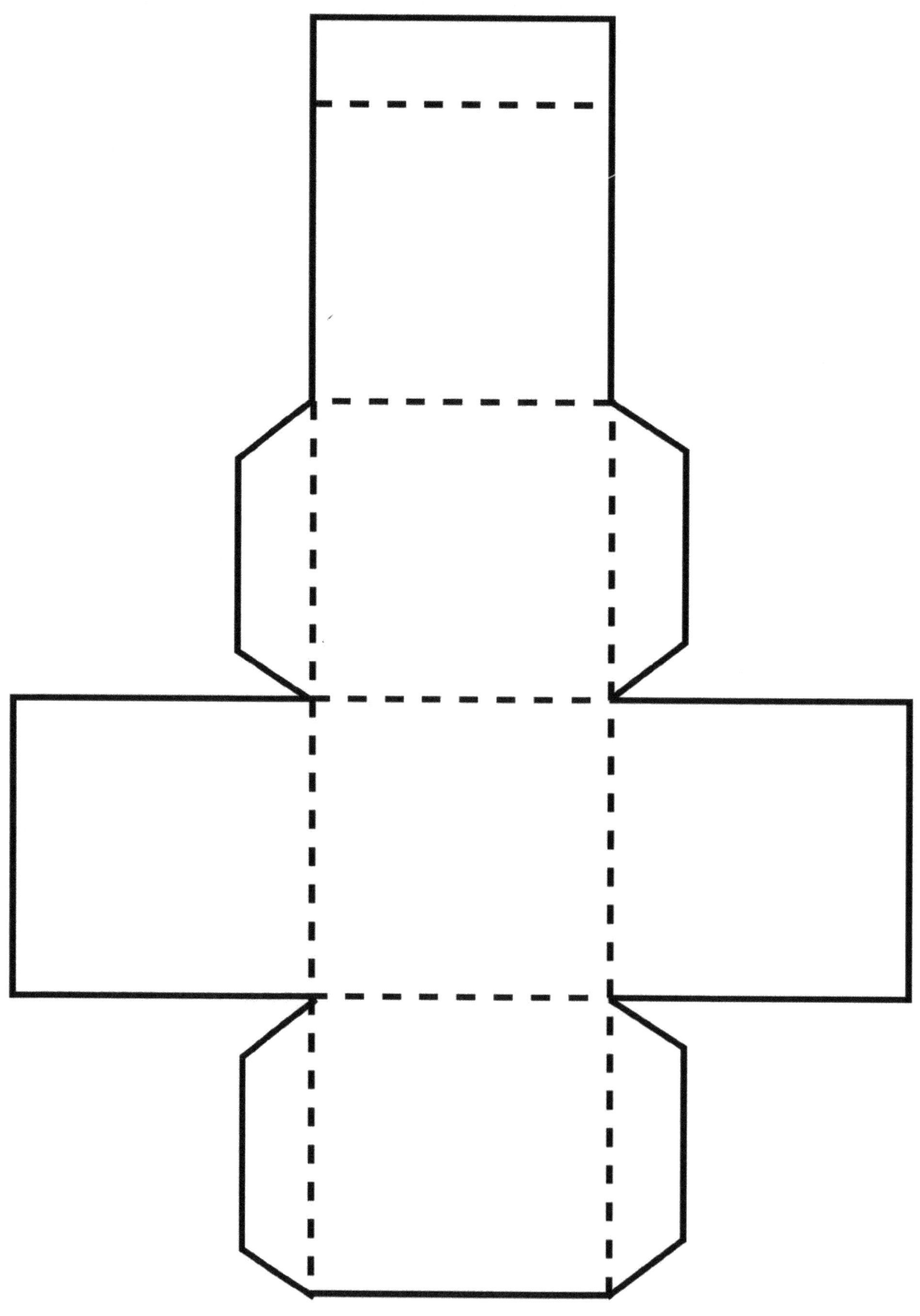

Jesus Clears the Temple

Scripture: John 2:13-22
Focus: Jesus has all authority.

Heart to Heart Teacher Devotion

Judges have authority in courtrooms. Police officers have authority on roads. Bosses have authority in offices. Teachers have authority in rooms. Parents have authority in homes. Does anyone have *ultimate* authority? Christians believe that Jesus has all authority. The Gospels tell of Jesus' amazing authority over weather, sickness, and even death. Thank God that the one who made the world has authority in your life!

Focus
Jesus has all authority.

Materials

Authority Role Play cards - see instructions below. **Skit**

Before the session use small blank index cards or blank squares of paper. Write one authority figure on each card:
- prime minister
- queen
- doctor
- headteacher
- fire fighter
- church pastor
- traffic police officer
- pop singer
- film actor
- YouTuber

Focus In

1 Use this activity to help children **explore people who have authority.**

Welcome

Welcome each child by name.

Authority Role Play

ASK: **What does 'authority' mean?** (accept answers) SAY: **Authority is a thing a person can have. It means they have power and can tell others what to do.** Give some examples - like a class teacher or parents. SAY: **Let's think about people who have authority.** Ask for a volunteer who would like to do some acting, and give the volunteer one of the Role Play cards. The volunteer can perform a few phrases to the rest of the group and the other children can guess what type of person they are. Ensure that everyone who wants to act has the chance to do so.

SAY: **Sometimes it can seem as if everyone has authority except ourselves. Whether you're young or old, there are always people who have some type of authority over you. Let's dig into God's Word and discover who has *all* authority.**

Focus
Jesus has all authority.

Explore His Word

2 Use these activities to help children **explain what Jesus did and what He said in the temple courts.**

Bible Background for the Teacher

Jews from all parts of the Greco-Roman world journeyed to Jerusalem to celebrate the Passover. Those who travelled long distances found it difficult to bring sacrificial animals with them, and cash offerings and the annual temple tax had to be paid in Tyrian shekels. As a result, a large trade of animal sales and currency exchange developed in the temple complex. The sellers enjoyed a complete monopoly over prices and exchange rates. Jesus found this situation unacceptable. The Passover was not intended as an occasion for priests to make money, and ordinary people were being exploited.

Jesus called the temple 'my Father's house' (John 2:16). In doing so, He claimed God as His Father and claimed authority over the temple and what happened there.

Bible Exploration   John 2:13-22

Ask a volunteer to stand by the timeline of Jesus' life and tell about the first four icons. SAY: **The Bible doesn't tell us much about Jesus as a child, but it does record that, at age 12, Jesus went with His parents to the temple in Jerusalem. Later, when Jesus was an adult, He was baptised and then was tempted by Satan. This is where we pick up God's story.** Ask a volunteer to stand by the map and show the city of Jerusalem.

Write 'John 2:13-22' on the board. Ask a volunteer to go to the board and circle the name of the Bible book (John). Ask another volunteer to underline the chapter number (2). Ask another volunteer to draw a box around the verse numbers (13-22). Remind children that the colon separates the chapter and verse numbers. Ask children to turn in their Bibles to John 2:13-22. SAY: **This event seems somewhat easy to understand. But listen carefully because there's a lot happening, and Jesus' words can be a little hard to understand.** Have volunteers read the verses aloud.

Distribute the Activity page *Jesus Clears the Temple*. Read the directions. Ask volunteers to read each sentence and say whether it's true or false. Let children suggest changes to make the false statements true. (Answers: 1=T; 2=F [Jesus was not happy]; 3=T; 4=F [they should leave]; 5=T; 6=F [three days]; 7=T; 8=T)

ASK: **What do you think was the tone in Jesus' voice when He told those selling animals and those exchanging money to leave?** (angry; upset)

Think about what Jesus said. What do you think surprised the crowds the most? (Jesus called the temple His Father's house)

What did Jesus say that the people didn't understand? (If the temple were destroyed, He would raise it in three days)

In this event, what two things do we learn that Jesus has authority over? (the temple; death)

SAY: **This event was one of the first things Jesus did to show people who He is. He clearly said that the temple is His Father's house; that means He's God's Son. He claimed, although no one understood it, that He would die and rise from the dead. Jesus showed throughout His life that He is more powerful than any president, king, or anyone. Only Jesus has *all* authority.**

Whiteboard, dry-erase marker, Bibles, Activity page *Jesus Clears the Temple* on page 124, pencils (optional: masking tape)

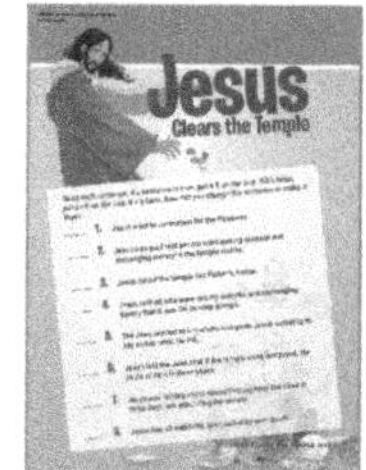

Make It Real

3 Use this activity to help children **discover what Jesus has authority over.**

Focus
Jesus has all authority.

The Authority of Jesus

SAY: **Get up and interview two people you don't know very well. Ask them to tell you something or someone they believe Jesus has authority over.** Give children a minute to do this; then ask them to sit down. Have several share what they found out in the interviews. Then have children look together at Activity page *The Authority of Jesus*. Have a volunteer read the first sentence, unscrambling the word. (nature)

ASK: **When is a time that Jesus had authority over nature?** (He calmed a storm; He walked on water; He fed over 5,000 people with a little bit of food.)

Materials
Activity pages *The Authority of Jesus* on pages 122-123, pencils, Bibles

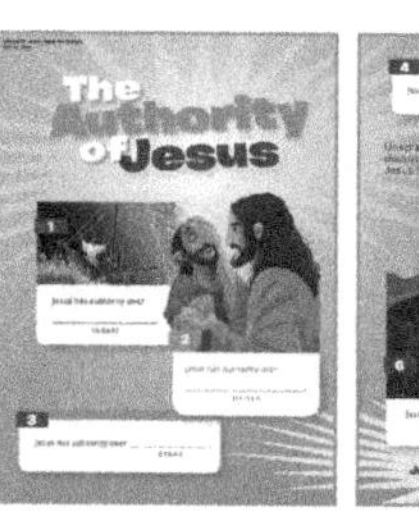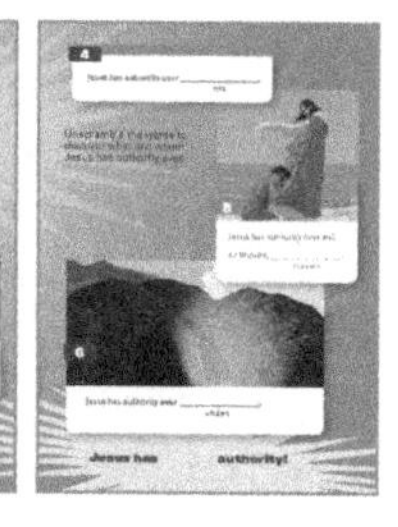

Do the same for all the others. (Answers: 2=illness; 3=Satan; 4=sin; 5=spirits; 6=death) If you have time, have children give other examples of when Jesus showed His authority over each.

ASK: **When did Jesus have authority over illness?** (He healed a man who couldn't see; He healed 10 men with leprosy)

When did Jesus have authority over Satan? (Jesus didn't give in to Satan's temptations)

When did Jesus have authority over sin? (He forgave the sins of the man who couldn't walk)

When did Jesus have authority over evil spirits? (He drove evil spirits out of a man)

When did Jesus have authority over death? (He rose from the dead; He raised Jairus's daughter)

Ask children how much authority Jesus has. (all!) Children should write 'all' on the blank line. SAY: **Only Jesus has *all* authority. And that makes Him, and Him alone, worth following, worshipping, and living for.**

Live It Out

4 Use this activity to help children **choose to remember that Jesus has all authority**.

Materials
none

Positions of Prayer

SAY: **A great thing for us to remember every day is that Jesus has all authority. Hard or scary things don't seem so bad when you remember that Jesus has all authority. When you sin, you can remember that Jesus has authority over sin and that He will help you to stop doing wrong things. When you have a hard time resisting temptation, remember that Jesus has authority over Satan and can help you to resist temptation.**

Ask children to gather for prayer. SAY: **When you pray, you're showing that you believe Jesus has all authority.**

ASK: **What are some prayer positions you could be in that would help you to remember that Jesus has all authority?** (heads bowed, kneeling, hands outstretched to Heaven)

Ask children to move away from each other as much as possible. Encourage them to each get into a prayer position of their choosing that will help them remember that Jesus has all authority. Once children are in position, ask them to pray silently, thanking Jesus that He has authority over nature, illness, Satan, sin, evil spirits, death—and everything! After a short time of silence, close in prayer.

The Authority of Jesus

1

Jesus has authority over

______________________.

tunaer

2

Jesus has authority over

______________________.

llsisen

3

Jesus has authority over ______________.

Stana

Jesus has authority over _________________.

n i s

Unscramble the words to discover what and whom Jesus has authority over.

5

Jesus has authority over evil, or impure, _________________.

r i p s i t s

6

Jesus has authority over _________________.

a h d e t

Jesus has _________ authority!

Jesus Clears the Temple

Read each sentence. If a sentence is true, put a **T** on the line. If it's false, put an **F** on the line. If it's false, how can you change the sentence to make it true?

______ **1.** Jesus went to Jerusalem for the Passover.

______ **2.** Jesus was glad that people were selling animals and exchanging money in the temple courts.

______ **3.** Jesus called the temple His Father's house.

______ **4.** Jesus told all who were selling animals and exchanging money that it was OK to keep doing it.

______ **5.** The Jews wanted to know who had given Jesus authority to say and do what He did.

______ **6.** Jesus told the Jews that if the temple were destroyed, He could raise it in three years.

______ **7.** Jesus was talking about himself rising from the dead in three days, not rebuilding the temple.

______ **8.** Jesus has all authority, even authority over death.

Jesus Teaches Nicodemus

Session 20

Scripture: John 3:1-17
Focus: God sent Jesus to save us.

Heart to Heart Teacher Devotion

'For God so loved the world . . . ' (John 3:16). What beautiful words Jesus spoke to Nicodemus! No wonder we memorise this passage and keep it close in our hearts. God loves you and me, with all our imperfections and inclinations to sin. God loves you and me, even though we don't always return that love to Him. God loves you and me— that's why God sent Jesus to save us. Thank God for His love!

Focus
God sent Jesus to save us.

Materials
3 copies of Activity page *Sin Cards* on page 130, scissors, paper, marker, sticky tape

Object Lesson

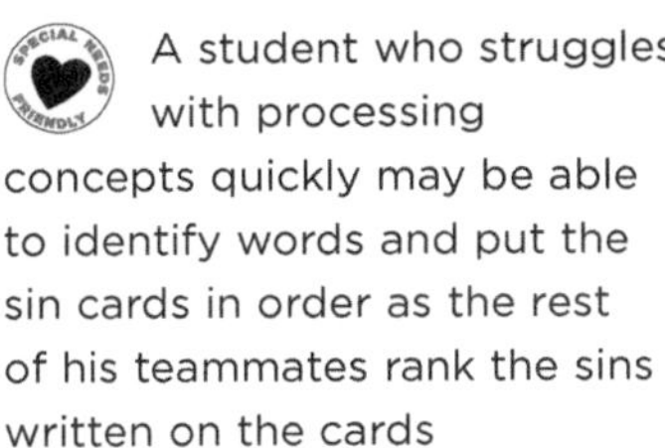

Teaching Tip
If children say that sins can't be ranked, just let them wrestle with this idea for a minute.

A student who struggles with processing concepts quickly may be able to identify words and put the sin cards in order as the rest of his teammates rank the sins written on the cards

Focus In

1 Use this activity to help children **explore what Jesus saves them from.**

Welcome

Welcome each child by name.

Sin Separates Us

Before the session, make three copies of the *Sin Cards* and cut them apart. Keep the sets separate. On a sheet of paper, write 'God' in large letters.

Divide the session into two groups. Give each group a set of the cards. SAY: **Each card has a sin written on it—something that God says is wrong.** Tell each group to work together and rank the sins in order, from what they believe is the worst sin to the least. Give groups only a minute or so to work. When time is up, let the groups explain their rankings. **Some of you were thinking that there is no difference to God when it comes to sin—and you're right. Sin is sin. Isaiah 59:2 tell us what sin does: 'Your iniquities have separated you from your God; your sins have hidden his face from you, so that he will not hear.' Sin, any sin, separates us from God—and that's a huge problem!** Place the 'God' paper on a wall. **Our sins separate us from God.** Throw your set of the *Sin Cards* onto the floor.

ASK: **What's the solution to our problem?** (Jesus saves us from our sins.)

SAY: **Jesus is the only solution to our sin problem. Today we'll hear an important leader tell what happened when he was wondering what to do about being right with God and getting into God's kingdom.**

Explore His Word

② Use these activities to help children **tell what Jesus and Nicodemus talked about.**

Bible Background for the Teacher

Nicodemus did not understand what it means to be 'born again'. The Greek word translated *again* means 'a second time' and 'from above.' To be born from above means to experience divine transformation as a child of God (John 1:12-13). Nicodemus, looking at things from an earthly perspective, thought that Jesus meant a person must be physically born a second time to enter the kingdom. Jesus clarified that a person must be born 'of water and the Spirit.' *Water* in John 3:5 could represent a number of things. But since Nicodemus was an Old Testament scholar, Jesus may have been using these words as they were sometimes used in the Old Testament: *water* meaning 'cleansing from impurity' and *Spirit* pointing to transformed hearts. *Water* and *Spirit* would also point toward the New Testament practice of baptism.

Salvation comes only through Jesus, the Son of Man, because He is the only human being who has come from Heaven and is therefore the only person who can fully reveal God to the world (John 1:14). Nicodemus gradually realised this, for he reappeared (7:50-51), insisting that the Pharisees listen to Jesus before condemning Him, and again (19:39) to help in Jesus' burial. Nicodemus seems to represent those who journey from misunderstanding to true faith.

Bible Exploration   John 3:1-17

ASK: **What New Testament books tell us about Jesus?** (Matthew, Mark, Luke, and John)
  What do we call Matthew, Mark, Luke, and John when we refer to them as a group of books? (Gospels)
  What are two things about Jesus that happened after He was baptised? (He was tempted; He cleared the temple)

SAY: **After Jesus cleared the temple, He stayed in Jerusalem to celebrate the Passover Festival. While there, the Scriptures tell us that many people saw the miracles Jesus did and believed in Him. This is where we pick up God's story.** Ask children to turn in their Bibles to John 3:1-17. **Listen carefully as we read about a meeting between Jesus and a man named Nicodemus. Some of it is easy to understand, but much of it is somewhat hard to understand. Let's see what we can learn about their meeting.** Have volunteers read the verses aloud.

Distribute Activity page *A Special Meeting*. Let children pair up and complete the page with their partners. When everyone is done, let pairs share their answers. (Answers: 1=teacher; 2=born; 3=old; 4=world, Son, life)

ASK: **What did you learn from the meeting between Jesus and Nicodemus?** Accept responses.
  What did Jesus say was needed for a person to enter the kingdom of God? (A person must be born again)
  What did Jesus say was *not* a reason God sent Jesus to the world? (to condemn the world)
  What did Jesus say were the reasons God sent Jesus into the world? (God loves us; God wants to save us so we can have eternal life with Him in Heaven)

Refer to the Bible time lines. SAY: **Throughout history, God's plan has been all about salvation. First He prepared for salvation. Then He sent salvation when Jesus came to earth. We know that God sent Jesus to save us. Let's find out how we can have eternal life in Heaven.**

Materials

Bibles, pencils, Activity pages *A Special Meeting* on pages 128-129

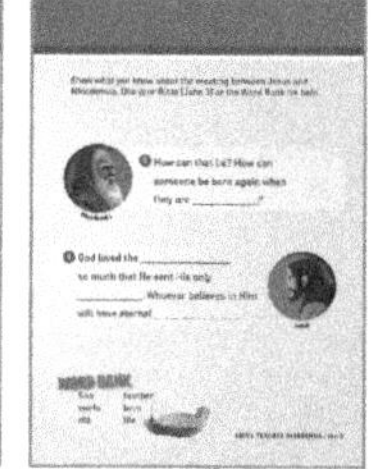

Teaching Tip

Some of the language in this Bible passage may be hard for young children to understand. Spend time answering their questions about what Jesus' words mean.

Focus
God sent Jesus to save us.

Make It Real

❸ Use this activity to help children **discover how to have eternal life in Heaven.**

Materials

small gifts bags (or boxes; 1 per student), paper, scissors, pen, Bibles, whiteboard, dry-erase marker

Object Lesson

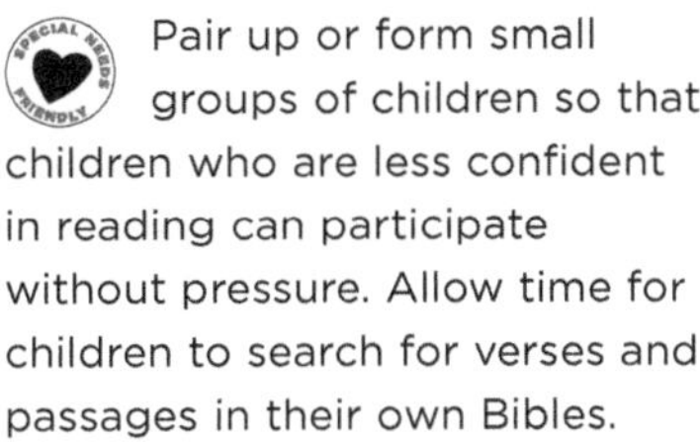
Pair up or form small groups of children so that children who are less confident in reading can participate without pressure. Allow time for children to search for verses and passages in their own Bibles.

God's Gift

Before session, cut paper into slips, one per student. On each paper, write one of these Scripture passages (it's OK to have duplicates): Ephesians 2:8-9; John 3:16; Romans 10:9; Romans 10:10; Acts 3:19; Acts 2:38; Romans 6:3-4. Put a slip of paper into each gift bag.

SAY: **Romans 6:23 says, 'The wages of sin is death, but the *gift* of God is eternal life in Christ Jesus our Lord.' Eternal life in Heaven is a gift; it's not something we earn. Let's find out more!** Give each student a gift bag. If you give out duplicate Scriptures, have those with duplicates work together. Children should look up their Scriptures and be prepared to read them. When everyone is ready, have the student (or group) with Ephesians 2:8-9 read first.

ASK: **Based on this Scripture, how would you finish this sentence: We are saved by _____ ?** (grace through faith) Then have the student (or group) with John 3:16 go next.

ASK: **Based on this Scripture, how would you finish this sentence: We are saved when _____ ?** (we believe in Jesus) Continue in the same way for the rest of the verses. Discuss any of the verses children don't understand.

SAY: **God sent Jesus to save us so that we could have the gift of eternal life in Heaven!**

Focus
God sent Jesus to save us.

Live It Out

❹ Use this activity to help children **respond to the offer of eternal life in Heaven.**

Materials

paper, scissors, markers (optional: heart stickers; you could use some other material for making the hearts, such as foil)

Art

To Whom Does Your Heart Belong?

SAY: **You can't earn eternal life because it's a gift! But it's up to you to accept it. If you haven't yet accepted God's gift, I hope you'll talk to your parents, a trusted adult who is a Christian, or me.** Distribute supplies. Tell children to cut out a heart that's big enough that they can write a sentence on it. **On your hearts, write 'My heart belongs to' and then finish the sentence. Think about that before finishing the sentence. If you're honest, some of you might write 'gymnastics' or 'drawing'. Some of you might write 'being popular' or 'having lots of friends'. Some of you might write 'my family' or 'Jesus'.** Encourage children to be honest and finish the sentence by writing whatever or whomever is most important to them. Children can also decorate their paper hearts.

Have children hold their paper hearts as they gather for prayer. SAY: **We have a lot to be thankful about when we remember that God sent Jesus to save us. No matter what you wrote on your paper heart, I hope and pray that you will always let your heart belong to Jesus by accepting God's gift of eternal life in Heaven.** Encourage children to pray silently and talk with God about the gift of salvation He gives through Jesus and about eternal life in Heaven. After a short time of silence, close in prayer.

A Special Meeting

Nicodemus

1 Rabbi, we know You are a

____

from God.

2 You cannot see God's kingdom unless you are _______________ again.

Jesus

WORD BANK

Son	teacher
world	born
old	life

Show what you know about the meeting between Jesus and Nicodemus. Use your Bible (John 3) or the Word Bank for help.

Nicodemus

3 How can that be? How can someone be born again when they are ______________?

4 God loved the ____________________ so much that He sent His only ______________. Whoever believes in Him will have eternal ____________________.

Jesus

WORD BANK

Son	teacher
world	born
old	life

HeartShaper Primary Blue Edition, Activity page
Permission is granted to reproduce this page for ministry purposes only—not for resale.

Sin Cards

Cut apart on the dotted lines.

Be jealous	Cheat
Lie	Steal
Hate	Disobey parents
Tell others a friend's secret	Boast
Use God's name disrespectfully	Murder
Be selfish	Want what others want
Practice witchcraft	Worship anything besides God

Jesus Heals

Scripture: Luke 4:31-32, 38-44
Focus: Jesus' power is greater than illness.

Heart to Heart Teacher Devotion

Consider the tiniest insect, the largest animal, the sun and the moon, the healing of sickness. God works in our lives in many ways, sometimes loudly displaying His power and other times quietly working in ways that we may never realise. Whatever the circumstances of life, let's worship Jesus and thank Him that His power is greater than anything!

Focus
Jesus' power is greater than illness.

Materials

whiteboard, dry-erase marker, paper, pencils, markers, coloured pencils, Bibles

Art

Rather than creating individual illustrations, create a session mural that reflects the miracles described in the Scriptures given. Assign to children with special needs parts of the mural that will be easier to draw (such as clouds or the sky), so that everyone can take part and be successful. Hang the mural in a public place in your church facility for all to see!

Focus In

① Use this activity to help children **explore examples of Jesus' healing.**

Welcome

Welcome each child by name.

Guess What I Drew

Before the session, write the following on the board: Matthew 8:2-4; Matthew 9:27-31; Mark 2:3-12; Luke 7:1-10; Luke 13:10-13; Luke 17:11-19; John 4:46-53; John 5:1-9.

Ask a few children to tell about a time when they were sick and what happened. Then give each child a sheet of paper. SAY: **When Jesus was on earth, the Bible tells us that He healed many people. The Scripture references listed on the board tell about a few of these miracles.** Tell children to choose one Scripture passage, read it, and illustrate one of the scenes from that passage. When everyone is finished, each of the children will show their drawings while the rest of the session guesses which miracle the person illustrated.

ASK: **Why did Jesus heal people?** (to help people know and believe He is God's Son; to show how powerful He is)

SAY: **Healing those who couldn't see or walk was definitely a great miracle! Today let's think about how Jesus' power is greater than illness.**

Explore His Word

② Use these activities to help children **explain how Jesus showed His power.**

Bible Background for the Teacher

The man named Simon in this passage is Simon Peter, one of Jesus' disciples. Jesus' ministry continued as He healed Peter's mother-in-law. Because it was the Sabbath, people waited until after sundown to carry their loved ones to Jesus for healing. Until sundown, Jews were not allowed to travel more than about two-thirds of a mile or to carry a burden. When Jesus laid His hands on people to heal them, it showed not only His concern, but that He was the source of healing power. It's interesting that the demons recognised Jesus as God's Son, even if the people didn't. Time after time it was evident that Jesus' power is greater than illness. The ability to heal and the ability to exorcise demons, then, go hand in hand as indications of Jesus' authority over sin and the spiritual world. While Jesus' ministry is characterised by compassion, His miracles primarily prove that His message is from God and that He is God's Son. The connection between miracles and the kingdom is explicit in Luke 11:20, where Jesus said that the healing He brings proves 'the kingdom of God has come upon you.'

Bible Exploration   Luke 4:31, 32, 38-44

Have a volunteer point out the town of Capernaum on the map from page 244. Tell children that Capernaum is the town in which today's Bible story takes place. Have children turn in their Bibles to Luke 4:31-32, 38-44. Have volunteers read the verses aloud. Encourage children to listen because they're going to act out what happened.

Ask for volunteers to play the parts of various Bible characters: Jesus, Simon Peter, Simon Peter's mother-in-law, people who were ill, and people who brought those who were ill to Jesus. If you have a small session, you wouldn't have to have children portray the people who brought those who were ill to Jesus. If you have some children who don't want to act, let them display the place signs on different walls. Read the Scripture passage, pausing as needed for children to act out what's going on. Encourage them to travel from place to place as indicated in the story. Those who speak in this passage—Jesus and the people who were healed of demons—could repeat their lines after you. When finished, thank everyone for their participation.

Distribute the Activity page *Jesus Heals*. Read the directions aloud, letting children work alone to complete the page. When children have finished, get volunteers to read and change each sentence, making it true. (Answers: 1=cross out 'Paul' and write 'Jesus'; 2=cross out 'Moses' and write 'Jesus'; 3=cross out 'not powerful' and write 'the Son of God'; 4=cross out 'bad' and write 'good'; 5=cross out 'singing' and write 'preaching')

ASK: **In this Scripture passage, how did Jesus show His power?** (healed Simon's mother-in-law by rebuking the fever; healed many people, including casting out demons and rebuking the demons)
Why did Jesus say He was sent to earth? (to proclaim the good news of the kingdom of God; to preach)
Why did Jesus do miracles? Accept responses.

Then have children turn in their Bibles to John 20:30-31. Ask a volunteer to read the verses aloud. SAY: **While it's true that Jesus had compassion for people, these verses say that Jesus mainly did miracles to prove who He is—to prove that He is the powerful Son of God. In today's Scripture passage we can definitely see that Jesus' power is greater than illness.**

Act It Out

Make It Real

3 Use this activity to help children **feel wonder and amazement at Jesus' power.**

Materials

scrap paper, masking tape, Activity pages *Jesus' Amazing Power!* on pages 134-135, pencils

 Remember that some children might struggle with throwing. Accommodate this by having different starting points from which to throw. Another option would be to have an adult come in and demonstrate weight lifting or other acts of strength. This would be fun for the children, and help them make connections with other adults in the congregation.

Amazing Power!

Place a long piece of masking tape on the floor, close to a wall. Give each child a piece of scrap paper. Tell children to wad up their papers and stand in a line approximately 5 metres from the tape line. Tell children that their goal is to get their paper wads across the line. To do so, they might need to use some power moves, such as hitting the paper as they would a tennis ball or rounders ball. SAY: **Ready? 1, 2, 3, show your power moves!** If that was too easy, have children back up and try it again. If it was too hard, have children move closer. Let children try this a couple times. **Some of you definitely have some amazing power moves, but that's nothing compared to Jesus' amazing power!** Have children turn to Activity page *Jesus' Amazing Power!* Ask a volunteer to read the Bible verses. Model the first answer together as an example, then ask children to work together in small groups to search the Bible references for clues. (Answers: 1=illness or disease; 2=nature; 3=blindness; 4=sin; 5=death)

ASK: **Who besides Jesus can *immediately* cure someone of disease or blindness? Who can make food instantly multiply to feed thousands? Who died and then rose from the dead?
What is a number between 1 and 10 to describe how powerful Jesus is compared with anyone else?** (Jesus' power is off the charts compared to anyone else's!)

SAY: **Jesus' power is greater than illness, nature, and even death! His amazing power helps us know and believe that He's God's Son.**

Live It Out

4 Use this activity to help children **worship Jesus because His power is greater than anything.**

Materials

whiteboard, dry-erase marker, paper, pencils, roll paper, markers

Media Option

Record children worshipping Jesus. Plan a time to show the videos to children along with their families. Be sure to get consent from parents.

 As children work in small groups, remind them to use kind words to each other so that each person's ideas will be accepted.

Your Choice of Worship

Write on the board in a column: Cheer, Rap, Prayer, Song, Poster, Dance.

SAY: **There is no one with greater power than Jesus. Jesus' power is greater than illness, nature, sin, death—anything! When you believe that no one can do the things Jesus did, there's only one response that's appropriate: to worship Him.**

Tell children that they get to choose how they want to worship Jesus. Have them look at the list on the board. SAY: **Decide which activity you'd like to do to worship Jesus.** Guide children to get into groups based on what they want to do. Give the cheer, rap, prayer, and song groups paper and pencils. Give the poster group a length of roll paper and markers. Encourage groups to use the focus of today's lesson— Jesus' power is greater than illness—along with other things they'd like to say about Jesus' power. Give children several minutes to work. When groups are done or time is up, have them present their worship to Jesus. Encourage children to continue worshipping Jesus all week, thanking Him for His power.

Jesus'
AMAZ

After hearing about a few of Jesus' miracles, finish the captions for the pictures.

3

Jesus is more powerful

than _______________________.

Mark 10:46-52

4

Jesus is more powerful

than _______________.

Matthew 1:18-21

5

Jesus is m

powerful

____

Matthew 28

W & Power!

Jesus is more

powerful than

____________.

Matthew 8:5-13

Jesus is more

powerful than

____________.

John 6:1-14

Jesus Heals

Change each sentence to make it true. Cross out the part of each sentence that's not true and write above it the word(s) that makes it true.

1. Paul healed Simon's mother-in-law of a high fever.

2. People brought to Moses lots of people who were sick.

3. The demons shouted to Jesus, 'You are not powerful.' The demons knew that Jesus was the Messiah.

4. 'I was sent to tell the bad news of the kingdom of God in other towns,' Jesus told the people.

5. Jesus kept on singing in the synagogues.

HeartShaper Primary Blue Edition, Activity page
Permission is granted to reproduce this page for ministry purposes only—not for resale.

Rather than photocopy this page you can download and print all activity pages in both colour and black & white from **www.heartshaper.co.uk**

Jesus Chooses 12 Apostles   Session 22

Scripture: Matthew 9:9; John 1:43-50; Luke 6:12-16
Focus: Jesus is worth following.

Heart to Heart Teacher Devotion

Singers, TV and film stars, and the president of the United States are the kind of people most likely to be followed on social media sites. Are they worth following? From Paul's perspective, people are worth following as long as they're following Christ. Let's remember that Jesus is worth following. Then we can follow those who follow Jesus.

Focus
Jesus is worth following.

Materials
none

Game

For a more visual activity, consider drawing a web on a board. Ask children to name good leadership qualities that you can add to the web. Show pictures of different people, and decide whether they are considered leaders (examples: pastors, teachers, politicians). Discuss how we follow these people.

Focus In

1 Use this activity to help children **explore what it means to follow someone.**

Welcome

Welcome each child by name.

Who's the Leader?

Ask a volunteer to leave the room. Have all the other children stand in a circle. Choose a leader. Explain that the leader does different movements that everyone must follow. The guesser will stand in the middle. The goal is to keep the guesser from guessing who the leader is. Tell children that as soon as the volunteer comes back in, they should start swinging their arms up and down; after that they should do whatever motions the leader does. Have the volunteer come back in and stand in the middle of the circle. Tell the volunteer he is to guess who the leader is that everyone is following. The guesser gets three guesses. Then play another round.

ASK: **Who are some people you follow?** (friends; sports celebrities; singers; YouTubers)
   How do you follow those people? (spend time with them; do what they say to do; try to be like them; watch them online; dress like them)

SAY: **We know that Jesus is worth following, so let's figure out how we can do that.**

Focus
Jesus is worth following.

Explore His Word

2 Use these activities to help children **explain how Jesus chose the 12 apostles.**

Bible Background for the Teacher

Originally, the disciples followed Jesus in the literal sense, travelling with Him and studying His teachings. Within Jesus' larger group of followers, Jesus chose 12 men to enjoy a uniquely intimate relationship with Him. *Apostle* comes from the Greek word *apostello* and literally means 'one sent out'. The title alludes to the

Great Commission (Matthew 28:18-20), in which Jesus sent His disciples into the world to preach the gospel and make disciples. The selection of the 12 men follows a typical Old Testament pattern: God calls the lowly to service. Logically, Jesus should have chosen the best-educated or most influential people to spread His message, but this was not the case. Four of the apostles were fishermen, one a tax collector, and Simon the Zealot was involved in a political group. Luke says that Jesus chose the men after a night of prayer but does not reveal His criteria. John and Matthew perhaps point to the true reason by indicating that the apostles responded without question to Jesus' simple call, 'Follow me.'

Bible Exploration   Matthew 9:9; John 1:43-50; Luke 6:12-16

Ask a volunteer to find these places on the map: Galilee, Bethsaida, and Nazareth. Tell children that these places are mentioned in today's Bible story. SAY: **It was time for Jesus to choose His special helpers. Jesus probably went to the richest cities and chose wealthy men. Let's find out how Jesus chose the men who would follow Him and spread the news about God's kingdom.**

Ask children to turn in their Bibles to Matthew 9:9. Have a volunteer read the verse aloud. Children can then turn to John 1:43-50. Have volunteers read those verses aloud. Then have children turn to Luke 6:12-16, and ask volunteers to read those verses aloud. Ask children if they have any questions about the Scripture passages. Then ask them to close their Bibles and pair up. SAY: **I'm going to retell the events about Jesus' choosing His followers. But I'm going to deliberately tell you some wrong things. When you and your partner hear something wrong, raise your hands. I'll call on a pair of you to tell what I said wrong and what I should have said.**

SAY: **Jesus saw Matthew sitting at a booth selling chickens.** (Wrong— Matthew was sitting at the tax collector's booth.) **Jesus told Matthew to follow Him. Matthew got up. He had to go and collect more tax money.** (Wrong—Matthew followed Jesus.) **Jesus went to Galilee, where He found Philip. Jesus told Philip to get Him something to eat.** (Wrong— Jesus asked Philip to follow Him.) **Philip was from Bethsaida. Philip found Nathanael and told him about the new movie that had just come out.** (Wrong—Philip told Nathanael about Jesus of Nazareth.) **Nathanael said, 'Can anything good come from Nazareth?' Philip said, 'Come and see.'**

SAY: **When Jesus saw Nathanael coming His way, Jesus said that He found lots of deceit, or dishonesty, in him.** (Wrong—Jesus said He couldn't find any deceit in him.) **On a certain day, Jesus went to a cave to pray.** (Wrong—it was a mountainside.) **Jesus spent 10 minutes praying to His Father.** (Wrong—He prayed all night.) **The next morning, Jesus called 30 men to follow Him and serve as His apostles.** (Wrong— He called 12 men.) **Jesus called Simon Peter, Andrew, James, John, Philip, Bartholomew, Matthew, Thomas, James son of Alphaeus, Simon the Zealot, Judas son of James, and Judas Iscariot.**

Ask children to look at Activity page *Jesus Chooses Apostles*. Have the same pairs work together to complete the sentences. (Answers: 1=tax; 2=follow; 3=Philip; 4=Nathanael; 5=dishonesty; 6=Son; 7=pray; 8=apostles) SAY: **Jesus didn't choose clever or wealthy men to be His apostles. He chose ordinary men. But these 12 men knew that Jesus is worth following; that's why they left everything and followed Him. Let's think about how *we* can follow Jesus.**

Materials

Jesus Ministry Map on page 326, Bibles, Activity pages *Jesus Chooses Apostles* on pages 140-141, pencils

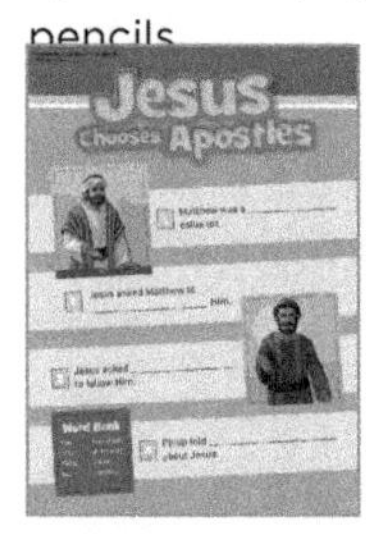
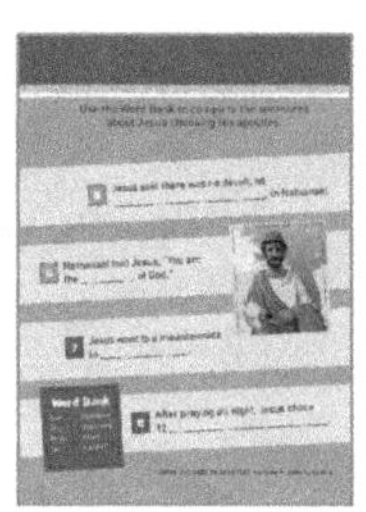

the *Jesus Ministry Map* poster can be downloaded in colour at **www.heartshaper.co.uk/resources**

Make It Real

❸ Use this activity to help children **discover how to follow Jesus.**

Materials

coarse salt, ground pepper, inflated balloon, wool cloth, whiteboard, dry-erase markers, Bibles

Science

Note

The balloon becomes negatively charged when it's rubbed with a wool cloth. Pepper jumps to the balloon because it's lighter than salt.

Take Action!

Scatter some salt and pepper onto the table. Ask children what they think will happen when you hold the balloon over the salt and pepper. Accept responses. As you do the experiment, nothing will happen. SAY: **Now I'm going to rub the balloon with this cloth.** Do so. **Watch what happens this time.** As you hold the balloon about an inch above the salt and pepper, the pepper jumps up to the balloon and sticks! **Rubbing the cloth on the balloon was an action I took. When we take action to follow Jesus, we'll stick as close to Him as the pepper sticks to this balloon!**

ASK: **How do we follow Jesus?** Accept responses.

Write these Scripture references in a column on the board: Acts 2:42; Colossians 3:12-14; Colossians 3:16; 2 Thessalonians 2:15; 1 John 3:23-24. Have volunteers look up these Scriptures and read them aloud. After each Scripture is read, ask a volunteer to come to the board and write beside the reference something in that passage that shows how to follow Jesus. Also be sure to ask questions about the verses to make sure children understand their meanings. SAY: **When you believe that Jesus is worth following, you'll want to follow Him. You'll want to stick as close to Jesus as the pepper stuck to this balloon!**

Live It Out

❹ Use this activity to help children **decide to follow Jesus.**

Materials

Activity page *Take the Challenge* on page 142, pencils

Pray

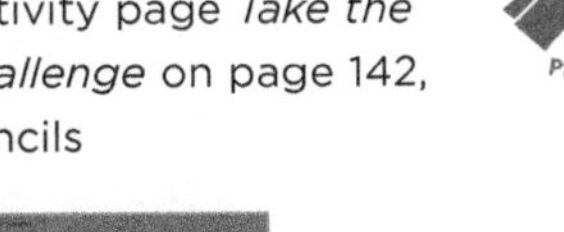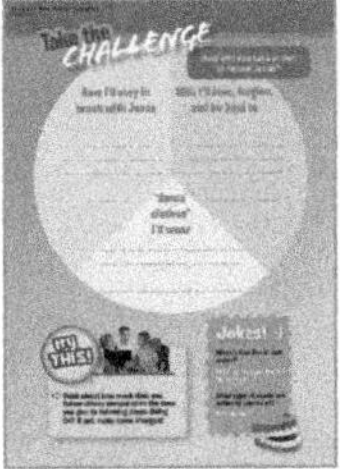

Take the Challenge

SAY: **I hope and pray that you'll decide to follow Jesus, because Jesus is worth following! He's the only one who's worth following for the rest of your life!** Ask children to look at Activity page *Take the Challenge*. Tell children to take a few minutes and write how they'll take action this week to follow Jesus. When everyone has finished, invite them to share what they've written.

Then ask children to gather for a time of prayer. Ask for three volunteers who are willing to pray aloud. Ask one volunteer to ask for God's help in staying in touch with Jesus. Ask another volunteer to ask for God's help in loving and forgiving others. Ask the last volunteer to ask for God's help in showing compassion and kindness to others. Encourage all the children to pray silently with the volunteers who are praying aloud. After the volunteers have prayed, close in prayer.

Jesus Chooses Apostles

1 Matthew was a ________________ collector.

2 Jesus asked Matthew to ________________ Him.

3 Jesus asked ________________ to follow Him.

Word Bank

Son	Nathanael
pray	dishonesty
Philip	follow
tax	apostles

4 Philip told ________________ about Jesus.

Use the Word Bank to complete the sentences about Jesus choosing His apostles.

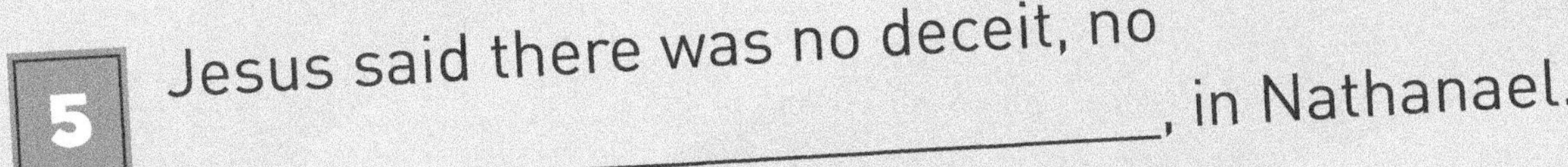

5 Jesus said there was no deceit, no _________________________, in Nathanael.

6 Nathanael told Jesus, 'You are the _________ of God.'

7 Jesus went to a mountainside to _________________.

Word Bank

Son	Nathanael
pray	dishonesty
Philip	follow
tax	apostles

8 After praying all night, Jesus chose 12 _________________________.

Take the CHALLENGE

How will you take action to follow Jesus?

How I'll stay in touch with Jesus

____
____
____
____
____
____

Who I'll love, forgive, and be kind to

____
____
____
____
____

'Jesus' clothes' I'll wear

____
____
____

try THIS!

➡ **Think about how much time you follow others compared to the time you give to following Jesus. Doing OK? If not, make some changes!**

Jokes! :)

Why do fish live in salt water?

Because pepper makes them sneeze!

What type of music are balloons scared of?

Pop music!

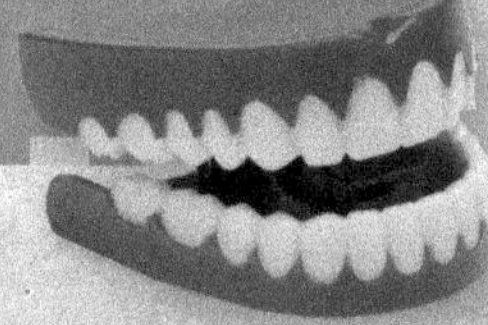

The Beatitudes

Scripture: Matthew 5:1-12
Focus: Jesus wants us to receive God's good gifts.

Heart to Heart Teacher Devotion

Most people love to give gifts for birthdays, or anniversaries, and especially at Christmas. In today's Scripture passage, commonly called the Beatitudes, God's gifts may not seem like typical gifts. And they're not! But God's gifts are the kind that last: Heaven, comfort, inheritance, being filled, seeing God, being called children of God. Praise God for His gifts!

Focus
Jesus wants us to receive God's good gifts.

Materials

whiteboard, dry-erase markers and eraser, watch

Game

Focus In

1 Use this activity to help children **explore gifts they like to receive.**

Welcome

Welcome each child warmly by name.

Giftionary

Divide the session into two teams. SAY: **Think about gifts you like to receive as we play a game of Giftionary.** Tell children how to play the game. You will choose which team goes first. That team sends a player to the board. The player whispers to you the gift he will draw, then draws it on the board. Those drawing cannot talk, and they can't include numbers or letters in their drawings. Teams get one minute to correctly guess the gift drawn. Right answers get 100 points. If a team does not guess correctly, the other team can guess. If correct, award that team 100 points. Then it's the other team's turn. Continue playing as time permits.

ASK: **If you could receive one gift today, what would you like it to be? Why?**

SAY: **Did you know that Jesus talked about receiving gifts from God? But the gifts Jesus talked about weren't the latest and greatest electronics, games, toys or phones. Let's dig into God's Word and find out about them.**

2 Use these activities to help children **name God's gifts and tell how to receive them.**

Bible Background for the Teacher

Jesus began this sermon, near the beginning of His ministry, with a series of statements about being 'blessed'. Some translations render it 'happy,' but being blessed is more than happiness. It is to experience the approval and favour of God, to receive God's good gifts. In the book of Matthew, 'the kingdom of heaven' means much more than being in God's presence after death. Jesus was declaring that He was establishing God's rule on earth. For those who are ready to submit to His reign, this sermon describes how life is to be lived.

Those who are poor in spirit place their utter reliance on God; their gift is the kingdom of Heaven (Matthew 5:3). Those who mourn over their sins receive the gift of comfort (v. 4). Those who are meek are humble, and willingly decline to assert their own rights or power; their gift is to inherit the earth (v. 5). Those who hunger and thirst for righteousness, to know God's right way, will be filled with blessings (v. 6). Those who are merciful, who are kind and forgiving, will be shown mercy by God (v. 7). Those who are pure in heart are blameless; they will see God (v. 8). Those who are peacemakers have harmony with others as their goal; they will be called children of God (v. 9). Those who are persecuted for following God will receive the kingdom of Heaven and enjoy a great reward in Heaven (vv. 10-12). The path to receiving God's good gifts is not easy. Were it not for God's help, we could not begin to undertake it or be successful.

Bible Exploration   Matthew 5:1-12

SAY: **Today's lesson tells about one of Jesus' first times of teachings. It's called the Sermon on the Mount, and the passage we're reading today is known as the Beatitudes.** Have children turn in their Bibles to Matthew 5:1-12. Have a volunteer read verses 1 and 2 aloud. **You'll notice as we read that the verses all begin with the word 'blessed'. Some people say the word *blessed* means the same thing as happy. But it's more than that. *Blessed* is to experience the approval and favour of God, to receive God's good gifts.** Have children listen as you read verses 3-12.

ASK: **What was Jesus teaching about?** Accept responses. At this point, don't correct children if they say something not quite right.

Give each child one or more cards from *The Beatitudes* activity page. Ask children to stand up.

SAY: **Quickly find who has the card that goes with yours and stand together.** If children have more than one card, they'll have to find creative ways to find their matches and stand together! After matches are found, let children read their matched verses aloud. Then ask children to sit down.

Distribute the Activity page *Teachings of Jesus*. Do the page together as a session. (Answers: 1=a, c; 2=a, b; 3=a, c; 4=b, c) **It's not a secret—Jesus wants us to receive God's good gifts! That's why He tells us how to receive them.**

Materials

Bibles, copies of Activity page *The Beatitudes* on page 148 (leave 1 intact; cut cards apart on the other one), scissors, Activity page *Teachings of Jesus* on page 146, pencils, sticky tape

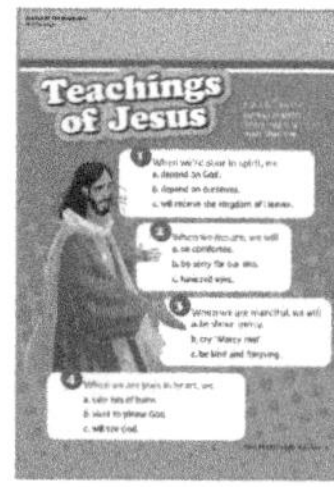

Make It Real

3 Use this activity to help children **identify ways they can choose to do what God says and receive His gifts.**

Materials
straws, paper, markers, scissors, tape

Game

You may want to pre-cut some circles. Offer assistance to children who struggle with fine-motor skills for drawing faces on the circles and taping them to straws.

Smiles or Frowns

Distribute supplies. Tell children to cut out two small circles. On one circle they should draw a smile face; on the other a frown face. Children should tape one to each end of a straw.

SAY: **I'm going to tell you about some children. If a child is doing what God says, quickly spin your straw to show the smile face. If a child isn't doing what God says, quickly spin your straw to show the frown face.
1. Emma is forgiving her friend for not inviting her to a party.** (smile)
2. David's two best friends are having another argument. He's sitting back, watching to see what happens. (frown) **3. Jayden is upset; he told his teacher a lie. He's going to tell his teacher about it tomorrow.** (smile) **4. Alyssa just heard some gossip about someone. She has decided not to tell anyone.** (smile) **5. Zach speaks up for Jesus all the time. Some children on his team laugh at him.** (smile) **6. Sophie likes to do her own thing. She doesn't really care if her parents or friends want her to do something else.** (frown) If you have time, let children make up situations to ask the session.

ASK: **How can you receive God's good gift of being called a child of God?** (be a peacemaker)
How can you receive God's good gift of seeing God? (be pure in heart)

SAY: **Remember, Jesus wants us to receive God's good gifts. And we'll receive God's good gifts when we choose to do what He says.**

Live It Out

4 Use this activity to help children **choose to receive God's good gifts.**

Materials
Activity page *Choose a Challenge* on page 147, pencils

Pray

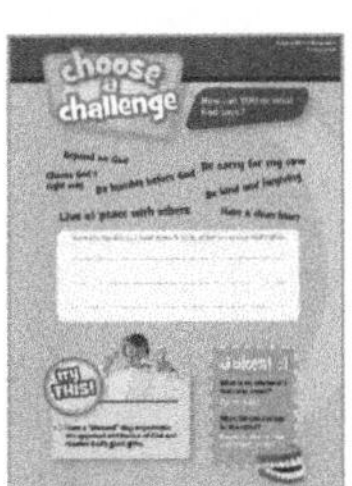

Choose a Challenge

SAY: **Jesus wants us to receive God's good gifts. We will, when we do what God says. Will you choose to do that?** Ask children to look at the Activity page *Choose a Challenge*. Read the instructions; then let children work in pairs, thinking about and writing things they need to work on. When everyone has finished, close with a time of prayer. SAY: **If we're honest about it, most of us probably need to work on ALL the things listed in the Choose a Challenge. When you think about it, that seems pretty hard: being kind to everyone, forgiving people who don't necessarily deserve it, living at peace with brothers and sisters, depending on God instead of ourselves, always choosing God's right way. Whew! How can you and I do that? We can't, unless we depend on God and ask for His help. Let's do that right now.**

Lead children in a time of directed prayer. Ask them to pray silently after your suggestions for prayer. SAY: **First, thank God for giving us good gifts.** Pause for a few seconds as children pray silently. **Thank God for the gift of the kingdom of Heaven.** Pause. **Thank God for the gift of comfort.** Pause. **Thank God for the gift of inheriting the earth.** Pause. **Thank God that He fills us.** Pause. **Thank God for His mercy.** Pause. **Thank God that we will see Him someday.** Pause. **Thank God that we can be called His children.** Pause. **Thank God for the reward that awaits us in Heaven.** Pause. **In Jesus' name, amen.**

Teachings of Jesus

Put a ✔ by the correct answers. There might be more than one.

1 When we're poor in spirit, we
a. depend on God.
b. depend on ourselves.
c. will receive the kingdom of Heaven.

2 When we mourn, we will
a. be comforted.
b. be sorry for our sins.
c. have red eyes.

3 When we are merciful, we will
a. be shown mercy.
b. cry 'Mercy me!'
c. be kind and forgiving.

4 When we are pure in heart, we
a. take lots of baths.
b. want to please God.
c. will see God.

choose a challenge

How can YOU do what God says?

Depend on God

Choose God's right way

Be humble before God

Be sorry for my sins

Be kind and forgiving

Live at peace with others

Have a clean heart

Here are the things I need to work on in order to receive God's gifts:

____

____

____

try THIS!

⇨ Have a 'blessed' day; experience the approval and favour of God and receive God's good gifts.

Jokes! :)

What is an astronaut's favourite snack?

Space chips!

What did one eye say to the other?

Between you and me, something smells!

The Beatitudes

Cut apart on the dotted lines.

"Blessed are the poor in spirit [those dependent on God],	for theirs is the kingdom of heaven."
"Blessed are those who mourn [those sorry for sin],	for they will be comforted."
"Blessed are the meek [those humble before God],	for they will inherit the earth."
"Blessed are those who hunger and thirst for righteousness [those who choose God's right way],	for they will be filled."
"Blessed are the merciful [those who are kind and forgiving],	for they will be shown mercy."
"Blessed are the pure in heart [those who have clean hearts],	for they will see God."
"Blessed are the peacemakers [those who live at peace with others],	for they will be called children of God."
"Blessed are those who are persecuted because of righteousness [those who are mistreated for living God's right way],	for theirs is the kingdom of heaven."
"Blessed are you when people insult you, persecute you and falsely say all kinds of evil against you because of me [those who are mistreated for living for Jesus].	Rejoice and be glad, because great is your reward in heaven, for in the same way they persecuted the prophets who were before you."

Jesus Calms a Storm

Session 24

Scripture: Matthew 8:23-27
Focus: Jesus is in control.

Heart to Heart Teacher Devotion
In this lesson, Jesus brings peace to a stormy sea and peace to His disciples. Jesus shows that He has power over nature, power over fear, power over any problem. When Jesus is in control of our lives, we have nothing to worry about or fear.

Focus
Jesus is in control.

Materials
large glass bowl, towel, measuring cup, measuring spoons, water, vinegar, baking soda, blue food colouring

Science

Reassure children that no one will get hurt. For children who may feel nervous watching the experiment up close, provide a place to view it from a distance.

Focus In

1 Use this activity to help children **explore times they've been afraid.**

Welcome

Welcome each child warmly by name.

Homemade Storm

ASK: **When are some times you've been afraid?** Accept responses.

SAY: **One thing that many people are afraid of is big storms. Let's make our own storm!** Have children gather around the bowl. Put a towel under the bowl. Let children help by pouring and measuring. Put one cup of water into the bowl. Add blue food colouring, if desired, to make it look more like a stormy sea. Pour in one cup of vinegar and stir. Then add one tablespoon of baking soda. As the ingredients mix, the water will become very bubbly and foamy.

SAY: **Today we're going to dig into God's Word to find out about a time when Jesus' friends were afraid of a storm. We'll also discover who can help us when we're afraid—and who is in control.**

Focus
Jesus is in control.

Explore His Word

2 Use these activities to help children **describe what happened when Jesus and His disciples were in a boat.**

Bible Background for the Teacher

The Sea of Galilee sits some 600 feet below sea level in the deep rift that forms the Jordan valley. After sunset, when cool air from the surrounding mountains meets the warm air rising from the lake, violent winds often arise suddenly and churn the surface of the sea.

Jesus interprets the disciples' cry for help as a lack of faith. Although they believe that Jesus can rescue them, they don't yet truly understand who He is. Jesus therefore criticised them for their 'little faith' (Matthew 8:26). No storm could disrupt God's plan. The disciples' response in Matthew 8:27 was typical of miracle accounts. The key to the episode lies in their unanswered question, 'What kind of man is this?' However, now the disciples have even more reason to know and understand that Jesus is in control.

Bible Exploration Matthew 8:23-27

Have a volunteer show the Sea of Galilee on the map. Tell children that this is where today's Bible story takes place. Stand by the Bible time line of Jesus' life. Point out the 'Beatitudes' icon. SAY: **Jesus continued teaching about God when He taught His disciples the Lord's Prayer. He spoke in parables and healed a centurion's servant. This is where we pick up God's story.**

Ask children to turn to Matthew 8:23-27. Have volunteers read the verses aloud. Then have children move their chairs to sit as if they were in a boat (or have children sit on the floor). If desired, you could use masking tape to make an outline of a boat in which the children could sit. You could also open a can of tuna fish to help create a sea-smelling room! SAY: **If you remember, some of Jesus' disciples had been fishermen. Probably all had travelled by sea many times. So when Jesus got into the boat, His disciples did too. Getting into a boat was a very normal thing to do. But while out on the Sea of Galilee, a huge storm came up. Let's pretend that we're in the boat too.** Tell children to sway back and forth as if being tossed by huge waves. Flash the overhead lights on and off.

SAY: **Hang on! We might drown! Wait a minute. Jesus is on the boat. The disciples looked for Jesus. Jesus was sleeping!** Tell children to keep swaying back and forth. **The disciples woke Jesus and said, 'Lord, save us! We're going to drown!'** (Matthew 8:25). **Jesus said, 'You men have such little faith. You know that I'm right here with you. Why are you afraid?' The disciples had nothing to say. Jesus got up and scolded the waves that were beating against the boat. He rebuked the strong winds that were blowing. Immediately, the storm was gone!** Children should stop swaying. **Jesus' disciples looked at each other in amazement. They couldn't believe it. How could Jesus speak to the waves and wind? And how could the waves and wind obey Him? What kind of man was this? The disciples did not yet understand how powerful Jesus is. They did not yet understand that Jesus is in control, even over winds and waves.**

Have children return to their seats. Distribute the Activity page *Jesus Calms a Storm*. Read the directions and do the page together. (Answers: 1=was sleeping; 2='We're going to drown! Save us!'; 3=men of little faith; 4=they immediately became calm; 5='What kind of man is this?')

ASK: **From this event, what did you learn about Jesus?** (He's powerful; He has control over nature)

    Why did Jesus scold, or rebuke, His disciples? (because they didn't have much faith; they were afraid)

    What is a number between 1 and 10, with 10 being the highest, to describe how much faith in Jesus you think you might have had if you had been in the boat? Accept responses.

SAY: **It can be easy to think badly about the disciples for not having much faith in Jesus and not understanding that Jesus is in control. But what if *we* had been in the boat? It's hard to know what we would have done. Let's think about times that we can put our faith in Jesus, knowing that He is in control.**

Materials
Activity pages *Jesus Calms a Storm* on pages 152-153, Bibles, masking tape, can of tuna fish

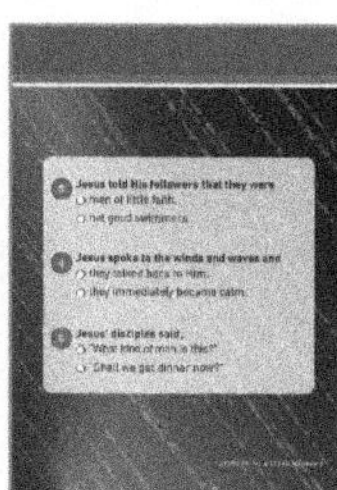

Make It Real

3 Use this activity to help children **discover times they can put their faith in Jesus.**

Materials

Activity page *Did You Know?* on page 154, pencils, Bibles

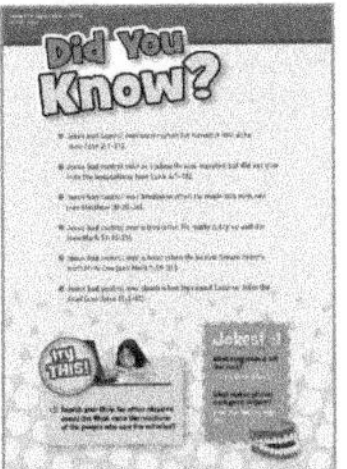

Did You Know?

Before the session, write these scenarios onto paper or card. Fold them over so the writing is not seen and put them into a bag.

• *Sarah has a Maths test at school* • *Sam has a Literacy test at school*
• *Jay is being bullied in the playground* • *Oliver's grandma is very sick*
• *Libby's dog has gone missing* • *Jo wants to join the football team or netball team or dance group but thinks she is not good enough* • *Layla's mum and dad are always arguing and she's worried*

Get children into pairs or threes.

SAY: **In the bag here I have some situations that could make you feel scared or worried - like the disciples felt during the storm. These are stormy moments in life. Think about what advice you would give these children about how they can put their faith in Jesus during these stormy times because he is in control.**

Let each group pull out a piece of paper from the bag and then discuss or write down their ideas. They can put the card back and pull out another if they finish quickly. Ask volunteers to tell the whole group about their suggestions.

Ask children to look at Activity page, *Did You Know?*

SAY: **Let's find out about other times when Jesus showed He was in control.**

Let children work together in pairs or groups and choose one or two of the Bible verses to look up and read.

Live It Out

4 Use this activity to help children **choose to put their faith in Jesus because He's in control.**

Materials

roll paper, pencils, markers, crayons, reusable adhesive

Faith Drawing

Before session, use a pencil to draw a large, simple boat outline on a long length of roll paper. Go over the outline with a black marker.

ASK: **We're all afraid at times. What will you do about that? Will you choose to put your faith in Jesus because you know and believe that Jesus is in control?** Allow time for children think to about these questions.

Lay the prepared roll paper on a table or on the floor. Tell children to draw themselves in the boat. **If you're choosing to put your faith in Jesus because He's in control, sign your name on or by your drawing.** When children are done with that, have them use crayons to draw waves beating against the ship. On top of the waves, tell children to use markers to write times when they need to put their faith in Jesus (as discussed in the Make It Real activities). Offer assistance with writing, as needed.

When children are done with the drawing, display it. For the prayer time, ask children to gather around the drawing. SAY: **I'm so glad that Jesus is in control. When rough storms of life come your way, I hope you'll choose to put your faith in Jesus, because He's the only one who is really in control.** Ask for volunteers to pray, thanking God that Jesus is in control.

Jesus Calms a Storm

1 **Jesus and His disciples were in a boat when a huge storm came up. Jesus**
- ○ was sleeping.
- ○ fishing.

2 **The disciples woke Jesus, saying,**
- ○ 'Jump overboard!'
- ○ 'We're going to drown! Save us!'

3 **Jesus told His followers that they were**

○ men of little faith.

○ not good swimmers.

4 **Jesus spoke to the winds and waves and**

○ they talked back to Him.

○ they immediately became calm.

5 **Jesus' disciples said,**

○ 'What kind of man is this?'

○ 'Shall we get dinner now?'

Did You Know?

- Jesus had control over water when He turned it into wine (see John 2:1-11).

- Jesus had control over evil when He was tempted but did not give in to the temptations (see Luke 4:1-13).

- Jesus had control over blindness when He made two men see (see Matthew 20:29-34).

- Jesus had control over a tree when He made it dry up and die (see Mark 11:12-21).

- Jesus had control over a fever when He healed Simon Peter's mother-in-law (see Mark 1:29-31).

- Jesus had control over death when He raised Lazarus from the dead (see John 11:1-44).

try THIS!

➪ **Search your Bible for other miracles Jesus did. What were the reactions of the people who saw the miracles?**

Jokes! :)

What song does a cat like best?

'Three Blind Mice'!

What makes pirates such good singers?

They can hit the high Cs!

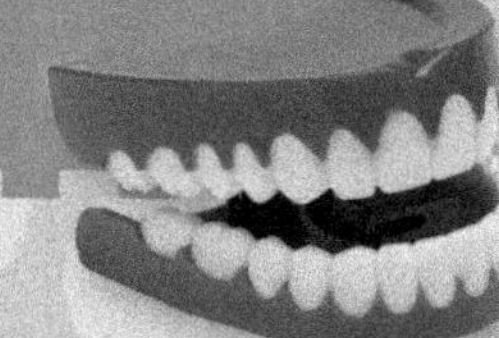

Jesus Feeds 5,000

Session 25

Scripture: John 6:1-14
Focus: Jesus meets our needs.

Heart to Heart Teacher Devotion
Did you know that the feeding of the 5,000 men, plus women and children, is the only miracle that's told in all four Gospels, except for the death, burial, and resurrection of Jesus? This miracle, along with all the others Jesus did, demonstrates His power and control over everything. While we bow in adoration before Him for His awesome power, we also humbly thank Him for meeting our daily needs.

Focus
Jesus meets our needs.

Materials
none

Action

For a more visual option, offer an object sort. Display on a tray items such as a drink can, bottle of water, medicine, a small doll house (or picture of a house), food items, a mobile phone. Have children sort the items according to WANTS and NEEDS.

Focus In

1 Use this activity to help children **explore some needs they have.**

Welcome
Welcome each child warmly by name.

Which Do You Need More?

SAY: **Let's think about things we need.** Ask children to stand and line up in the middle of the room. **I'm going to call out two things. If you think you need the first thing I call out, take two steps to your left. If you think you need the second thing I call out, take two steps to your right. After everyone has decided, take two steps back to the middle. Here's the first set.**

ASK: **Which do you need more—a brother or sister** (step to the left) **or a friend** (step to the right)**?** Pause as children take two steps away from the middle, then take two steps back. Other things to call out:
Breakfast or lunch?
A notebook or a pencil?
A tablet or a mobile phone?
Clothes from a discount store or expensive, name-brand clothes?
An ice cream cone or vegetables?
A bottle of water or a sports drink?
A huge mansion or a tiny flat?

ASK: **What's the difference between needs and wants?** (We need some things in order to live; The things we want, we don't really need)
What needs do we have? (food, water, shelter, clothing, love)

SAY: **We sometimes mix up our needs and wants, don't we? Let's dig into God's Word to learn about our needs and who can meet them.**

Explore His Word

2 Use these activities to help children **tell about Jesus' feeding the crowd.**

Bible Background for the Teacher

The feeding of the 5,000 is one of the few events recorded in all four Gospels. John highlights the abundance of the miracle. Jesus asks Philip, who is from the nearby town of Bethsaida (John 1:44), where they might purchase food. The question is ridiculous, for 200 denarii (eight months' wages) would not feed the crowd, which may have numbered over 10,000, given that 5,000 men were present. The feeding of the 5,000 has two purposes in John's narrative. First, as a miraculous sign it reveals that, as Jesus met the needs of the crowd, Jesus meets our needs. Second, it introduces Jesus' discussion of himself as the bread from Heaven who gives eternal life to those who receive Him (John 6:32-58).

Bible Exploration   John 6:1-14

SAY: **Since today's Bible story is a familiar one to many of you, let's act it out to help us understand more about what Jesus did and what Jesus' disciples and the crowd must have been thinking and feeling.** Choose volunteers to act out the parts of Jesus, Philip, Andrew, and the boy. If you have a large session, other volunteers can play the parts of the other disciples and the crowd. **As I read about this event, act out your part the best you can. You can repeat your lines after me if you want to.** Read John 6:1-14 aloud, pausing often so children can act it out. If desired, give the child playing the boy a small basket to carry, and the disciples 12 baskets to pick up the leftovers. When finished, thank everyone for participating. Ask children to look at Activity page *Philip's Journal*. Have volunteers read the sentences, completing the ones that have missing words. (Answers: bread; Andrew; fish; 5,000; thanked; 12)

SAY: **The feeding of the 5,000 is one of the few events recorded in all four Gospels. Many times the Gospel writers wrote about the same events that happened in Jesus' life, describing them in slightly different ways. We call these similar passages** *parallel* **passages.** Draw parallel lines on the board to illustrate this concept. SAY: **Jesus loved the people and had compassion for them. That's why He met their needs. The same is true today. Jesus loves us and has compassion for us. That's why He continues to meet our needs.**

Materials

Bibles, whiteboard, dry-erase marker, Activity page *Philip's Journal* on page 160, pencils (optional: small basket for the boy's lunch, 12 baskets for leftovers)

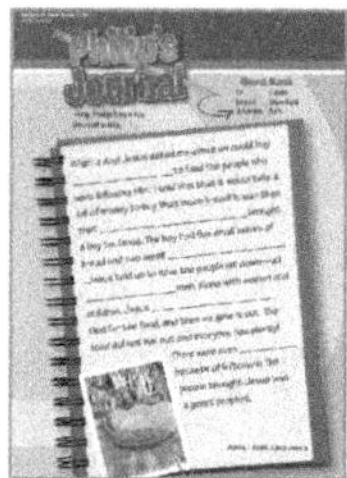

Media Option

Go to www.biblegateway.com and play a dramatised reading of the Bible verses.

Make It Real

3 Use this activity to help children **explore their biggest needs and identify ways Jesus meets those needs.**

Materials

scrap paper, pencils, small container, Activity pages *Our Biggest Needs* on pages 158-159 (optional: bread, margarine, jam, paper plates, napkins)

Teaching Tip

As a fun tie-in to the Bible story, you could let children enjoy some bread and margarine or jam while doing this activity. Be sure to check for allergies, and have an alternative snack available.

Our Biggest Needs

Give each child a piece of scrap paper. SAY: **On your paper, write your biggest need.** Tell children that these will be read aloud, but they are not to put their names on the papers. **Fold your papers and put them in the container.** Mix up the papers and read them. Depending on what children wrote, say something like: **I wonder if those are really our *biggest* needs. Let's see what God's Word says about that.** Ask children to look at Activity page *Our Biggest Needs*, and read the instructions. Either work together as a session or divide the session into small groups. Each small group could take a need, look up the Scripture, and be prepared to complete the sentences. (Answers: 1=life, love; 2=sins; 3=Jesus, saved; 4=peace; 5=eternal) Then tell children to think of their own biggest needs and write them at the bottom of the page.

SAY: **Our biggest needs aren't having the latest video games or jeans. What we really need is forgiveness, grace, peace, love, and salvation, to name a few really big needs. Let's be thankful that Jesus meets our needs.**

Focus
Jesus meets our needs.

Live It Out

4 Use this activity to help children **thank Jesus for meeting their needs.**

Materials

Large sheets or roll paper, sticky tape, pencils (or coloured pencils)

Before the Session

If short on time, you can prepare the basic text on the prayer posters before the session or have children write them and decorate them during the session.
• Jesus, thank you for LOVE
• Jesus, thank you for FORGIVENESS
• Jesus, thank you for PEACE
• Jesus, thank you for GRACE
• Jesus, thank you for FOOD and WATER
• Jesus, thank you for HOME
• Jesus, thank you for AIR
• Jesus, thank you for SALVATION
A blank poster

Prayers of Thanks Posters

SAY: **Whether our needs are big or small, Jesus meets our needs. Our biggest needs—things like forgiveness, grace, salvation—can only be met by Jesus. Let's thank Him for meeting our needs.**

SAY: **We are going to create nine posters. On each poster will be a prayer, thanking Jesus for meeting one of our needs. When we've finished making them, we'll display them on the walls. When you go to each poster, read the prayer, then silently pray it. Then you can either put your name or your initials somewhere on that poster. You could also write 'Thanks!' or 'Thank You' or something else that's appropriate. As soon as you're finished with one poster, move on to the next.** Show children the poster that doesn't have a need on it. **If you would like to thank Jesus for meeting another need that's not listed on any of the posters, write it on this poster.** Tell children that this is a serious time to thank Jesus for meeting their needs. There should be no talking out loud, only silent prayers being offered. Tell children to sit down when they're finished.

1

We need
LOVE.
Read 1 John 3:16 and Romans 8:39.

Jesus met this need by laying down His

_______________ for us. Nothing can

separate us from His _______________.

OU
B

See v
Jesus

M
N

____

____

____

2

WE NEED
FORGIVENESS.
Read Acts 2:38.

Jesus meets this need by offering

forgiveness of our _______________

when we repent and

are baptised.

3

G

Read

Jesus meets th

come through

grace of Jes

WORD BANK

Jesus	love
life	eternal
peace	saved
sins	

~~GGEST~~ NEEDS

's Word says about
our biggest needs.

We need
SALVATION.
Read John 3:16.

Jesus meets this need because when
we believe in Jesus, we will have
_________________ life.

5

4

We need
PEACE.
Read Acts 10:36.

Jesus meets this need because
_________________ comes through Him.

S

____

____

____

eed
CE.
nd Acts 15:11.

ause grace and truth
_______. Through the
_________________.

Philip's Journal

Help Philip finish his
journal entry.

Word Bank

12	5,000
bread	thanked
Andrew	fish

What a day! Jesus asked me where we could buy
________________ to feed the people who
were following Him. I told Him that it would take a
lot of money to buy that much bread! It was then
that ________________________ brought
a boy to Jesus. The boy had five small loaves of
bread and two small ________________________.
Jesus told us to have the people sit down—all
________________ men, along with women and
children. Jesus ________________________
God for the food, and then we gave it out. The
food did not run out and everyone had plenty!
There were even ________________
baskets of leftovers! The
people thought Jesus was
a great prophet.

The Good Samaritan

Session 26

Scripture: Luke 10:25-37
Focus: Jesus wants us to help others.

Heart to Heart Teacher Devotion
The Samaritan man commended by Jesus had learned to love a neighbour as much as he loved himself. You may come in contact this week with someone who is hurting. You can choose to love that person as much as you love yourself, or you can ignore the person's needs and go on your way. Maybe you'll remember Jesus' parable, change your plans, and offer to help. If you do, you will be a good neighbour!

Focus
Jesus wants us to help others.

Materials
(optional: pictures of helping/not helping situations)

Action

Something More!
Let children take turns acting out ways they help others. Have the rest of the session guess what is being done to help someone.

Focus In

1 Use this activity to help children **explore helping others.**

Welcome
Welcome each child warmly by name.

Helping or Not Helping

Have children gather in a circle. Teach children an action for the word *help*—one hand lifts the other hand up to represent the concept of helping. Explain that you will be describing (or showing pictures of) different situations. The children are to do the action for *help* if the sentence describes someone helping. They are to shake their heads no if it describes someone not helping.

SAY: **Maria saw a girl at school fall and scrape her knee. Maria took her to the nurse's office.** (helping; show sign)
Anna played games while her sister cleaned their room. (no)
Ethan forgot to help with the washing up, so his dad had to do it. (no)
Lily's friend couldn't play until she did some chores. Chantel left and asked another friend to play with her. (no)
Antone told a friend who was lonely about Jesus. (helping)

Ask children to share ways they help others. SAY: **We're going to learn that Jesus wants us to help others.**

Explore His Word

2 Use these activities to help children **talk about what Jesus taught on helping others.**

Bible Background for the Teacher

The road from Jerusalem to Jericho was 17 miles long, and it descended from about 2,500 feet above sea level to about 800 feet below sea level. After leaving Jerusalem, a traveller would pass through Bethany. After leaving Bethany, there were no other settlements along the way. It was a rocky, rough area with many caves and drop-offs. It was known as a road where bandits hid.

Priests and other religious leaders travelled frequently between Jericho, a priestly city, and Jerusalem, the site of the temple. Priests and Levites were religious leaders. They could be expected to help a person in need. The Samaritans and the Jews were not on friendly terms. By answering the man's question with a parable, Jesus was able to disarm prejudice and prevented objection to any conclusion but the obvious one.

Bible Exploration   Luke 10:25-37

SAY: **Today's Bible story comes once again from the book of Luke.** Write 'Luke 10:25' on the board. Help children turn to Luke 10:25 in their Bibles, and ask for a volunteer to read the verse.

The man who asked Jesus a question was a teacher of God's law. When Jesus answered the man, Jesus told a story. Some things in Bible times were different from how they are today. Let's look at a few pictures before we hear Jesus' story. Show 12g. **Strips of cloth were often used as bandages because the people did not have plasters like we have today.** Show 12h. **Medicine was different too. There were no tubes of antibiotic cream to put on a cut or bruise. Instead, oil was poured from a bottle. The oil was good for soothing the skin and taking away soreness.** Show 12i. **The places where people stayed when they travelled were different too. There were no hotels, but there were places called inns where people could stay. Most travellers provided their own food and sleeping mats. Having some money would have been important.**

Now that we know more about the way things were done in Bible times, let's act out the story that Jesus told. Choose six volunteers to act out the Bible story. Introduce the story characters and give each volunteer one of the name cards to wear. If you are not using real props, place cards 12g–12i in the backpack and give the bag to the Samaritan, who can remove the cards as the items are used during the story.

Explain that you will read the Bible story and show the Teaching Picture *The Good Samaritan*. Children who are wearing the name cards should act out the story as it is told. Give prompts as needed. Note: If you have a small session, provide toy people figures and let the children move the figures as you read.

When the Bible story is finished, thank those who acted out the story. **As you just heard, Jesus finished His story by asking a question. Jesus asked, 'Who do you think was a neighbour to the man who had been robbed and beaten?' Who would like to answer Jesus' question?** Call on a volunteer to answer.

The man gave Jesus a good answer. He said, 'The one who helped him was his neighbour.'

Materials

whiteboard, dry-erase marker, Bibles, Activity page *The Good Samaritan Story Name Cards and Props* on page 164, scissors, wool, backpack, Teaching picture *The Good Samaritan* on page 165 (optional: gauze bandage roll, small bottle with lid, coins)

Before Session

Cut 60cm lengths of wool; tie a piece to each name card so children can wear the name cards around their necks. If using real props, place the gauze, bottle with lid, and coins in the backpack.

Make It Real

3 Use this activity to help children **name ways they can help others.**

Materials
Activity page *Jesus Teaches us Game Cards* on page 166, basket 

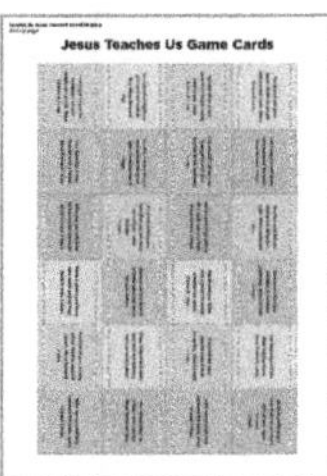

 Consider placing a child with special needs on a team with an assistant (or with a group of children who understand the child's particular challenges).

'Jesus Teaches Us' Game

SAY: **Let's play the 'Jesus Teaches Us' game and learn more about sharing and helping.** Have the children form two teams. Have the teams line up on opposite sides of the room, facing each other. Let the teams take turns choosing cards from the basket. Team members should work together to give a response or do as the card says. The goal is to see how quickly the two teams can meet in the center of the room.

When the teams meet, members of opposing teams should give each other high fives. SAY: **When we work together, we help each other and can finish a task or reach a goal more quickly. We should do our best to work together and help each other. Jesus wants us to help others.**

Live It Out

4 Use this activity to help children **help someone.**

Materials
craft paper, colouring pencils (or washable markers), scissors, hole punch, wool

Something More!
Let children trace around their feet and think of ways to help others by using their feet.

Helping Hands

SAY: **We have learned that Jesus wants us to help others, and we've named ways we can help others. What is the one part of our bodies we use most often to help others?** (hands) Distribute the craft paper and colouring pencils. Ask the children to help each other trace around one of their hands on the paper. Tell children that they each should write (or draw) inside their hand outline a way that they will help someone by using their hands. Then children can cut out their hand outlines, punch holes in the tops, and string with wool, forming reminders that can be hung up.

Have children bring their completed hand reminders to a closing prayer time. Let children share how they will help others this week, and encourage them to follow through on what they are planning to do. Encourage children to pray and promise God that they will do their best to help others.

PRAY: **Thank You, God, for Your Son, Jesus, who taught us how important it is to help others. Help us as we work together to help others. In Jesus' name, amen.**

The Good Samaritan Story Name Cards and Props

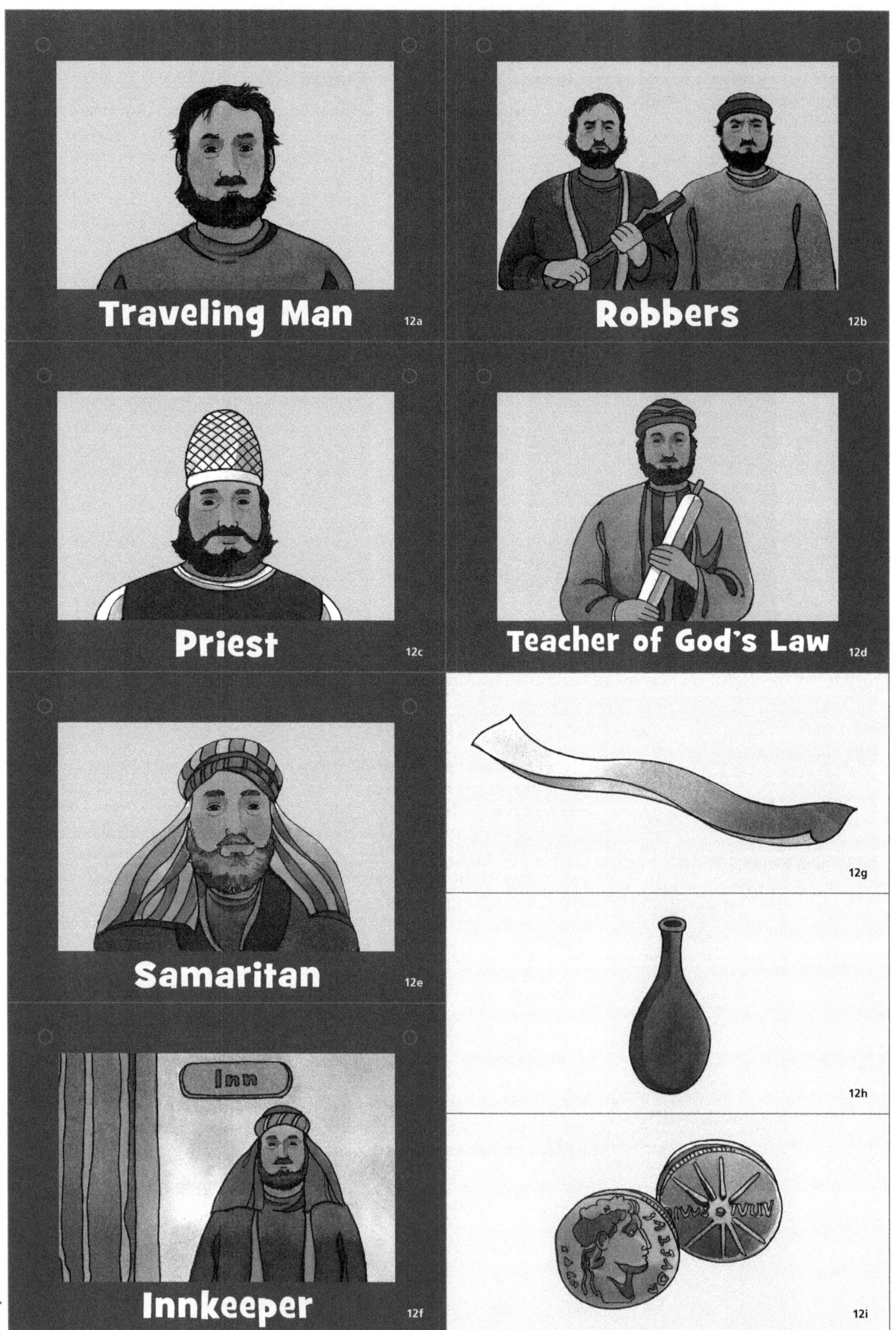

HeartShaper Primary Blue Edition, Activity page
Permission is granted to reproduce this page for ministry purposes only—not for resale.

Rather than photocopy this page you can download and print all activity pages in both colour and black & white from **www.heartshaper.co.uk**

The Good Samaritan

HeartShaper Primary Blue Edition, Activity page
Permission is granted to reproduce this page for ministry purposes only—not for resale.

Jesus Teaches Us Game Cards

- You shared and gave some clothes to people who needed them. Move forward 1 step.
- Tell a way you will share with someone this week. Move forward 2 steps.
- You forgot to help by drying the dishes last night. Move backward 1 step.
- Name something you shared with someone yesterday. Move forward 2 steps.
- You helped your little sister tidy her room. Move forward 1 step.
- Name something you have that you can share with others. Move forward 2 steps.

- You shared your new pens with the girl sitting next to you. Move forward 1 step.
- You wouldn't share your new game with your brother. Move backward 1 step.
- Name a person you know who could use your help. Move forward 2 steps.
- You shared your Bible with a guest in Sunday school group. Move forward 1 step.
- If you helped your parents make dinner yesterday, move forward 1 step.
- Tell a way you will help someone this week. Move forward 2 steps.

- You helped a neighbour put out their rubbish bins. Move forward 1 step.
- You didn't share the last two cookies with your sister. Move backward 1 step.
- Name something you have that you can share with others. Move forward 2 steps.
- Name a way you helped at home yesterday. Move forward 2 steps.
- If you helped and made your bed this morning, move forward 2 steps.
- You helped cheer up a friend who was sick. Move forward 1 step.

- You forgot to put the newspaper on your neighbour's porch. Move backward 1 step.
- You shared your new football with a friend. Move forward 1 step.
- Tell a way you will share with someone this week. Move forward 2 steps.
- Name a person you know who could use your help. Move forward 2 steps.
- You helped your Sunday school teacher pass out papers. Move forward 1 step.
- Tell a way you will help someone this week. Move forward 2 steps.

Peter's Confession

Scripture: Matthew 16:13-17
Focus: Jesus is the Son of God.

Heart to Heart Teacher Devotion

Jesus was such a great question asker; He knew how to cut through issues and get to the heart of matters. Why are you anxious? Where is your faith? Why do you worry? The question in this week's Scripture is one that Jesus asks us too: 'Who do you say I am?' (Matthew 16:15). Since your answer is no doubt the same as Peter's—that Jesus is the Son of the living God—that means that living for Jesus is top priority in your life. In other words, you're living for Jesus and there's no plan B!

Focus

Jesus is the Son of God.

Materials

slips of paper, pencils

Game

For children who have language issues, offer assistance with writing as needed. Post the childrens lists in the room after the game.

Focus In

1 Use this activity to help children **explore who Jesus is.**

Welcome

Welcome each child warmly by name.

This Is Who I Am

Distribute paper and pencils. SAY: **Let's play a game called This Is Who I Am. Make a list of words that describe who you are, such as son, daughter, football player, good friend. Try to write at least four or five things.** Give children a minute or so to do this. When time is up, collect the papers. Tell children that after you read the first paper, they should guess who wrote it. When a correct guess is made, the person whom the paper describes should say, 'This is who I am.' The person who is first to guess it correctly can read the next paper. Keep playing in the same way, making sure that all the children who want to read have the opportunity to do so.

ASK: **Using one or two words, who would you say Jesus is?** Accept responses.
How do you know who Jesus is?

SAY: **Let's keep thinking about who Jesus is as we dig into God's Word.**

Explore His Word

2 Use these activities to help children **tell about Jesus' feeding the crowd.**

Bible Background for the Teacher

Jesus came directly to the point. He wanted to know who the disciples thought He was. They had the most opportunity to hear Him teach. They had seen more miracles than anyone else. They had spent the most time with Him. What was their answer? We don't know whether the question was in some way directed at Peter, but he was the first to respond to Jesus. He boldly proclaimed that Jesus is the Messiah, God's Son. Jesus commended Peter's response and pointed out that his understanding didn't come from human reasoning, as the other suggestions had, but from being in tune with God. Peter's confession didn't mean that he understood everything about Jesus, but it did mean that he had caught the main point. In the same way, we must grasp this basic understanding of who Jesus is before we can move on to accept Him as Saviour and Lord.

Bible Exploration   Matthew 16:13-17

Ask children to look at the table of contents in their Bibles (either a printed Bible or a Bible on a tablet computer, phone, or e-reader) and find the book of Matthew. Have children turn to Matthew 16:13-17. Ask volunteers to read the verses aloud. Then have a volunteer point out Caesarea Philippi on the map and another volunteer point out the 'Peter's confession' icon on the Bible time line. While referring to the icons on the time line, SAY: **Jesus did many miracles when He lived on earth. He healed a man who couldn't walk. He also fed over 5,000 people with only five loaves of bread and two fish. This is where we pick up God's story.**

SAY: **Let's dig a little deeper into this event in the life of Jesus.** Choose a volunteer who will read the Bible verses aloud.

Distribute the Activity page *Peter's Confession*. Read the directions, and have volunteers read the three sentences, filling in the blanks. (Answers: 1=servant; 2=spoke; 3=5,000) SAY: **Peter and the other disciples had heard Jesus teach about God and had seen Him do miracles.**
ASK: **When Jesus asked His disciples who people thought He was, how did they answer?** (John the Baptist; Elijah; Jeremiah; another prophet)
Why do you think people thought Jesus might be one of those men? (Those men also spoke for God; those men also had power from God)
How did Peter answer Jesus? Have a volunteer read the last sentence, filling in the blanks. (Messiah, Son, living)
How was Peter able to know that Jesus is the Messiah, the Son of the living God? (God told him)

SAY: **Jesus being the Messiah, the Son of the living God, is what makes Him different from anyone else who has ever lived. Jesus is not just a good teacher or a prophet. Jesus is God's Son, the Saviour for all people. Let's dig deeper to discover reasons why we know that Jesus is the Son of God.**

Materials

Bibles, Bible map from page 106, Bible time lines, Activity page *Peter's Confession* on page 172, pencils, reusable adhesive (optional: tape)

Skit

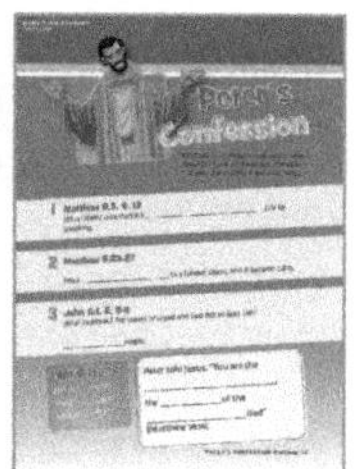

Teaching Tip

Slow down the time on the Activity Page by letting older children help younger ones in pairs or small groups.

Make It Real

3 Use this activity to help children **discover how we know Jesus is God's Son**.

Materials

whiteboard, dry-erase marker, Activity pages *Jesus is God's Son* on pages 170-171, pencils, Bibles

 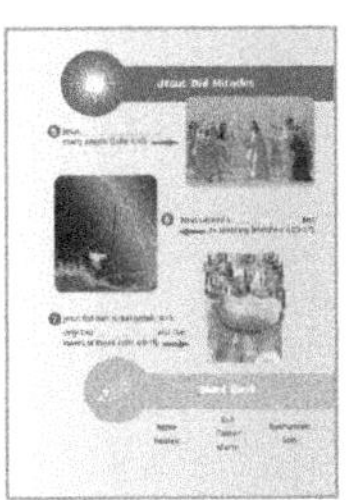

How do you know that . . .

1. **the sun rises in the east and sets in the west?** (can see it)
2. **blue and yellow make green?** (can try it)
3. **10 + 10 equals 20?** (learned it in school)
4. **ice cream is yummy?** (Everyone knows that!)

How Do You Know?

Group the session into two teams. SAY: **Let's play a game called How Do You Know?** Ask each team to send one player to stand by you. The player who says 'I know!' first, gets to answer. If correct, that team gets 10 points. If not, the other team can answer and get the points. Keep score on the board. Continue for a few rounds. The narrow column has a few possible questions. **Now let's discover some reasons why we know Jesus is the Son of God.** Give out Activity page *Jesus Is God's Son*. Divide the session into three groups (or pairs). Assign one group the Jesus Fulfilled Old Testament Prophecies section; another, the Jesus Called God His Father section; and the last, the Jesus Did Miracles section. Groups should work together to look up the Scriptures and finish their sentences. When ready, let the groups read their sentences. All children can write the correct answers in their leaflets. (Answers: 1=Bethlehem; 2=Son; 3=Father; 4=name; 5=healed; 6=storm; 7=fish)

ASK: **When someone asks you why you believe that Jesus is God's Son, what can you say?** (Jesus fulfilled the Old Testament prophecies about a ruler; Jesus called God His Father; Jesus did amazing miracles)

SAY: **These are just a few of the many reasons why we know that Jesus is the Son of God.**

Live It Out

4 Use this activity to help children **express who they believe Jesus is**.

Materials

roll paper, markers, reusable adhesive

 Consider having each group make their poster without telling them to create the 'best' poster. Non-competitive environments for art activities are important, especially for children with special needs.

Convincing Posters

SAY: **Peter confessed that Jesus is the Messiah, the Son of the living God. Did you know that many times when people choose to accept Christ as their Saviour, they are asked to say the same words that Peter said to Jesus?**

Divide the session into small groups (or pairs). Give each group a length of roll paper and markers. SAY: **Now it's your turn to answer Jesus' question. Who do you believe Jesus is? Each group's challenge is to create the best poster with convincing statements about who you believe Jesus is. Talk about it as a group; then create your poster.** When groups are done, have them display their papers on the wall. Ask everyone to gather around the papers. Let group members read what they wrote.

SAY: **You have a choice to believe that Jesus is the Son of God or to believe that He is not. I hope and pray that each of you will truly believe that Jesus is the Son of God and live for Him every day of your life.** Close with a time of prayer. Ask for volunteers to pray. Encourage them to express in their prayers who they believe Jesus is.

1 The ruler would be born in Bethlehem (Micah 5:2). → Jesus was born in ________________________ (Luke 2:4-7).

2 The ruler would be a son, given by God and born of a virgin (Isaiah 7:14; 9:6). → Jesus is God's __________, born of a virgin (Luke 1:26-38).

Jesus Called God His Father

3 Jesus said, 'I . . . speak just what the ____________________ has taught me' (John 8:28).

4 Jesus said, 'The works I do in my Father's ____________________ testify about me' (John 10:25).

Jesus Did Miracles

5 Jesus ___________________________
many people (Luke 4:40). ➡

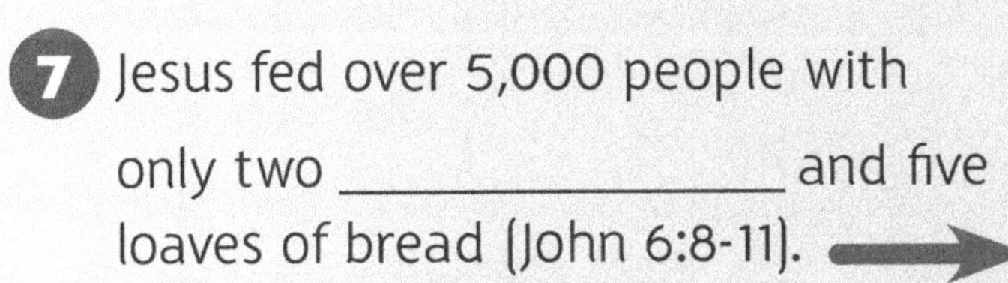

6 Jesus calmed a __________________ just
⬅ by speaking (Matthew 8:23-27).

7 Jesus fed over 5,000 people with

only two ________________ and five

loaves of bread (John 6:8-11). ➡

Word Bank

name

fish
Father

healed

storm

Bethlehem
Son

Peter's Confession

What led up to Peter's confessing who Jesus is? Look up these Scriptures to find out. Use the Word Bank for help.

1 Matthew 8:5, 6, 13

Jesus healed a centurion's _________________________ just by speaking.

2 Matthew 8:23-27

Jesus _________________ to a furious storm, and it became calm.

3 John 6:1, 2, 8-11

Jesus multiplied five loaves of bread and two fish to feed over

_________________ people.

Word Bank

Messiah	spoke
living	5,000
servant	Son

Peter told Jesus, 'You are the

_________________________,

the _________________ of the

_________________ God'

(Matthew 16:16).

Jesus' Transfiguration

Session 28

Scripture: Luke 9:28-36
Focus: Jesus is worth listening to.

Heart to Heart Teacher Devotion

Do you like to listen to music or comedy, news or sport? There is plenty to listen to each day—and some of it really isn't worth listening to! Through the clutter of noise comes the voice of the one who is truly worth listening to. With authority, yet compassion, comes the voice of Jesus: 'I love you. Trust me. Follow me. I'm preparing a place in Heaven for you.' Thank God that Jesus is worth listening to.

Focus
Jesus is worth listening to.

Focus In

1 Use this activity to help children **explore how they know whom to listen to.**

Welcome

Welcome each children warmly by name.

Listen to My Voice

Before the session, create a simple obstacle course in your room. Use masking tape to identify the edges. Put a few chairs (or waste paper bin, etc.) on the outside of the taped path.

Show children the obstacle course. Choose a volunteer who is willing to try the obstacle course. Blindfold the volunteer and turn the person around a few times. SAY: **If you listen to my voice, I will get you through the obstacle course. Sounds easy, doesn't it? Well, it won't be because everyone else will be talking too. But remember—listen only to my voice.** Tell the rest of the children they can say anything they want, including giving wrong instructions to the blindfolded person, but they can only talk using their 'indoor' voices. When finished, ask the volunteer whether it was hard to listen to the right voice. If time permits, let another volunteer try the obstacle course.

ASK: **When are some times it's hard to know whom to listen to?** Accept responses.
How do you decide whom to listen to?

SAY: **Let's see what God's Word says about who is worth listening to.**

Materials

masking tape, chairs and other objects for obstacle course, blindfold

Action

Note

Safety first—don't let the blindfolded volunteer run into anything.

Focus
Jesus is worth listening to.

Explore His Word

2 Use these activities to help children **describe the events of Jesus' transfiguration.**

Bible Background for the Teacher

Jesus took Peter, James, and John with Him to a mountain to pray, where He gave them a glimpse of His true glory. Jesus' change of form was a visible transformation. The true glory of Jesus was presented in a manner that the apostles could see with their own eyes. It wasn't a vision or a dream. Unlike many of the miracles that the disciples witnessed, this one involved the very person of Jesus. Perhaps this difference in the nature of the miracle explains the terror of the disciples that is mentioned in the description of the event given in Matthew 17:1-8 and Mark 9:2-8.

The voice of God brought the scene to its proper focus: Jesus. Jesus is clearly identified as God's Son, God's chosen, and the one to listen to.

Bible Exploration   Luke 9:28-36

Have children turn in their Bibles to Luke 9:28, and have a volunteer read the verse aloud. SAY: **About eight days earlier, Peter had confessed that Jesus is God's Son. Jesus had told His disciples that He would soon have to suffer. As I tell you more about what happened that day on the mountain, I'll stop once in a while. When I stop, make the face you think that person might have made at that moment, and freeze your face.** Read Luke 9:28-29. SAY: **As Jesus prayed to His Father, something miraculous happened. Show on your face how Jesus might have looked as His face changed, and freeze your face!** Look at the children' faces. **While we don't know how Jesus' face changed, it must have been something to see!**

Read verses 30-31. SAY: **As Jesus' appearance changed, or transfigured, two men appeared with Him: Moses and Elijah. Moses had been a great leader of the Israelites. Elijah had been a great prophet for God. Both had been dead for quite a long time. Show on your face how Moses and Elijah might have looked as they talked with Jesus, and freeze your face!** Look at the children' faces. **They might have been concerned because they knew what would soon happen to Jesus.**

Read verse 32. SAY: **Show on your face how Peter, John, and James looked as they woke up and saw Jesus transfigured, standing with Moses and Elijah.** Look at the children' faces. **They may have been afraid, confused, amazed, or maybe all those emotions!** Read verse 33. **Peter just had to say something! He suggested putting up three shelters, or buildings, for Jesus, Moses, and Elijah. Show on your face how Peter might have looked as he said this, and freeze your face!** Look at the children' faces. **It seems as if Peter didn't want the men to leave.**

Read verse 34. SAY: **Peter was still speaking, when a cloud covered them. Show on your face how the disciples felt, and freeze your face!** Look at the children' faces. **They were afraid!** Read verse 35. **The voice was the voice of God! God told the disciples to listen to His Son, Jesus.** Read verse 36. **After God spoke, Moses and Elijah were gone. Show on your face how the disciples might have looked after everything that had just happened, and freeze your face!** Look at the children's faces. **We don't know, but we can imagine what they were thinking and feeling. They had seen Jesus changed, or transfigured, standing with two men of God who had been dead for a long time. They had heard God say that Jesus was His Son and that they should listen to Him. What a day it had been!** Thank children for their participation.

Ask children to look at Activity page *Jesus' Transfiguration*. Ask children to explain what *transfiguration* means. (change in form or appearance) Have volunteers read the questions and answer them. (Answers: 1=c; 2=b, c; 3=a, b, c) SAY: **God said that Jesus is His Son and that Jesus is worth listening to. Will you listen to Jesus?**

   Jesus' Transfiguration **Session 28**

Focus
**Jesus is worth
listening to.**

Make It Real

3 Use this activity to help children **discover ways to listen to Jesus.**

Materials
Activity pages *How Can You Listen To Jesus?* on pages 176-177, pencils

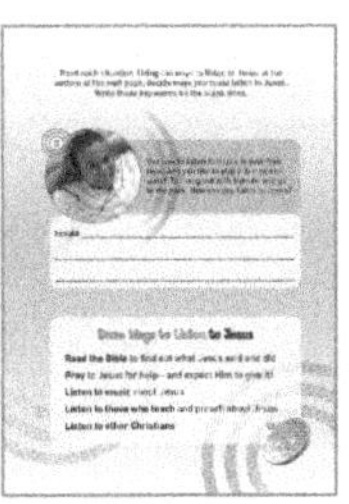

Note
Tell children that listening to others who believe in Jesus can, many times, help us understand His Word better. Listening to music about Jesus can help us want to know Him better and bring to our minds truths from His Word.

Repeat the Beat

Clap a short and simple rhythmic beat. Have children repeat the beat. Try a few more, each beat getting a little more complicated. Comment on the children' listening skills. SAY: **God wants us to have good listening skills too, not so we can repeat beats, but to listen to Jesus, because Jesus is worth listening to. Let's discover ways to do that.** Hand out Activity page *How Can You Listen to Jesus?* Read the directions, and have a volunteer read the first situation. **If you were in that situation, how could you listen to Jesus? Look at the list of ideas at the bottom of the page.** Read the ideas and explain them. See the narrow column.

SAY: **Choose one way or several ways that you could listen to Jesus in the first situation. Write those key words on the blank lines.** Have volunteers share what they wrote. Then let children complete the other two situations individually or in pairs. When children are ready, let volunteers read the situations and tell what key words they wrote down. **God told us to listen to Jesus. So let's be sure to do it!**

Focus
**Jesus is worth
listening to.**

Live It Out

4 Use this activity to help children **plan to listen to Jesus.**

Materials
Bibles

Before the session print out or write out these Bible references in large letters on separate pieces of paper. Display the papers around your room. If you have younger children print out the text of the actual Bible passage so that they can be accessed and read easily by an older child or helper.

- Mark 8:34-38
- Mark 9:33-35
- Mark 12:28-31
- Luke 12:22-26
- Luke 15:1-7
- John 14:1-4

The Listening Challenge

SAY: **When you need to know what you should do in a situation, Jesus is worth listening to. When you're sad or worried about something, Jesus is worth listening to. When someone is sick, Jesus is worth listening to. Anytime is a good time to listen to Jesus!** Show children the verses you have written out on paper or posted around the room. SAY: **In pairs, choose one of these Bible verses, look it up in the Bible and read together what Jesus is saying.**

ASK: **What is Jesus saying in these verses that we need to listen to?** Guide children to think about what these verses mean.

Do the same with a few more Scriptures. Then challenge children to look up the rest of the Scriptures during the week. SAY: **As you read these Scriptures, listen to what Jesus is saying to you through them. Maybe He is asking you to do something for Him or helping you to know how you should treat others. Whatever He is saying, Jesus is worth listening to.** Have children gather for a time of prayer. PRAY: **Dear God, thank You for listening to us as we talk to You. Help us to always take time to listen to You. Bring to our minds people we should pray about and things You want us to do. In Jesus' name, amen.**

How Can You LISTEN to JESUS?

1

You're worried that you're not very popular. Someone told you that you would be more popular if you didn't hang out with that child no one else talks to. How can you listen to Jesus?

I could ______________________________________

____

____

2

Your mum is unwell and in hospital. You're worried that she will never get better. How can you listen to Jesus?

I could ______________________________________

____

____

Read each situation. Using the ways to listen to Jesus at the bottom of the next page, decide ways *you* could listen to Jesus. Write those key words on the blank lines.

3

You love to listen to music in your free time. And you like to play video games, watch TV, hang out with friends, and go to the park. How can you listen to Jesus?

I could ____

____

____

Some Ways to Listen to Jesus

Read the Bible to find out what Jesus said and did

Pray to Jesus for help—and expect Him to give it!

Listen to music about Jesus

Listen to those who teach and preach about Jesus

Listen to other Christians

Jesus' Transfiguration

Circle the correct answers. There might be more than one for each question.

1 Who did Jesus take up onto a mountain to pray with Him?

a. All 12 disciples

b. Anyone who wanted to go

c. Peter, John, James

2 As Jesus prayed, what happened to His appearance?

a. He became very tall.

b. His face changed.

c. His clothes became as bright as lightning.

3 From the cloud, what did God's voice say?

a. Jesus was His Son.

b. God had chosen His Son.

c. Listen to Jesus.

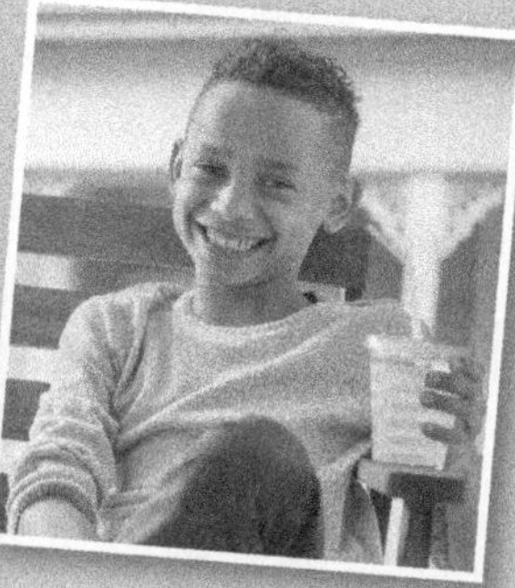

Jesus Raises Lazarus

Session 29

Scripture: John 11:1-7, 17, 34-45
Focus: Jesus' power helps us believe in Him.

Heart to Heart Teacher Devotion
God's Word presents Jesus as one who is humble and meek, yet can control sickness, storms, and death itself. Jesus had compassion for people, yet commanded evil spirits to depart. Jesus showed His power to help us know who He is, and believe in Him. As you consider the challenges facing you this week, remember the power of the one who brings the dead to life, and renew your belief and faith in Jesus.

Focus
Jesus' power helps us believe in Him.

Materials

blanket large enough for everyone to comfortably stand on (or use masking tape or rope to mark off an area in which children can stand)

Teaching Tip
If you have a really large session, you'll need more than one blanket.

Trust can be a tricky concept, especially for children whose trust in adults or peers has been damaged. As an alternative, create on a whiteboard a 'trust web' that lists qualities of people who are trustworthy. Have children reflect on who in their lives are trustworthy people, based on the qualities listed.

Focus In

1 Use this activity to help children **explore people they believe in.**

Welcome
Welcome each child warmly by name.

Blanket Stand
ASK: **Who do you believe in? Who do you trust and have faith in?**
Accept responses.

Place the blanket on the floor, and ask all the children to stand on it. SAY: **If I fold the blanket in half, do you believe, or trust, that all of you can work together to stand on it? Let's try it!** Have children move off the blanket. Fold it in half and then children can step back onto it. Encourage the children to work together. **If I fold it in half again, do you believe, or trust, that all of you can work together to stand on it?** Do so, encouraging the children to work together. Keep folding until it's too small for all the children to stand on. **It was good to see you all believing in and trusting each other to figure out how to stand on the blanket each time.**

ASK: **Who are some people you would *always* believe in, or have trust in?** Accept responses.

SAY: **We believe in and trust people when they care about us and help us. Now let's discover some reasons to believe in Jesus.**

Explore His Word

2 Use these activities to help children **describe the events surrounding the raising of Lazarus.**

Bible Background for the Teacher

Mary, Martha, and Lazarus were very close to Jesus. Many people believe that their home was Jesus' home whenever He was in the area of Bethany, which was just west of Jerusalem. We know for certain that Jesus was their honoured guest at dinner on at least two occasions (see Luke 10; John 12).

Most people would say that Jesus arrived in Bethany too late. In fact, some of the people who were gathered to comfort Mary and Martha criticized Him for not getting there earlier so that He could have healed Lazarus (John 11:37). Interestingly, Martha, whom Jesus earlier rebuked for her lack of focus on Him, showed the greatest faith in this circumstance. She was convinced not only that Jesus could have kept Lazarus from dying but also that He still could do something to change the situation (v. 22). We see Jesus' deep compassion as He saw the suffering of others (v. 33) and His own tears joined theirs (v. 35). Even more importantly, we see Jesus' power. Just by speaking, He called Lazarus out of the tomb and back from the dead. Lazarus's return proves Christ's victory over the grave, a victory that would be extended to Jesus' own resurrection. This display of Jesus' power helped many believe in Him.

Bible Exploration   John 11:1-7, 17, 34-45

Ask a volunteer to stand by the map and point out Bethany. Tell children that Bethany is where today's Bible story takes place. Ask children to turn in their Bibles to John 11. Have volunteers read verses 1-3, 6-7, 17, 34-36, 38-45. Show children the empty tomb photo from page 324. **Lazarus was buried in a tomb similar to this one. Tombs were cut from stone. The body would be laid inside, and a stone covered the opening.**

ASK: **How long had Lazarus been dead when Jesus raised him back to life?** (four days)
How did Jesus feel about His friend's death? (Jesus cried, so He must have been sad; we know Jesus loved Lazarus)

Choose volunteers to act out the parts of some of the Bible characters in this story (Jesus, Lazarus, Mary, Martha). One or more children can be Jesus' disciples, and one or more children can be the Jewish people. (If possible, provide Bible-times costumes for children to wear.) You can tell the story in your own words, read it from your Bible, or play a dramatised version of it from the Internet. Whatever you do, give time for children to act. If the actors want to, they can repeat their lines after you. When finished, thank the children for their participation.

Hand out the Activity page *Jesus Raises Lazarus*. Read the directions. Let children pair up and do the page together. When children are done, let pairs of volunteers read the sentences, saying what they changed to make the sentences true. (Answers: 1=cross out 'left right away' and write 'stayed where He was for two more days'; 2=cross out 'hated' and write 'loved'; 3=cross out 'Peter' and write 'God'; 4=cross out 'had no faith' and write 'believed'.)

ASK: **How did this miracle show how powerful Jesus is and that Jesus is God's Son?** (Jesus called God His Father; only God or His Son has enough power to raise someone from the dead)

SAY: **The miracles Jesus did helped the people in His time believe in who He is. The same is true for us. Knowing Jesus' power helps us believe in Him too. When we realise just how powerful Jesus was when He was on earth—and still is—it helps us believe in Him.**

Materials

Activity Page *Bible Map* on page 324, Teaching Picture *Burial Tomb* on page 208, Bibles, Activity page *Jesus Raises Lazarus* on page 184, pencils (optional: Bible-times costumes)

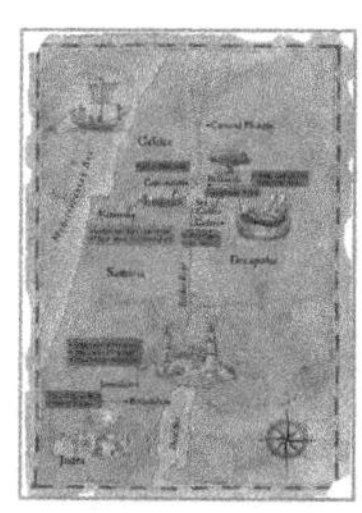

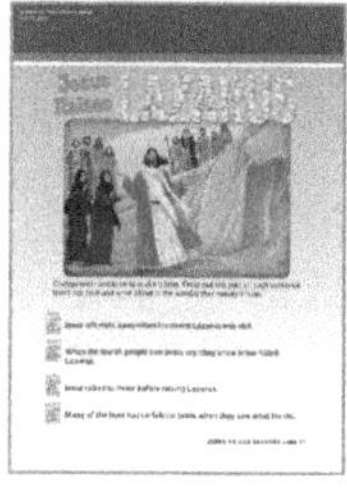

Media Option

You can go to a website such as www.biblegateway.com and play a dramatised reading of the Bible verses.

Make It Real

3 Use this activity to help children **discover why they can believe in Jesus.**

Materials

Activity pages *Thinking About Jesus' Power* on pages 182-183, pencils, Bibles

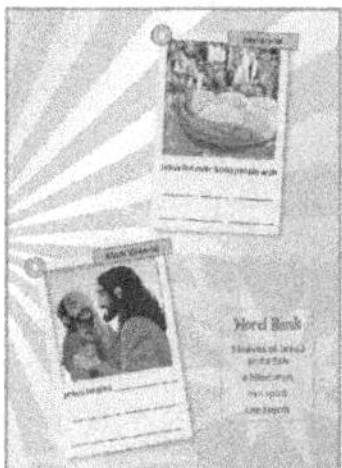

Thinking About Jesus' Power

Divide the session into small groups. SAY: **In your groups, come up with one good reason that you could give others to help them believe in Jesus.** Give children a minute to work on this. Have groups share their reasons. Lead a discussion about the reasons children gave. Then hand out Activity page *Thinking About Jesus' Power*. Assign each small group to look up one of the Scriptures and finish the caption. If you don't have four small groups, assign more than one Scripture to each group. When groups have finished, let them tell how they finished the captions. Invite all the children to finish the captions in their page as they are discussed. (Possible answers: 1=Jesus healed a man of an evil spirit. 2=Jesus calmed a storm. 3=Jesus fed over 5,000 people with five loaves of bread and two fish. 4=Jesus healed a blind man.)

ASK: **What's one big reason you can believe in Jesus?** (Jesus is powerful)

Over what does Jesus have power? (sickness, nature, death, everything)

How powerful would you say Jesus is? (He has more power than anyone or anything)

SAY: **There are lots of reasons to believe in Jesus. Knowing about Jesus' power helps us believe in Him.**

Live It Out

4 Use this activity to help children **believe in Jesus.**

Materials

pencils

Before the session write out the following challenges on separate pieces of card or paper and display them around the room.
• Read the Bible
• Help at home
• Tell others about Jesus
• Trust Jesus
• Share Jesus' love with others
• Pray

Choose a Challenge

SAY: **After Jesus raised Lazarus from the dead, many of the people who had seen the miracle believed in Jesus. They saw Jesus' power and then they believed in Him. Jesus' power helps us believe in Him too! Jesus doesn't ask us to believe in Him without giving us some great reasons. One of the reasons we can believe in Jesus is because of His awesome power. No one but God's Son could do the things He did and the things He continues to do.**

ASK: **How about you? Do you believe in Jesus? If you do, how will you show it?** Accept responses.

SAY: **Decide how you will show that you believe in Jesus. I've written some ideas to help you. Choose at least one of these ways, or come up with your own ideas.** If children want to tell what they're choosing to do, let them share that with everyone. Close with a time of prayer. Encourage volunteers to pray, expressing their belief in Jesus.

Thinking About Jesus' Power

Read the Bible verses.
Finish the captions by telling
about Jesus' power.

1

Jesus healed a man of

____

____

2

Jesus calmed __________________

____

HeartShaper Primary Blue Edition, Activity page
Permission is granted to reproduce this page for ministry
purposes only—not for resale.

Rather than photocopy this page you can download
and print all activity pages in both colour and
black & white from **www.heartshaper.co.uk**

3

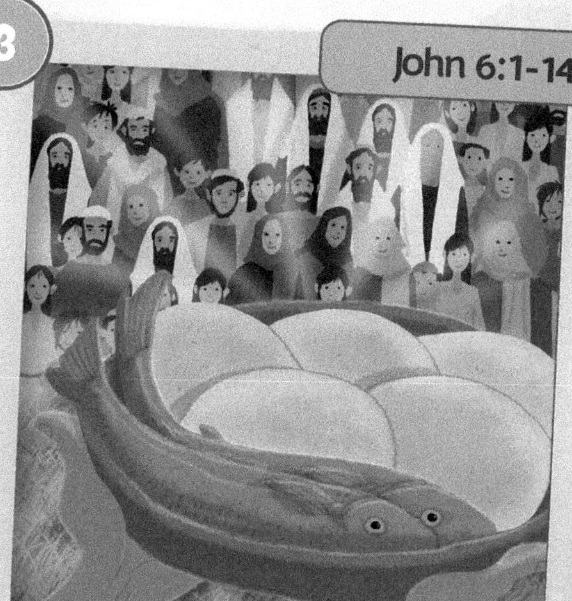

Jesus fed over 5,000 people with

____

____

4

Jesus healed ______________

____

____

Word Bank

5 loaves of bread
and 2 fish

a blind man

evil spirit

the storm

Jesus Raises LAZARUS

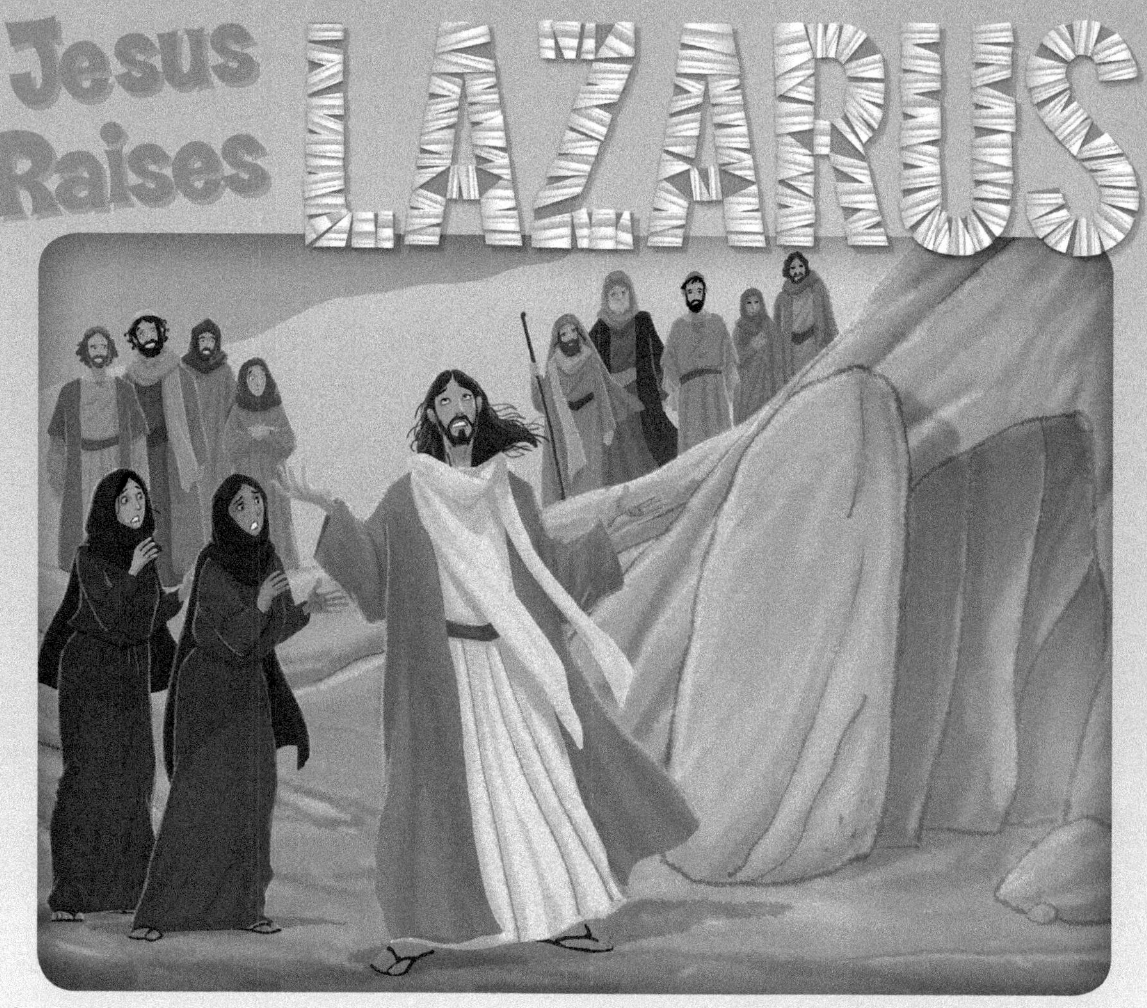

Change each sentence to make it true. Cross out the part of each sentence that's not true and write above it the word(s) that makes it true.

 Jesus left right away when He heard Lazarus was sick.

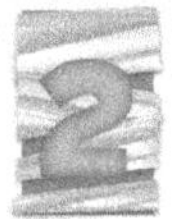 When the Jewish people saw Jesus cry, they knew Jesus hated Lazarus.

 Jesus talked to Peter before raising Lazarus.

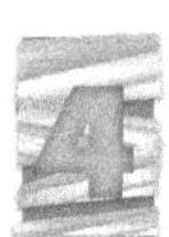 Many of the Jews had no faith in Jesus when they saw what He did.

The Greatest Commandments Session 30

Scripture: Matthew 22:34-40
Focus: Jesus wants us to love God and others.

Heart to Heart Teacher Devotion
Sometimes we think that living the Christian life is a complicated process. Jesus took special care to make His instructions as concise and as simple as possible: love God with all your being, and love your neighbour as you love yourself. When we follow these commands, the rest will fall into place.

Focus
Jesus wants us to love God and others.

Materials
roll paper, sticky tape, colouring pens

Art

Teaching Tip
If you have a large session, display more than 2 lengths of roll paper.

Focus In

1 Use this activity to help children **explore different kinds of love.**

Welcome
Welcome each child warmly by name.

Love Posters
Before the session, display two lengths of roll paper on the walls of the room. Label one paper, 'People We Love.' Title the other paper, 'Things We Love.'

SAY: **Think of people you love. I'm sure that includes family members and friends. Also think about things you love, from stuff you own to food to places you like to go.** Draw children' attention to the papers. **On the 'People We Love' poster, draw at least one person you love. On the 'Things We Love' poster, draw at least one thing you love.** When time is up, comment on the people and things the children drew.

ASK: **How is the love you have for your parents different from the love you have for pizza?**
How is the love you have for a friend different from the love you have for a pet?

SAY: **We use the word** *love* **to describe how we feel about a lot of things. Let's find out what Jesus said about love.**

Explore His Word

2 Use these activities to help children **name the two greatest commandments.**

Bible Background for the Teacher

The Pharisee who questioned Jesus was an expert in the law himself (Matthew 22:35). From the description of this incident as recorded in Mark 12, we get the idea that, unlike some of the other questions, this one was motivated by a real desire for an answer. The question literally asks, 'What kind of commandment is greatest?' The Pharisees debated whether the negative (what not to do) or the positive (what to do) commandments were more important. Therefore, the question tested two things: Jesus' knowledge of the law and His conformity to the thinking of the Pharisees. In His answer, Jesus tried to get the Pharisees' focus away from observable actions and onto the training of their hearts and minds and wills.

Jesus' answer (quoting Deuteronomy 6:5) indicates not only the importance of this particular command but also the reason for obeying all God's commands: complete, wholehearted love for Him. Jesus also quoted Leviticus 19:18 to make clear the importance of loving other people. If we have God's love in our hearts, following His way will come naturally.

Bible Exploration   Matthew 22:34-40

Materials
Bibles

SAY: **God sent salvation when Jesus came to earth. After Jesus was baptised, He began His ministry of teaching people about God. He called disciples to follow Him and learn from Him. He performed miracles to help people know that He is God's Son. Jesus even raised Lazarus from the dead and made a man who couldn't see be able to see! This is where we pick up God's story.**

Ask children to turn in their Bibles to Matthew 22:37-40. Ask volunteers to read the verses aloud. Then ask a volunteer to read verses 35-36.
SAY: **This Scripture gives us the context, or the setting, in which Jesus said these important words.**

ASK: **What was the man who was asking the question an expert in?**
(the law, he was a lawyer) Have a volunteer read verse 37.

ASK: **From where did Jesus get His answer?** (the Old Testament)
How can we find out where in the Old Testament Jesus got His answer? (look it up)

SAY: **Jesus wants us to love God and others, because when we do, we'll live at peace with God and with those around us. Jesus wants us to love God and others, because when we do, we'll live the best kind of life possible—a life lived for God!**

Make It Real

3 Use this activity to help children **discover ways they can love God and others.**

Materials

feathers (1 per child), timer, Activity pages *Loving God and Others* on pages 188-189, pencils

 Before distributing the feathers, model what the children are to do so they will see how difficult the task is. For children with breathing issues, offer roles such as timekeepers and judges.

Loving God and Others

Give each child a feather. SAY: **Just by blowing with your mouth, keep your feather in the air for one minute. You can't touch your feather in any way. Ready? Go!** Keep time. Congratulate those who completed this very hard task. Have children get into small groups as they sit down.

SAY: **It seems as though that would have been an easy thing to do, but it wasn't. It can seem easy to love God and others, but sometimes it just isn't.** Ask children to look at Activity page *Loving God and Others.* Read the directions, and have children complete the page on their own or, if you have a mixed age class, pair older children with younger ones. They can get some ideas from the first page of their leaflets. When everyone is finished, ask volunteers to share what they've written. (Possible answers: 1=being kind to her, or not getting angry with her; 2=asking parents to pick you up so you can go to church services; 3=telling the truth; 4=forgiving the friend, explaining how upset you are without anger.)

ASK: **When are times that it may be hard to love God?**
When are times that it's hard to love others?

SAY: **Even when it's not easy, Jesus wants us to love God and others. When we do, we'll be keeping the greatest commandments!**

Live It Out

4 Use this activity to help children **commit to showing love to God and others.**

Materials

wool (or string) in 3 colours, scissors, tape

Extra time
Use Activity page *My Top 3* on page 190 to help children to plan three ways they can show love to God and others.

 Some children will find braiding and tying knots difficult due to the fine motor skills and coordination needed. Support them to adapt the task to their abilities.

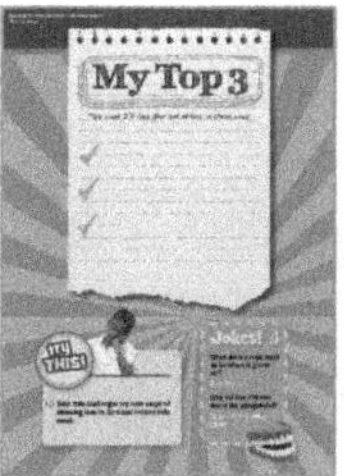

Love Commitment Bracelets

SAY: **Since we know that Jesus wants us to love God and others, let's plan on doing that. As you make love commitment bracelets, think about specific ways you'll show love to God and others this week. One colour of lacing will help you remember to love God, another colour will help you remember to love others, and the third colour will help you remember that *you* are the one loving God and others.**

Each child needs three 30cm lengths of wool, each in a different colour. Here are the directions: **Hold the three strands together and tie a knot at one end. Tape the knot to the table, and lay the three lengths of wool straight out. Braid the three lengths together and tie a knot at the end.** Offer help with the fine-motor aspects of this task as needed. Children can help each other put on their bracelets and tie the two ends together.

Ask children to wear their bracelets as they gather for a time of prayer. SAY: **Wear your bracelets this week and let them remind you to love God and others. Let's talk to God right now about that. Silently talk to God and tell Him some ideas you have for loving Him and others. Ask for His help too.** Ask children to bow their heads and silently talk to God. After a short time of silence, close in prayer.

Loving God and Ot

How can you show love to God and others throughout your day? Write what you think you could do.

Your sister ate all your favourite cereal. You can't believe it! This is the second time she's done that. You decide to show love to your

sister by _______________________

____

____

2 You get invited to a pizza party sleepover. Your friend said that everyone will sleep in on Sunday morning, then go ice skating. You decide to show love to God by

____

____

____

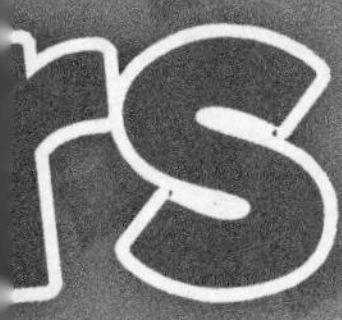

3

You didn't complete your maths homework. You are tempted to lie and tell your teacher that you were sick last night and didn't feel like doing it. You decide to show love to your teacher and God by

____

____

____

4

Your best friend broke your brand-new game controller, and he didn't even offer to buy you a new one! You feel like shouting at him! You decide to

show love to God by _________

____

____

How will **you** show love?

HeartShaper Primary Blue Edition. Activity page

189

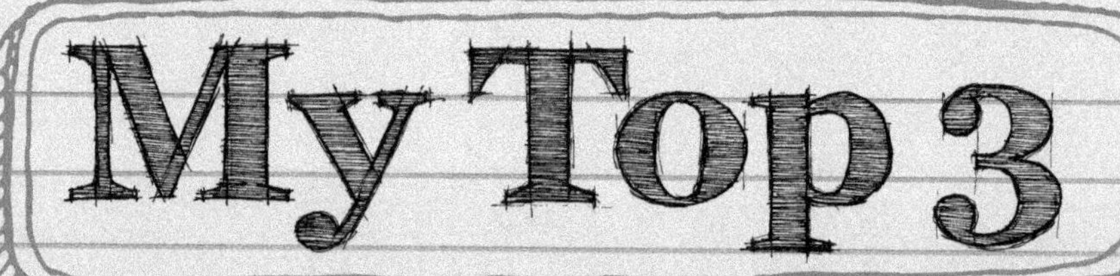

This week I'll love God and others in these ways:

▷ **Take this challenge: try new ways of showing love to God and others this week.**

Jokes! :)

What does a rock want to be when it grows up?

A rock star!

Why did the chicken cross the playground?

To get to the other slide!

Parable of the 10 Virgins

Session 31

Scripture: Matthew 25:1-13
Focus: Jesus wants us to be ready for His return.

Heart to Heart Teacher Devotion

We get ready for work, we get ready for meetings, we get ready to go to bed. We are constantly getting ready for something. For the Christian, that's even more true. Each day finds us getting ready for the return of Jesus: praying, reading God's Word, serving others, and living out our faith. Help your children know that although the journey on this earth is sometimes hard, the reward of Heaven is greater than we can imagine.

Focus
Jesus wants us to be ready for His return.

If you have a child with special needs, suggest actions that the person is able to do alone or with a partner.

Materials
2 sets of identical items needed to get ready for school (toothbrushes, washcloths, combs, small bowls of cereal, plastic spoons, shirts, books, pencil case, school bag.)

Action

Focus In

① Use this activity to help children to **practise getting ready.**

Welcome

Welcome each child warmly by name.

Get Ready Relay

Have children get into two teams and line up. Tell each team to select a person they will get ready for school. Ask those selected to go to the opposite side of the room, and place a set of the gathered items by each person. SAY: **Time for the Get Ready Relay! Each team has a friend who needs to get ready for school—and your teams will help the friend do just that. When I say 'Go,' the first person in line should walk over to your team's friend and quickly choose an item that will help your friend get ready for school. If it's a toothbrush, brush your friend's teeth; then bring me the toothbrush. If it's a washcloth, pretend to wash your friend's face; then bring me the washcloth. Do something similar with each item. The team who uses all the items first wins! Ready? Go!**

ASK: **How well do you like getting ready to: go to school; take a test; eat lunch; go to bed?**

SAY: **In today's lesson, Jesus tells a parable about getting ready. Let's see what God's Word says.**

Focus
Jesus wants us to be ready for His return.

Explore His Word

② Use these activities to help children **explain Jesus' parable.**

Bible Background for the Teacher

Matthew 24 includes a discussion of the second coming of Christ. In chapter 25, Jesus tells three related parables, stressing the importance of being ready for Jesus' return. The first story Jesus told involves 10 virgins taking part in a marriage celebration. They were part of the group that would accompany the groom to the wedding feast. The lamp bowl held a wick that had been soaked in oil and would burn when lit, drawing on the oil supply. The young women fit into two groups: the wise (those who were prepared) and the foolish (those who were not). The difference was the jars of oil brought by the wise. The wise women were ready even if things didn't go exactly as planned.

Unfortunately, when the foolish women realised that they weren't ready, it was too late. While they were away trying to buy more oil, the groom came and the wedding feast began. By the time they arrived at the feast, no more guests were being admitted. They were left on the outside—in the dark, away from the groom, missing the feast. Jesus finished the parable with a clear statement of its message: 'Therefore keep watch, because you do not know the day or the hour (Matthew 25:13).' All Christians eagerly await Christ's return. But we must be ready for His return at any moment, and we must help others prepare. We don't want anyone to be on the outside—in the dark, without Jesus, for eternity.

Bible Exploration   Matthew 25:1-13

SAY: **Jesus taught people about God, like the time He taught about the greatest commandments. Today's lesson is about another time Jesus taught about God. This time, Jesus taught using a parable.**

ASK: **What is a parable?** (a story that has a deeper meaning; a story that helps people think about things in a new or different way)

SAY: **Jesus' parable, His story with a deeper meaning, is about a wedding celebration. Wedding celebrations in Jesus' time were different from weddings today. In this story, there were 10 young women, 10 virgins, who would accompany the groom to the wedding feast. The young women would hold lamps, or lamp bowls, with wicks soaked in oil that would burn when lit.** Show children the photos of the lamp and jar of oil from the Activity page *Be Ready for Jesus.* **Keep all this in mind as we read this parable.** Ask children to turn in their Bibles to Matthew 25:1-13. Have volunteers read the verses aloud.

ASK: **Who does the groom in the story represent?** (Jesus)
   Who do the women in the story represent? (people, both wise and foolish)
SAY: **Let's do some acting. You won't be acting alone, but acting as part of a group.** Divide the session into two groups. Have the groups stand together. Designate one group as the foolish women and the other group as the wise women. **When your group is talked about, all of you in that group should pretend to do what was said. Or when your group says something, all of you in that group should say those words after me. Ready?** Read Matthew 25:1-13. Pause in places where children should act out what's happening. In places where groups will say something, read it in short phrases so children can repeat the words. When finished, thank everyone for participating, and have children sit down.

Distribute the Activity page *Digging Deeper.* Read the directions. Ask volunteers to read the sentences, telling which are the correct answers. (Answers: 1=a; 2=b; 3=a; 4=a)

ASK: **Why did Jesus tell this parable?** (to help people get ready for His return, because we don't know when Jesus will come back)
   According to this parable, how can we be wise and not foolish? (be ready for Jesus' return)
   Why is it important to be ready for Jesus' return? (People who aren't ready won't go to Heaven.)

SAY: **Jesus wants us to be ready for His return—that's why He told this story. Jesus wants us to live forever with Him in Heaven. I want that, and I hope you do too!**

Make It Real

3 Use this activity to help children **want to be ready for Jesus' return.**

Materials
Activity page *Ready or Not?* on page 196, pencils, Bibles

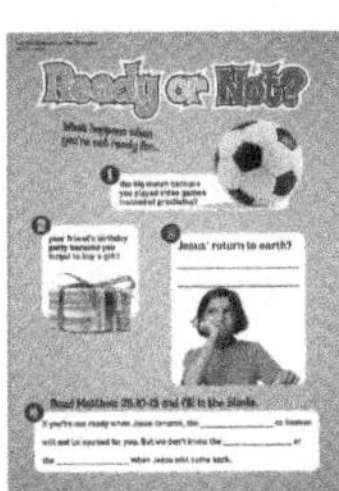

Teaching Tip
The concept of Jesus' return can be abstract and sometimes difficult for young children to grasp. Try to balance the hope and excitement of Jesus coming again without a worry or anxiety of *not* being ready.

Ready or Not?

Ask children to look at Activity page *Ready or Not?*

ASK: **What happens when you're not ready for the sports game or match because you didn't train or practise?** (you won't play or perform well)

Ask volunteers to read questions 2 and 3, letting children respond. SAY: **Not being ready for some things can be a big problem.** Draw children's attention to question 4, reading the question. Ask children to turn in their Bibles to Matthew 25:10-13, and have volunteers read those verses aloud. **As I read these next sentences, call out the words that go in the blanks.** (Answers: door, day, hour, ready)

SAY: **Jesus wants us to be ready for His return; that's why He told this parable. Let's plan to be ready!**

Live It Out

4 This activity will help children **remember to live ready for Jesus' return!**

Before the session
Write out the directions for the recipe on two index cards

Craft

Materials
large mixing bowl, spoon, 170g softened margarine, 170g caster sugar, 3 tablespoons unsweetened cocoa powder, ½ teaspoon vanilla essence, 1 tablespoon water, 150g of crispy rice cereal, icing sugar, paper plates, index card, pen, Bible

Be sure to check for food allergies. Have an alternative snack available

Recipe Risk

Make sure children wash their hands. Keep the cereal hidden from children. Display all the other ingredients. Ask different children to read the recipe steps and follow them.

Directions:
1. Put softened margarine in bowl. 2. Add sugar. 3. Mix well. 4. Add cocoa, vanilla, and water. Mix. 5. Add cereal. 6. Shape mixture into small balls. 7. Roll in confectioners' sugar. Keep in refrigerator.

When you come to #5, SAY: **Oops! I knew I forgot something! I'm sorry; we can't make this after all!** Apologize for not being prepared with all the ingredients. Let children complain for a while. **See what happens when you're not prepared? You can't do what you need to do. It's the same way with the return of Jesus. It would be very upsetting not to be ready for that—a lot more upsetting than not having all the ingredients you need for a recipe. After all, we want to spend eternity in Heaven with Jesus! Fortunately, I *do* have the missing ingredient, so let's continue making the snack.** As children finish making the snack and enjoy it, read Matthew 25:10-13.

ASK: **What don't we know about Jesus' return?** (We don't know the day or hour when He will return.)

When children have finished, close with a time of prayer. Encourage volunteers to pray, asking God to help them live ready for Jesus' return.

Be Ready For Jesus

lamp

jar of oil

Digging Deeper

Dig deeper into Jesus' parable. Circle the correct answers.

1. In Jesus' parable, five women were called wise because they

   a. had oil in jars, along with their lamps.

   b. remembered to bring their lunches.

2. When the news came that the bridegroom was coming, the five foolish women

   a. just kept sleeping.

   b. didn't have enough oil to keep their lamps burning.

3. When the bridegroom came, the five women who were ready

   a. went with the groom to the wedding banquet.

   b. went home again.

4. Jesus told this parable to remind us to be ready

   a. for His return, because we don't know when He will come back to earth.

   b. for anything!

Ready or Not?

What happens when you're not ready for...

1 the big match because you played video games instead of practising?

2 your friend's birthday party because you forgot to buy a gift?

3

Jesus' return to earth?

____

____

Read Matthew 25:10-13 and fill in the blanks.

4 If you're not ready when Jesus returns, the _________________ to Heaven will not be opened for you. But we don't know the _________________ or the _________________ when Jesus will come back.

The Lord's Supper

Session 32

Scripture: Mark 14:12-26
Focus: Jesus wants us to remember Him.

Heart to Heart Teacher Devotion
What helps you remember good times—photos, special objects, a journal? What helps you remember all the things you need to do each day—an app on your phone, a calendar, a paper and pencil list? We need things to jog our memories, and Jesus knew that. Bread and fruit of the vine were the items Jesus chose—simple items available to anyone, anywhere. Jesus wants us to remember Him and what He did on the cross for us. We do so humbly, with love and gratefulness in our hearts.

Focus
Jesus wants us to remember Him.

Focus In

1 Use this activity to help children **explore ways they remember special people and events.**

Welcome
Welcome each child warmly by name.

Remembering 
Before the session, put on one item of clothing that you can take off (such as a sweater or hat). Hold a couple of items such as a glue bottle, stapler, or paper clip. Greet the children as they come in. Then, as children are talking to each other, quietly put those items where children can't see them.

ASK: **Who remembers what I was wearing at first that I no longer have on? How about what I was holding that I'm no longer holding?** Accept responses.

SAY: **Sometimes it's easy to remember things, while other times it's pretty hard.** Give each child a copy of the Activity page *Remembering* from page 202 and a pencil. Read the instructions. Tell children to complete the page on their own or pair up with someone. When children have finished, let volunteers tell how they matched Column A to Column B. (Answers: 1=c; 2=e; 3=a; 4=b; 5=d) **It's good to have things to help us remember special people and events. Let's find out how Jesus wants us to remember Him.**

Materials
items to wear and hold, copies of Activity page *Remembering* on page 202 (1 per child), pencils

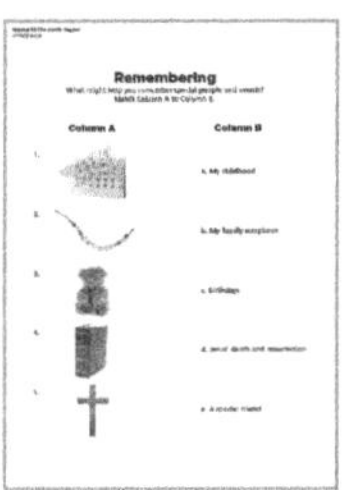

Focus
Jesus wants us to remember Him.

Explore His Word

2 Use these activities to help children **explain how Jesus planned for us to worship and remember Him.**

Bible Background for the Teacher
Jesus sent two of His disciples to prepare for the Passover. Luke tells us that the two chosen were Peter and John (Luke 22:8). Jesus' instructions to them included following a man carrying a jar of water. While this may seem vague to us, it would have been very unusual to see a man carrying a jar of water since,

during that time, women typically performed this task. Jesus' reference to 'my guest room' (Mark 14:14) may mean that He had made prior arrangements with the man. Jesus knew that the room would be adequate for the feast and that it was ready, possibly implying that all yeast had been removed, which was one requirement for the place where the feast was held.

Jesus knew that His time with His disciples was short. John 13 gives a much more detailed version of the teaching that takes place, but Mark focuses on two topics of discussion: Jesus' betrayal and the institution of the Lord's Supper. One attempts to end Jesus' ministry, while the other continually calls it to memory. Luke stresses the idea that the Lord's Supper is a remembrance of Jesus (Luke 22:19). In addition, Jesus points out that the Lord's Supper looks forward to His followers' eternal connection to Him (Matthew 26:29).

Bible Exploration   Mark 14:12-26

SAY: **Holidays have special meanings attached to them. The Jewish people had a special holiday to remember a special event—it was, and still is, called Passover. Passover reminds Jewish people of the time when God rescued the Israelites from slavery in Egypt. This was an important holiday to Jesus too. During the last Passover celebration that Jesus was a part of, He gave His disciples a new feast to celebrate so they could remember something very important.**

Ask a volunteer to stand by the map and point to the city of Jerusalem. Tell children that Jerusalem is the city where today's Bible story took place. Ask children to turn in their Bibles to Mark 14:12-26, and have volunteers read those verses aloud.

SAY: **It was time for Jesus and His disciples to celebrate the Passover. Jesus told two of His disciples, Peter and John, to go into Jerusalem. There they would find a man who would show them a large upstairs room where they could prepare for Passover. And that's what they did. Let's pretend that you all are Jesus' disciples, there in that upstairs room with Him.** If possible, have children sit on the floor. Another adult or a child can pretend to be Jesus, or you can do it. **When you hear that the disciples did something, either do it or pretend to do it.** Tell children and the person portraying Jesus to recline, to lay back propped up on one arm. **When you hear that the disciples expressed emotion, show it on your face or with other gestures.** When finished, thank everyone for participating, and have children return to their seats.

Distribute the Activity page *Remember Jesus*. Have volunteers read each sentence aloud and tell whether it's true or false. If a sentence is false, ask a volunteer to make it true. (Answers: 1=F (Passover); 2=T; 3=T; 4=F; 5=T.) SAY: **Eating bread and drinking grape juice were parts of the Passover meal. Jesus took those two parts and made a new celebration**

ASK: **What do we call that celebration?** (Communion; the Lord's
   Supper)
  What does the bread help us remember? (Jesus' body) Show
   children the Communion elements your church uses.
  What does the juice help us remember? (Jesus' blood)
  Why do we take part in Communion, or the Lord's Supper? (to
   remember what Jesus did for us by dying on the cross)

SAY: **Christians today continue to participate in Communion, or the Lord's Supper, because Jesus wants us to remember Him. Let's discover why it's such an important thing to do.**

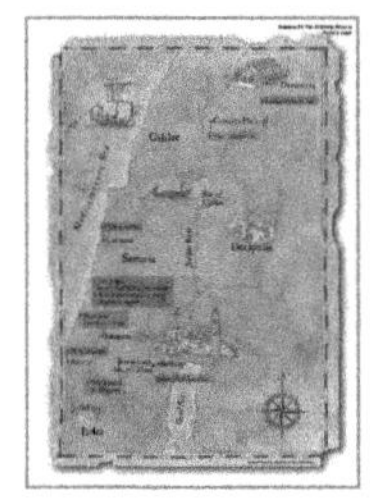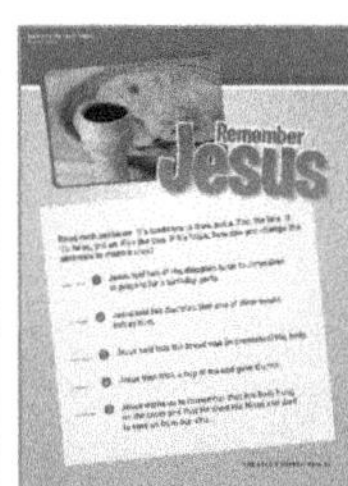

Make It Real

③ Use this activity to help children **discover why the Lord's Supper is important to Christians.**

There's Only One Way

Materials
washing-up liquid, red food colouring, small container, clear bowl filled with water, ground black pepper, paper towels

Object Lesson 

When talking about the blood of Jesus, use matter-of-fact terms, with the emphasis being on forgiveness. Too much 'bloody talk' can become scary for children with anxiety issues. And some children may overthink the gore of the story.

Before session combine some washing-up liquid and red food colouring in a small container.

Set the bowl of water on the table where everyone can see it. Put some paper towels under the bowl. SAY: **This bowl of water represents our lives. The black pepper represents sin.** Ask children to name some sins. As each sin is named, sprinkle a little pepper into the water. **Each of us sins and does wrong things. There is only one way to make our lives pure before God.** Pour or drop some of the prepared red soap into the center of the water filled with pepper. The pepper should quickly go to the sides of the bowl. **Because Jesus is God's Son, He is perfect. He took the punishment we deserve, by dying for us on the cross. His blood gets rid of our sins and makes us acceptable to God.**

ASK: **Why is it important for Christians to participate in the Lord's Supper, or Communion?** (It helps us remember that Jesus' body hung on the cross and that He shed His blood for us to save us from our sins; we don't want to forget what Jesus did for us)

SAY: **Jesus wants us to remember His dying on the cross—with bread and juice—because it helps us remember the most important thing anyone has ever done for us!**

Live It Out

④ Use this activity to help children **observe the Lord's Supper appropriately.**

Communion Helps

Materials
Bibles, roll paper, markers, reusable adhesive, Activity page *Prayer Prompts* on page 201, pencils

Pray

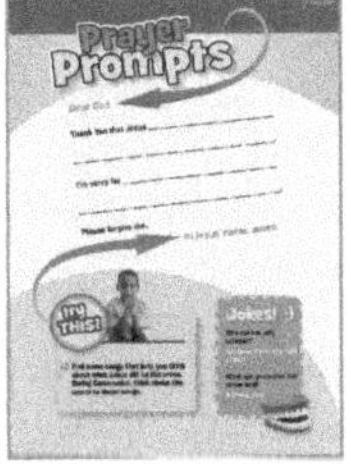

For children who have difficulty participating in writing activities, suggest options such as drawing pictures or symbols.

Have children turn in their Bibles to 1 Corinthians 11:23-29. Ask volunteers to read those verses aloud. SAY: **Participating in Communion is a serious thing. Let's see if we can help each other know what we should think about, do, and pray during the Lord's Supper.** Divide the session into three groups (or pairs). Give each group a length of roll paper and markers. Ask one group to make a list of things people should *think about* during Communion. Another group should make a list of things people could *do* during Communion. The last group should write out a few prayers people could *pray* during Communion. When groups are done, have them display their papers on a wall. Read their ideas, making sure children understand that participating in the Lord's Supper is a serious time to remember what Jesus did for us on the cross. **Remember, Jesus wants us to remember Him when we participate in Communion.**

Ask children to look at the Activity page *Prayer Prompts*. Ask them to take a few moments and write a prayer that they might pray during the Lord's Supper. Encourage them to thank Jesus for dying on the cross (for taking the punishment for their sins) and to ask for forgiveness for the wrong things they've done. When children are done, encourage them to silently pray their prayers to God. After a brief time of silence, close in prayer.

Read each sentence. If a sentence is true, put a *T* on the line. If it's false, put an *F* on the line. If it's false, how can you change the sentence to make it true?

_____ **1** Jesus told two of His disciples to go to Jerusalem to prepare for a birthday party.

_____ **2** Jesus told His disciples that one of them would betray Him.

_____ **3** Jesus said that the bread was [represented] His body.

_____ **4** Jesus then took a cup of tea and gave thanks.

_____ **5** Jesus wants us to remember that His body hung on the cross and that He shed His blood and died to save us from our sins.

Prayer Prompts

Dear God,

Thank You that Jesus _______________________________

_______________________________.

____

I'm sorry for _______________________________

_______________________________.

____

Please forgive me.

In Jesus' name, amen.

try THIS!

➡ **Find some songs that help you think about what Jesus did on the cross. During Communion, think about the words to those songs.**

Jokes! :)

Why did the jelly wobble?

Because it saw the milk shake!

What can you serve but never eat?

A tennis ball!

Remembering

What might help you remember special people and events?
Match Column A to Column B.

Column A   ## Column B

1. 

a. My childhood

2. 

b. My family scrapbook

3. 

c. Birthdays

4. 

d. Jesus' death and resurrection

5. 

e. A special friend

The Ultimate Miracle

Scripture: Mark 14:43-46; 15:16-20, 33-34, 37-39, 43, 46; 16:1-7
Focus: Celebrate Jesus' resurrection!

Heart to Heart Teacher Devotion
What celebrations do you enjoy the best—birthdays, weddings, or graduations? How do you celebrate—with cake, presents, or being with family and friends? Take time to celebrate the ultimate miracle: Jesus' resurrection! How will you celebrate it? Will you thank God for sending Jesus, praise Jesus for His amazing power, or tell someone the good news about Jesus? How about all three . . . and more?

Focus
Celebrate Jesus' resurrection!

Materials
plastic eggs that pull apart, slips of paper, pencils  *Action*

Ask children to work in pairs to accommodate any special needs.

Media Option
Let children go online and search for 'Easter traditions.' They'll find information on how some Easter traditions began.

Focus In

1 Use this activity to help children **explore traditions of the Easter season.**

Welcome

Welcome each child warmly by name.

Egg Roll!

Give each child a plastic egg, a slip of paper, and a pencil. SAY: **Write on your paper an Easter tradition. This can be something that comes to your mind when you think of the Easter season, or something that people do during the Easter season. When you have finished, put your paper inside your egg and close the egg.** When children have finished, get them to hold their eggs and stand in a line across the room from you. Tell children to remember the colour of their eggs. **On the count of three, roll your eggs toward me. 1, 2, 3, roll!** When the eggs have stopped rolling, tell children to go to the eggs and choose one that's a different colour than theirs. They should read the paper inside their eggs, find other children who wrote the same thing, and stand together. Have groups of children share what's written on their eggs.

ASK: **Which of these traditions does your family do?**
      Why do you celebrate Easter?
      What other reasons would some people have for celebrating Easter?

SAY: **While the Easter season has many traditions associated with it, let's dive into God's Word and see what it says about why we celebrate.**

Focus
Jesus wants us to remember Him.

Explore His Word

2 Use these activities to help children **tell about Jesus' death and resurrection.**

Bible Background for the Teacher

As Jesus prayed, Judas and a crowd of men came to arrest Jesus. Judas's kiss was meant to identify Jesus in the darkness. The kiss was a customary greeting between a disciple and a rabbi. Pilate, the procurator (provincial governor), sentenced Jesus to crucifixion, a particularly gruesome capital punishment. The sky darkened as Jesus hung on the cross, then Jesus finally and willingly laid down His life for ours. Early Christians recognised that the torn temple curtain symbolized the direct access to God that Christ made possible (Hebrews 10:20).

Early on Sunday morning, a group of women, disciples of Jesus, went to the tomb. Spices were used to prepare bodies for burial, but this had been skipped in the rush to bury Jesus before the Sabbath. The women were mainly concerned about gaining entry to the tomb, but the tomb was already open. The man at the tomb, undoubtedly an angel, had an unexpected message: Jesus was dead, but is now risen! The women, and later the other disciples, now knew the certainty of this fact that would forever change their lives—and ours!

Bible Exploration Mark 14:43-46; 15:16-20, 33-34, 37-39, 43, 46; 16:1-7

Before the session, cut a long length of roll paper so that children can illustrate today's Scripture verses. Divide the paper into four equal sections, and draw a line to separate the sections. Write the following Scripture references in this order on the paper, one per section: 1—Mark 15:33-34, 37-39; 2—Mark 15:43, 46; 3—Mark 16:1-3; 4—Mark 16:4-7.

Jesus taught people about God and performed miracles. Many people loved Him and followed Him. But some people didn't like Him. Some people even hated Him. This is where we pick up God's story. Ask a volunteer to stand by the map and point out Jerusalem. Tell children that today's story takes place in Jerusalem. Have children turn in their Bibles to Mark 14:43-46. Have volunteers read those verses aloud. **One of Jesus' followers, Judas, betrayed Him, leading to the arrest of Jesus. Let's discover what happened that evening and in the days that followed. First, let's see how Jesus was treated.** Have volunteers read Mark 15:16-20 aloud.

SAY: **In the next scene, it is Friday, and Jesus was on the cross.** Have volunteers read verses 33-34 and 37-39. **Even the Roman centurion knew at that moment that Jesus is God's Son. In the next scene, we see what happened after Jesus died.** Have volunteers read verses 43 and 46. **Joseph put Jesus' lifeless body into a tomb, rolling a stone over the entrance.** Show the photo of a burial tomb on Activity Page 208. **The next scene takes place three days later on a Sunday morning.** Have volunteers read Mark 16:1-3. **The women knew about the stone over the opening in the tomb and wondered who would move it for them.** Have volunteers read verses 4-7. **The angel told the women the best news of all—that Jesus was no longer dead but had risen from the grave! The women went and told the disciples what had happened!**

Ask children to look at Activity page *He Has Risen!* Read the directions. Ask a volunteer to read the first sentence and choose the correct answer (the Son of God). Do the same with the other sentences. (Answers: 2=in a tomb cut out of rock; 3=had been rolled away; 4=Jesus had risen and was no longer in the tomb; 5=go tell Jesus' disciples)

ASK: **If you had been one of Jesus' disciples, how do you think you might have felt, or what would you have thought, after Jesus had died on the cross and was buried in the tomb?** (I would have felt sad; I might have wondered why I had followed Him)
If you had been one of Jesus' disciples, how do you think you would have felt, or what would you have thought, after Jesus rose from the dead? (happy, surprised, couldn't believe it)

SAY: **The women told the disciples that Jesus was alive! Now it's your turn to tell that same good news. Today you get to tell about Jesus'**

Materials

Activity Pages:
Bible Map on page 207,
Burial Tomb on page 208,
He Has Risen! on page 206,
pencils, roll paper, scissors,
markers, sticky tape

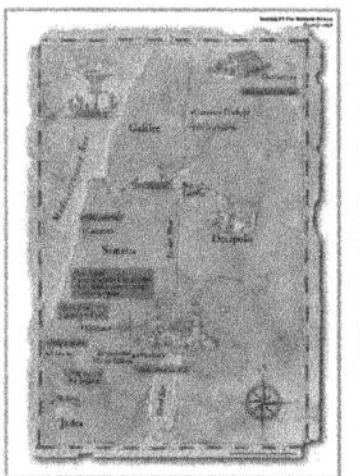

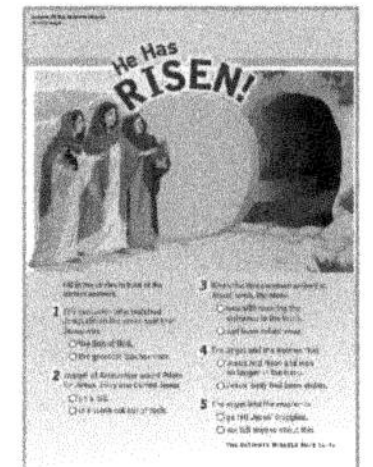

The Ultimate Miracle **Session 33**

resurrection by illustrating what happened. Divide the session into four groups (or pairs). Assign each group one of the four sections on the roll paper to illustrate. If you have a large session, divide into additional small groups and give each group a smaller Scripture portion. SAY: **We can celebrate Jesus' resurrection because it's the ultimate miracle! Jesus died and rose to show His power over sin and death. And that's worth celebrating!**

Focus
Jesus wants us to remember Him.

Make It Real

3 Use this activity to help children **discover what Jesus' death and resurrection mean for them**.

Materials
container of coloured water, saucer, towel, short candle, matches (or lighter), glass, coin, Bibles  *Science*

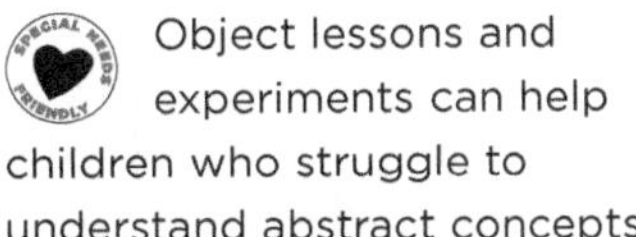 Object lessons and experiments can help children who struggle to understand abstract concepts.

He Took Our Sins

Do this experiment where everyone can see the action. Place the saucer on a towel. Place the coin on the edge of the saucer. SAY: **The coin represents us. The coloured water represents our sins.** Pour the water onto the saucer until the coin is submerged. **The candle represents Jesus.** Stand the candle in the middle of the saucer and light it. **The flame represents the life of Christ.** Tell children to watch carefully, as you take the glass and place it over the lighted candle. Within a few seconds, the flame will consume all the oxygen in the glass and go out. However, it will have created a vacuum, which, in turn, will draw the water up inside the glass (thus surrounding the candle), leaving the coin dry and 'free'. **On the cross, Jesus gave up His life, taking our sins on himself, so we could go free.** Have children turn in their Bibles to John 3:16-17. Have a volunteer read the verses aloud.

ASK: **Based on these verses, what does Jesus' death and resurrection mean for you?** (God sent Jesus because He loves us; When I believe in Jesus, I'll be saved and have eternal life in Heaven)

SAY: **What Jesus did means that when you accept Jesus as your Saviour, one day you too can rise from the dead and live in Heaven forever.**

Focus
Jesus wants us to remember Him.

Live It Out

4 Use one of these activities to help children **celebrate Jesus' resurrection**.

Materials
roll paper, markers, scissors, sticky tape, coloured paper, snack  *Action*

Teaching Tip
If you have any guests or other children who aren't sure what to write, quietly offer ideas to them.

 Some children with special needs may have difficulty formulating ideas or writing their ideas on paper. Be ready to offer assistance as needed.

Good News Worth Sharing

Before the session, cut a large cross from roll paper. Display it on a wall.

SAY: **The angel told the women at the tomb to go and tell the disciples that Jesus was no longer in the grave. We too are to go and tell others about Jesus. Let's think about how we can celebrate Jesus' resurrection by telling others about Him.** Hand out the coloured paper and markers. Tell children to tear a paper shape and write on it something they know about Jesus that they could tell others. Let children enjoy a favourite snack as they work. When they're ready, children can attach their papers to the cross.

When all the papers are on the cross, ask children to gather around the cross. SAY: **The good news of Jesus is worth sharing! And the best thing we call tell others is that Jesus died on the cross for all people, then rose from the tomb.**

Fill in the circles in front of the correct answers.

1 The centurion who watched Jesus die on the cross said that Jesus was

○ the Son of God.

○ the greatest teacher ever.

2 Joseph of Arimathea asked Pilate for Jesus' body and buried Jesus

○ on a hill.

○ in a tomb cut out of rock.

3 When the three women arrived at Jesus' tomb, the stone

○ was still covering the entrance to the tomb.

○ had been rolled away.

4 The angel told the women that

○ Jesus had risen and was no longer in the tomb.

○ Jesus' body had been stolen.

5 The angel told the women to

○ go tell Jesus' disciples.

○ not tell anyone about this.

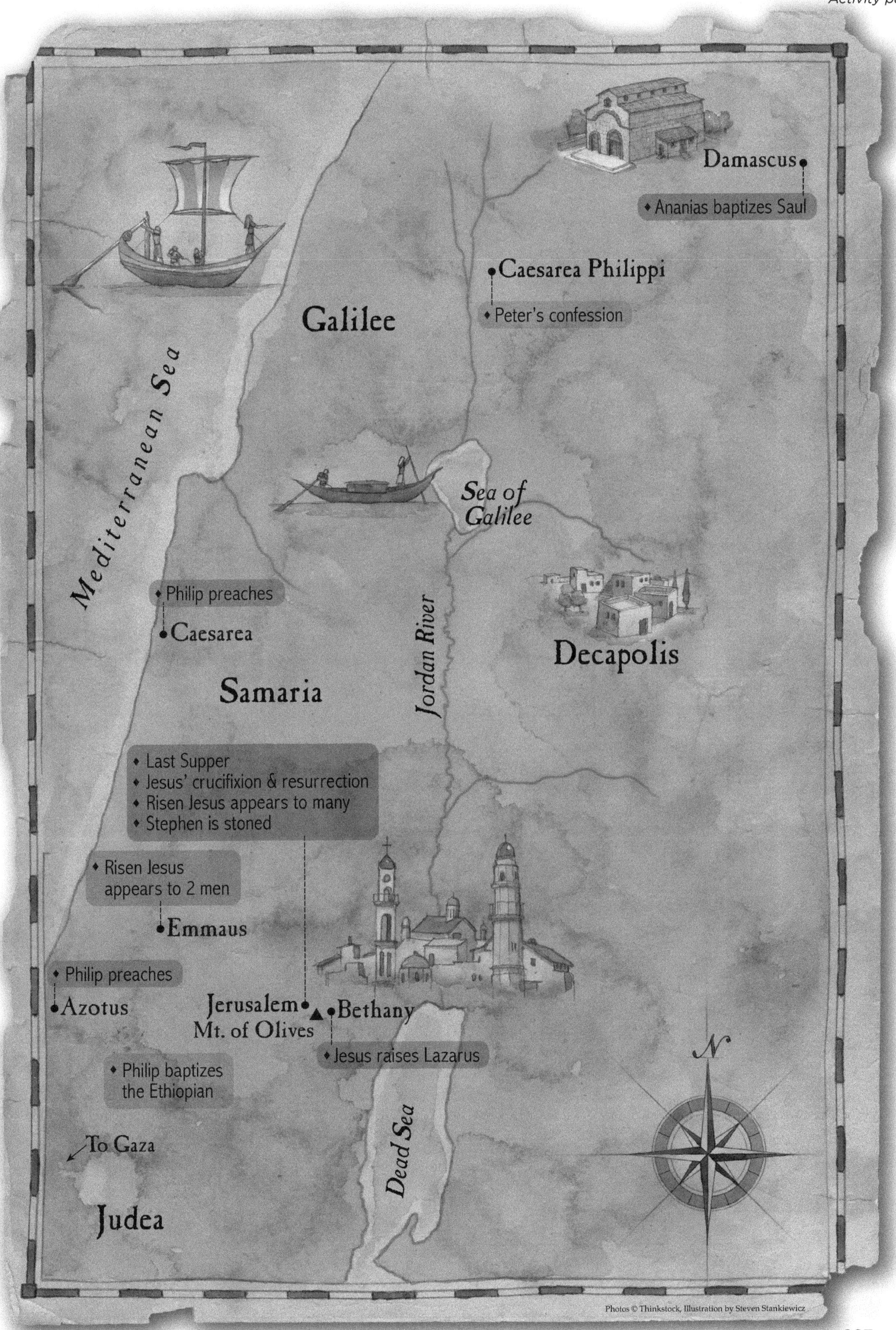

Photos © Thinkstock, Illustration by Steven Stankiewicz

HeartShaper Primary Blue Edition, Activity page
Permission is granted to reproduce this page for ministry purposes only—not for resale.

The Road to Emmaus

Session 34

Scripture: Luke 24:13-35
Focus: Jesus gives us hope.

Heart to Heart Teacher Devotion

The book of Psalms is a good one to turn to when we're searching for hope. 'We wait in hope for the LORD; he is our help and our shield' (Psalm 33:20). 'Why, my soul, are you downcast? Why so disturbed within me? Put your hope in God, for I will yet praise him, my Saviour and my God' (42:5). Of course, the greatest source of hope is Jesus. 'God has given us new birth into a living hope through the resurrection of Jesus Christ from the dead' (1 Peter 1:3).

Focus
Jesus gives us hope.

Materials
whiteboard, dry-erase markers, timer

Game

Focus In

1 Use this activity to help children **discuss things they hope for.**

Welcome

Welcome each child warmly by name.

Draw It Fast!

SAY: **Think about something you hope for. It might be something you hope to buy, something you hope will happen, or something you hope you get to do. Get that in mind as we play a game of Draw It Fast!** Divide the session into two teams. Have a volunteer from one of the teams whisper to you what she's going to draw. Tell the volunteer to start drawing something she hopes for. Her team has 30 seconds to guess what it is. Award 10 points for correct answers. If her team doesn't guess correctly, let the other team guess. Play as time permits.

ASK: **What is hope?** Accept responses. **The dictionary says that hope is 'to expect with confidence' or 'to desire with expectation of obtaining something.' Hope is the 'feeling of excitement about something we are waiting for.'**

SAY: **Today's Bible story is one about hope. Let's dig into God's Word and see how two men found out that Jesus gives us hope.**

Focus
Jesus gives us hope.

Explore His Word

2 Use these activities to help children **tell about Jesus' death and resurrection.**

Bible Background for the Teacher

Some followers of Jesus were leaving Jerusalem, perhaps to avoid the danger from the Jews (see John 20:19). As two of them walked toward the village of Emmaus, they discussed the events of the week, trying to make sense of all that had happened. They were joined by Jesus but did not recognise Him. They were amazed that the stranger did not seem to know about Jesus' trial and death. Their description of the events reveals that their understanding of the crucifixion was limited because of their expectations for the Messiah. Their hope was that Jesus would redeem Israel by restoring the Davidic kingdom—with accompanying power, wealth, and glory—while ridding the promised land of all foreigners, especially the Romans. That was their hope, and they had spent the last three days thinking about how Jesus' death had dashed that hope.

Jesus spoke to them, using the Scriptures to show that the Old Testament writers had described a Messiah who would suffer and die before establishing His kingdom. Luke does not tell us which Scriptures Jesus used, but Isaiah 53 and Zechariah 12 come to mind as possible examples. When the followers reached Emmaus, they persuaded Jesus to accept their hospitality and stay for a meal. Even though He was a guest, Jesus took the role of host, breaking the bread for distribution. Immediately they recognized Jesus' presence, perhaps by the way He broke the bread. Christians today recognize Jesus' presence in the breaking of bread of the Lord's Supper on the Lord's Day. The two disciples immediately returned to Jerusalem, even though it was dark. There they found the disciples rejoicing in the knowledge that Jesus was indeed risen!

Bible Exploration   Luke 24:13-35

Ask a volunteer to stand by the map and point out Emmaus and Jerusalem. Tell children that today's Bible story takes place in these locations. Ask another volunteer to stand by the Bible time lines and point out the icon for 'Jesus appears to many.' SAY: **As you can see, we're nearing the end of the Bible time lines about Jesus. After His resurrection, Jesus appeared to many people. This is where we pick up God's story.** Ask children to turn in their Bibles to Luke 24:13-14. Have volunteers read those verses aloud.

ASK: **What were the two men talking about?** (Jesus' death, burial, and resurrection)

SAY: **In today's Bible story, there are lots of feelings expressed.** Give each child a copy of the Emoticons activity page and scissors, and tell them to cut on the dotted lines. **When you think someone was sad, hold up that card. When you think someone was happy, confused, or overjoyed, hold up one of those cards. Follow along as I read, or just listen to the rest of this story. Be sure to hold up your emoticon cards during the story.** Read Luke 24:15-35. Pause in places where children should hold up their cards. When finished, ask children to look at the Activity page *On the Road*. Do the page together, or let children complete it on their own. (Answers: 1=Jesus; 2=women, tomb; 3=Scriptures, bread; 4=Jerusalem.) **Cleopas and the other man were disciples of Jesus. But they lost hope because they didn't really understand who Jesus is.** Note: If time allows, ask two volunteers to act out this eyewitness account of what happened on the road to Emmaus. The actors can use the completed activity as a script.

ASK: **How do you think you would have felt, had you been on the road that day with Cleopas and the other disciple?**
   What brought hope back to the two men? (Jesus explaining the Scriptures to them; seeing Jesus alive again)
   How did the two men show their restored hope? (They returned to Jerusalem to tell the disciples that Jesus had risen)

SAY: **After Jesus showed himself alive and explained the Scriptures to Cleopas and the other disciple, their hope was restored. They were beginning to understand, in the right way, how Jesus gives us hope.**

Materials
Bible map from Session 33, Activity page *Emoticons* on page 214, scissors, Bibles, Activity page *On The Road* on page 212, pencils

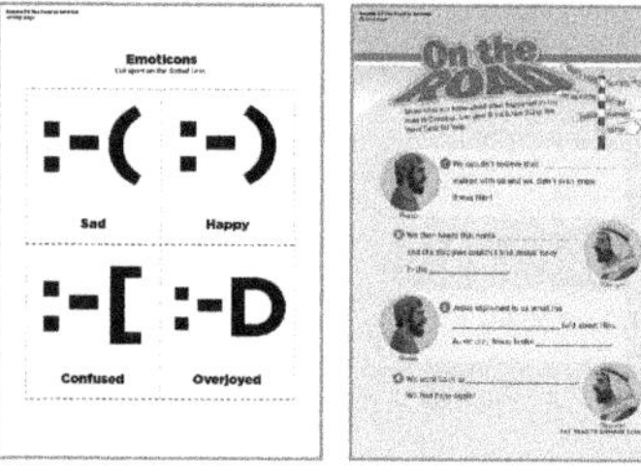

Media Option
You can go to a website such as www.biblegateway.com and play a dramatised reading of the Bible verses.

Make It Real

3 Use this activity to help children **understand why Jesus' resurrection gives us hope.**

Materials
Empty tomb poster on page 208, Activity page *Hope Through Jesus' Resurrection* on page 213, pencils, Bibles, markers

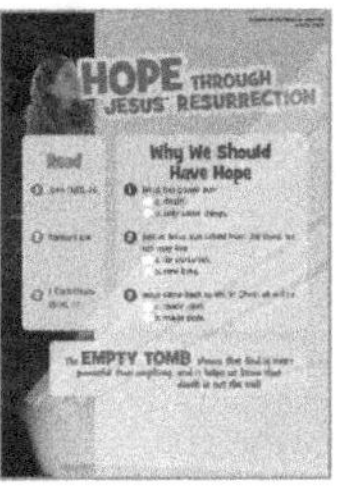

Jesus Gives Hope

Show children the empty tomb poster, and read the question on the poster. SAY: **Let's dig into God's Word to find out the answer to this important question.** Ask children to look at Activity page *Hope Through Jesus' Resurrection*. Assign one or more of the Scriptures to a pair of children to look up. Pairs should also work together to complete their sentences. When children are ready, have each pair read its Scripture and sentence. Encourage all children to check the right ending to each sentence. (Answers: 1=death; 2=new lives; 3=made alive) SAY: **These are just a few of the reasons why Jesus' resurrection gives us hope.**

Draw children' attention back to the poster. SAY: **Why does Jesus' resurrection give *you* hope? Choose one of the ideas from the activity leaflet or come up with your own. When you have your idea, use a marker to write it on the bottom of the poster.** When children have finished, read their ideas aloud.

SAY: **We said earlier that *hope* is the 'feeling of excitement about something we are waiting for.' Because of His death and resurrection, Jesus gives us hope, real hope, that one day we will live with Him in Heaven. Now *that's* exciting!**

Live It Out

4 Use this activity to help children **express their hope in Jesus.**

Materials
pencils, paper

Rather than limiting this activity to writing, offer a few more choices. Here are some ideas: Choose from pre-printed Scriptures and pictures. Make greeting cards that symbolise messages of hope. Choose a worship CD to play and listen to it quietly. Pray for someone who needs the hope of Christ.

Expressions of Hope

SAY: **Right now you have the opportunity to write a poem, prayer, song, or rap expressing your hope in Jesus, thanking Him that His resurrection gives us the hope of someday living in Heaven with Him.** Let children work either alone or with a partner. When children have finished, ask volunteers to read their poems and prayers or perform their songs and raps for the rest of the session.

Ask children to gather for a time of prayer. Encourage the children to silently pray to God the words of their poems, prayers, songs, and raps. After a brief time of silence, PRAY: **Dear God, thank You that just as Jesus was raised from the dead, we too can live new lives. Thank You that because of Jesus' resurrection, we have an inheritance in Heaven that will never go away. Thank You that Jesus gives us hope. In Jesus' name, amen.**

On the ROAD

Show what you know about what happened on the road to Emmaus. Use your Bible (Luke 24) or the Word Bank for help.

Cleopas

1 We couldn't believe that ___________________ walked with us and we didn't even know it was Him!

2 We then heard that some ___________________ and the disciples couldn't find Jesus' body in the ___________________.

Other man

Cleopas

3 Jesus explained to us what the ___________________ said about Him. As we ate, Jesus broke ___________________.

4 We went back to ___________________. We had hope again!

Other man

HOPE THROUGH JESUS' RESURRECTION

Read

1. John 11:25, 26

2. Romans 6:4

3. 1 Corinthians 15:20, 22

Why We Should Have Hope

1. Jesus has power over
   - a. death.
   - b. only some things.

2. Just as Jesus was raised from the dead, we too may live
   - a. for ourselves.
   - b. new lives.

3. Jesus came back to life. In Christ all will be
   - a. made alive.
   - b. made poor.

The **EMPTY TOMB** shows that God is more powerful than anything, and it helps us know that death is not the end!

Emoticons
Cut apart on the dotted lines.

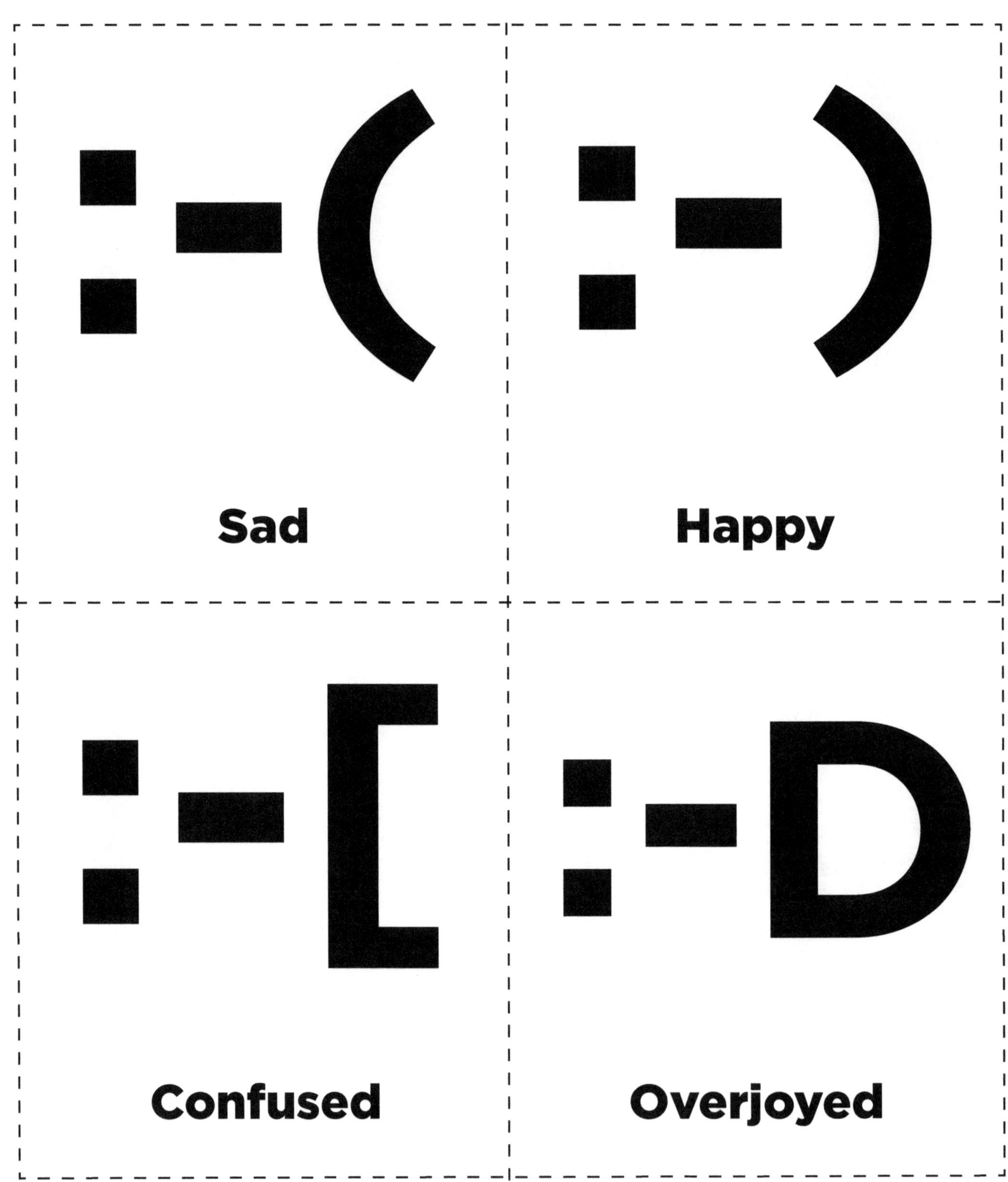

The Great Commission

Scripture: Matthew 28:16-20; Acts 1:6-11
Focus: Jesus commands His disciples to go and make disciples.

Heart to Heart Teacher Devotion

As Jesus spoke the final words to His faithful disciples, He promised them His abiding presence. That promise is for us too! As you go and make disciples week by week, teaching the children in your session, the Holy Spirit is with you, giving help and guidance. May you continue to be faithful to this life-changing mission!

Focus
Jesus commands His disciples to go and make disciples.

Materials
wrapped sweets or dried fruit, Bible

Game

Focus In

1 Use this activity to help children **explore what a disciple of Jesus does.**

Welcome

Welcome each child warmly by name.

A Disciple or Not?

Get children into pairs and have sweets or fruit ready to hand out. SAY: **I'm going to read you some situations. If you think the child in the situation is a disciple of Jesus, make a capital *D* with your fingers.** Have children try that. **If you think the person is *not* a disciple of Jesus, make an *X* with your fingers.** Have children try that. Tell children to work together in pairs because when the correct answer is a *D* and *both* of them make that letter, they each get a treat.

Situations: 1. **Charlie made friends with the new boy in school and invited him to church services.** Pause for children to make a *D*; give them a treat. 2. **Gabriella gossiped about her best friend.** Pause for children to make an *X*. 3. **Isaac told a lie. He then told his mum about it, asked her to forgive him, and asked God to forgive him.** (*D*) 4. **Amy chose to share some of her toys and clothes with some children who don't have much.** (*D*) 5. **Luke forgot to study for a test, so he looked at a friend's paper.** (*X*) 6. **Megan loves to draw pictures. Every week she and her mum take her drawings to people who live in a nursing home.** (*D*)

SAY: **Disciples of Jesus are people who believe that He's God's Son, obey His commands, and follow Him.** Read 1 John 5:1-3. **Let's dig into God's Word to see what it says about disciples.**

Focus
Jesus commands His disciples to go and make disciples.

Explore His Word

2 Use these activities to help children **tell about Jesus' last day on earth.**

Bible Background for the Teacher

The word that is translated into 'make disciples' is an imperative, and is the primary focus of the command. The words 'go', 'baptising' and 'teaching' derive their force from the command to 'make disciples', and describe how the disciples are to do it. 'In the name of' means that in baptism new disciples identify themselves with the person, character, and purpose of God. Disciples of Jesus make every effort to share with friends, neighbours, and strangers the good news about Jesus; to baptise; and to teach them about living for Christ. Jesus promised His continuing presence with the disciples as they went to do what would sometimes be difficult work. In Acts, Jesus reveals that the Holy Spirit would be the agent for His continued presence, empowering them to go and make disciples in Jerusalem and throughout the entire world.

Bible Exploration   Matthew 28:16-20; Acts 1:6-11

Ask a volunteer to stand by the map and point out Galilee. Tell children that today's Bible story takes place somewhere in Galilee. Ask another volunteer to stand by the Bible time lines and point out the icon for Jesus' resurrection. SAY: **As you can see, we're nearing the end of the Bible time line about Jesus. After His resurrection, Jesus appeared to many people, including the two men on the road to Emmaus. This is where we pick up God's story.**

Ask children to turn in their Bibles to Matthew 28:16-20, and have volunteers read the verses aloud. SAY: **This story is about Jesus' last day on earth. Jesus had told His eleven disciples to meet Him in Galilee. Let's pretend that we're part of that group of disciples and go to the mountain. We'll imagine that we actually see Jesus. React as you think you might have if you had been one of the eleven disciples that day.** Ask children to stand and move to another part of the room. **We're here at the mountain Jesus asked us to come to. Look, there's Jesus! We worship You, Jesus.** Encourage children to worship Jesus by lifting their hands to Him, bowing, or saying something like 'We praise You, Jesus!'.

Read aloud the verses from Acts and show the teaching poster of the Ascension.

ASK: **If you had really been one of Jesus' disciples, how do you think you would have felt, or what would you have thought, after Jesus gave you those final instructions and then went up into Heaven?** Accept responses.

Ask children to look at the Activity pages *Great Commission and Ascension*. Read the instructions. Assign a small group or pair one of the sentences to rewrite to make it true. When children are ready, let them read their sentences and tell how to make them true. (Answers: 1=cross out '30' and write '11'; 2=cross out 'were afraid of' and write 'worshipped'; 3=cross out 'enemies' and write 'disciples'; 4=cross out 'wash' and write 'baptise'; 5=cross out 'never' and write 'always'; 6=cross out 'money' and write 'power'; 7=cross out 'London' and write 'Jerusalem'; 8=cross out 'rainbow' and write 'cloud'; 9=cross out 'purple' and write 'white'; 10=cross out 'Moses' and write 'Jesus') SAY: **We call Jesus' last words the Great Commission. It's a command, or instruction. This command, though, wasn't just for those eleven disciples. Jesus commands—*all* His disciples to—go and make disciples. And that includes us!**

Materials
Bible Map from Session 33 on page 207, *Ascension Poster* downloadable file, Bibles; Activity pages *Great Commission and Ascension* on pages 218-219; pencils

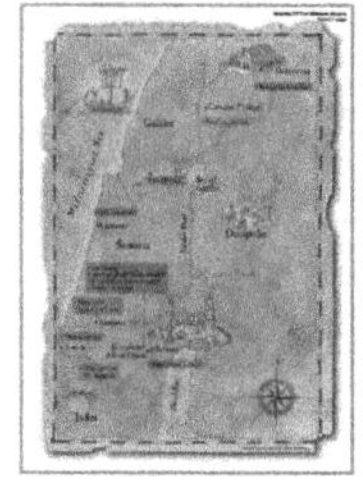

The *Ascension Poster* poster can be downloaded at **www.heartshaper.co.uk/resources**

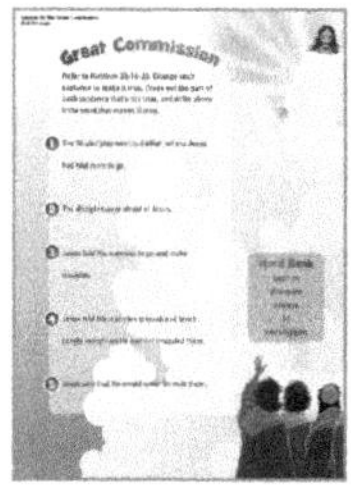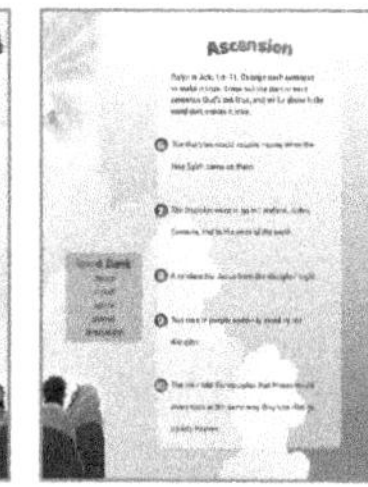

Make It Real

 Use this activity to help children **tell why everyone needs to be a disciple of Jesus.**

Materials
2 helium-filled balloons,
2 regular balloons,
ribbon, Bibles

 Consider the children in your session when talking about being in Heaven for eternity. Some children with separation anxiety may be frightened by this concept. Rephrasing and simply saying that we will always be with Jesus may be more reassuring to them.

When You're a Disciple 

Before the session, purchase 2 helium-filled balloons with ribbons. Fill two regular balloons with air and tie a length of ribbon to each balloon. Hold the balloons so children can't tell that some are filled with air and some are filled with helium.

ASK: **Why does everyone need to be a disciple of Jesus?** Accept responses.

SAY: **When Jesus told His disciples to go and make disciples of all nations, it wasn't a suggestion; it was a command.** Have children turn in their Bibles to Acts 2:38 and Romans 6:23, and have volunteers read those verses aloud. **When you accept Christ as your Saviour and become one of His disciples, your sins are forgiven and you receive the Holy Spirit. Without Jesus as our Saviour our sins are not forgiven and we don't have the Holy Spirit.** Release the balloons filled with air. **But when you're a disciple, you'll have eternal life in Heaven.** Release the balloons filled with helium. **These second balloons are a symbol for us when we have the life Jesus gives us - as his disciples. That's why Jesus commands His disciples to go and make disciples. He wants everyone to spend eternity with Him in Heaven!**

Live It Out

 Use this activity to help children **plan to go and make disciples.**

Materials
Activity page *Make Disciples for Jesus* on page 220, pencils

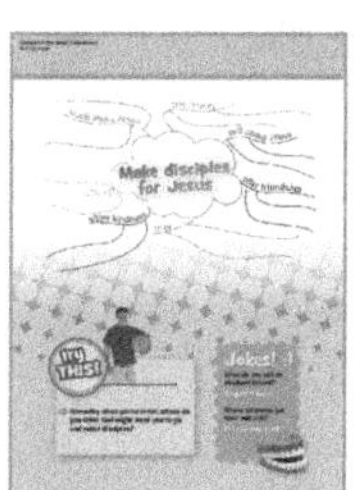

Making Plans

SAY: **Since Jesus commands His disciples to go and make disciples, let's plan some ways to do that.** Hand out Activity page *Make Disciples for Jesus*. Ask children to look at the ways listed of making disciples. **Think about a few people who don't know God or know much about God, people whom you could serve. Write their names on the lines by the word 'serve'.** Tell children to do the same for the others. As they work, discuss these questions:

ASK: **How could praying help others become disciples of Jesus?
Who could you teach about Jesus?** Help children think into the future a little too.
How could showing kindness or offering friendship help others become disciples of Jesus?

When children have finished, encourage them to follow through on their plans. Then PRAY: **Dear God, we are so glad to know You. Thank You for what Jesus did for us so that our sins could be forgiven, and that one day we can live with You in Heaven. Help us to do all we can to help others become disciples of yours. In Jesus' name, amen.**

Great Commission

Refer to Matthew 28:16-20. Change each sentence to make it true. Cross out the part of each sentence that's not true, and write above it the word that makes it true.

1 The 30 disciples went to Galilee, where Jesus had told them to go.

2 The disciples were afraid of Jesus.

3 Jesus told His enemies to go and make disciples.

4 Jesus told His disciples to wash and teach people everything He had commanded them.

5 Jesus said that He would never be with them.

Word Bank

baptise

disciples

always

11

worshipped

Ascension

Refer to Acts 1:6-11. Change each sentence to make it true. Cross out the part of each sentence that's not true, and write above it the word that makes it true.

6 The disciples would receive money when the Holy Spirit came on them.

7 The disciples were to go to Londonv, Judea, Samaria, and to the ends of the earth.

8 A rainbow hid Jesus from the disciples' sight.

9 Two men in purple suddenly stood by the disciples.

10 The men told the disciples that Moses would come back in the same way they saw Him go up into Heaven.

Word Bank

Jesus

cloud

white

power

Jerusalem

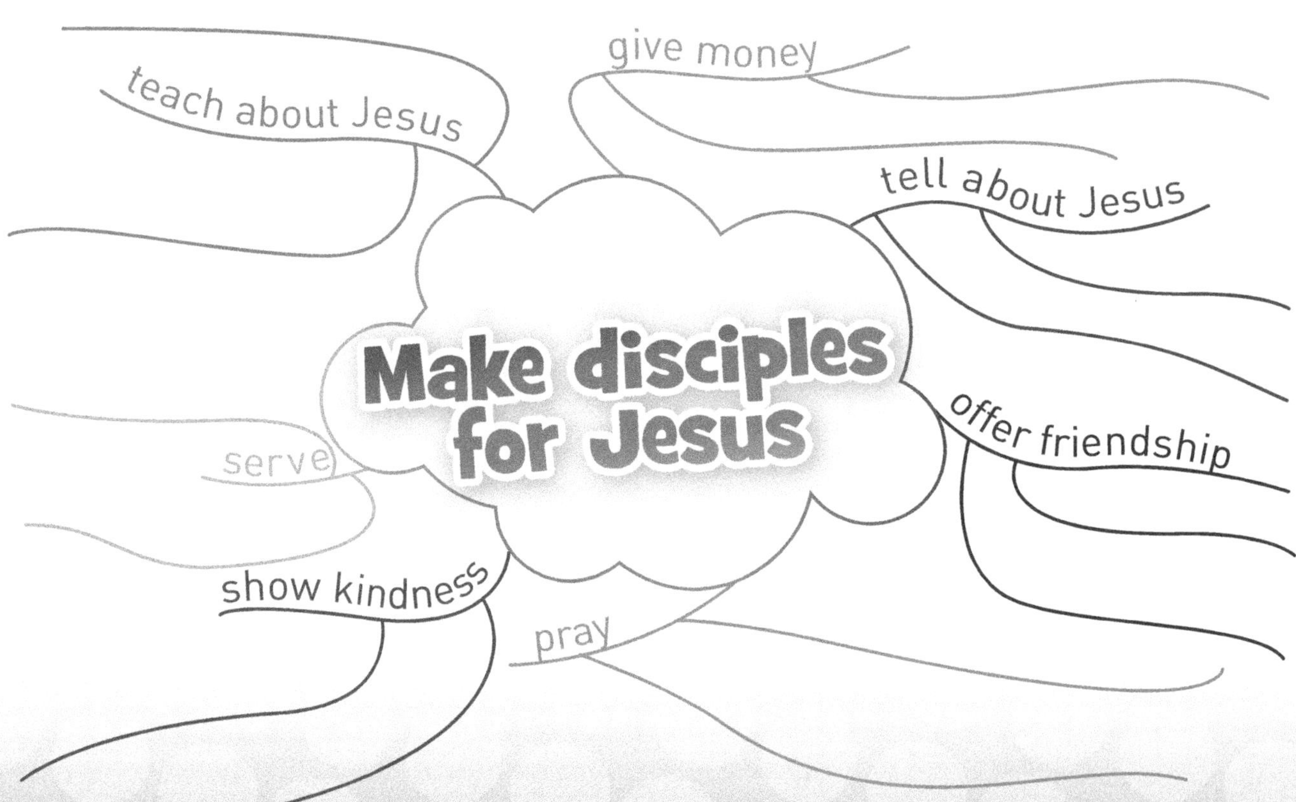

Jokes! :)

What do you call an elephant in bed?

A heavy sleeper!

Where do sheep get their hair cut?

At a baa-baa shop!

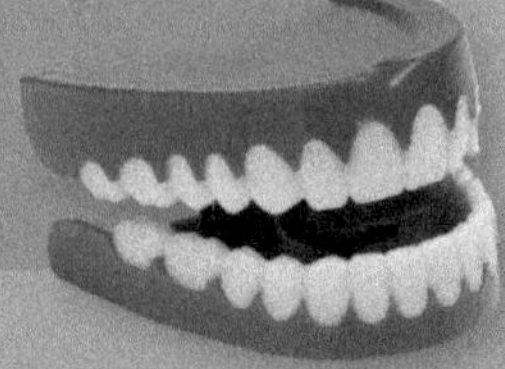

Stephen is Killed

Session 36

Scripture: Acts 6:8-15; 7:51-60; 8:1a
Focus: God helps us to be faithful.

Heart to Heart Teacher Devotion
Maybe you've heard of Jim Elliot, Nate Saint, Ed McCully, Peter Fleming, and Roger Youderian. These faithful young men were killed in 1956 while trying to evangelize the Huaorani people in Ecuador. But God doesn't just ask *missionaries* to be faithful—that's job No. 1 for *all* Christians. While we have many cares and concerns in this life, the one that matters most is our relationship to God. May your faithfulness to God shine brightly so your children can see it and model it.

Focus
God helps us to be faithful.

Materials
none

Action

 If you have children with physical limitations, be sure to give options for motions they can do.

Focus In

① Use this activity to help children **explore situations that require us to be faithful.**

Welcome

Welcome each child warmly by name.

Why Be Faithful?

ASK: **What does it mean to be faithful?** (keep promises; do what you're supposed to do; show support, be loyal)

Ask children to stand up. SAY: **Let's think about situations that require us to be faithful.** Tell children that you'll name a situation. Tell them to squat low if it only requires a little bit of faithfulness, stand up more if it requires some faithfulness, and stand on tiptoes if it requires a whole lot of faithfulness. 1. **Playing an instrument**. Pause between situations for children to change positions. 2. **Keeping your promises. 3. Doing your chores at home. 4. Being a child. 5. Playing on a team. 6. Being a friend.**

ASK: **Why do you need to be faithful when playing an instrument or playing on a team?** (You have to practise and keep going to get better.)
Why do you need to be faithful when keeping your promises? (If you don't keep your promises, no one will ever trust you.)

SAY: **Let's dig into God's Word and see what it says about being faithful to Him.**

Focus
God helps us to be faithful.

Explore His Word

② Use these activities to help children **explain what happened to Stephen.**

Bible Background for the Teacher

Stephen was one of the men chosen to help carry out the ministry of the church in Jerusalem. He was 'full of God's grace and power' (Acts 6:8) and was actively engaged in preaching the gospel. Stephen's message also showed that because of Jesus' sacrifice, the temple and its sacrifices were not enough to reconcile sinful people to a holy God. This message was strongly opposed by many Jews since the temple was the center of their worship. The 'Synagogue of the Freedmen' (v. 9) was made up of Jews who had migrated to Jerusalem from North Africa and the province of Asia in modern Turkey, and its members were among Stephen's most vocal critics. Unable to refute the gospel message, they resorted to false witnesses to bring charges against him to the Sanhedrin (the Jewish ruling council). As the charges were made, Stephen's face reflected the peace of someone who knows the comfort of God's presence.

As Stephen defended his message, he reminded the members of the Sanhedrin that God had dealt with the Jews throughout the centuries (Acts 7:1-50). As he reached the culmination of his defence (beginning with v. 51), he accused the Jewish leaders of being just like their ancestors, who repeatedly resisted God's attempts to bring them closer to Him. Their ancestors had responded by killing the prophets, while the leaders of Stephen's day had responded by killing Jesus. The charge that the leaders were disobedient to God's law, followed by Stephen's description of Jesus at God's right hand, was too much. Acting as a mob, they were determined to kill Stephen. Stephen remained faithful and full of God's grace, even as he faced death. Stephen stands as a remarkable example for us all.

Bible Exploration   Acts 6:8-15; 7:51-60; 8:1a

Ask children to turn in their Bibles to Acts 6:8-10. Have volunteers read the verses aloud.

SAY: **Stephen was one of the men chosen to help carry out the ministry of the church in Jerusalem. He was full of God's grace and power. Stephen taught that it was Jesus' sacrifice—not the temple or any sacrifices made there—that forgives sin. There were some men who didn't like Stephen's saying that, but these men couldn't stand up against Stephen since the Holy Spirit was guiding him.** Tell children that the rest of this Bible story has some high points—meaning that something good happens. When they hear a high point, they should raise their hands up high. Have children do that. When they hear some low points—meaning that something not so good happens—they should put their hands down low. Have children do that. When they hear about so-so times—meaning that something not really good or bad happens— they should put their hands in between. Have children do that.

Ask for a volunteer or two to stand in front and lead everyone in doing the motions. Read Acts 6:8-15; 7:51-60; and 8:1a aloud. Pause as needed so children can do the motions. Emphasise and explain any parts that children seem confused about. When finished, SAY: **There seemed to be a lot of low points in that story. But really, they turned out to be high points. God helped Stephen remain faithful to Him. When it would have been easier for Stephen to give up preaching about Jesus, Stephen kept preaching. He told the people what they needed to hear. God rewarded Stephen's faithfulness by allowing him to look into Heaven, seeing the glory of God and Jesus standing at the right hand of God. Even while being stoned to death, Stephen asked God to forgive the people doing it.**

Distribute the Activity page *Stephen Is Faithful*. Let pairs of children do the page together, or do it as a session. (Answers: 1=False, bad; 2=broken, killed; 3=Jesus, hand.)

ASK: **Why do you think Stephen stayed faithful to God?** (Stephen loved God and was close to God; he knew that the most important thing he could do was to stay faithful to God.)

SAY: **Just as God helped Stephen be faithful, God helps us be faithful too.**

Materials
Bible map from page 207, Bibles, Activity page *Stephen is Faithful* on page 224, pencils

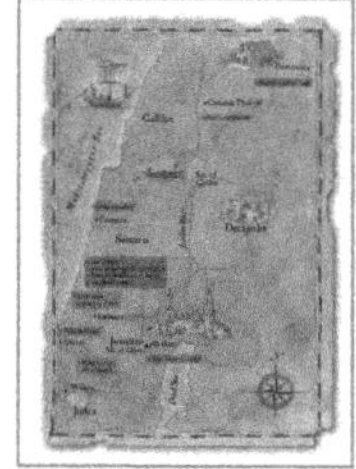

Make It Real

3 Use this activity to help children to **identify specific situations in which they need to be faithful to God.**

Materials

Activity page *Faithful to God* on page 225, Bibles 

 If you have children who struggle with transitions and staying on task, you may want to go straight into the role play and skip the board activity. This can help to manage good behaviour.

Teaching Tip

Some children don't like to act. If no one in the group wants to act, let children read their situation and talk about their ideas.

Faithful to God

Have children stand up. SAY: **Be faithful to me; obey what I say. Stare at the board for 30 seconds without blinking.** Comment on how they do. Then SAY: **Be faithful to me; obey what I say. Stare at the board for 30 seconds without talking, laughing, or blinking.** Again, comment on how they do. **Aren't you glad God doesn't ask us to be faithful in such silly ways?** Have children look at the Activity page *Faithful to God*. Divide the session into small groups (or pairs). Assign each group one of the situations to read and ask them to come up with an ending or response showing them being faithful to God. When ready, let groups act out their situations. After each group has finished, discuss the situation and talk about why it can be hard to be faithful. After all groups have performed, ask these questions:

ASK: **What is a number between 1 and 10, with 10 being the highest, to describe how important is it to be faithful to God?** Accept responses. Hopefully, children will say 10.
Why do you say that? After children have responded, ask them to turn in their Bibles to Revelation 2:10. Have a volunteer read the verse aloud, starting with 'Be faithful.'

SAY: **Being faithful to God is what the Christian life is all about. That's why God helps us to be faithful to Him.**

Live It Out

4 Use this activity to help children to **name a situation in which they need help being faithful and ask for God's help.**

Materials

Activity page *Praying Well* on page 226, pencils 

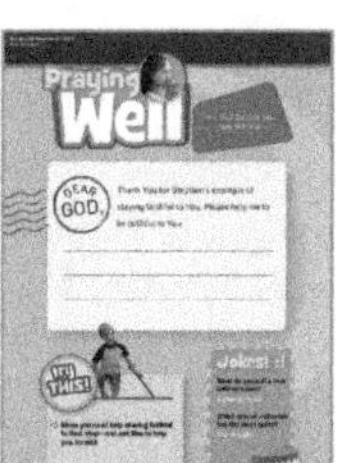

Praying Well

SAY: **I hope you're beginning to understand how important it is for us to stay faithful to God. No matter the situation or how hard it is, God helps us be faithful.** Ask children to stand in the middle of the room. **Think of a situation in which you need help being faithful to God. If it's with a friend, go to ___ (point to a corner). If it's with a brother, sister, or cousin, go to ___ (point to a different corner). If it's with parents, go to ___ (point to a different corner). If it's with someone else or a situation that involves only you, go to ___ (point to a different corner). Now that everyone is in a corner, bow your head and pray silently about your situation. Ask God to help you stay faithful to Him.**

After a brief time of silence, have children sit down and work in pairs on the Activity page *Praying Well*. Encourage them to write their prayers, asking for God's help in staying faithful. Close in prayer.

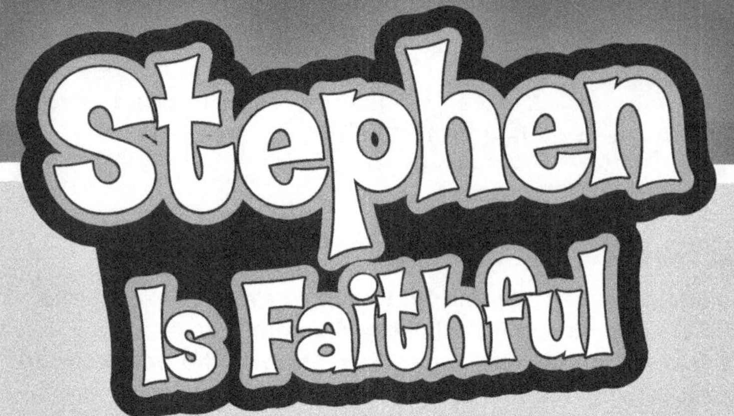

Write the correct words into the gaps to complete the sentences.

> ### Word Bank
> false   broken
> Jesus   killed
> bad   hand

1 __________________ witnesses said that Stephen spoke __________________ words about Moses and God.

2 Stephen told the people that they had __________________ the law and had __________________ the righteous one, Jesus.

3 God let Stephen see His glory and __________________ standing at God's right __________________.

Faithful to God

For each situation, come up with an ending or response showing the children being faithful to God.

1 You love your parents— but really? All they do is nag you about cleaning up your room. Nag, nag, nag! You've got other things to do besides cleaning your room.

2 You really mean to pray and read your Bible every day. You really do! But you're so busy! You and your friend both made the soccer team, and you practise a lot. Plus you have homework and other stuff to do.

3 Your best friend is spending the night. You're watching a favourite programme. You remember that you talked about this show in Sunday school. Everyone agreed that it isn't a very good one for followers of Jesus to watch.

Praying Well

Ask God to help you stay faithful.

DEAR GOD,

Thank You for Stephen's example of staying faithful to You. Please help me to be faithful to You _______________________

____

____

____

try THIS!

➡ **When you need help staying faithful to God, stop—and ask Him to help you. He will!**

Jokes! :)

What do you call a bear with no teeth?

A gummy bear!

Which side of a cheetah has the most spots?

The outside!

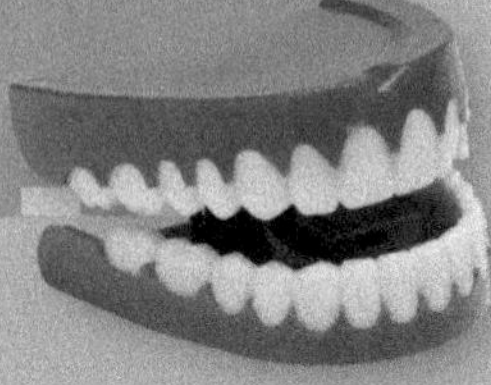

Philip and the Ethiopian
Session 37

Scripture: Acts 8:26-40
Focus: God helps us explain His Word to others.

Heart to Heart Teacher Devotion
For thousands of years, God prepared for salvation. When salvation came through Jesus, His disciples were given the command of spreading the gospel throughout the world. That's our command! As you prepare to teach, ask for His help in understanding passages that aren't easy to understand, and thank Him that He helps you explain His Word to the children He has entrusted to you.

Focus
God helps us explain His Word to others.

Materials
copies of Activity page 
Pop Quiz! on page 230 *Activity Page*
(1 per child), pencils

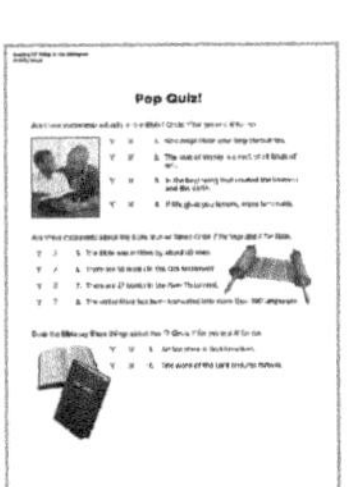

Focus In

1 Use this activity to help children **identify what they know about the Bible.**

Welcome

Welcome each child warmly by name.

Pop Quiz!

Distribute copies of the *Pop Quiz* Activity page. SAY: **Let's see what you know about the Bible. Don't worry if you don't know much about the Bible yet. That's why we're here—so all of us can learn more!** Read the statements aloud as children mark their papers. Tell children that no one has to see their papers. When finished, let volunteers read the statements and give their answers. (Answers: 1=N; 2=Y [1 Timothy 6:10]; 3=Y [Genesis 1:1]; 4=N; 5=T; 6=F; 7=T; 8=T; 9=Y [2 Timothy 3:16]; 10=Y [1 Peter 1:25])

ASK: **How have you learned about the Bible?**
How can you keep learning about God's Word?

Be sure to personalize this next part to fit you. SAY: **The more I read and study the Bible, the more I learn. When I was younger, I didn't understand some things I understand now. And I'm sure there are things that I will understand better in the future. The same can be true for you!**

Focus
God helps us explain His Word to others.

Explore His Word

2 Use these activities to help children **tell about Philip's meeting with the Ethiopian.**

Bible Background for the Teacher

Philip was one of the first men to serve in the ministry of the church. He was 'full of the Spirit and wisdom' (Acts 6:3). His ministry included evangelism, telling others about Jesus Christ. The first part of chapter 8 tells of Philip's work among the Samaritans. As that work concluded, an angelic messenger sent Philip from Samaria to one of the less travelled roads that ran southwest from Jerusalem toward Gaza. Along the road he observed a man travelling in a chariot. The occupant of the vehicle was a treasury officer for Kandake (or Candace), the queen of Ethiopia. He had travelled far from his home to worship at Jerusalem. The man was probably quite wealthy, since he had his own copy of Scripture (which was quite a luxury in the first century!) and a driver for his chariot.

The man was reading, but not understanding, Isaiah 53. His interest in spiritual matters allowed Philip to approach and offer to help him understand the Scriptures. Philip showed that the text predicted a Messiah who would suffer and offer himself on behalf of His people, and Philip explained that Jesus fulfilled that prophecy. The actual words of Philip are not preserved in the text, but he evidently discussed baptism, for the Ethiopian immediately asked to be baptised when they came to a place with water. Note that some later manuscripts include an additional verse (Acts 8:37). God called on Philip to go out from where he was working and look for an opportunity to tell someone about Jesus. Because Philip did what God wanted him to do, the Ethiopian became a Christian. As God led Philip north to Azotus, the Ethiopian went home rejoicing. He was returning home with forgiven sins, a new life in Christ, a personal relationship with God, and hope for eternity.

Bible Exploration   Acts 8:26-40

Have a volunteer stand by the map and point out Jerusalem, Gaza, and Azotus. Tell children that these places are in today's Bible story.

SAY: **The book of Acts tells the history of the early church. Philip was one of the men chosen to help take care of the people in the church who were needy. Philip became a great preacher, telling many people about Jesus.** Ask children to turn in their Bibles to Acts 8:26, and have a volunteer read it aloud. Refer again to the map. **Now God had another job for Philip. One of God's angels told that message to Philip.**

Choose two volunteers who would like to pantomime the action while you read the Scripture; one can portray Philip and the other can portray the Ethiopian. Give the volunteer portraying the Ethiopian a paper scroll. (Provide Bible-times costumes, if desired.) Tell the rest of the session to listen for Philip obeying God or doing something good. When they hear that, they should say, 'Way to go, Philip!' Read Acts 8:26-40, pausing for the children to act and for the rest of the children to respond. When finished, thank everyone for participating. Distribute the activity pages, and have children look at *Philip Explains God's Word*. Read the directions, and let children complete the page on their own or in pairs. When children have finished, let volunteers read the sentences, including the right endings. (Answers: 1=Jerusalem to Gaza; 2=the queen's treasury; 3=good news about Jesus; 4=baptised the man; 5=preaching about Jesus)

The Ethiopian was reading from Isaiah, and Philip explained that Old Testament passage to the man. Then Philip told him about Jesus. That meant that Philip had read and studied God's Word. He was prepared to explain God's Word and share his faith in Jesus. If time allows, ask a volunteer to read *Philip's Post* from Activity page 232. Encourage children to respond to the post.

ASK: **What about you? If you had been in that situation, would you have been prepared and ready to explain God's Word?** Accept responses.

SAY: **God gave us His Word so we could read and study it together. Like Philip, when we're in a situation to help others learn from the Bible, God helps us explain His Word to others. I depend on His help as I teach you. And when you help others learn from the Bible, God will help you too!**

Materials

Bible map from page 207, Bibles, sheet of paper (rolled up as a scroll), Activity page *Philip Explains God's Word* on page 231, pencils, Bible with cross-references (optional: 2 Bible-times costumes)

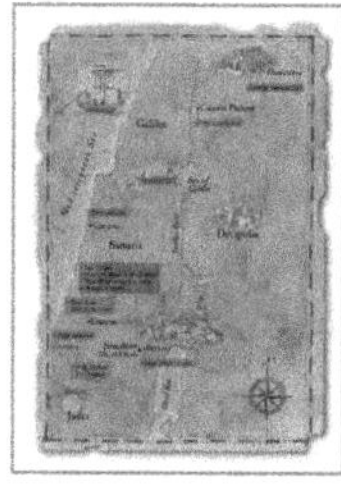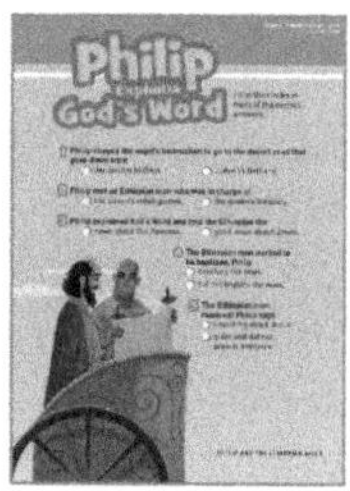

Media Option

If you have a laptop or tablet computer, show children how they can go to a Bible website such as www.biblegateway.com to do searches. Type in part of Acts 8:32-33; it will reference Isaiah 53:7-8.

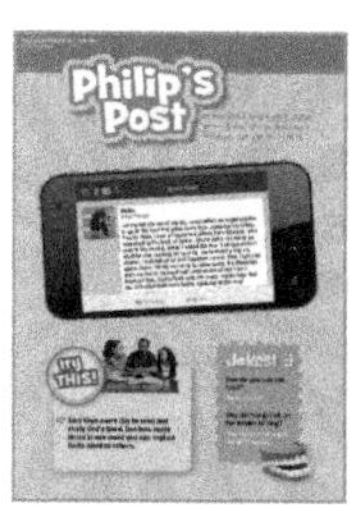

Focus
God helps us explain His
Word to others.

Make It Real

3 Use this activity to help children **think about real life situations in
which to explain God's Word.**

Materials
none

Listen

Before the session,
search the Internet to
find pictures you can print
that show the various items
mentioned in the story (armour
of God poster, pizzas, Bible,
praying hands, church worship
service, Communion elements).
The pictures will help to keep
the children' attention and give
them a point of reference.

Zach's Story

SAY: **God helps us explain His Word to others when we look for those
opportunities.** Tell children to listen as you read a short story about
Zach. When they hear an opportunity Zach has for explaining God's
Word to someone, they should open their hands as if holding a Bible.
SAY: **Brandon is spending the weekend at Zach's. Zach has a poster
on his bedroom wall that shows the armour of God. Brandon asks
Zach about it.** Pause. Children should open their hands as if holding a
Bible. Ask how Zach could use this opportunity to explain God's Word.
**Zach's mum bought pizzas for dinner. The boys were ready to dive in,
when Zach's dad reminded them what God's Word says about being
thankful.** Pause. Ask how Zach could use this opportunity to explain
God's Word. **Brandon went to church services with Zach and his family.
Afterward, Brandon asked Zach why everyone ate the little pieces
of bread and drank grape juice.** Pause. Ask how Zach could use this
opportunity to explain God's Word.

SAY: **I don't know what *your* story will look like this week, but I hope
and pray that you'll remember that God helps us explain His Word to
others.**

Focus
God helps us explain His
Word to others.

Live It Out

4 This activity will help children to **look for opportunities to explain
God's Word to someone.**

Materials
snack cut into heart
shapes (cookies, brownies,
or Rice Krispies bars),
resealable plastic bags, coloured
index cards, markers, clear tape,
Bible

Food

Heart-Shaped Snack Fun

Before doing this activity, have children wash their hands. SAY:
**God helps us explain His Word to others when we look for those
opportunities.** Show children the heart-shaped snack, and distribute
supplies. **A fun way of explaining God's Word to others can be through
this fun snack.** Tell children to put a heart-shaped snack into a plastic
bag. Let children eat a snack while they work. Have each child write the
following, or something similar, on an index card: 'Ask me what John
3:16 has to do with this snack.' Ask for someone to say John 3:16 from
memory or read it. Tell children that they will tape their completed
cards onto their bags. During the week, they are to each give a bag to
someone who doesn't know God or know much about Him. **When you
give away the snack, hopefully the person will ask you, 'What does
John 3:16 have to do with this snack?'**

ASK: **When you hear that question, what will you say?** (The snack is
heart-shaped, and John 3:16 talks about God's love.)

SAY: **I hope and pray that you'll remember that God helps us explain
His Word to others. Take advantage of any and all opportunities you
have of explaining God's Word to others.** Encourage volunteers to pray,
asking God for opportunities to explain His Word to others and for His
help in doing that.

Pop Quiz!

Are these statements actually in the Bible? Circle *Y* for yes and *N* for no.

Y N 1. God helps those who help themselves.

Y N 2. The love of money is a root of all kinds of evil.

Y N 3. In the beginning God created the heavens and the earth.

Y N 4. If life gives you lemons, make lemonade.

Are these statements about the Bible true or false? Circle *T* for true and *F* for false.

T F 5. The Bible was written by about 40 men.

T F 6. There are 50 books in the Old Testament.

T F 7. There are 27 books in the New Testament.

T F 8. The entire Bible has been translated into more than 500 languages.

Does the Bible say these things about itself? Circle *Y* for yes and *N* for no.

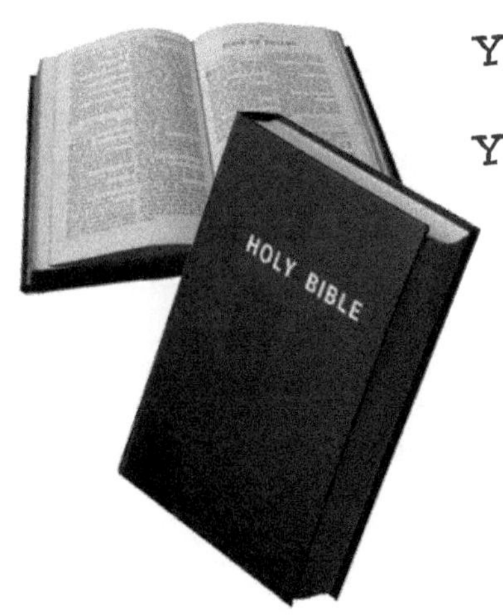

Y N 9. All Scripture is God-breathed.

Y N 10. The word of the Lord endures forever.

Philip Explains God's Word

Fill in the circles in front of the correct answers.

1 **Philip obeyed the angel's instruction to go to the desert road that goes down from**
- ○ Jerusalem to Gaza.
- ○ Judea to Bethany.

2 **Philip met an Ethiopian man who was in charge of**
- ○ the queen's video games.
- ○ the queen's treasury.

3 **Philip explained God's Word and told the Ethiopian the**
- ○ news about the Romans.
- ○ good news about Jesus.

4 **The Ethiopian man wanted to be baptised. Philip**
- ○ baptised the man.
- ○ did not baptise the man.

5 **The Ethiopian man rejoiced! Philip kept**
- ○ preaching about Jesus.
- ○ quiet and did not preach anymore.

Philip's Post

If you like Philip's post, put a ✔ on 'Like.' If you will share his post, put a ✔ on 'Share.'

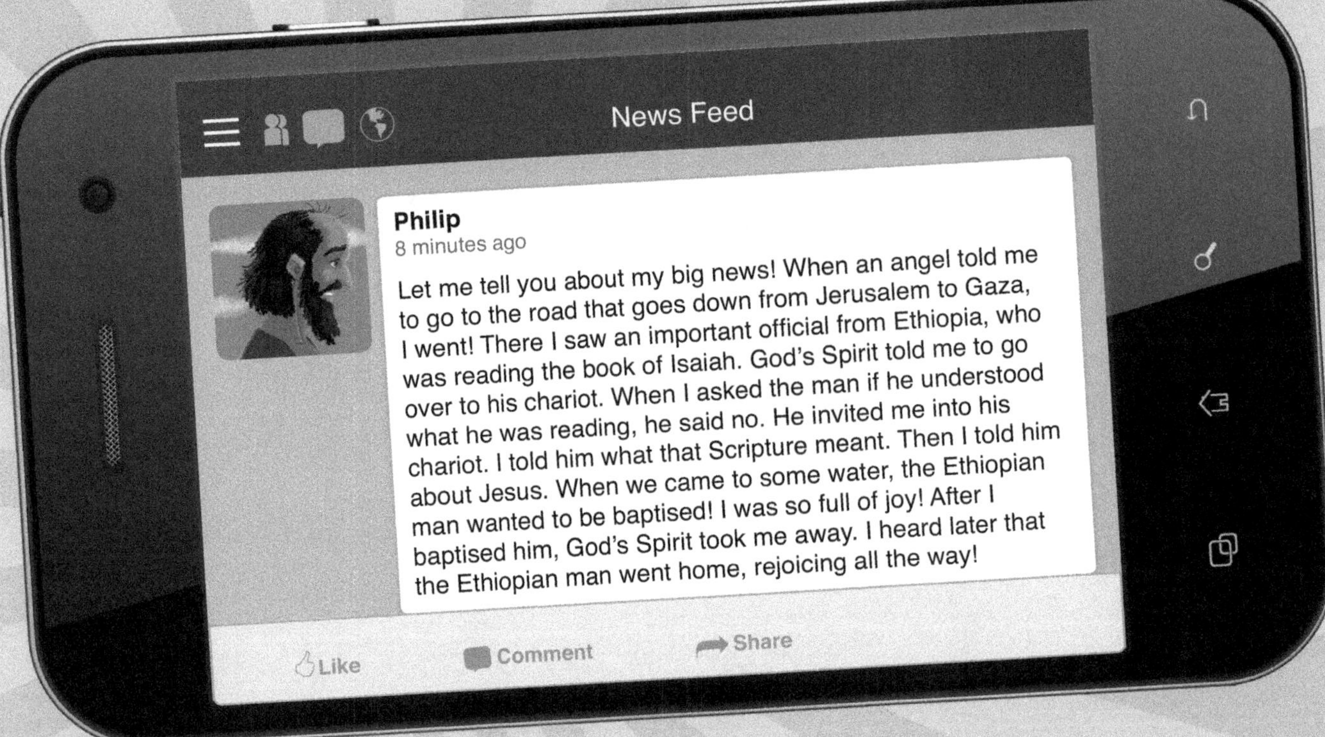

try THIS!

⇨ **Take time every day to read and study God's Word. See how many times in one week you can explain God's Word to others.**

Jokes! :)

How do you buy cat food?

Purrrrrrr can!

Why did the girl sit on the ladder to sing?

She wanted to reach the high notes!

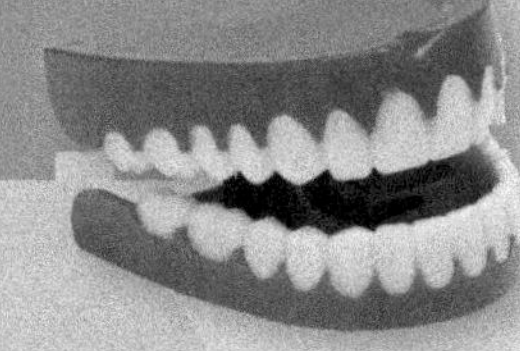

Saul's Conversion

Session 38

Scripture: Acts 9:1-19
Focus: God is a life changer!

Heart to Heart Teacher Devotion
Saul (later known as Paul) was known for the threats and harm he brought on those who would dare follow Jesus. No one would ever have guessed that one day he would become one of those followers. And Paul didn't just become someone following Jesus in the shadows. No! He became a leader and one of the most vocal followers, telling everyone, everywhere about Jesus. Only God's power and grace can change a life like that!

Focus
God is a life changer!

Materials
bedsheet (or a very large towel), ball, timer

Game

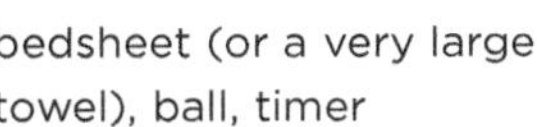
Model what children are to do, and lead in a couple of practice rounds. To help all children (including those with impulse difficulties), review rules for being gentle, keeping the ball on the sheet, and so on.

Focus In

1 Use this activity to help children to **identify ways God can change people's lives.**

Welcome

Welcome each child warmly by name.

Changing Directions

Ask children to stand in a circle. Place the bedsheet in the middle of the circle and ask children to hold it up with both hands. SAY: **This is a game about changing directions. I'll place the ball on the sheet and say 'Go left'. Use your arms to move the sheet so the ball will roll in a circle around the sheet to your left until I tell you to change direction and say 'Go right'. I'll time how long it takes for the ball to change directions. Your goal is to get faster and faster each time.** When children understand the game, place the ball on the sheet. Play as time permits. Then have children sit down. **That was a fun game about changing directions. But today we're talking about the kind of change that happens inside people.**

ASK: **What are some ways God can change people's lives?** Accept responses.
    Can God change us to be more loving, even to our brothers and sisters?
    Can God change us to think better thoughts?
    Can God change us so we are patient?

SAY: **God is in the business of changing lives. In fact, you could say that God is a life changer! Let's dig into God's Word and learn about two men who needed to make a change.**

Explore His Word

2 Use these activities to help children **describe the changes in the lives of Saul and Ananias.**

Bible Background for the Teacher

As a result of the persecution, many Christians left Jerusalem. When Saul learned that some had gone to Damascus in Syria, he went there to seek and destroy the believers. Saul sincerely believed that he was doing God's work, based on the assumption that God hated Jesus and the church. Saul (now called Paul) retells the story of his conversion, with additional details, in Acts 22:3-21 and 26:4-23. The trip to Damascus involved travelling about 150 miles. As the group neared the city, Saul was struck down by the brilliance of a heavenly light, and Jesus spoke to him. Saul's friends led him to Damascus, where he fasted, prayed, and waited for some further word from God. In a vision, the Lord reassured Ananias that Saul's condition was real and that God had plans to use Saul as a missionary to the Gentiles. When Ananias did what God asked, Saul's sight was restored and he was baptised.

Bible Exploration   Acts 9:1-19

Give each child an index card and marker pen. Tell children to draw a large arrow on their cards. Then have a volunteer show Damascus and Jerusalem on the map. Tell children that these cities are where today's Bible story takes place. Have children turn in their Bibles to Acts 9:1-19. **This is where we pick up God's story. Let's read about a man who needed a big change and another man who needed a change too.** Have children lay their arrow cards in front of them. **Whenever you hear about someone undergoing a change, take your arrow card and point it in the opposite direction.** Ask volunteers to read Acts 9:1-2.

ASK: **Who did Saul plan to take as prisoners?** (people who followed Jesus)

    Why do you think he was doing that? (Saul thought he was doing God's will; Saul hated Christ and His church)

Have volunteers read verses 3-9. Ask children to describe what happened to Saul. Then have volunteers read verses 10-14.

ASK: **Who was Ananias?** (disciple of Jesus)

    To whom did the Lord want Ananias to go? (Saul)

    Why didn't Ananias want to do it? (He had heard what Saul was doing to Christians, and he knew that Saul had come to Damascus to do the same things)

Have volunteers read verses 15-16. Ask children to put in their own words why the Lord wanted Ananias to go to Saul. Then read verse 17. Pause; see if children turn their arrow cards to the opposite direction.
SAY: **Ananias didn't want to go to Saul. But when God told him to and explained why, Ananias did. He underwent a change of heart and obeyed God.** Children should turn the direction of their arrow cards. Read verses 18-19. **Saul, a man who was harming Christians, became a Christian! That has to be the biggest change a person could ever make!** Children should turn the direction of their arrow cards. Hand out Activity page *Saul's Journal.* Ask volunteers to read each sentence, filling in the blanks. (Answers: Damascus; light; ground; three; Ananias; baptised)
SAY: **Saul was perhaps the church's greatest persecutor. But things changed, and Saul, who was later called Paul, became one of the church's greatest teachers. God is a life changer!**

Materials

Bible map on page 207, Bibles, index cards, markers, *Listen*
Activity pages *Saul's Journal* on pages 236-237, pencils

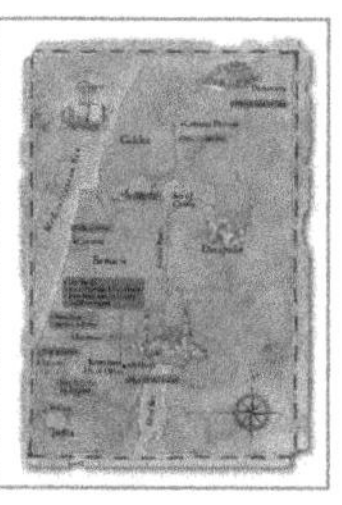

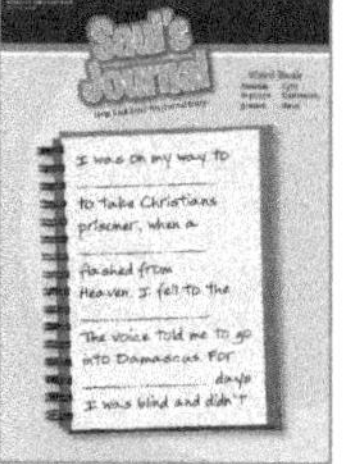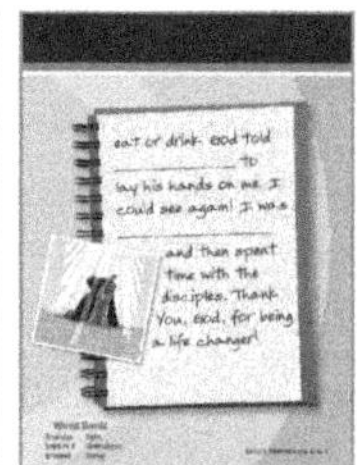

Media Option

You can go to a website such as www.biblegateway.com and play a dramatised reading of the Bible verses.

Make It Real

3 Use this activity to help children **understand ways they need to let God change their lives.**

Materials

paper, pencils, colouring pencils, markers, Bibles

Art

When having children work in groups, consider assigning roles so that everyone is included and gets to participate in the process.

Design an Ad

SAY: **People noticed a big change in how Saul acted and spoke. That can happen for you too. When you let God change you, others will see a difference in how you act and speak too.** Tell children that they get to design an advert for a magazine or website that would help people know about ways God could change their lives. There are three things that each ad must include: the main thought from a Scripture that you will provide, at least one arrow, and the words 'God is a life changer!' Let children work in small groups (or pairs). Distribute supplies. Give each group one of these Scripture references: 1 Corinthians 13:4; Galatians 6:10; Ephesians 4:25; Ephesians 6:1-2; Philippians 4:8; Colossians 3:13. When the groups are done, let children present their ads. After each ad is presented, ask questions such as the following, tailoring them to fit the Scriptures and thoughts presented:

ASK: **Is being patient and kind a way that you need to let God change your life? In what situations do you find it hard to be patient and kind?**
SAY: **When it's hard being patient with your sister or brother, remember that God is a life changer! When you're tempted to lie, remember that God is a life changer!**

Live It Out

4 Use this activity to help children to **ask God to change their lives.**

Materials

roll paper, scissors, sticky tape, coloured paper, pencils, clear tape (or masking tape)

Pray

Teaching Tips

Have the group stand far enough away from the cross during prayer so no one is tempted to remove a note. After prayer, take down the cross and notes.

Extra Time

If there is time, have children to use the Activity page *Prayer Prompts* on page 238.

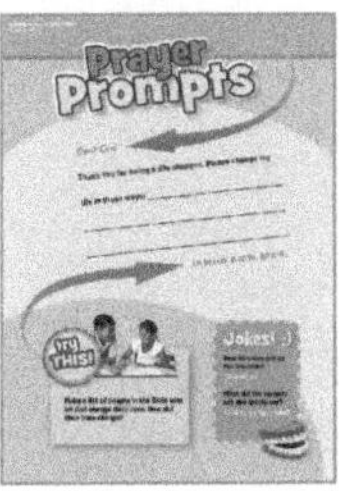

Ask the Life Changer!

Before the session, cut a large cross from roll paper. Display it where children can reach it. Coloured paper cut into small squares, enough for each child to have three or four pieces. Lay some tape near the cross.

SAY: **Because we know that God is a life changer, let's ask Him to change us, and help us to make changes in our lives so we can be more like Him.** Encourage children to write on each paper a way they want to ask God to change their lives. When they're finished, have children fold their notes and tape them onto the cross.

When children are done, have them gather around the cross for a time of prayer. PRAY: **Dear God, thank You for being a life changer. Thank You for changing my life, giving me purpose, hope, and joy. In Jesus' name, amen.**

Saul's Journal

Help Saul finish his journal entry.

Word Bank

Ananias	light
baptised	Damascu
ground	three

I was on my way to

____

to take Christians
prisoner, when a

____

flashed from
Heaven. I fell to the

__________________.

The voice told me to go
into Damascus. For

__________________ days

I was blind and didn't

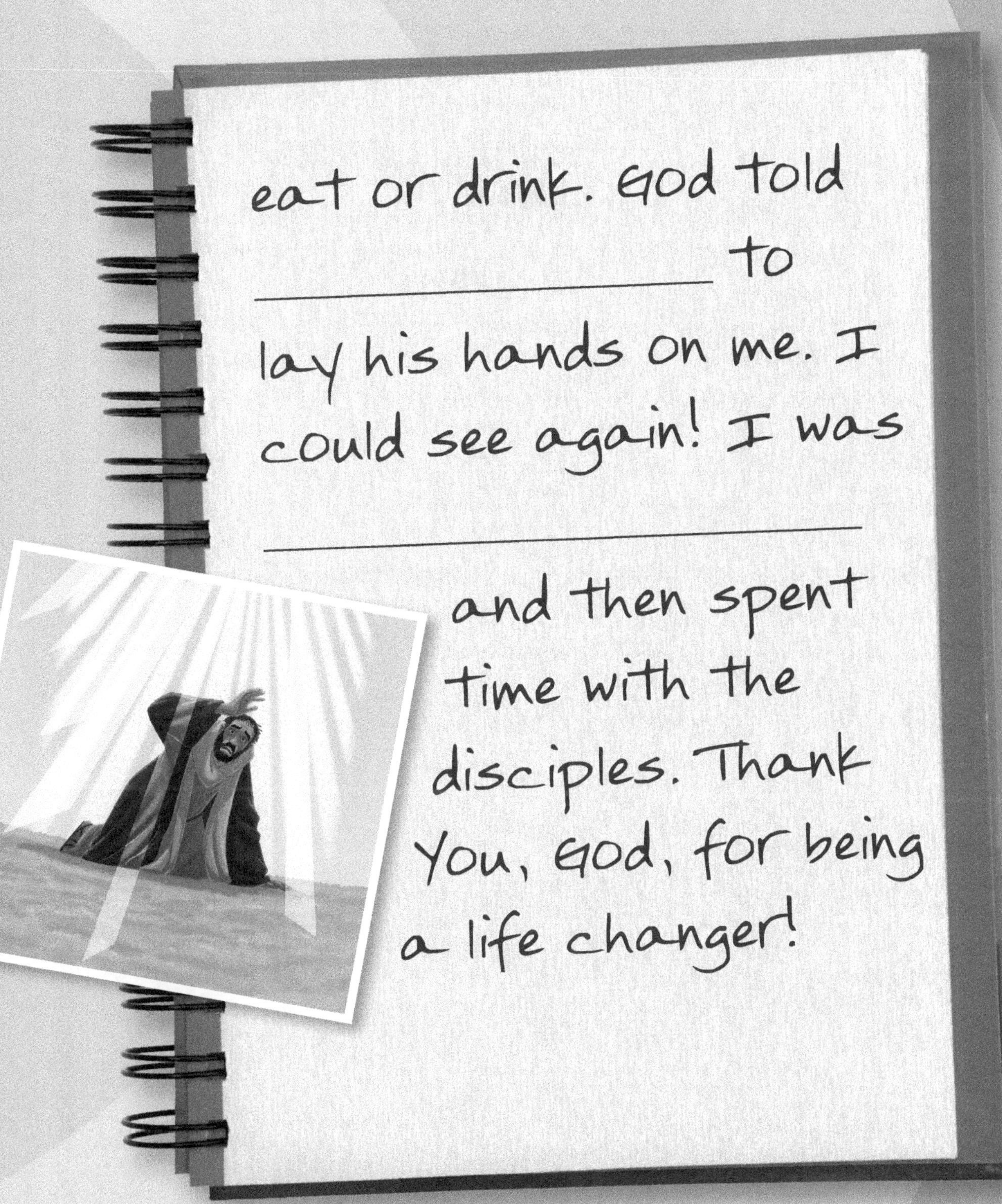

Word Bank

Ananias	light
baptised	Damascus
ground	three

HeartShaper Primary Blue Edition, Activity page
Permission is granted to reproduce this page for ministry purposes only—not for resale.

Prayer Prompts

Dear God,

Thank You for being a life changer. Please change my

life in these ways: _______________________________

____

____.

In Jesus' name, amen.

try THIS!

Make a list of people in the Bible who let God change their lives. How did their lives change?

Jokes! :)

How do trees get on the Internet?

They log in!

What did the tornado ask the sports car?

Want to go for a spin?

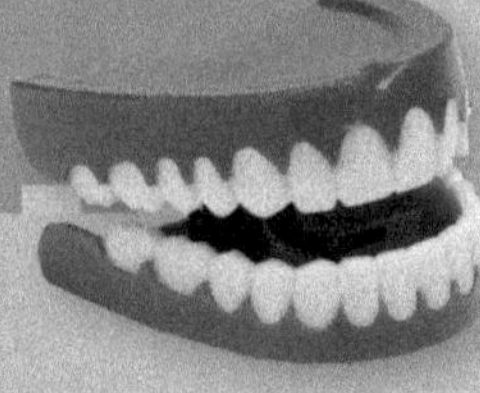

Paul and Barnabas Teach About Jesus

Session 39

Scripture: Acts 14:1-20
Focus: Do everything for Jesus.

Heart to Heart Teacher Devotion

Have you ever met people who wanted Jesus as *part* of their lives, but not in *all* parts of their lives? That certainly isn't how Paul and Barnabas lived, is it? Wherever they were and whatever they were doing, they did everything for Jesus. When it would have been easier to stop speaking about Jesus, they spoke even more boldly. Let's follow their example and do everything for Jesus.

Focus
Do everything for Jesus.

Materials
none

Action

Teaching Tips
If you have time, call out more situations or let children make up some.

Visual prompts can help some children stay focused. Consider bringing these objects to show as you read the situations: a pair of trainers, homework page, toothbrush, dish and towel. Use your hand to gesture which is left and which is right to help children.

Focus In

1 Use this activity to help children to **explore the motives behind what they do.**

Welcome
Welcome each child warmly by name.

Why Do It?

ASK: **If I asked you what your *motive* is for eating food, what would you say?** (to stay alive; food tastes good)
What does the word *motive* mean? (a need or desire that causes a person to act)

Ask children to stand on an imaginary line, one behind the other. SAY: **Let's think about our motives. I'll read a situation with two different motives. Move to the left or right, based on which motive you think you would have in that situation. If neither would be your motive, stay on the line.**
1. **I would buy the newest trainers that everyone is wearing (a-move to the left) to impress my friends, or (b-move to the right) so I could run faster and jump higher.**
2. **I would do extra homework to (a-move to the left) please my teacher, or (b-move to the right) make my parents happy.**
3. **I would brush my teeth after meals so (a-move to the left) there's no green stuff in my teeth, or (b-move to the right) my teeth would stay healthy.**

SAY: **Our motives are important. Let's think more about our motives, especially our motives in living for Jesus.**

Explore His Word

2 Use these activities to help children **tell what Paul and Barnabas did for Jesus.**

Bible Background for the Teacher

When resistance against the gospel mounted, Paul and Barnabas did not give up. After learning about a plot to stone them to death, they escaped to Lystra, a small country town used by the Romans as a military outpost. Here they met a man whose condition is described in some detail so as to establish how great a miracle Paul and Barnabas performed. Once the Lystrans knew about the healing, they began to treat Paul and Barnabas with a respect owed only to God. A garlanded bull was brought for sacrifice as the Lystrans prepared to worship the missionaries as gods. Paul and Barnabas, however, courageously stood up for right against this enthusiasm, even though the particular dialect of Lystra presented a barrier to communication. Paul and Barnabas used the occasion to preach the gospel of a living God who made all things.

Bible Exploration Acts 14:1-20

Before the session, cut out the figures from the Activity page map on page 244. The figures will be used in most lessons, so be sure to keep them available for the following sessions.

SAY: **The book of Acts tells the history of the early church; it's the only New Testament book of history.** Ask children to turn in their Bibles to Acts 14:1, and have a volunteer read the verse aloud. Have another volunteer show where these places are on the map: Iconium, Lystra, Derbe, and Antioch. Tell children that these places are mentioned in today's Bible story. Let another volunteer attach the Paul and Barnabas figures near Iconium.

SAY: **Listen or follow along in your Bibles as I read verses 1-20. You will all be part of the crowd, listening to Paul and Barnabas. When I hold up a sign, either say or do what it says. Listen to these exciting, yet dangerous, times for Paul and Barnabas as they teach about Jesus.** Read verse 1; then hold up Sign #1, prompting children to read it together. Read verses 2-4; then hold up Sign #2, prompting the girls to read the first part, and the boys to read the second part.

Read verse 5; then hold up Sign #3, prompting children to do what the sign says. Read verses 6-7. Have a volunteer move the Paul and Barnabas figures on the map between Lystra and Derbe. Read verses 8-20, encouraging children to do any actions that go along with the words.

Hand out Activity page *Paul and Barnabas*. Read the directions. Ask children to work together in small groups. (Answers: 1=Jesus; 2=stone; 3=Derbe; 4=walk; 5=Hermes; 6=food; 7=Paul; 8=Barnabas)

ASK: **What did Paul and Barnabas do for Jesus?** (taught boldly; healed in Jesus' name; endured lots of hard times for Jesus)
> **Why do you think Paul and Barnabas taught boldly about Jesus, healed in Jesus' name, and endured lots of hard times for Jesus? What were their motives?** (they loved God; they knew how important it is for everyone to know about Jesus; they wanted people to turn to the living God who made everything)

SAY: **If Paul and Barnabas had not loved God, they would not have kept teaching about Jesus. Now let's think about why we should do everything for Jesus.**

Materials

Activity page map on page 244, reusable adhesive, Bibles, Activity pages *Paul and Barnabas* on pages 242-243, pencils

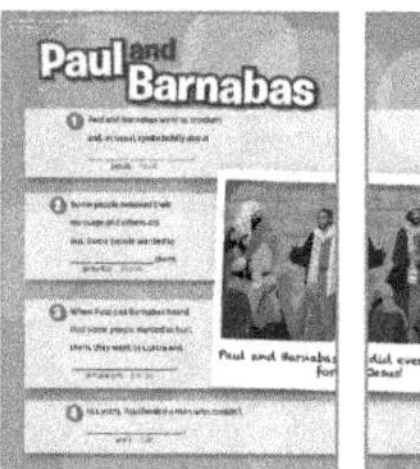
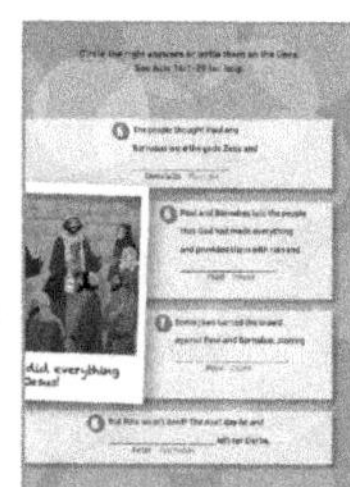

Before the Session
Write or print the following 5 signs to use during the Bible reading:
Sign 1 Yes, we believe
Sign 2 Girls say 'We believe!' Boys say 'We don't believe'
Sign 3 Act out picking up a stone, ready to throw it.

Make It Real

3 Use this activity to help children **tell why it's important to do everything for Jesus.**

Materials
balloon

Game

A Game with a Motive

Before this activity, take one child aside. Tell them that during the game they are to try to catch the balloon or try to nudge it out of children's hands but not to tell what they're doing.

Inflate the balloon. Have children sit or stand in a circle. SAY: **Let's pretend that this balloon represents good things we can do for Jesus. As you throw it, think about something good you can do for Jesus. Say it out loud if you want to.** Tell children to throw the balloon from person to person around the circle and keep it going as long as possible. Begin the game. Of course, children will complain and not understand what's going on. After several children have had the balloon taken away, stop the game, and tell everyone what was going on.

ASK: **What was the motive of our friend who interfered with the game?**
  (She tried to take the balloon)
  What should be our motives when doing good things for Jesus?
  (to show Jesus how much we love Him; to help others get to know Jesus too, even when people may try to stop us)

SAY: **Let's show Jesus how much we love Him, and let's help others get to know Him as we do everything for Jesus.**

Live It Out

4 Use this activity to help children to **choose to do everything for Jesus.**

Materials
paper, pencils, colouring pencils

Write

Everything for Jesus

Distribute paper and pencils. Tell children to write 'Doing everything for Jesus!' in the middle of their papers: SAY: **Think about your week, where you will go and what you will do. Write those places on different areas of your paper. Include your home and the church building. You might include a sports field, friends' homes, restaurants, shops, and other places. Write down as many as you can think of. This week, your challenge is to do everything for Jesus, showing Jesus how much you love Him and helping others get to know Him too. Think first about your home.**

ASK: **As you do your chores, how can you show that you love Jesus?**
  (do them without complaining; do them before being asked to; do extra chores)

SAY: **Decide what you'll do, and write your ideas under 'home'.** Encourage children to do the same for several places where they will be this week. Close with a time of prayer. PRAY: **Dear God, help us to do everything for Jesus whether we're at home, with friends, involved in sports and other activities, or wherever we are. We love You, and we want others to know and love You too. In Jesus' name, amen.**

Paul and Barnabas

1 Paul and Barnabas went to Iconium

and, as usual, spoke boldly about

________________________.

Jesus   food

2 Some people believed their

message and others did

not. Some people wanted to

________________them.

pray for   stone

3 When Paul and Barnabas heard

that some people wanted to hurt

them, they went to Lystra and

________________________.

Jerusalem   Derbe

4 In Lystra, Paul healed a man who couldn't

________________________.

walk   talk

5 The people thought Paul and Barnabas were the gods Zeus and

_______________________.

Donatello   Hermes

6 Paul and Barnabas told the people that God had made everything and provided them with rain and

_______________________.

food   floods

7 Some Jews turned the crowd against Paul and Barnabas, stoning

_______________________.

Paul   Peter

8 But Paul wasn't dead! The next day he and

_______________________ left for Derbe.

Peter   Barnabas

N
S
E
W
•Rome
ITALIA
SICILIA
•Malta
MACEDONIA
Thessalonica•
Berea•
Samothrace•
•Philippi
•Neapolis
•Troas
•Thyatira
GALATIA
Corinth•
•Athens
Patmos—
Cnidus—
CRETE •Salmone
•Ephesus
Iconium•
Lystra•
•Derbe
•Antioch
Mediterranean Sea
Black Sea
CYRENE
EGYPT
JUDEA
Jerusalem•
•Antipatris
Caesarea•
CYPRUS
SYRIA

Lydia's Conversion

Session 40

Scripture: Acts 16:11-15
Focus: Respond positively to God's Word.

Heart to Heart Teacher Devotion
As a teacher, have you ever been sure that a lesson would be exciting and life changing, only to be disappointed that the children didn't listen—let alone responded? Don't worry; children hear more than you realise. And as you sow the seeds of the gospel, the Holy Spirit works in people's lives—including the children in your session— and helps people respond positively to God's Word.

Focus In

1 Use one or both of these activities to help children **identify ways people can respond to God's Word.**

Welcome

Welcome each child warmly by name.

A Rock and a Sponge

Have children gather where they can see the object lesson clearly. Put a rock in one bowl and a sponge in the other bowl. Have a volunteer slowly pour some water over the sponge until it's thoroughly soaked. Have another volunteer pick up the sponge and wring it out, keeping it over the bowl.

ASK: **Would you say that the sponge soaked up or resisted the water? Why?** (soaked up; the sponge absorbed, or drew in, the water.)

Have a volunteer slowly pour some water over the rock in the other bowl. Have another volunteer pick up the rock and try to wring it out, keeping it over the bowl.

ASK: **Would you say that the rock soaked up or resisted the water? Why?** (resisted; the rock did not soak up the water at all.)

SAY: **When it comes to God's Word, people respond differently too. Some people respond very positively, 'soaking up' God's Word. Some resist God's Word, not wanting anything to do with it. Many people respond somewhere in between. Let's discover how someone called Lydia in the Bible responded to God's Word.**

Explore His Word

② Use these activities to help children **tell how Lydia responded to God's Word.**

Bible Background for the Teacher

In Philippi there was evidently no synagogue, and some women met for prayer outside the city, at a site probably near the Gangites River about a mile south of the city. Here Paul met Lydia, a businesswoman whose trade brought her into contact with the rich and powerful of the Roman Empire. As 'a dealer in purple cloth', she produced the expensive material often used by royalty, and she was prosperous enough to own a home that could lodge travelling missionaries (16:15).

Paul recognised in Lydia a spiritual sensitivity. That she is called 'a worshipper of God' (Acts 16:14) helps us understand her relationship to Judaism. She was not a convert or a pagan; like Cornelius she was a Gentile who was informally connected to Judaism, representing a group often referred to as worshippers of God or 'God-fearing' (10:2). She knew the Scriptures, and her heart was receptive to God's leading. So Paul and his friends discussed the gospel with her, and, as He always does with sincere people, God used truth to open her heart. Lydia chose to respond positively to God's Word. What happened next is very familiar in Acts. Faith is followed by baptism, which was also part of Paul's message. The 'members of her household' need not include infants, since a wealthy woman like Lydia might have other adult family members and servants living with her. Her faith was seen in her generous offer to give the missionaries lodging in her home.

Bible Exploration   Acts 16:11-15

Ask a volunteer to stand by the map and point out places in today's Bible story: Troas, Samothrace, Neapolis, Philippi, Macedonia, and Thyatira. The volunteer can move the Paul, Silas, and Timothy figures from place to place, finally placing them near Philippi.

Ask children to turn in their Bibles to Acts 16:1. Have volunteers read verses 1 and 4. SAY: **Paul, Silas, and Timothy were travelling from town to town, teaching and preaching about Jesus.** Ask volunteers to read verses 11-12. **Let's listen and find out what happened in Philippi.** Choose three volunteers who are willing to read, and give them each a copy of the 'Lydia's Story' Activity page along with a name sign to hold or wear. Have them stand and read the parts. When finished, thank them for their participation.

Hand out Activity page *Lydia Responds*. Read the directions and do the page together. (Answers: 1=c; 2=a; 3=b; 4=a) SAY: **Let's think about how Lydia responded to Paul's teaching from God's Word.**
ASK: **Did Lydia pay attention to God's Word? How do you know?** (yes, it says she listened)
　　How did Lydia respond positively to God's Word? (She listened; she was baptised; she showed hospitality by inviting Paul and his companions to stay at her house.)

SAY: **Even though we don't know exactly what Paul taught, we know the results. No doubt Paul told the women the good news about Jesus: how Jesus died on the cross to save us from our sins, was buried, then rose from the dead on the third day. Because Lydia and her household were baptised, Paul must have taught what the apostle Peter taught on the Day of Pentecost as recorded in Acts 2:38: 'Repent and be baptised, every one of you, in the name of Jesus Christ for the forgiveness of your sins. And you will receive the gift of the Holy Spirit.' Lydia did respond positively to God's Word. I hope each of us will too.**

Materials
Bible map from session 39, reusable adhesive, Bibles, Activity pages *Lydia's Story* on pages 248-249, Activity page *Lydia Responds* on page 250, pencils

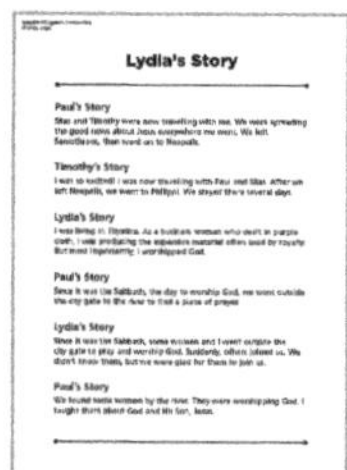

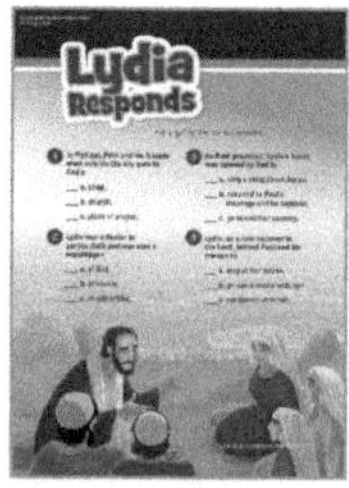

Media Option
Go to www.biblegateway.com or a similar website and play a dramatised reading of the Bible verses.

Before the session
Write out these three name signs for children to hold or wear when they are reading their parts:
Paul
Lydia
Timothy

Focus
**Respond positively to
God's Word.**

Make It Real

3 Use this activity to help children **discover how they can respond
positively to God's Word.**

Materials
cress seeds, resealable
plastic bags, Bibles 
Object Lesson

Media Option
Search online for 'video of cress
seeds growing.' You may find a
fun video you could show the
session.

Before the Session
Put a handful of cress seeds into
each resealable bag (one bag
per child).

Responding Positively

Give each child a bag with cress seeds. Ask whether any children
have planted cress seeds (or any kind of seeds) before. If so, let those
children talk about what it takes for seeds to grow. (water; light; good
soil; air; time) SAY: **You could say that when seeds grow they are
responding positively to water, light, good soil, air, and time. Let's
go to the Bible and find out how we can respond positively to God's
Word.** Assign these Scriptures to individuals or pairs of children to look
up and be ready to read to the session: Psalm 119:11, 34, 97; Luke 11:28;
Acts 17:11; 1 Timothy 4:13. When children are ready, have them read their
Scriptures aloud.

ASK: **How can we respond positively to God's Word?** (listen and hear it;
study it; memorise it; think about it; obey it)
**What way of responding positively to God's Word is something
you need to do or do more of?**

SAY: **Let's follow Lydia's example and respond positively to God's
Word.** Encourage children to take their seeds home and plant them.

Focus
**Respond positively to
God's Word.**

Live It Out

4 Use this activity to help children to **choose to respond positively
to God's Word.**

Materials
index cards, pencils 
Write

Consider providing
drawing paper and
markers for children who
struggle with writing or are non-
writers.

Write It and Do It

SAY: **Lydia is a great example of someone who listened to God's
Word and responded positively to it. She obeyed God's Word and
was baptised. Then she showed hospitality by inviting Paul and his
companions to stay at her house. How will you respond positively to
God's Word?** Distribute index cards. Ask children to write or draw one
or more things on their cards that they will do this week to respond
positively to God's Word. As needed, review some ideas with them:
listen to God's Word, read the Bible, obey God's Word, memorise Bible
verses, and think about what God's Word says.

On the other side of their index cards, invite children to write a prayer to
God, asking for His help as they try to always respond positively to His
Word. When finished, close with prayer. Encourage children to plant the
seeds. SAY: **As you check on your seeds each day, ask God to help you
respond positively to His Word.**

Lydia's Story

Paul's Story

Silas and Timothy were now travelling with me. We were spreading the good news about Jesus everywhere we went. We left Samothrace, then went on to Neapolis.

Timothy's Story

I was so excited! I was now travelling with Paul and Silas. After we left Neapolis, we went to Philippi. We stayed there several days.

Lydia's Story

I was living in Thyatira. As a businesswoman who dealt in purple cloth, I was producing the expensive material often used by royalty. But most importantly, I worshipped God.

Paul's Story

Since it was the Sabbath, the day to worship God, we went outside the city gate to the river to find a place of prayer.

Lydia's Story

Since it was the Sabbath, some women and I went outside the city gate to pray and worship God. Suddenly, others joined us. We didn't know them, but we were glad for them to join us.

Paul's Story

We found some women by the river. They were worshipping God. I taught them about God and His Son, Jesus.

Lydia's Story

Lydia's Story

I listened as Paul preached. It was wonderful to hear the good news about Jesus! I had to respond to Paul's message.

Timothy's Story

When Paul was done preaching, Lydia and the members of her household were baptised! What a wonderful day!

Paul's Story

I thanked God that He used me to tell Lydia and the other women about Jesus.

Lydia's Story

I thanked God that He sent Paul and the others to Philippi. I invited Paul and his friends to come and stay in my house.

Timothy's Story

Lydia was so kind to invite us to come to her house.

Paul's Story

We went to Lydia's house because we knew she was a believer in the Lord.

Lydia's Story

I'm so grateful that Paul and his friends came to Philippi. My life was changed forever!

Put a ✔ by the correct answers.

1 In Philippi, Paul and his friends went outside the city gate to find a

____ a. shop.

____ b. church.

____ c. place of prayer.

2 Lydia was a dealer in purple cloth and was also a worshipper

____ a. of God.

____ b. of money.

____ c. of celebrities.

3 As Paul preached, Lydia's heart was opened by God to

____ a. sing a song about Jesus.

____ b. respond to Paul's message and be baptised.

____ c. go to another country.

4 Lydia, as a new believer in the Lord, invited Paul and his friends to

____ a. stay at her house.

____ b. go see a movie with her.

____ c. eat dinner with her.

Paul and Silas in Prison

Session 41

Scripture: Acts 16:16-40
Focus: Live for Jesus, even in difficult situations.

Heart to Heart Teacher Devotion

Whether you live in a big city or a tiny town, living for Jesus can be challenging. Maybe you have friends who don't understand the time you give to Jesus and His church. Maybe you have family members who make fun of you for not going to questionable places of entertainment. Maybe your spouse or boss just doesn't get why you do the things you do. It's OK. Definitely, not maybe, God will reward your faithfulness as you live for Jesus, even in difficult situations.

Focus
Live for Jesus, even in difficult situations.

Materials
Activity pages *Difficult Situations* on pages 254-255, paper, pencils

Discuss

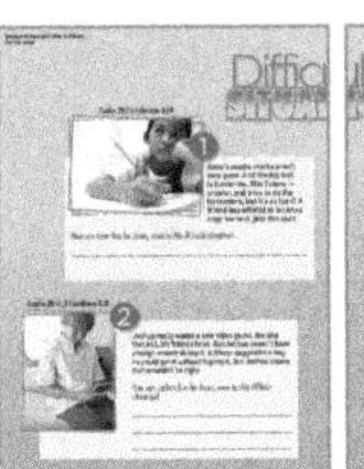 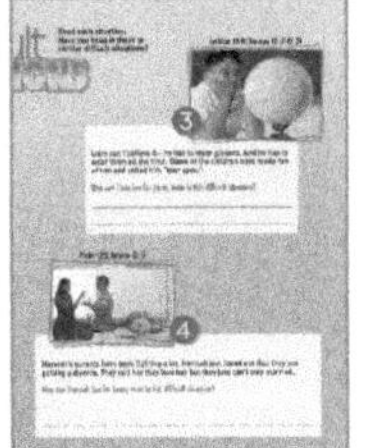

Focus In

1 Use this activity to help children to **identify difficult situations that happen in their lives.**

Welcome

Welcome each child warmly by name.

Most to Least

Hand out the Activity page *Difficult Situations*. Ask volunteers to read each of the situations aloud. Tell them not to read the sentences that ask how the children can live for Jesus. Then divide the session into small groups (or pairs), and give each group a sheet of paper and a pencil. SAY: **In your groups, rank these four situations from what you think is the most difficult situation to what you think is the least difficult situation. Write the childrens' names to identify each situation.** (Example: If a group thinks that Adrian's situation is the hardest, they should write '1=Adrian.') Give groups time to work. When groups are done, let children read their rankings.

ASK: **What's a difficult situation you have faced or someone you know has faced?** Accept responses.

SAY: **As we think about difficult situations today, we'll discover that we can live for Jesus, even in difficult situations.**

Focus
Live for Jesus, even in difficult situations.

Explore His Word

2 Use these activities to help children **tell how Paul and Silas lived for Jesus during a difficult situation.**

Bible Background for the Teacher

While on the second missionary journey, Paul and Silas encountered a female slave 'who had a spirit' (Acts 16:16). The spirit shouted that Paul and Silas were 'servants of the Most High God' (v. 17). The spirit gave the girl the ability to predict the future, which gave her owners the ability to make a lot of money. Paul's exorcism parallels cases when Jesus cast out evil spirits who spoke truth about Christ (see Mark 5:7-8). The exit of the spirit meant the exit of the owners' profits, so the owners invented some charges about unlawful customs to justify taking the missionaries before the magistrates. They encouraged an attack on Paul and Silas, leading to a beating that Paul remembered years later as one of his hardships for Christ (2 Corinthians 11:25). Paul and Silas were then locked up in the dark, inner cell, their legs in stocks.

Nevertheless, their joy and hope moved them to pray and sing to God, who sent an earthquake that shook the jail and freed the prisoners from their chains. The jailer assumed all had escaped and that he must face the Roman death sentence for jailers who lost their prisoners (see Acts 12:19). Paul's assurance prevented the jailer's suicide, and the jailer asked about salvation. Paul's answer compares well with the response to converts elsewhere in Acts (see 16:14-15; 18:8): he must believe in the Lord Jesus. Then the jailer was baptised. He showed that his faith was sincere by washing the wounds of Paul and Silas and feeding them at his house. When the magistrates tried to get the prisoners to leave the city, Paul exerted the pressure of his Roman citizenship. It was his way of showing the unfairness of their treatment in Philippi and removing any stain on the reputation of the gospel.

Bible Exploration   Acts 16:16-40

Have children turn in their Bibles to Acts 16:16. Ask a volunteer to read verse 16. Choose volunteers to act out some or all of these parts: Paul, Silas, the slave girl, owners of the slave girl, and the jailer. One or more children can be the crowd, one or more children can be the magistrates, and one or more children can be the other prisoners. (If possible, provide Bible-times costumes for children to wear.) You can tell the story in your own words, read it from your Bible, or play a dramatised version of it from the Internet. Whichever you do, give time for children to act. If the actors want to, they can repeat their lines after you. When finished, thank the children for their participation.

ASK: **If you had been in the same difficult situations as Paul and Silas, what do you think you would have done in prison? What would you have done when given the opportunity to escape from prison?** Accept responses.

Ask children to look at Activity page *Even in Prison*. Ask volunteers to read each sentence, then say what they would change in each sentence to make it true. (Answers: 1=cross out 'treated well' and write 'beaten'; 2=cross out 'danced' and write 'prayed'; 3=cross out 'all' and write 'none of'; 4=cross out 'Timothy' and write 'Silas'; 5=cross out 'idols' and write 'God')

ASK: **How did Paul and Silas live for Jesus, even in difficult situations?**
(They prayed and sang while in prison; they did not escape from prison when the earthquake caused the prison doors to fly open and their chains to come loose; they told the jailer about Jesus and how to be saved; they baptised the jailer and his family.)

SAY: **Paul and Silas were in some really difficult situations, probably more difficult and challenging situations than we'll ever face. They were beaten because they lived for Jesus. They were thrown into prison because they lived for Jesus. And yet they remained faithful, living for Jesus every step of the way. Paul and Silas chose to live for Jesus, even in difficult situations. They knew that nothing else was as important as living for Jesus. I hope that each of us will make that same choice.**

Materials
Bible map on page 244, reusable adhesive, Bibles, *Act It Out* Activity page *Even in Prison* on page 256, pencils (optional: Bible-times costumes)

Media Option
Record children acting out the Bible story. Let them watch it before leaving. Be sure to get consent from parents/carers.

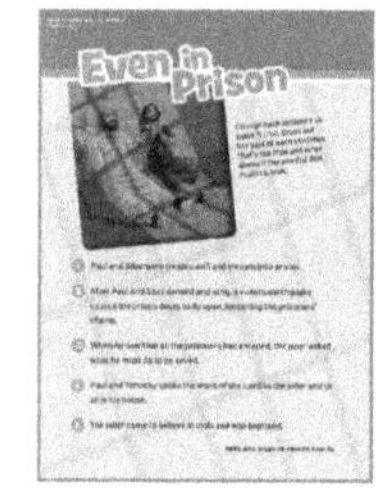

Make It Real

3 Use this activity to help children **discover ways they can live for Jesus, even in difficult situations.**

Materials

items children have with them (or items in your room), Activity pages *Difficult Situations* used earlier in the session, on pages 254-255, pencils, Bibles

Teaching Tip

If you have an uneven number of children, you can be someone's partner.

Difficult Situations

Ask children to find several unbreakable items that could be thrown around, such as coins, socks, and combs. Or let them use paper clips, tape rolls, and other items in the room. Have children pair up, stand about four feet apart, and throw one item back and forth. When pairs have mastered that, have them add a second item, throwing the items without stopping. Then challenge them to add a third item, then a fourth item. SAY: **Throwing and catching three, four, or more items seems fairly impossible without a lot of practice. That's kind of how living for Jesus can be. When we're in difficult situations, living for Jesus can, at times, seem fairly impossible.**

Ask children to look again at the Activity page *Difficult Situations*. Assign one or more situations to each pair of children. Tell children to read their assigned situations and the Scriptures listed. Then they should write on the lines how the children in their situations can live for Jesus. When all the children are ready, let them read their situations aloud, along with their answers. (There could be various ANSWERS: 1=don't steal answers, but do her own work; 2=don't covet, or really want, what others have; do right in God's eyes; 3=don't seek revenge, but love others; do right; 4=obey parents because it pleases God; 5=put hope in God; be patient; keep praying) SAY: **These are great ways to live for Jesus, even in difficult situations.**

Live It Out

4 Use this activity to help children **talk with God about how they want to live for Jesus, even in difficult situations.**

Materials

paper, scissors, clear tape, markers, reusable adhesive (or pushpins)

Before the Session

Cut sheets of paper into four long strips, each strip the same size. You'll need at least one strip per child.

 Be ready to offer help with writing or fine motor tasks as necessary.

Prayer Chain

SAY: **Paul and Silas are great examples of how to live for Jesus, even in difficult situations. They were in chains in prison, yet they sang and prayed to God. They were beaten and their feet were in stocks, yet they lived for Jesus.**

Each of us will go through difficult times when it's hard to live for Jesus. That's when we need to be like Paul and Silas and keep talking to God and praising Him. Let's make a chain, a prayer chain, to remind us to live for Jesus, even in difficult situations. Give each child one strip of paper. Ask children to write on their strips some of the difficult situations they're going through or others are going through (and that they won't mind others seeing). Some children might want to do a second strip of paper.

When children have finished, ask them to gather for a time of prayer, holding their strips of paper. Encourage children to silently talk to God and ask for His help so they can live for Jesus, even in difficult situations. After a brief time of silence, close in prayer. Then have children make a long chain of their strips. Put the prayer chain on a wall or bulletin board in your room.

Exodus 20:15; Ephesians 4:28

1

Anna's maths marks aren't very good. And the big test is tomorrow. She listens in session and tries to do the homework, but it's so hard! A friend has offered to let Anna copy her test, just this once.

How can Anna live for Jesus, even in this difficult situation?

____

____

Exodus 20:17; 2 Corinthians 8:21

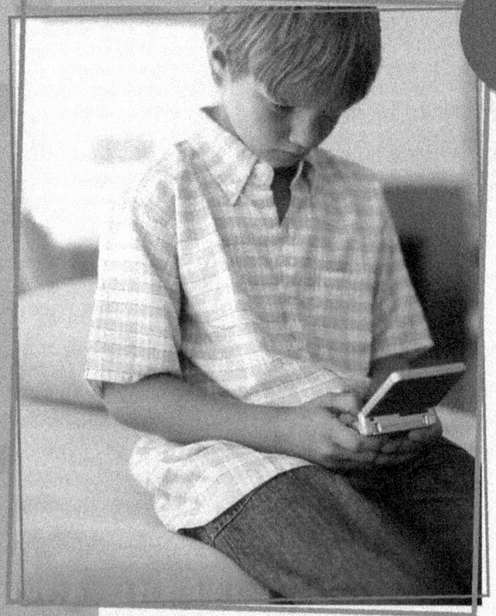

2

Joshua really wants a new video game, the one that ALL his friends have. But Joshua doesn't have enough money to buy it. A friend suggested a way he could get it without buying it. But Joshua knows that wouldn't be right.

How can Joshua live for Jesus, even in this difficult situation?

____

____

Leviticus 19:18; Romans 12:17-19, 21

3

Liam can't believe it—he has to wear glasses. And he has to wear them all the time. Some of the children have made fun of him and called him 'four eyes.'

How can Liam live for Jesus, even in this difficult situation?

____

____

Psalm 42:5; Romans 12:12

4

Hannah's parents have been fighting a lot. Hannah just found out that they are getting a divorce. They told her they love her but they just can't stay married.

How can Hannah live for Jesus, even in this difficult situation?

____

____

Change each sentence to make it true. Cross out the part of each sentence that's not true and write above it the word(s) that makes it true.

1. Paul and Silas were treated well and thrown into prison.

2. After Paul and Silas danced and sang, a violent earthquake caused the prison doors to fly open, loosening the prisoners' chains.

3. When he saw that all the prisoners had escaped, the jailer asked what he must do to be saved.

4. Paul and Timothy spoke the word of the Lord to the jailer and to all in his house.

5. The jailer came to believe in idols and was baptised.

Eutychus Raised

Session 42

Scripture: Acts 20:7-12
Focus: God comforts His followers.

Heart to Heart Teacher Devotion

God shows His care and comfort in both big and small ways. His daily expressions of care can sometimes get overlooked in light of the more dramatic, but He is always there, comforting in ways we may not be aware of. God can work through e-mails, hugs, prayers and thoughtful words to bring comfort. Let's thank Him for bringing comfort, even in the midst of a hectic day.

Focus
God comforts His followers.

Materials

large bag filled with items (cereal box [representing food], stuffed animal, Bible, blanket, mobile phone, book, football or tennis ball, music CD, picture of parents [representing families], picture of children [representing friends])

Children with anxiety or sensitivity issues may be hesitant to reach inside a bag full of unknown items. You could pull out the item so they can see it first.

Focus In

1 Use this activity to help children **explore ways people are comforted.**

Welcome

Welcome each child warmly by name.

Bag of Comfort

Have children gather in a circle. SAY: **In this bag are all kinds of items that represent things or people that could bring us comfort. Whether we're sad or frustrated or upset, we all need to be comforted at one time or another. Volunteers can reach into the bag, take one item, and tell how it could bring comfort to someone.** Have the first volunteer reach into the bag and take out an item. Be sure that all children who want to participate have the opportunity.

ASK: **What are some things you like to have or like to do when you need to be comforted?** Accept responses.
What are some ways your family and friends comfort you?

SAY: **Let's see what the Bible says about a time when some people needed to be comforted.**

Focus
God comforts His followers.

Explore His Word

2 Use these activities to help children **tell what happened when the believers in Troas came together.**

Bible Background for the Teacher

Paul and Silas were on Paul's third missionary journey when they boarded a boat at Philippi bound for Troas. The phrase that says they 'came together to break bread' (v. 7) implies the observance of the Lord's Supper, though the context provides clues that a full meal may have been included (see 20:11; compare 1 Corinthians 11:20-22).

The occasion demanded that time be taken to listen to Paul, but as the hours wore on, one worshipper, Eutychus, had trouble keeping his eyes open. The mention of the lamps may help us understand the young man's difficulty, since the burning oil would have produced a warm and heavy air. Sitting on a window ledge with no glass made the situation dangerous, and the fall to the ground below killed him. Paul wasted no time in rushing to the boy's assistance. The apostle 'threw himself on' Eutychus and raised him from death. The same divine power that had energised Peter's ministry in Joppa when Tabitha was raised to life (Acts 9:36-43) was now at work in Troas in the ministry of the apostle Paul. After such an event, the disciples found new reasons to go back upstairs and worship God through the breaking of bread and listening to Paul teach from God's Word.

Bible Exploration   Acts 20:7-12

Ask a volunteer to stand by the Bible time line and point out the icon for 'Paul & Silas in prison.' Ask who would like to summarise that Bible story. Then SAY: **This is where we pick up God's story.** Ask a volunteer to stand by the map and point out the cities you mention. **Paul and other disciples of Jesus continued traveling and telling everyone about Jesus. They had traveled to Thessalonica, Berea, Athens, Corinth, and Ephesus. In today's lesson, they are in Troas.** Have another volunteer move the Paul figure to Troas. **Paul has been in Troas for seven days. Today's account begins on the last day of his stay there, a Sunday, when the Christians at Troas gathered to worship God. Let's find out what happened.** Have children turn in their Bibles to the contents page. For Bibles on a tablet, phone, or e-reader, children can open to the contents page. Ask them to look in the New Testament section and find the book of Acts.

Have children turn in their Bibles to Acts 20:7-12, and have volunteers read the verses aloud. Invite any questions about the Scripture passage. Remind children that back in Bible times windows did not have glass. Then ask children to close their Bibles and pair up. SAY: **I'm going to retell the events we just read about. But I'm going to deliberately tell you some things that are wrong. When you and your partner hear something wrong, raise your hands. I'll call on a pair of you to tell what I said wrong and what I should have said. Ready? On the second day of the week, the Christians met together.** (Wrong—It was the first day of the week, Sunday.) **The Christians met together to break bread, to partake of the Lord's Supper, and worship God. Jonah spoke to the people because he was leaving the next day.** (Wrong—It was Paul.) **Paul talked on and on until 2:00 in the morning.** (Wrong—It was midnight.) **There were lots of lamps in the upstairs room where they were meeting. A young man named Ethan sat in a window located on the third story.** (Wrong—It was Eutychus.)

SAY: **Eutychus went to sleep and fell to the ground. He was OK!** (Wrong—He was dead.) **Paul went to Eutychus, threw himself on him, and put his arms around him. Paul told everyone not to be afraid. Eutychus was already in Heaven.** (Wrong—Eutychus was alive.) **Paul, Eutychus, and all the believers went back upstairs. Paul kept talking until daylight; then he stayed another week.** (Wrong—Paul left.) **The people were comforted because Michael was alive.** (Wrong—It was Eutychus.) Ask children to look at Activity page *Paul and Eutychus.* Ask volunteers to read the sentences, filling in the blanks with the correct words. (Answers: 1=first; 2=midnight; 3=sleep; 4=dead; 5=bread; 6=comforted)

ASK: **Why did the Christians in Troas need to be comforted?** (Eutychus had fallen out of the window and died.)
  How did God comfort them? (God worked through Paul to bring Eutychus back to life.)

SAY: **God comforts His followers, and that's what He did when He worked through Paul to bring Eutychus back to life.**

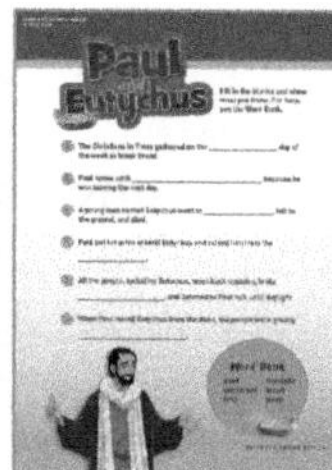

Make It Real

3 Use this activity to help children **discover ways God comforts His followers.**

Materials

Activity page *God Gives Comfort* on page 261, pencils, whiteboard, whiteboard marker pen.

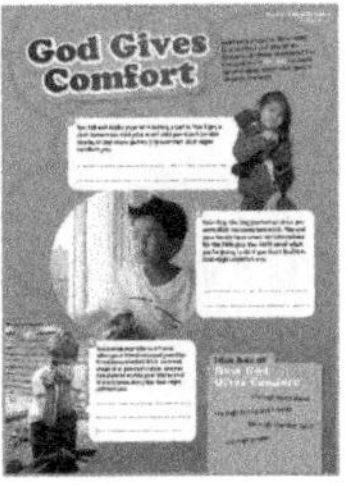

God Gives Comfort

SAY: **God brought a lot of comfort to His followers when He worked through Paul to bring Eutychus back to life. Let's think about ways God comforts His followers today.** Form two teams. Hand out Activity page *God Gives Comfort*. **Look at situation 1.** Have a volunteer read it aloud. **That's a tough situation! Huddle up in your teams and come up with at least one specific way that God might comfort you in that situation. There are general ideas listed in the Idea Box. But your ideas must be specific. For each good, specific idea, your team gets 100 points.** When teams are ready, let them share their ideas. Keep track of points on the board. Tell children to choose the ideas they like best and write them in their activity leaflets. Do the same for the other three situations.

ASK: **When has God comforted you through family and friends? through the Holy Spirit? through Scriptures? through prayer?** If children have a hard time coming up with times, tell them to think about times they've been sad or going through a tough time.

SAY: **Knowing that God comforts His followers can help us get through tough times that come our way.**

Live It Out

4 Use this activity to help children **thank God for the comfort He gives and share His comfort with others.**

Materials

Activity page *Comfort Challenge* on page 262, pencils, Bible

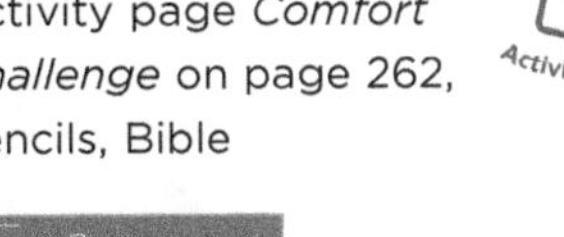

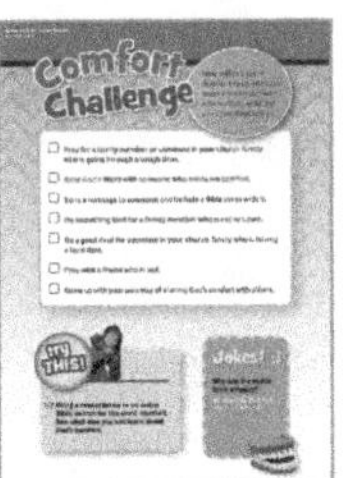

Comfort Challenge

SAY: **One way God comforts His followers is through other Christians. God can work through *us* to bring His comfort to others.** Ask children to look at Activity page *Comfort Challenge*. Read the directions, and give children time to put ticks next to the ways they'd like to try thanking God for His comfort and sharing it with others. Let volunteers share a few things they checked. SAY: **I noticed that for most of these you don't need to go anywhere different from where you already go. I noticed that these are all things children your age can do. I noticed that some of you already do some of these things! I noticed that all of these need your time. And of course, I noticed that when you do these things, you're showing you believe that God comforts His followers.**

Ask children to gather for a time of prayer. Read 2 Corinthians 1:3-4 aloud. Then have several volunteers pray aloud. Encourage some to thank God for the many ways God comforts His followers. Encourage others to ask for God's help in sharing His comfort with others. Invite all children to pray silently with those who are praying aloud. Encourage children to follow through on their plans of sharing God's comfort with others.

Fill in the blanks and show what you know. For help, see the Word Bank.

1. The Christians in Troas gathered on the _________________ day of the week to break bread.

2. Paul spoke until _________________________________ because he was leaving the next day.

3. A young man named Eutychus went to _________________, fell to the ground, and died.

4. Paul put his arms around Eutychus and raised him from the

   _________________.

5. All the people, including Eutychus, went back upstairs, broke

   _________________________, and listened to Paul talk until daylight.

6. When Paul raised Eutychus from the dead, the people were greatly

   _____________________________.

Word Bank

dead	midnight
comforted	bread
first	sleep

Rather than photocopy this page you can download and print all activity pages in both colour and black & white from **www.heartshaper.co.uk**

God Gives Comfort

Read each situation. How might God comfort you, one of His followers, in these situations? You can look in the Idea Box for some general ideas. Write your specific ideas on the lines.

1 You fell and broke your arm during a game. You'll get a cast tomorrow, and your mom said you won't be able to play in any more games this summer. God might comfort you

____

____

2 Your dog, the dog you've had since you were little, ran away last week. You and your family have searched everywhere for the little guy. You don't know what you're going to do if you don't find him. God might comfort you

____

____

____

3 You loaned your bike to a friend. When your friend returned your bike, it had been wrecked. It's in such bad shape that you can't ride it. And you had planned to ride your bike to your friend's home every day. God might comfort you

____

____

Idea Box of How God Gives Comfort

through God's Word

through family and friends

through the Holy Spirit

through prayer

HeartShaper Primary Blue Edition, Activity page
Permission is granted to reproduce this page for ministry purposes only—not for resale.

Comfort Challenge

How will you thank God for His comfort and share His comfort with others? Put a ✔ by the ones you want to try.

- ☐ Pray for a family member or someone in your church family who is going through a tough time.

- ☐ Read God's Word with someone who needs His comfort.

- ☐ Send a message to someone and include a Bible verse with it.

- ☐ Do something kind for a family member who is sad or upset.

- ☐ Do a good deed for someone in your church family who is having a hard time.

- ☐ Pray with a friend who is sad.

- ☐ Come up with your own way of sharing God's comfort with others.

try THIS!

⇨ **Using a concordance or an online Bible, search for the word *comfort*. See what else you can learn about God's comfort.**

Jokes! :)

Why was the maths book unhappy?

Because he had too many problems!

When should a mouse carry an umbrella?

When it's raining cats and dogs!

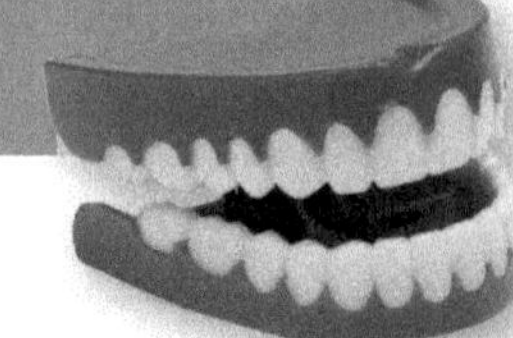

Plot to Kill Paul

Scripture: Acts 23:1-12, 16-24, 31
Focus: God encourages and protects His followers.

Heart to Heart Teacher Devotion

When the cares of everyday life weigh us down, there's no encouragement like the encouragement God gives through His Word, His Holy Spirit, and other people. When we need protection from Satan's fiery darts, there's no protection like the protection God gives through His power. As we daily look to God for encouragement and protection, He will provide!

Focus
God encourages and protects His followers.

Materials
none

Action

Media Option
Go online to www.british-sign.co.uk which shows British Sign Language.

Focus In

1 Use this activity to help children **explore ways people encourage and protect each other.**

Welcome

Welcome each child warmly by name.

Encourager or Protector?

Show children an action for *encourage*: both hands push forward as if pushing someone forward. Have children practice that. Then show them an action for *protect*: the hands, clenched into fists, cross and are locked in a defensive position. SAY: **I'm going to read some situations. If a situation tells about a person encouraging someone, do the action for *encourage*. It if tells about a person protecting someone, do the action for *protect*.** Read the situations from the printable file.

• Sara noticed that a girl at school looked like she was falling off the play equipment. Sara ran over to see if she needed help. *(protect)*
• Steven patiently listened while his friend told him about a problem at home. *(encourage)*
• James ran over to help his sister when a bully picked on her. *(protect)*
• Megan showed support to a friend who didn't make the cricket team. *(encourage)*

ASK: **How do people encourage each other?** (listen; support; say 'You can do it'; help; motivate someone to do something)
How do people protect each other? (keep someone from getting hurt; keep someone safe from bullies; follow rules)

SAY: **Let's dig into the Bible and see what happened when one of God's followers needed encouragement and protection.**

Explore His Word

2 Use these activities to help children **describe what happened when some Jews plotted against Paul.**

Bible Background for the Teacher

Paul now stood before the same assembly that had crucified Jesus and martyred Stephen (Matthew 26:59; Acts 6:15). Nevertheless, because he knew the doctrinal divisions between the Sadducees and Pharisees in the Sanhedrin, Paul proclaimed his background as a Pharisee and his strong belief in the resurrection of the dead.

Paul remained a prisoner. The voice of Jesus came to Paul during the night, encouraging Paul that he would also teach about Jesus in Rome. Protection from the Lord also came by means of Paul's nephew. In a rare glimpse into Paul's family life, Luke records how the son of Paul's sister heard about a plot to murder his uncle and how he reported this to the Roman commander. Claudius Lysias sprang into action, ordering that Paul be transported to Caesarea by a detachment of 470 soldiers (23:23-24) in order to make sure that this Roman citizen was not harmed by mob action.

Bible Exploration   Acts 23:1-12, 16-24, 31

Ask children to turn to Acts 23:1. Have a volunteer show where these places are on the map: Jerusalem, Rome, Caesarea, and Antipatris. Tell children that these places are mentioned in today's Bible story. Let another volunteer attach the Paul figure by Jerusalem. Direct childrens' attention to the 'Eutychus raised' icon on the Bible time line. SAY: **After Paul raised Eutychus from the dead, he continued travelling, teaching about Jesus everywhere he went. Then he went to Jerusalem. Paul was arrested for teaching about Jesus, but then released. The Roman commander wanted to find out why Paul was being accused by the Jews. This is where we pick up God's story.** Have a volunteer read Acts 23:1 aloud. **The Sanhedrin was the Jewish supreme court. Let's find out what happened to Paul and why he needed God's encouragement and protection.**

Choose seven or more volunteers to read or act it out. You'll need volunteers to act (or read) the parts of Paul, people near Paul, Pharisees, voice of the Lord, centurion, commander, and Paul's nephew. When finished, thank the children for their participation. Let a volunteer move the Paul figure on the map from Jerusalem to Antipatris.

Ask children to look at Activity page *The Plot Against Paul*. Have volunteers read the sentences, choosing and reading the correct answers. (Answers: 1=the resurrection of the dead; 2=Pharisees; 3=take courage; 4=eat or drink; 5=barracks; 6=ambush him; 7=200; 8=carried out) Encourage everyone to circle the correct answers.

ASK: **How did God encourage Paul?** (The Lord spoke to Paul and told Paul that he would speak about Him in Rome.) Be sure that children understand that this meant Paul's life, at this time, would be spared, and he would live to travel to Rome to tell people there about God.

    How did God protect Paul? (God worked through Paul's nephew, the centurion, and the commander to protect Paul. The commander ordered that Paul be taken during the night so the Jews who were going to ambush and kill him wouldn't have the opportunity.)

SAY: **God encourages and protects His followers today too. Let's discover how He might do that.**

Materials
Bibles, Bible map from page 244, reusable adhesive, Activity pages *The Plot Against Paul* on pages 266-267, pencils

Make It Real

3 Use this activity to help children **discover ways God encourages and protects His followers.**

Materials

apples, knife, 2 plates, lemon juice, Bibles 

Object Lesson

Before the Session

Preferably up to an hour before the session begins, cut an apple into slices. Put several slices on each plate. Pour lemon juice over the apple slices on one plate.

God's Preservers

Show children both plates of apple slices. The slices without lemon juice should be noticeably brown.

ASK: **Why do you think that the apples on one plate look great, but the others look brown and yucky?** Accept responses.

SAY: **I put a preservative, or preserver, of lemon juice on the great-looking apple slices. The other apples didn't get the preserver.** Give out apple slices for children to enjoy. **The ways that God encourages and protects His followers are like a preservative, or preserver.** Ask volunteers to read Romans 1:12 and 15:4. **God encourages us through the Scriptures and through each other's faith. When we're discouraged because of a situation at school or home, we can look to the Bible for help. When we need encouragement to speak up for Jesus, we can look at the faith others have.** Ask volunteers to read Psalm 40:11 and 2 Thessalonians 3:3. **God protects us by His love and faithfulness and by the strength He gives us. When we need protection from bad stuff on the internet, God can surround us with His love and faithfulness. When we need protection from people saying bad words about us, God can give us strength to deal with it wisely.**

Focus
God encourages and
protects His followers.

Live It Out

4 Use this activity to help children **ask for God's encouragement and protection.**

Materials

Activity Page *Shields* on page 268 (each child needs 1 shield), card stock, scissors, markers, foil, glue sticks, pencils, Bibles 

Craft

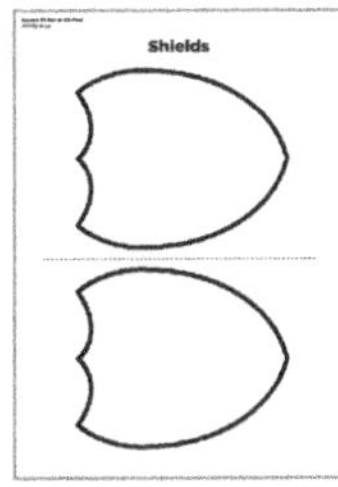

Shield Reminders

SAY: **Paul needed God's encouragement and protection, and so do we. We all go through times of discouragement and times when we need protection.** Give each child a shield. **This shield can help you remember to ask for God's encouragement and His protection.** Tell children to turn in their Bibles to 2 Thessalonians 2:16-17; 3:3. They can write those Scriptures (or key phrases) on one side of their shields. Then children can cut foil to cover the other side, gluing it onto their shields.

SAY: **Hold up your shields, and together we'll read the Scriptures you wrote on them. Then silently pray, asking God for His encouragement and protection in specific situations.** After a brief time of silence, close in prayer.

Before the Session

Make copies of the shields on card stock.

 Offer to assist with fine-motor skills as needed. Have extra copies available, in case children need have another try on their shields.

The Plot Against Paul

Show what you know about what happened to Paul. Circle the correct answers.

1. Paul told the Sanhedrin that he had fulfilled his duty to God and was on trial because of his hope in rainbows / the resurrection of the dead.

2. When a big dispute broke out between the Sadducees and the Pharisees / Philistines, the commander ordered that Paul be taken into the barracks.

3. The Lord told Paul to sing / take courage because Paul would testify about Him in Rome.

4. The Jews plotted against Paul. They decided not to laugh or cry / eat or drink until they had killed Paul.

5 When Paul's nephew heard about the plot to kill Paul, the nephew went to the barracks / park and told Paul.

6 Paul's nephew told the commander about the plot to kill Paul. Forty Jews were waiting to give him a party / ambush him.

7 The commander ordered that 2 / 200 soldiers, 70 horsemen, and 200 spearmen deliver Paul safely to Governor Felix during the night.

8 The soldiers carried out / disobeyed their orders. They took Paul during the night to Antipatris.

Shields

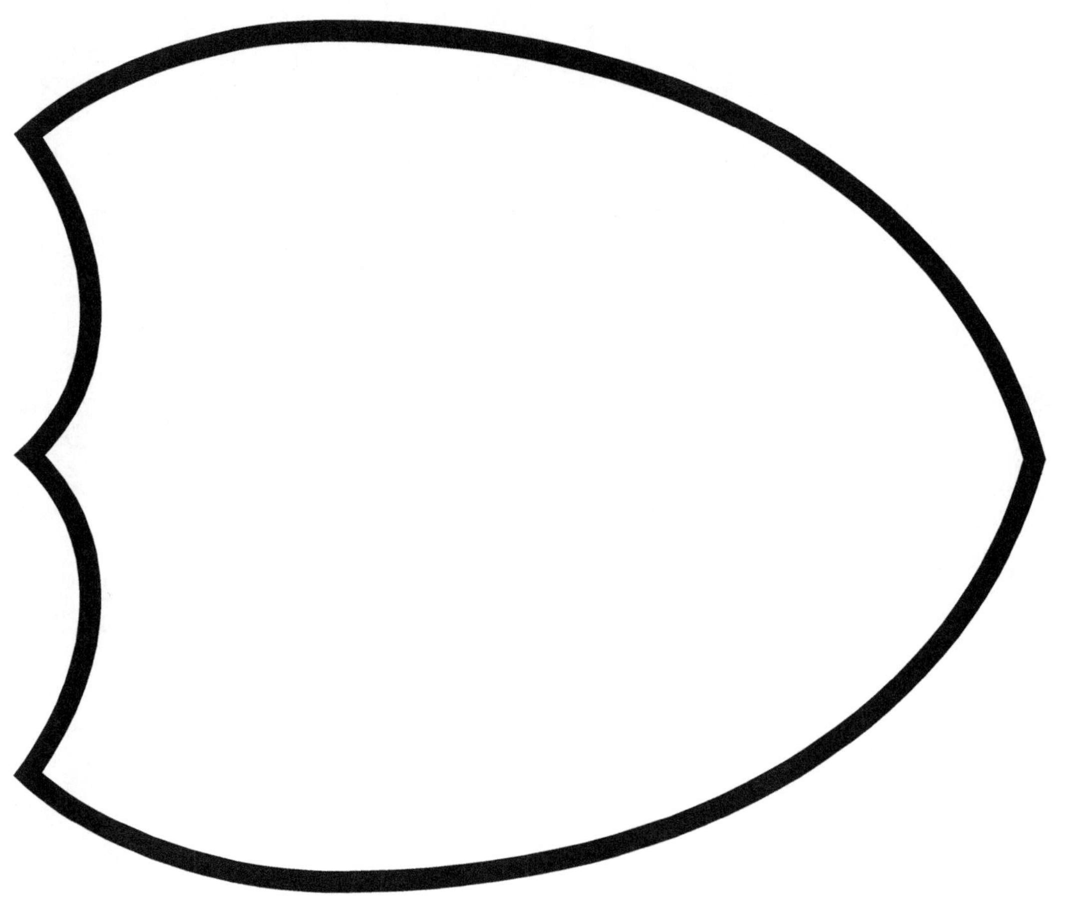

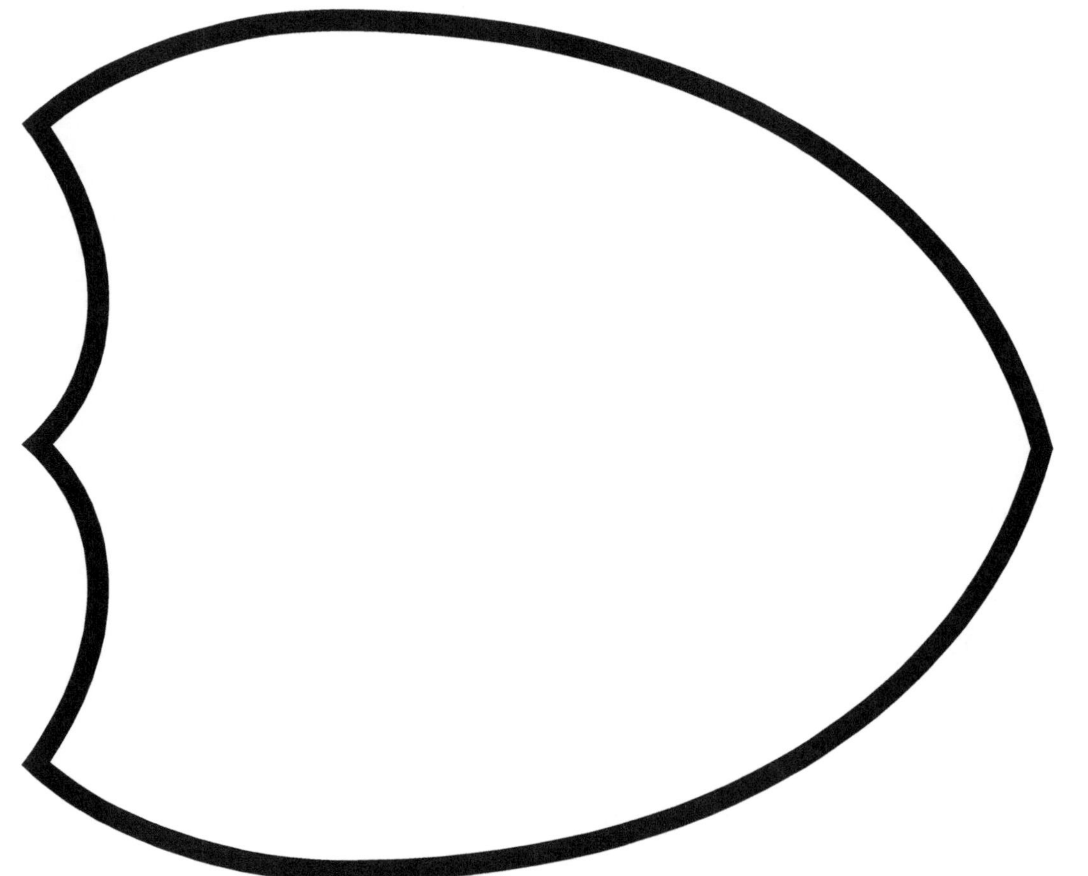

Paul's Journey to Rome

Session 44

Scripture: Acts 27:1, 6-7, 9-11, 13-15, 18-25, 41-44; 28:16, 30-31
Focus: God knows how things will turn out.

Heart to Heart Teacher Devotion

Have you ever seen the back side of a tapestry or something that's been embroidered? It's usually messy, isn't it? You would think that whatever is on the other side would be equally messy—but it's not. The other side is the beautiful finished picture. Sounds like our lives, doesn't it? Through the day in and day out of living, our lives can seem messy. But when our lives as followers of Christ are finished, we'll see the beautifully completed picture. That's why we trust the one who knows how things will turn out.

Focus
God knows how things will turn out.

Materials
self-stick notes, pencils

Write

Teaching Tip
Some children may write about the serious ill-health of a family member. Be sensitive to this and check whether or not they want to post their note up.

Focus In

❶ Use this activity to help children **explore situations in which they don't know how things will turn out.**

Welcome

Welcome each child warmly by name.

How Will It Turn Out?

Give each child several self-stick notes. SAY: **Write on each note a situation where you don't know how it will end. Maybe it's a big sports match this week or whether or not a friend is moving or your family holiday. It can be any situation that you don't know how it will turn out.** Tell children to stick their finished notes on a wall (or wherever you want the notes to go).

SAY: **Now decide how to group the notes. Maybe you can put all of the friend-related situations together, all the family stuff together, all the sports stuff together, and so on.** After children have grouped the notes, talk about the groupings and some specific situations. **Look at all the times we *don't* know how things will turn out. Let's dig into God's Word to find out who *does* know how things will turn out.**

Focus
God knows how things will turn out.

Explore His Word

❷ Use these activities to help children **tell about Paul's journey to Rome.**

Bible Background for the Teacher

Because Paul appealed to Caesar (25:11), he was transported as a prisoner to Rome from Caesarea. Paul was boarded on a Roman merchant grain vessel sailing against the prevailing winds on its way to Rome. The danger in this voyage was the time of year, and Roman sea-lanes were considered closed from the late autumn months to early spring. Paul's ship was sailing 'after the Day of Atonement' (v. 9), which was a day of fasting observed as a Jewish holiday in late September or early October.

Reaching the south shore of the island of Crete, it seemed as if the 'gentle south wind' was just what they needed. But after setting sail, a typhoon-like wind struck the vessel with such force that they could not even turn the ship, and they were helplessly 'driven along'. For fourteen days (Acts 27:27) this storm had the crew doing everything possible to keep the vessel afloat, including passing cables under the hull (v. 17) and throwing overboard the cargo to keep the ship high in the water (vv. 18-19). Meanwhile, God promised Paul that he would stand before Caesar, and Paul passed this encouragement on to the crew and prisoners. After the ship ran aground on Malta and all 276 were saved, they waited three months for another vessel. Arriving in Rome, Paul was placed in light Roman custody, which allowed him to receive visitors. The last words of Acts tell us that Paul continued preaching about the kingdom of God without hindrance for two whole years.

Bible Exploration   Acts 27:1, 6-7, 9-11, 13-15, 18-25, 41-44; 28:16, 30-31

Have a volunteer stand by the map and point out Italy, Rome, Cnidus, and Crete. Tell children that these places are mentioned in today's Bible story. Have another volunteer stand by the Bible time line and point to the 'Instructions from Romans' icon.

Ask children to turn in their Bibles to Acts 26:32-27:1. SAY: **Since Caesar was in Rome, that's where Paul, as a prisoner, headed. The journey to Rome would be a long one—no train or plane or car to get there. The journey had some high points—meaning that something good happened. When you hear about a high point, raise your hands up high.** Have the children do this. **The journey also had some low points— meaning that something not so good happened. When you hear a low point, put your hands down low.** Have the children do this. **The journey also had some so-so times, meaning that something not really good or bad happened. When you hear about a so-so time, put your hands in between.** Have the children do this.

Ask for a volunteer or two to stand in front and lead everyone in doing the motions. Have another volunteer move the Paul figure on the map as you read. Read the Scripture passage aloud. Pause where needed so that children can do the motions. Emphasise and explain any parts the children seem confused about. Make sure you emphasise Acts 27:25 and Acts 28:16, 30-31. When finished, thank everyone for participating. Hand out the Activity page *Paul's Journal*. Have volunteers read the sentences, filling in the blanks or let children do it together in small groups. (Answers: storm; angel; faith; Rome; soldier; Jesus)

ASK: **What were some low points in today's Scripture passage?** (Paul was a prisoner; the centurion didn't listen to Paul; a dangerous storm came up)
  What were some high points? (An angel of God spoke to Paul and told him not to be afraid; when the ship ran aground, Paul and everyone on board were saved; Paul was allowed to live by himself, and for two years he preached about God)
  Who knew how things would turn out for Paul? (God)
  In the middle of the storm, how did Paul show that he trusted God? (Paul said that he had faith in God, that everything would happen just as the angel had told him)

SAY: **Paul lived an exciting, yet dangerous, life for God. While he seldom knew how things would turn out, Paul served the only one who does! Paul learned time after time that God knows how things will turn out. That helped Paul trust God, whether as a prisoner on a ship in the middle of a dangerous storm, or in a rented house in Rome.**

Materials
Bible map from page 244, sticky tape, Bibles, Activity pages *Paul's Journal* on pages 272-273, pencils

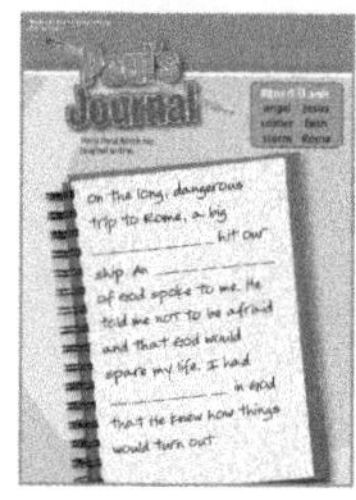
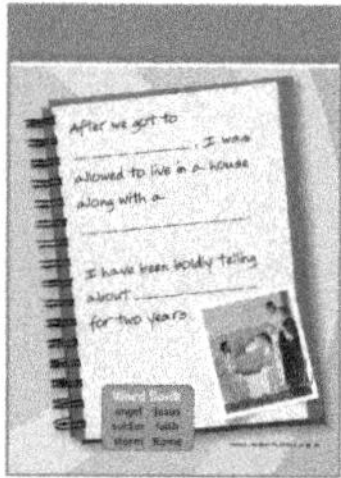

Media Option
Go to www.biblegateway.com or a similar website and play a dramatised reading of the Bible verses.

Make It Real

3 Use this activity to help children **discuss situations in which they need to have faith in God.**

Materials

very sour sweets or slices of lemon, roll paper (1 length per each group), pencils, markers

Object Lesson

This multisensory activity will engage most children. Consider that some children really won't try the lemon slice. Then follow up with a sweet fruit or sweet hard-boiled sweet for the 'sweet truth.' Be careful of food allergies or intolerances.

Sour Situations

Ask a volunteer to taste a sour sweet or lemon slice while the other children watch. Whisper to the volunteer to exaggerate his or her reaction to the sourness, making a sour face. SAY: **Even though Paul was in a really difficult, or sour, situation, I don't think he made a sour face—because he said that he had faith in God. Paul trusted God and had faith that things would turn out as God said they would. When do we need to have faith in God?**

Divide the session into two groups, and give each group a length of roll paper, pencils, and markers. Give each child a sour sweet or lemon slice. Explain that, as children taste it, each group is to create a poster.

SAY: **Your posters are to answer two questions:** 1. **What sour situation has someone in your group been in that required faith in God to get through it?** 2. **How did having faith in God make a difference?** Tell children they can write out their responses, draw their responses, or do both. If some groups finish early, encourage them to list or draw more situations. When the groups have finished, let them share their posters.

SAY: **While we seldom know how things will turn out, we can serve the only one who does know! Remembering that God knows how things will turn out will help us have faith in Him.**

Live It Out

4 Use this activity to help children **develop a plan for having faith in God.**

Materials

jigsaw puzzle with box, whiteboard, dry-erase markers and erasers

Object Lesson

For children with cognitive disabilities, consider one-on-one help. Ask yes and no questions, or provide a modified activity that will be more understandable.

Teaching Tip

If you prefer not to do Puzzling Lives activity or you have extra time, use the Activity page *Paul's Post* on page 274.

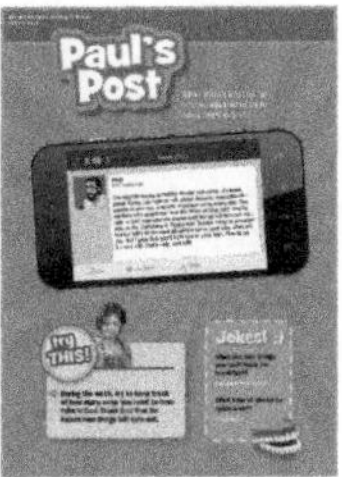

Puzzling Lives

Give each child a puzzle piece. Be sure not to let children see the box lid. Ask children to look at just their puzzle pieces and guess what the finished puzzle looks like. After children take a few guesses, talk about how they have to trust you that their puzzle pieces will fit together and that the pieces form a puzzle. Then reveal the box lid showing the finished puzzle. SAY: **Our lives are sort of like puzzle pieces. We don't know how things will turn out, because we only see little pieces of what's going on. That's where faith in God comes in. We should have faith because God knows how things will turn out and we don't! That was true of Paul's life, and it's true of our lives too.**

SAY: **Let's think about things we can do to show faith in God, especially in tough situations. When you have an idea, get a marker and write your idea on the board.** Tell children they can work with a partner if they'd like to. (Possible responses: think about the situation; see what the Bible says; pray about it; talk to a parent or other trusted Christian adult; trust God and do what He wants you to do) When children are finished, summarise their ideas and add any important ideas children may have left out. Close your session time in prayer. SAY: **Pray silently, and thank God that He knows how things will turn out. Ask God to help you stay faithful, no matter what comes your way.** After a brief time of silence, close in prayer. If possible, allow children to take home their puzzle pieces as reminders of the day's lesson. Children may want to print 'Have faith' or 'God knows' on the back of their pieces.

Paul's Journal

Help Paul finish his journal entry.

On the long, dangerous trip to Rome, a big ______________ hit our ship. An ______________ of God spoke to me. He told me not to be afraid and that God would spare my life. I had ______________ in God that He knew how things would turn out.

After we got to
______________, I was
allowed to live in a house
along with a
______________.

I have been boldly telling
about ______________
for two years.

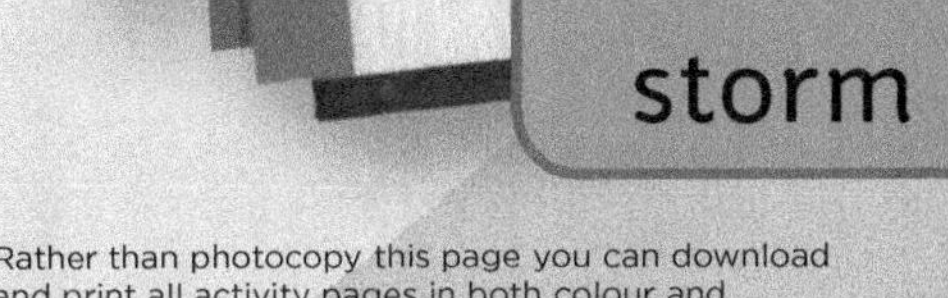

Word Bank

angel	Jesus
soldier	faith
storm	Rome

Read Paul's post as he encourages all of us to have faith in God.

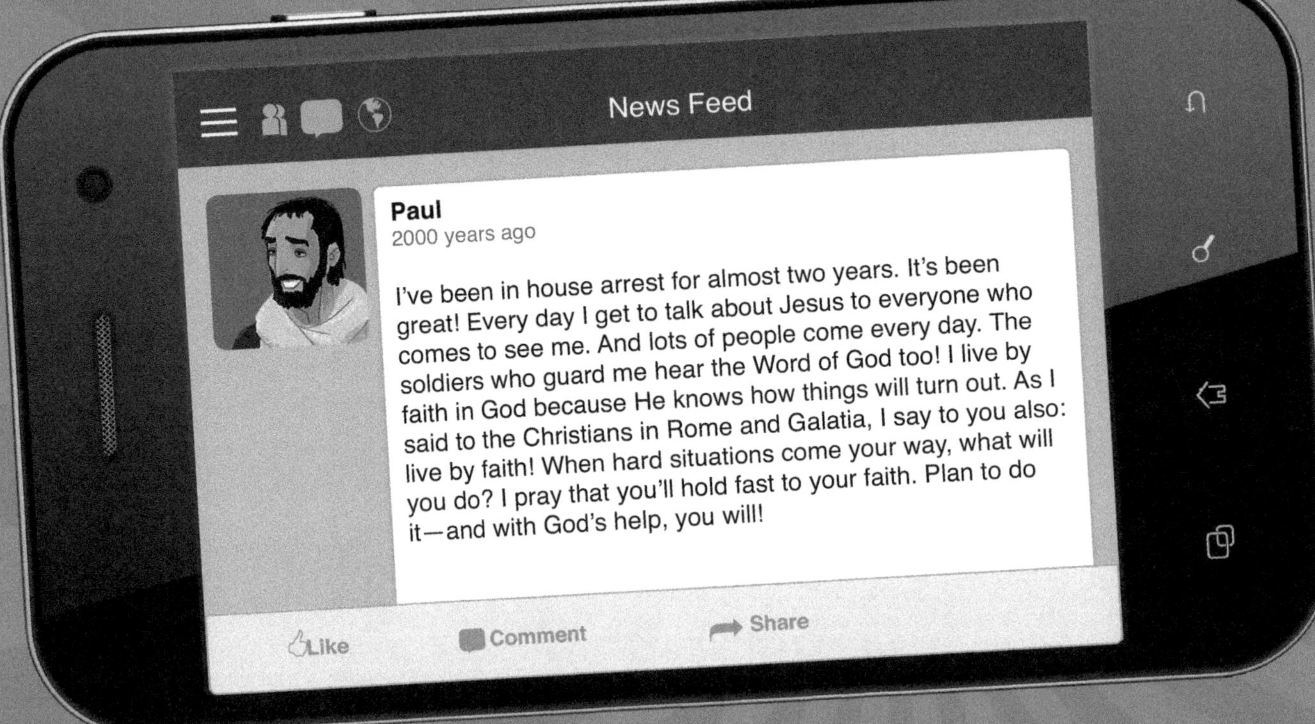

➡ **During the week, try to keep track of how many ways you need to have faith in God. Thank God that He knows how things will turn out.**

Jokes! :)

What are two things you can't have for breakfast?

Lunch and dinner!

What kind of shoes do spies wear?

Sneakers!

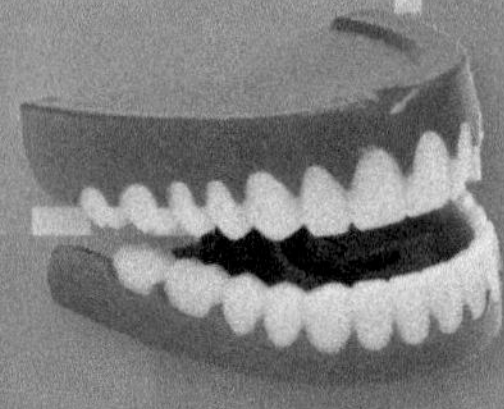

Paul Tells About Jesus in Rome

Scripture: Acts 28:11-17, 23-24, 30-31; Philippians 1:12-13
Focus: We can tell about Jesus in everyday places.

Heart to Heart Teacher Devotion

Today's lesson takes us to Paul's home in Rome—a temporary one, but a home. True to form he acted no differently than the Bible tells us he acted in other places—he started telling everyone about Jesus! Paul wrote letters to old friends, but he also talked with those people who showed up at his home. No matter what, when, or where, Paul testified of Jesus. May God help us to do nothing less, as nothing matters more!

Focus
We can tell about Jesus in everyday places.

Materials
none

Game

Added Fun!
Steps for the game can include baby steps, giant steps, or scissor steps. Children will also enjoy steps such as a frog leap, crab walk, or kangaroo hop. If time allows, let the children take turns being the soldier.

Focus In

(1) Use this activity to help children **explore what life might have been like for Paul in Rome**.

Welcome

Welcome each child warmly by name.

'Soldier, May We?'

Have children gather, and explain that they are going to play a game. In this game the leader is a soldier. Have the children line up on the opposite side of the room. Let the children take turns asking 'Soldier, may we _______?' and filling the blank with a suggested movement. For example, one child might ask, 'Soldier, may we take five steps forward?' You can reply, 'Yes, you may' or 'No, you may not, but you may take _______ instead' and add a suggestion. All the children must then do whatever you command, even if it leads them farther from the goal of reaching you. Eventually give approval to a request that allows all children to reach you.

ASK: **How did it feel to have to get my permission for every move that you made?**

SAY: **In today's Bible story, soldiers guarded Paul in his house. These soldiers allowed Paul to tell others about Jesus. We can tell others about Jesus in everyday places too.**

Explore His Word

2 Use these activities to help children **tell what Paul did when he was under house arrest in Rome.**

Bible Background for the Teacher

The last two chapters of Acts record the fulfillment of Paul's great desire to go to Rome. Paul was sent to Rome for his trial, since he was a citizen of Rome by birth. Once in Rome, Paul was allowed to live in a rented home. He seemed to have more freedom than a regular prisoner, although there was always a soldier to guard him. While a prisoner, Paul wrote letters to churches and spent time talking to the Jewish leaders. Though the book of Acts comes to a sudden end, the writer, Luke, summarises by saying that Paul continued to preach boldly about Jesus.

Bible Exploration   Acts 28:11-17, 23-24, 30-31; Philippians 1:12-13

Help children turn to Acts 28:11, and ask for a volunteer to read the verse. SAY: **Paul was sent to Rome to be put on trial.** Point to the Bible map. **Let's find out why Paul was in Rome and why there was always a soldier to guard him. Listen for how Paul told about Jesus.**

It all started when Paul was telling people about Jesus. Paul was in the temple in Jerusalem, and men started shouting lies about him. Since Paul was a Roman citizen, he had the right to have the emperor of Rome be the judge at his trial. That's why Paul was sent by ship all the way to Rome, the capital city. When Paul finally made it to Rome, he lived in a rented house for two years. Paul was still a prisoner, so a soldier always guarded Paul as he waited for his trial to begin. Paul probably had chains on his wrists or ankles.

Let's find out what Paul did. Ask a child to open the first scroll. Read what is written on the scroll: 'Paul wrote letters.' **Paul couldn't travel to churches to tell them about Jesus, but he could write letters to the churches. Paul sent letters that told the people the right way to live. These letters are now some of the books in the New Testament. So Paul is still helping people learn about Jesus!**

What else could Paul do in his house? Open the second scroll, and read it: 'Paul welcomed and talked to guests.' **Every day people came to Paul's house and he explained things about God and Jesus. Some people believed, and some did not. But Paul kept on talking about Jesus. Paul did something else to tell about Jesus too.** Open the third scroll and read it: 'Paul set an example for the guards.' **Even though there was always a Roman soldier guarding Paul, Paul boldly told those who came to see him about the kingdom of God. Soon all the palace guard had heard about Jesus!**

Why could Paul do all these things for Jesus? Let's open one more scroll. It will tell us something Paul wrote. Open the fourth scroll and read it: 'I can do all this through him who gives me strength' (Philippians 4:13). **Paul could do all these things because he trusted Jesus, and Jesus gave him strength!**

Hand out the Activity page *Paul Tells About Jesus* on page 279 and do the page together as a big group.

Materials

whiteboard; dry-erase marker; Bibles; Map of Paul's Travels from page 244; 4 rubber bands; marker; reusable adhesive (or self-adhesive magnetic strip)

Before the Session

Photocopy and cut out the 4 scrolls included on the *Paul's Everyday Way* Activity page on page 278. Roll and put a rubber band around each page, making the pages resemble rolled scrolls. Number the scrolls 1 to 4 so you will know the order in which to open them. Display the Bible map on a wall, bulletin board, or whiteboard.

 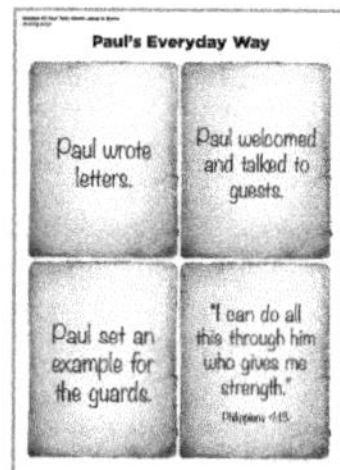

Materials

Activity page *Paul Tells About Jesus* on page 279, pencils (optional: whiteboard, dry-erase markers and erasers)

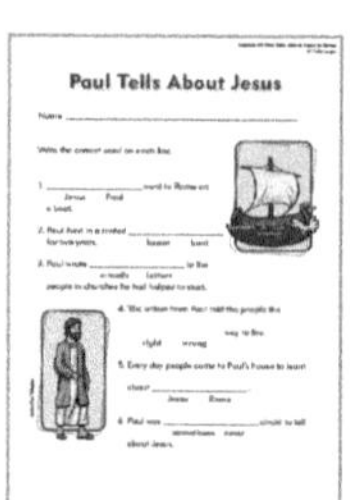

Make It Real

3 Use this activity to help children **discuss ways they can tell about Jesus in places where they are each day.**

Materials
Activity page *How Will You Tell?* on page 280

Discuss

Teaching Tip
Be prepared to give suggestions for ways to tell about Jesus in different places. For example, at their homes children could tell about Jesus by watching a video about Jesus and then talking about it, or by reading a Bible storybook to a brother or sister. Remind children that the example they set is a good way to tell about Jesus too.

How Will You Tell?

SAY: **We've learned that Paul told about Jesus in different ways while in his home in Rome. Let's name ways we can tell about Jesus in everyday places we go.** Distribute Activity page *How Will You Tell?* from page 280. SAY: **Let's imagine that the picture on this page shows where we live. We'll stop at each place in the town and see if we can name ways we can tell about Jesus in these everyday places.** Have the children find the house. Let a couple of children share a way to tell about Jesus at home. Look at another place on the page, and let the children share ways they can tell about Jesus in that place. Continue until you have talked about all the places pictured.

SAY: **It might not always be easy to share about Jesus. If we ask God for His help, He will give us the strength we need. Then we can tell about Jesus in everyday places—every day!**

Live It Out

4 Use this activity to help children **choose a way to tell about Jesus today.**

Materials
mobile phone, sheet of paper and marker pen, Bible (or Bible storybook), sheet of paper with the words 'My Example' written on it

Pray

Teaching Tip
Offer children a choice of going to one of the prayer locations or gathering with you for the prayer time. Emphasise that it's OK not to choose a specific way to tell about Jesus if they are uncertain about what that means or how to do it.

The Choice Is Yours

Have the children gather for a special prayer time. SAY: **We've learned that there are lots of ways we can tell about Jesus in everyday places. You need to choose how you will tell about Jesus today.** Show the items you have gathered. Tell the children you will place the items in four locations. If they choose to talk or use a phone to tell about Jesus, they should go the phone. If they will write a card or draw a picture, they can go to the paper and marker. Children who want to read a Bible verse or Bible storybook to tell about Jesus can move to that item. If they will tell about Jesus by the example they set, they should gather at the paper that says 'My Example.' Assist any child who needs individual help in choosing or moving to one of the four locations.

When children have chosen the ways they will tell about Jesus, lead in a closing prayer.

Paul's Everyday Way

Paul wrote letters.

Paul welcomed and talked to guests.

Paul set an example for the guards.

'I can do all this through him who gives me strength.'

Philippians 4:13

Paul Tells About Jesus

Name ____

Write the correct word on each line.

1. ________________________ went to Rome on

   Jesus   **Paul**

   a boat.

2. Paul lived in a rented ________________________
   for two years.   **house**   **boat**

3. Paul wrote ________________________ to the

   e-mails   **letters**

   people in churches he had helped to start.

4. The letters from Paul told the people the

   ________________________ way to live.

   right   **wrong**

5. Every day people came to Paul's house to learn

   about ________________________.

   Jesus   **Rome**

6. Paul was ________________________ afraid to tell

   sometimes   **never**

   about Jesus.

Art by Ron Wheeler

How Will You Tell?

Look at the picture. Talk about all the places where you can show
Jesus' love to others. What can you do to talk about Jesus?

Stand Firm in the Lord

Session 46

Scripture: Philippians 1:27-29; 2:12-16; 4:1, 4, 13, 19
Focus: Stand firm in the Lord.

Heart to Heart Teacher Devotion

Has life been hard for you lately, or has it been smooth sailing? Are you full of hope, or feeling hopeless? Whatever season you're in right now, take a moment and commit anew to stand firm in the Lord. Read Philippians 4:4, 13, 19. When are you to rejoice? Always! What can you do through Christ? Everything! How many of your needs does Jesus meet? All! Show your thanks by standing firm in the Lord.

Focus
Stand firm in the Lord.

Materials
none

Action

If you have children in your group with physical disabilities consider changing the activity. Using an electric fan on low setting, place the different items in front of it one by one: feather, tissue paper, piece of cardboard, brick. Ask children which one 'stood firm' and didn't move.

Focus In

1 Use this activity to help children **explore what it means to stand firm.**

Welcome

Welcome each child warmly by name.

Don't Give In!

Ask children to stand and form a circle. SAY: **Interlock your arms, stand firmly on both feet, and hold on! I'm going to try to break through your arms, but you are to stand firm. Don't give in, maintain your ground, dig your heels in, and stand firm!** Try to break through in several places. Then you can join the circle and have a volunteer try to break through. Encourage children to stand firm! After a few rounds, have children sit down. **You did a great job of not giving in, of standing firm.**

ASK: **If you were to stand firm in your belief that your school's football or netball team is the best team in the league, what would that mean?** (that I would never change my mind about that; that I wouldn't give up believing that)

If you were to stand firm in your belief that your favourite ice cream is the best flavour ever, what would that mean? (to not give in or change my mind when others challenge my belief; to keep believing that no matter what)

SAY: **Let's dig into God's Word and see what it says about standing firm.**

Explore His Word

Focus
Stand firm in the Lord.

2 Use these activities to help children **discuss the Scriptures about standing firm in the Lord.**

Bible Background for the Teacher

Philippians is a positive, upbeat letter written by a Roman prisoner—Paul the apostle. Today's text opens with the words 'Whatever happens' (Philippians 1:27). From shipwreck to floggings to hunger to exposure, Paul experienced intense suffering for preaching the gospel to those who didn't want to hear it (2 Corinthians 11:23-28). But through it all Paul was able to stand firm, and now he was challenging the Philippian Christians to do the same. Paul reminded his readers that belief in Christ and suffering for Christ often go hand in hand (Philippians 1:29).

Bible Exploration   Philippians 1:27-29; 2:12-16; 4:1, 4, 13, 19

Ask children to follow along as volunteers read Philippians 1:27-29.
SAY: **Paul wrote this letter to the church in Philippi. He told them that whatever happened, he wanted them to stand firm in the Lord as they shared the gospel with others. There would be people who opposed them, but they were to stand firm. They would suffer for Jesus, but they were to stand firm.**

Next, have children turn to chapter 2, verses 12-16. Ask children to follow along as volunteers read these verses. **Paul told the Christians in Philippi to keep obeying God, because God would work through them. Paul told them not to complain or argue, so they would stand out for the Lord like bright stars.**

Finally, have children turn to chapter 4, verses 1, 4, 13, 19. Ask children to follow along as volunteers read these verses. SAY: **Paul wanted the Christians in Philippi to stand firm in the Lord. They were to rejoice because they could do everything through God who gave them strength and met all their needs in Jesus.**

ASK: **Are these Scriptures just for the Christians in Philippi? If not, who are they for?** (no; they are for all Christians, including us)
SAY: **You're right! These Scriptures are for us too. So, let's dig deeper into these verses.**

Hand out the Activity page *Standing Firm*. Read the directions. Let children pair up to do the page or do it by themselves. When everyone has finished, ask volunteers to read the sentences and give their answers. (Answers: 1=a; 2=b, c; 3=a, b; 4=a; 5=a, c) SAY: **In good times and bad, Christians are not to give up or change our minds about living for God. We are not to give in, but hold on to what we believe. When we do stand firm, God will give us strength and meet all our needs.**

Materials
Bible map from previous sessions on page 244, Bibles, scissors, pencils, Activity page *Standing Firm* on page 285

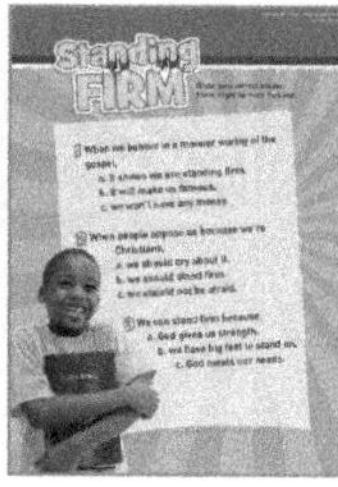

Make It Real

3 Use this activity to help children **want to stand firm in the Lord.**

Materials

cookie sheet (or flat pan), polystyrene cup, 10 small rocks, hair dryer, whiteboard, dry-erase marker, Bibles 
Science

Teaching Tip

Always try experiments before the session! Make sure that the low setting on your hair dryer won't blow away the rocks. If it does, you'll need bigger rocks.

Standing Firm

Put the cookie sheet where everyone can see it, and turn it over. Have a child place the stones on it. Have another child break the foam cup into 20 pieces and place those pieces on the cookie sheet. Stand approximately three feet from the cookie sheet. Turn the hair dryer on low and aim it toward the cookie sheet. The foam pieces should blow off, but not the rocks.

ASK: **Based on what we've talked about today, what could the foam pieces represent?** (people who don't stand firm in the Lord) **What could the rocks represent?** (people who do stand firm in the Lord)

Live It Out

4 Use this activity to help children to **commit to stand firm in the Lord.**

Materials

Activity Page *Tough Times* on page 284, scissors 
Act It Out

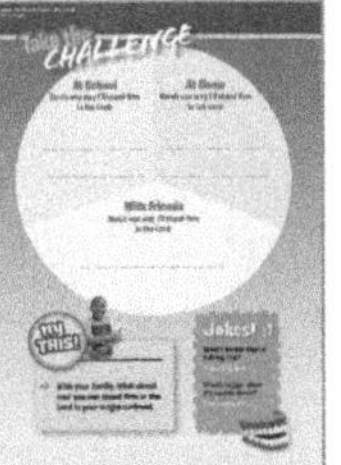

Teaching Tip

If you have a small session, choose one or two of the situations for children to do.

Extra Activity

Take the Challenge

SAY: **Think about how *you* will stand firm this week.** Use Activity page *Take the Challenge* on page 286. Provide assistance as needed to children who struggle with putting their thoughts into writing. When children are done, let volunteers share what they wrote.

Tough Times

Before the session, cut apart the cards on the Activity page *Tough Times*.

SAY: **It can seem easy to stand firm in the Lord when life is easy. But what about the tough times? Will you continue to stand firm in the Lord?** Ask for volunteers who would like to do some acting. Divide the situations among those children. Children who don't like to act can join in on the situations that require several children. They can be part of the crowd of children without having to talk or act. After a few minutes, have groups present their skits.

SAY: **There will be times when it's hard to stand firm in the Lord. That's when you need to pray and read God's Word even more than usual.** Ask children to gather for prayer. Tell children that you'll lead them in prayer. When you pause, they can respond by saying out loud, 'I will stand firm in the Lord.' Tell children it's OK if they don't feel comfortable saying that out loud. PRAY: **Dear God, when people make fun of me for praying before I eat . . .** Pause as children respond, 'I will stand firm in the Lord.' **When it seems like I'm the only child who doesn't swear or use God's name disrespectfully . . .** Pause as children respond. **When everyone else goes to a party I'm not allowed to go to . . .** Pause as children respond. **When all the children are talking about a violent video game I don't have . . .** Pause as children respond. **Thank You, God, for listening to our prayers. Help us to always stand firm. In Jesus' name, amen.**

Tough Times

Cut apart on the dotted lines.

1 Kid, 2 Parents

Your dad tells the family that he's lost his job. And your mum has been sick a lot lately. You have been praying and asking God to help, but you don't see Him answering your prayers. You're ready to give up on God.

Act out how you will stand firm in the Lord.

Several Kids

You go to Sunday school and church services every week. And you're on a sports team. A few kids on your team make fun of you for going to "little baby" Sunday school. They make fun of you at every practice.

Act out how you will stand firm in the Lord.

Several Kids

You're finally hanging out with the "popular" group of kids. But they're planning to do something you know wouldn't be right to do. You really want to fit in with this group.

Act out how you will stand firm in the Lord.

1 Kid, 1 Grandma

You're at your grandma's home for the weekend. She went to bed early because she wasn't feeling well. You want to check out some of the TV programmes your parents don't let you watch.

Act out how you will stand firm in the Lord.

Standing FIRM

Circle each correct answer.
There might be more than one.

1 When we behave in a manner worthy of the gospel,
- a. it shows we are standing firm.
- b. it will make us famous.
- c. we won't have any money.

2 When people oppose us because we're Christians,
- a. we should cry about it.
- b. we should stand firm.
- c. we should not be afraid.

3 We can stand firm because
- a. God gives us strength.
- b. we have big feet to stand on.
- c. God meets our needs.

HeartShaper Primary Blue Edition, Activity page
Permission is granted to reproduce this page for ministry purposes only—not for resale.

Take the CHALLENGE

At School
Here's one way I'll stand firm
in the Lord:

____

____

____

At Home
Here's one way I'll stand firm
in the Lord:

____

____

____

With Friends
Here's one way I'll stand firm
in the Lord:

____

____

____

try THIS!

➡ **With your family, think about how you can stand firm in the Lord in your neighbourhood.**

Jokes! :)

What's better than a talking dog?

A spelling bee!

What's bigger when it's upside-down?

The number 6!

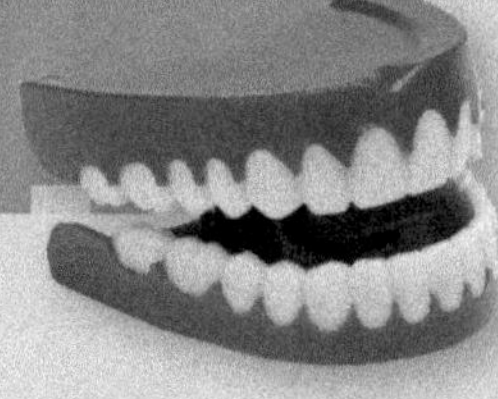

Jonah and the People of Nineveh

Scripture: Jonah 1:1-4, 7, 11-12, 15, 17; 2:1, 10; 3:1-10
Focus: God is a forgiving God.

Heart to Heart Teacher Devotion

Aren't you glad that forgiveness is part of God's nature? Look how God's forgiveness weaves its way through the book of Jonah. Jonah disobeyed God, then repented. God forgave; then Jonah obeyed. The people of Nineveh were wicked and violent, then repented. God forgave; then the people turned from their wicked ways. God's forgiveness still weaves its way through our lives today. Our disobedience, when followed by repentance, leads to God's forgiveness. Thank God!

Focus
God is a forgiving God.

Materials
copies of Activity Page *Forgiveness Word Cards* page 292 (1 copy per small group), scissors

Game

Remember that not all children can read fluently in the primary years. Provide pictures that illustrate the words, if possible.

Focus In

1 Use this activity to help children **explore what forgiveness looks like.**

Welcome

Welcome each child warmly by name.

What Forgiveness Is

Before the session, make one copy of the *Forgiveness Word Cards* Activity Page for each small group and cut apart the cards. Keep the cards for each group separate.

Divide the session into small groups (or pairs). Give each group a set of cards. SAY: **Let's see what you know about forgiveness. When I say go, place the headings 'Forgiveness' and 'Not Forgiveness' on the table. Let's see which group can be the first to place all the word cards under the correct headings. Ready? Go!** Let the group that finishes first tell which word cards they placed under 'Forgiveness'. Then ask a few children to tell which word card they think best describes forgiveness.

ASK: **When is a time you forgave someone?** Accept responses.
When is a time someone forgave you?
How do you feel when you either offer forgiveness or receive it from someone?

SAY: **Let's keep thinking about forgiveness as we dive into God's Word.**

Focus
God is a forgiving God.

Explore His Word

2 Use these activities to help children to **describe the events surrounding God's instructions to Jonah.**

Bible Background for the Teacher

Jonah's message of doom as recorded in Jonah 3:4 left no apparent room for God to change His mind. The Ninevites, however, understood that God might forgive them if they repented. They did so, showing their sorrow for sin in ways well-known in the ancient Near East: they wore rough sackcloth and fasted. Moreover, they went a step further than usual by imposing a fast on their livestock and putting sackcloth on their farm animals. This radical act showed their extreme revulsion at their sin and paved the way for God's forgiveness. God's universal love stands in contrast to Jonah's narrow nationalism. Jonah thought pagan Gentiles were unworthy of God's attention, but God showed him in no uncertain terms that He loves non-Israelites as much as Israelites.

Bible Exploration   Jonah 1:1-4, 7, 11-12, 15, 17; 2:1, 10; 3:1-10

Ask children to look in the contents pages of their Bibles and find the book of Isaiah. SAY: **The books of Isaiah to Malachi are books of Prophecy. One of God's prophets was Jonah.** Ask children to find his name in the list. Help children as needed as they turn to Jonah 1:1.

SAY: **You may be pretty familiar with Jonah's life. But listen up as we read; you may discover some things you've not really heard or understood before. Then we'll illustrate scenes from Jonah's life.** Ask for three volunteers who are willing to read from the Bible. Assign one to read the Lord's words (Jonah 1:2 and 3:2); one to read Jonah's words (1:12 and 3:4); and one to read the sailor's words (1:7 and 1:11). You can read all the other text.

As you and the volunteers read the Scripture passages aloud, encourage everyone to follow along in their Bibles. When finished, thank the volunteers. Then tell children that they're going to illustrate some scenes from Jonah's life. Divide the session into six groups (or let children work independently). Give each group a length of roll paper and markers. Assign these scenes: 1. Jonah running away and getting on a ship; 2. Jonah being thrown into the sea and a fish swallowing him; 3. Jonah inside the fish, praying; 4. Jonah being vomited onto dry land; 5. Jonah in Nineveh preaching about God; 6. The people of Nineveh repenting. When groups are done, display the scenes in order on a wall. Let groups talk about what they drew. Then distribute the Activity Page and have children look at *Jonah's Journey*. Have volunteers read the questions and give answers or let children do it together in pairs. (Answers: 1=b, c; 2=a, c; 3=a; 4=c)

ASK: **What do you find surprising about the real-life story of Jonah?**
Accept responses.
What are you learning about God from this story?

Refer to the illustrated scenes. SAY: **When we read about and study Jonah, many times we focus on his disobedience, then his obedience. And that's a good thing to do. But think for a moment about God— think about how forgiving He was. When Jonah disobeyed God in a pretty big way, God could have given up on Jonah. The people of Nineveh are described as being wicked—God certainly could have given up on them.**

SAY: **When Jonah repented and when the people of Nineveh repented, God forgave them. And it's still true today that God is a forgiving God. When we repent after doing wrong, God will forgive us. The real-life story of Jonah shows that God is a forgiving God. He longs for us to repent after we sin. God forgives us when we repent and turn our lives around, obeying Him.**

Materials

Bible time lines, Bibles, 6 lengths of roll paper, markers, reusable adhesive, Activity page *Jonah's Journey* on pages 290-291, pencils

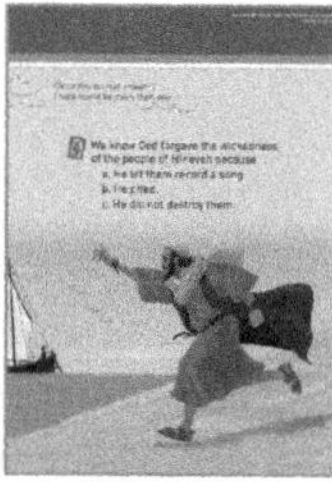

Media Option

Go to www.biblegateway.com and play a dramatised reading of the Bible verses.

Make It Real

3 Use this activity to help children **discover that God's forgiveness follows repentance.**

Materials
whiteboard, dry-erase marker, lesson 1, pencils, Bibles

Discover

Sum It Up!

Group the session into two teams. Ask each team to send one player to stand by you. SAY: **Let's play a quick game called First This, Then That. I'll start by saying something like this: First breakfast, then . . . The first player who shouts out something that could happen next—such as brushing teeth or school or lunch—gets 10 points for his team.** See the narrow column for things you can name. Possible responses are in parentheses. Make sure everyone gets a turn.

For the Game
Some ideas: socks (shoes); reception (year 1); learning addition (learning subtraction); phonics (learning to read); snow (snowman); game (fun); number 3 (number 4); going to the supermarket (eating); shopping (buy something). Make up more as needed.

ASK: **What comes first: repentance or God's forgiveness?** (repentance)
Does God want to forgive our sins? Why do you say that? (Yes, there are lots of Scriptures that say God wants to forgive us.)

SAY: **Just as God longed for Jonah and the people of Nineveh to repent, He longs for us to repent, because God is a forgiving God. When we repent, He forgives!**

Live It Out

4 Use this activity to help children **repent and ask for God's forgiveness.**

Materials
balloons, pencils

Object Lesson

Balloon Prayers

Give each child a balloon. SAY: **Blow a big breath into the balloon for each thing you think of that you want to say 'sorry' to God about.** Tell children to then hold their balloons closed but not to tie them off. **Bow your heads and ask for God's forgiveness.** After a short time of silence, tell children to let go of their balloons.

SAY: **Like the air going out of your balloon, your life contained sin, wrong things you had done. When you repented, God took away your sins and forgave you. Just as Jonah and the people of Nineveh experienced God's forgiveness, you've experienced God's forgiveness too.** Close in prayer.

 **1** The first time God told Jonah to go to Nineveh, Jonah

    a. obeyed God.

    b. ran away from the Lord.

    c. got on a ship headed for Tarshish.

 **2** The second time God told Jonah to go to Nineveh, Jonah

    a. had just come out of a huge fish.

    b. couldn't decide what to do.

    c. obeyed God.

 **3** We know God forgave Jonah's disobedience because

    a. God gave Jonah another opportunity to obey Him.

    b. Jonah became famous.

    c. Jonah could tell great fish stories.

Circle the correct answers.
There might be more than one.

4 We know God forgave the wickedness of the people of Nineveh because

a. He let them record a song.

b. He cried.

c. He did not destroy them.

HeartShaper Primary Blue Edition, Activity page

Forgiveness Word Cards

Cut apart on the dotted lines.

Forgiveness 	Not Forgiveness 
Patient	Impatient
Give up feeling bad	Continue to feel bad
Everything is better	Everything is not better
Kind	Not kind
Let go of hard feelings	Hold on to hard feelings
Let go of anger	Hold on to anger
Let go of hatred	Hold on to hatred

Esther Saves Her People
Session 48

Scripture: Esther 2:5-7, 17; 3:1, 5-6; 4:1, 5, 7, 14-17; 5:1-4; 7:1-6, 9-10; 8:11, 15-16; 9:28
Focus: God works through us when we're courageous for Him.

Heart to Heart Teacher Devotion

Who would you say is courageous for God? Maybe it's the young man who becomes a missionary in a country halfway around the world. Maybe it's the TV star who speaks up for God. Maybe it's the sports celebrity who gives God the credit for her success. Maybe it's . . . you! 'Who knows but that you have come to your royal position for such a time as this?' (Esther 4:14).

Focus
God works through us when we're courageous for Him.

Materials
Activity Page *Courage Needed* on page 298 (1 set of 3 cards per child), scissors

Act It Out

Be careful when using an activity that quantifies which feat requires the most courage. For a child with a brain injury, riding a bike might take a lot of courage, while it is easy for the child who is physically healthy. Moderate the discussion carefully, reminding children how to use kind and encouraging words.

Focus In

1 Use this activity to help children **explore what courage is.**

Welcome

Welcome each child warmly by name.

Courage Needed

Give each child a copy of the Activity page *Courage Needed*. Tell children to cut apart the cards. Ask volunteers to read aloud the text on the cards. SAY: **Which of these situations do you think would require the most courage? Make your choice; then stand up holding that card.** Tell children to find others who made the same choice and stand together. Tell each group to prepare to act out the situation on its card, particularly why that situation would require a lot of courage. When groups are ready, let them act out their situations.

ASK: **When are some times you've had to have courage at school? at home? in your street? during a sports event?** Accept responses.

SAY: **Let's keep thinking about courage as we dig into God's Word.**

Focus
God works through us when we're courageous for Him.

Explore His Word

2 Use these activities to help children **describe how Esther saved her people from destruction.**

Bible Background for the Teacher

The Babylonians destroyed Jerusalem and deported people from Judah around 600 BC. While some returned and rebuilt Jerusalem nearly 70 years later, many others and their descendants never returned to the homeland. The book of Esther tells of some of these Jewish people who lived scattered throughout the Persian Empire.

Esther's husband, Xerxes I, ruled about 485–464 BC. By this time many Jews had assimilated to Persian culture so thoroughly that Esther could keep her nationality secret until she bravely revealed it (Esther 2:10; 7:3-4). The account revolves around a plot by the wicked Haman to destroy all the Persian Jews because of his grudge against Esther's cousin, Mordecai. Besides telling the story of Esther's courage and her choice to stand up for what was right, the book of Esther explains the origin of the festival called Purim ('lots'), which Jewish people still celebrate today.

Bible Exploration
Esther 2:5-7, 17; 3:1, 5-6; 4:1, 5, 7, 14-17; 5:1-4; 7:1-6, 9-10; 8:11, 15-16; 9:28

SAY: **Many things happened after the prophets told about Jesus' birth. The Babylonians took many of the Israelite people captive to Babylon, which at some point became part of the Persian Empire.** Ask children to turn in their Bibles to the contents page. Ask them to find the book of Esther in the Old Testament section.

Have children turn in their Bibles to Esther 2. SAY: **The book of Esther tells of some of the Jewish people who lived in the Persian Empire. Let me give you a little background. The wife of King Xerxes had been removed from being queen. The advisers of King Xerxes wanted him to find a new queen. So they set up a competition to find him a wife.** Have volunteers read Esther 2:5-7, 17 aloud. **Esther, who was Jewish, became the new queen! Let's find out what happened next.**

Read the Bible passages aloud to children. Allow them to ask you questions about parts they may not understand. Distribute the Activity Page *Esther's Journal*. Have volunteers read the sentences and complete them. (Answers: Jewish; Mordecai; queen; Xerxes; Haman; protect; Purim)

ASK: **What did Esther do that took great courage?** (She went to see the king even though it was against the law and she could have been killed)
   What happened because of Esther's courage? (The Jewish people were allowed to protect themselves; the Jews did not die)
   If you had been in Esther's situation, what do you think you would have done? Accept responses.

SAY: **Esther found out an important truth—God works through us when we're courageous for Him!**

ASK: **Who else was courageous for God? How?** (Mordecai was courageous when he refused to bow and worship Haman)

SAY: **Mordecai found out the same important truth—that God works through us when we're courageous for Him. Esther was queen; Mordecai was just a regular guy. But both were courageous for God. And God worked through them. God works through *us* when we're courageous for Him too!**

Materials 
Bible time lines, Activity page *Esther's Journal* on page 296, pencils

Skit

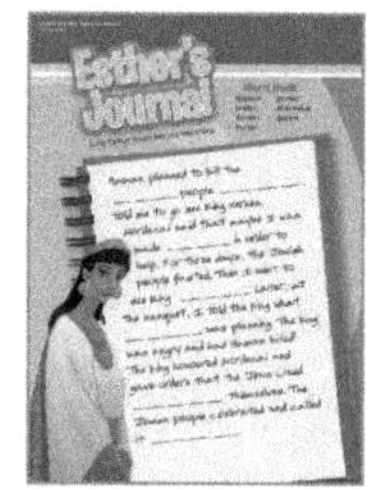

Media Option
Go to www.youtube.com and type in 'Esther the girl who became queen.' You may find a video clip you'd like to use.

Make It Real

3 Use this activity to help children **discover what courage for God might look like.**

Materials
Bibles, whiteboard, dry-erase marker, roll paper, markers 

 Allow children to have some thinking time before they share in their small groups ways they might be courageous. The extra time will help children who struggle to process their thoughts quickly.

Courageous Children Needed!

ASK: **If you were courageous for God this week, what would you do?** Accept responses, but help children know that courage for God means doing the right thing even when others don't, standing up for God even when it's hard, sharing their faith, etc.

Ask children to turn in their Bibles to Psalm 56:11, and have a volunteer read it aloud. Also have volunteers read 1 Corinthians 16:13-14 and 2 Timothy 2:1, 3 aloud. Write key words from the verses on the board. Divide the session into small groups (or pairs) and give each group a length of roll paper and markers. Challenge each group to create an advertisement looking for children who will be courageous for God. The adverts should include real ways children can be courageous for God. Encourage children to use some ideas from the Bible verses. When groups are ready, let each group present its advert.

SAY: **When you're courageous for God, you might get laughed at and friends might unfriend you. You might suffer for God. But it's worth it! When you place your trust in God, you don't need to be afraid. Like He did with Esther and Mordecai, God works through us when we're courageous for Him too!**

Live It Out

4 Use this activity to help children **commit to being courageous for God.**

Materials
Activity page *My Courage Journal* on page 297 

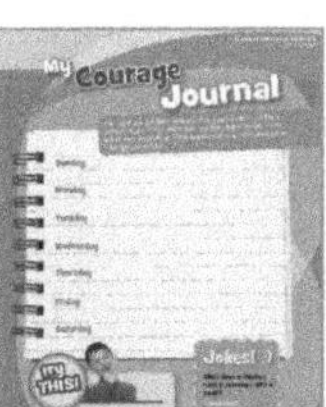

My Courage Journal

SAY: **Esther and Mordecai were courageous for God. And God worked through them. God works through *us* when we're courageous for Him too! Will you commit to being courageous for God?**

Hand out Activity page *My Courage Journal*. Read the directions aloud. SAY: **Here's your challenge—look for ways to be courageous for God every day this week. Write what you did. Maybe it was something quite big, or maybe it was something rather small. That's OK! God works through us in lots of ways when we're courageous for Him!**

Have children gather for a time of prayer. Ask children to think of one way that they can be courageous for God this week. Encourage all children to share, but don't force anyone who doesn't want to. After the children have shared, PRAY: **Dear Father in Heaven, thank You for letting us know about people like Esther and Mordecai, who were so courageous for You. Help us want to be that courageous for You. Help us look for times that we can stand up for You. Help us do the right thing even when others don't. Help us find ways to share our faith with others. In Jesus' name, amen.**

Esther's Journal

Help Esther finish her journal entry.

Word Bank

Haman	protect
Jewish	Mordecai
Xerxes	queen
Purim	

Haman planned to kill the ___________ people. ___________ told me to go see King Xerxes. Mordecai said that maybe I was made ___________ in order to help. For three days, the Jewish people fasted. Then I went to see King ___________. Later, at the banquet, I told the king what ___________ was planning. The king was angry and had Haman killed! The king honoured Mordecai and gave orders that the Jews could ___________ themselves. The Jewish people celebrated and called it ___________.

My Courage Journal

Each day, ask yourself, *How was I courageous for God?* Then write what you did. It might be something big or small. It's OK either way. Remember—God will work through you when you're courageous for Him!

Sunday

Monday

Tuesday

Wednesday

Thursday

Friday

Saturday

try THIS!

➡ **Interview some friends and family members. Ask how they've been courageous for God. When you hear something you could do—try it!**

Jokes! :)

What does a chicken have in common with a band?

Drumsticks!

What did the maths book say to the other maths book?

I've got a lot of problems!

Courage Needed
Cut apart on the dotted lines.

Eating a food you've never tried before	Helping a classmate that everyone laughs at	Facing a parent after you did something wrong
Eating a food you've never tried before	Helping a classmate that everyone laughs at	Facing a parent after you did something wrong
Eating a food you've never tried before	Helping a classmate that everyone laughs at	Facing a parent after you did something wrong

True Wisdom

Scripture: James 1:2-3, 5-6, 12; 2:15-17; 3:13-18; 4:1-3, 7-8a, 10, 17
Focus: God gives wisdom to those who ask.

Heart to Heart Teacher Devotion

Wisdom is the knowledge of what is proper or reasonable; of having good sense or sound judgment. While we may possess wisdom at times, there are certainly other times when we're anything but wise. James tells us we're wise when we live a good life and do good deeds with humility. Need help being wise? Humble yourself, and ask God. Only He gives true wisdom.

Focus

God gives wisdom to those who ask.

Materials

copies of Activity Page *Words of Wisdom* on page 304 (1 per small group), pencils

Discuss

Focus In

1 Use this activity to help children **discover the meaning of *wisdom*.**

Welcome

Welcome each child warmly by name.

Words of Wisdom

Help children get into small groups (or pairs). Give each group a copy of the Words of Wisdom page and pencils. Tell groups to read the words of wisdom on the page together. Then each group should work together to write their own words of wisdom. They can also illustrate their wise words. Give groups time to work. When children are ready, let group members read their words of wisdom and show their drawings.

ASK: **What does it mean to have wisdom?** (to have good sense; to know what to do and do it)

SAY: **A wise person is someone who understands what's really important in life. Let's keep thinking about wisdom as we discover that God gives wisdom to those who ask.**

Explore His Word

2 Use these activities to help children to **summarise what James says about wisdom.**

Bible Background for the Teacher

The book of James has many parallels to the teachings of Jesus, who is wisdom personified (1 Corinthians 1:24, 30). Faith is key to Christianity. But if faith is not demonstrated and applied to everyday living, James says that faith is dead (James 2:17). It's of no value to say that we care for the hungry if we don't give them something to eat (vv. 15-16). Perhaps James was recalling Christ's compassion for hungry people in Matthew 15:32. Why do we as Christians fail to act on our faith in practical ways? James says that our faith is often squelched by selfishness (James 3:14, 16; 4:1-3). He warns that 'such 'wisdom' does not come down from heaven but is earthly, unspiritual, demonic' (3:15).

Bible Exploration   James 1:2-3, 5-6, 12; 2:15-17; 3:13-18; 4:1-3, 7-8a, 10, 17

Materials

Use the *Bible Timelines* from the back of this book.

Ask children to look at the table of contents in their Bibles (either a printed Bible or a Bible on a tablet, phone, or e-reader) and find the book of James in the New Testament section.

SAY: **The book of James is thought to have been one of the earliest books written in all the New Testament. While many events are placed in the Bible in the order they happened, some are not.** Have a volunteer point out the 'Saul's conversion' icon on the time line. **Saul, better known as Paul, became a follower of Jesus. Then the apostle Peter raised Tabitha from the dead, taught a Gentile man named Cornelius about Jesus, and escaped from prison, where he had been held for teaching about Jesus.** Then have the volunteer point out the 'True wisdom' icon. **This is where we pick up God's story.** Ask children to turn in their Bibles to James 1. Have volunteers read verses 2-3, 5-6, and 12 aloud.

ASK: **When we need wisdom, what are we to do?** (ask God)
According to these verses, when are some times that we'll need wisdom? (when we face trials; when we go through tough times)

Divide the session into small groups (or pairs). SAY: **I'm going to read a section of Scripture, then ask you a question. Your group will work together to answer that question.** Read James 2:15-17. Encourage children to follow along as you read.

ASK: **Based on this Scripture, what are some wise things we should do and shouldn't do?** Ask each group to work together, then have the groups share their answers. When groups are done, read James 3:13-18 aloud.
Based on this Scripture, what are some wise things we should do and shouldn't do? Ask each group to work together, then have the groups share their answers. When groups are done, read James 4:1-3, 7-8a, 10, 17 aloud.
Based on this Scripture, what are some wise things we should do and shouldn't do? Ask each group to work together, then have the groups share their answers.

Make It Real

3 Use this activity to help children **discover ways to live wisely**.

Materials
Activity pages *Living Wisely*
on pages 302-303, paper,
pencils, markers

Teaching Tip
If you have a small session, do
the situations together.

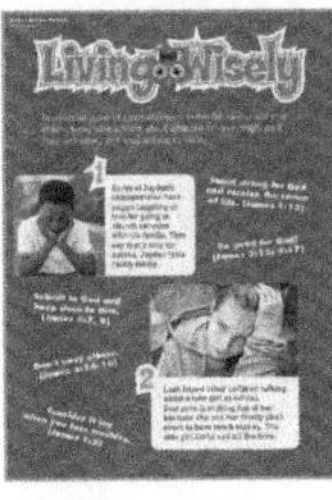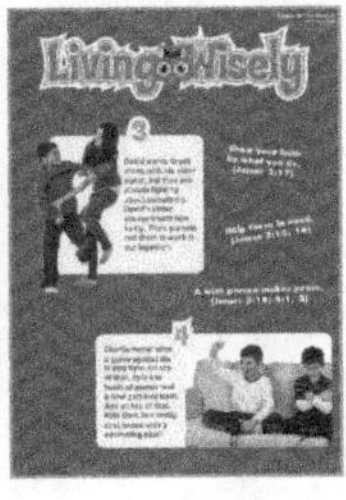

Tell It, Draw It, or Act It

SAY: **No matter how wise we think we are, there's probably room for all
of us to be wiser. Let's discover some ways each of us can live wisely
for God every day.** Hand out Activity page *Living Wisely*. Read the
directions. Divide the session into pairs or small groups, assigning one
of the situations to each pair or group. **Read your situation. Discuss two
things: how the person could act wisely and how the person could act
not so wisely. Then it's your choice—you can draw, act or talk about
either the person acting wisely or not wisely.**

Provide paper, pencils, and markers. Encourage children to get some
ideas from the Bible verses from the book of James. When children
are ready, let them do their acting, show their drawings, or give their
responses. SAY: **It can be challenging to live wisely for God, so let's ask
God because God gives wisdom to those who ask.**

Live It Out

4 Use this activity to help children **ask God for wisdom**.

Materials
Pre-prepared Wisdom
Walk Posters, reusable
adhesive

 It may be helpful to
provide a bit more
structure for some children,
rather than telling them that
they can walk around the room
in any order they choose.
Coloured self-stick notes can be
used to help children remember
where they have been.

Wisdom Walk

Before the Session
Prepare A4 posters to stick to the walls of your children's area. Write
one prayer on each poster.

1. Dear God, help me to live wisely for You at school.
2. Dear God, help me to live wisely for You at home.
3. Dear God, help me to live wisely for You when I'm going through
    hard times.
4. Dear God, help me to live wisely for You by helping people in need.
5. Dear God, help me to live wisely for You when I'm tempted to be
    jealous.
6. Dear God, help me to live wisely for You and not fight or quarrel
    with others.
7. Dear God, help me to live wisely for You by staying close to You.

Display the Wisdom Walk posters around your room.

SAY: **Do you really believe that when you ask God for wisdom, He
gives it? I hope you do, because that's what God's Word says!** Draw
children's attention to the Wisdom Walk posters displayed in your room.
**In just a moment, you get to go on a prayer walk. Go to each of the
Wisdom Walk posters in any order you choose. Read each poster; then
pray about what's on each poster. The posters will guide you to ask
God for wisdom. God gives wisdom to those who ask—so let's ask Him.**
Tell children that when they're done praying, they should take a seat and
wait quietly until everyone is done. As children leave, challenge them to
live wisely for God every day.

A printable set of posters for the Wisdom Walk can be found at
www.heartshaper.co.uk

Living Wisely

Read about some children who want to live for God—and that means living wisely. Think about what the children might do if they act wisely or if they act not so wisely.

1

Some of Jayden's sessionmates have begun laughing at him for going to church services with his family. They say that's only for babies. Jayden feels really lonely.

Stand strong for God and receive the crown of life. (James 1:12)

Do good for God! (James 3:13; 4:17)

Submit to God and keep close to Him. (James 4:7, 8)

Don't envy others. (James 3:14-16)

Consider it joy when you face troubles. (James 1:2)

2

Leah heard other children talking about a new girl at school. Everyone is making fun of her because she and her family don't seem to have much money. The new girl looks sad all the time.

Living Wisely

3

David wants to get along with his older sister, but they are always fighting about something. David's sister always treats him badly. Their parents tell them to work it out together.

Show your faith by what you do. (James 2:17)

Help those in need. (James 2:15, 16)

A wise person makes peace. (James 3:18; 4:1, 2)

4

Charlie never wins a game against his friend Kyle. On top of that, Kyle has loads of games and a new game-system. And on top of that, Kyle lives in a really cool house with a swimming pool!

Words of Wisdom

Read these words of wisdom from children. What do you think? Are these children wise?

Never try to hide broccoli
in a glass of milk.

When you want something
expensive, ask your
grandparents.

Never dare your little brother to
paint your family's car.

Don't ever be too full for dessert.

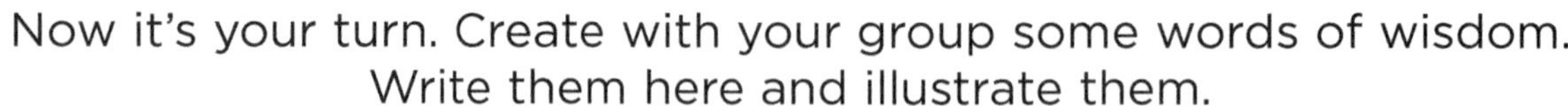

Now it's your turn. Create with your group some words of wisdom.
Write them here and illustrate them.

Live Godly Lives

Session 50

Scripture: Titus 2:6-8, 11-14; 3:1-8
Focus: Do good for God.

Heart to Heart Teacher Devotion

'Do something good,' says the parent to the child. 'Do something good,' says the Heavenly Father to us, His children. Do good for God by helping a neighbour who is struggling. Do good for God by encouraging a widow. Do good for God by guiding the children in your session to know and love Him more and more. We've been saved to do good for God. Let's do all the good we can—all for God!

Focus In

Focus
Do good for God.

① Use this activity to help children **explore what it means to do good.**

Welcome

Welcome each child warmly by name.

Materials
none

Action

 This activity may be difficult for children with sensory issues. Rather than getting together in tight groups, children can work together to make murals that show good things they have done for others.

If You've Ever

Have children stand up. Designate an open area where groups of children can gather. SAY: **I'm going to call out actions. If you've ever done an action I name, quickly go to the open area and form a tight group with the others who have done it. Count to five together; then return to where you were standing.**

SAY: **Played with a younger sibling or a child on your street.** Pause between sentences for children to form tight groups, then return to where they were standing. **Cleaned your room without complaining. Kept a promise. Helped a friend with a project. Prayed for others. Helped a new child at school. Made a card for someone who was sick. Helped at an animal shelter. Forgave someone. Helped a neighbour. Shared some toys or clothes with children who don't have much.**

ASK: **What was the same about all these actions?** (the actions were all about doing good)
    What does it mean to do good? (to be kind or nice; to help someone; to do the right thing)

SAY: **Let's dig into God's Word to see what it says about doing good.**

Explore His Word

Focus
Do good for God.

② Use these activities to help children **explain why the Bible says we should do good for God.**

Bible Background for the Teacher

Titus is a letter that was written by the apostle Paul to a fellow missionary friend named Titus (Titus 1:1, 4). Titus was with Paul when he visited the island of Crete. When Paul left Crete, Titus remained behind for the purpose of helping the church (v. 5). A fundamental component of organising a congregation in New Testament times was the appointing of elders. Many of the qualifications for an elder center around whether or not the candidate lives a godly lifestyle (vv. 6-9). Titus himself was also instructed to be an example and demonstrate Godly living (2:7). Good examples not only benefit Christians but unbelievers as well. On the one hand, some non-Christians are drawn to the Lord by the lives of Christians who win the right to share their faith (3:1-2). Of course, any goodness that unbelievers see in us comes from God.

Bible Exploration Titus 2:6-8, 11-14; 3:1-8

In this week's lesson, we'll read what Paul wrote to a fellow Christian and missionary, a man named Titus. Have a volunteer stand by the map and point out Crete. **Titus was in Crete when Paul wrote to him. This is the last lesson we'll have that comes from the letters Paul wrote. This is where we pick up God's story.**

Ask them to look in the New Testament section and find the book of Titus. Ask children to turn to Titus 2:6-8, and have volunteers read the verses aloud. SAY: **Paul wrote to Titus to tell him something very important that can be summed up in four words: do good for God! But Paul also tells him *why* he should do good for God. Of course, it's also why *we* should do good for God. Let's see what we can discover.**

SAY: **Listen and follow along as I read Titus 2:6-8, 11-14, and 3:1-8. I'll pause after every verse. If you hear a reason *why* we should do good for God, raise your hand. You can tell us the reason, and I'll write it on the board.** Read slowly, and help children understand important points of these verses. Group what you write on the board so you can *later* draw an outline of a cross around the words. Children should raise their hands after these verses: 2:7—set an example; 2:8—so others will have nothing bad to say about us; 2:11—God gave us salvation; 2:13—waiting for Jesus to return; 2:14—Jesus redeemed, or saved, us; 3:5—Jesus saved us and gave us the Holy Spirit; 3:7—we're justified by grace and have hope of eternal life.

SAY: **We should do good for God because of what God did for us when He sent Jesus to die on the cross for our sins.** Draw a cross outline around what you've written on the board. **The *cross* is the reason to do good. We are saved, through what Jesus did on the cross, in order to do good. We are saved to do good for God!** Hand out the Activity page *Doing Good for God*. Do the page together as a session, letting volunteers read the sentences and fill in the blanks. (Answers: 1=example; 2=eager; 3=life; 4=good)

ASK: **Why should Christians do good for God?** (to set an example for others; God saved us to do good)

SAY: **Always remember that we're saved to do good for God!**

Materials
Bible map on page 244, reusable adhesive, Bibles, whiteboard, dry-erase marker, Activity Page *Doing Good for God* on page 309, pencils

Make It Real

3 Use this activity to help children **discover ways to do good for God.**

Materials

Activity Page *Doing Good Cards* on page 308, scissors, masking tape, Activity page *Ways to Do Good for God* on page 310, pencils

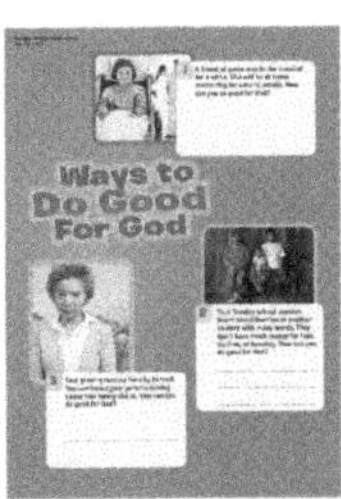

Ways to Do Good for God

Before the session cut apart the cards on from the Activity Page *Doing Good Cards*. If you have a large session, make two copies of the cards.

Without showing children the cards, tape one card on the back of each child. SAY: **The card on your back tells one way to do good for God. Without looking, you have to guess what your card says. To find out what it says, get up and ask questions. But you can only ask questions that can be answered either yes or no.** Give children these examples: **Is it something you do outside? Is it something you do with others?** Tell children to call out 'Doing good for God' when they have guessed it correctly. Play until all children have figured out their cards. Then they can remove the cards from their backs. Ask children to read their cards aloud, then place the cards on the table where everyone can see them.

Hand out Activity page *Ways to Do Good for God*. Read the directions. SAY: **Read the situations and think about them. How could you do good for God? Write down a few ideas for each one.**

Live It Out

4 Use this activity to help children to **plan to do good for God.**

Materials

fun-size packs of sweets or bag of grapes.

Be sure to check for food allergies. Provide an alternate snack as needed.

It's Sweet to Do Good!

SAY: **We have been saved to do good for God! That makes me want to do all the good I can—all for God! I hope you do too! Let's plan right now some sweet ways we will do good for God. Remember, these are everyday kind of things you can do at home, at school, and in your neighbourhood.**

Give each child a small handful of sweets or grapes. SAY: **Take turns to say aloud one way you can plan to do good for God in this coming week. Then you can eat one sweet or grape each time you say a way.** Make sure children pause and listen to one another and not just chomp away on all their sweets/grapes at once.

Have children gather for prayer. Invite volunteers to pray, thanking God for sending Jesus to save us from our sins, and asking for God's help as they do good for Him.

Doing Good Cards

Cut apart on the dotted lines.

Pray for someone who is sick.	Obey the teacher's rules.
Spend time with a friend who is sad.	Save your money to give to God.
Make friends with a kid who seems lonely.	Spend time with your grandad or grandma.
Leave the last piece of cake for someone else.	Donate toys and clothes to a family in need.
Clean your room without being asked.	Read to a younger sibling or cousin.
Be nice to someone who wasn't nice to you.	Help a friend at school who is having trouble with a subject.

Doing Good for God

Fill in the blanks and show what you know! Use your Bible or the Word Bank for help.

1 We should set a good ________________________ by doing what is good. (Titus 2:7)

2 Christians belong to Jesus and are ________________ to do good. (Titus 2:14)

3 As Christians, we have the hope of eternal ______________. (Titus 3:7)

4 Those who trust in God should do what is ______________. (Titus 3:8)

Word Bank

life   good
example   eager

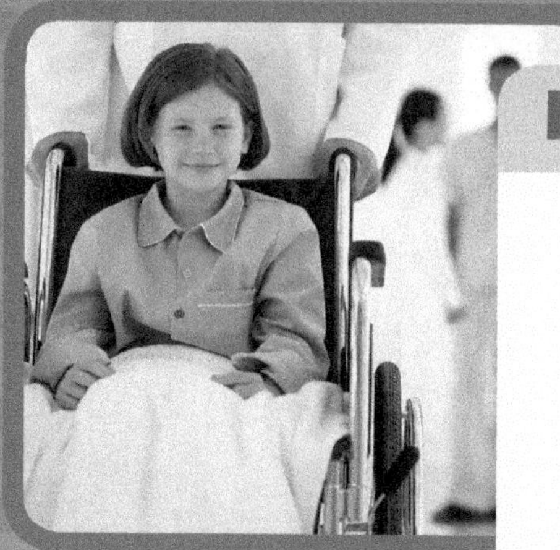

1 A friend of yours was in the hospital for a while. She will be at home recovering for several weeks. How can you do good for God?

____

____

____

Ways to Do Good For God

2 Your Sunday school session heard about families in another country with many needs. They don't have much money for food, clothes, or housing. How can you do good for God?

____

____

____

3 Your great-grandma lives by herself. You overheard your parents talking about how lonely she is. How can you do good for God?

____

____

____

Jesus Will Return

Scripture: Revelation 1:1-3, 7-8; 2:10b; 3:3, 11; 22:12-14, 16, 20-21
Focus: Jesus is coming soon!

Heart to Heart Teacher Devotion

While we know Jesus as a gentle shepherd and friend, He is also the one who will come with the clouds, commanding them and all of nature. Every eye, whether those eyes have believed in Jesus or not, will see Him when He returns. For believers, what a glorious day it will be to see the 'Alpha and the Omega . . . who is, and who was, and who is to come, the Almighty' (Revelation 1:8).

Focus
Jesus is coming soon!

Materials
none

Act It Out

 Make this activity more concrete for children who struggle with the concept of time (present versus future). Show a calendar and have the children write (or dictate) what is going to happen in the week ahead that makes them happy. Then they can act out or give clues that describe one of those events.

Focus In

❶ Use this activity to help children **explore things they are anticipating.**

Welcome

Welcome each child warmly by name.

I Can't Wait Charades

SAY: **Think about something you can't wait for, something you're really looking forward to. Think about how to act it out without talking. It might be a holiday, getting a pet, having your own money, getting a place on a sports team, flying in a plane, playing a musical instrument, or jumping off a high diving platform. It can be anything you're really looking forward to, whether tomorrow, next week, or way out in the future.** Ask a volunteer to stand up and act out what she's anticipating. Let the rest of the session guess what she's acting out. Let everyone who wants to act have the opportunity.

SAY: **We know when some things we're anticipating and looking forward to will happen. But other things we don't know. Let's dig into God's Word and learn about something that's going to happen, but no one knows when.**

Focus
Jesus is coming soon!

Explore His Word

❷ Use these activities to help children **describe what Revelation says about Jesus' return.**

Bible Background for the Teacher

The apostle John referred to himself as a 'brother and companion in the suffering' (Revelation 1:9). John received the visions recorded in Revelation while under Roman imprisonment on Patmos—an island 60 miles southwest of Ephesus. Although Christians of John's day were facing martyrdom, the symbolic messages of Revelation encourage suffering Christians of all eras to remain faithful until Jesus returns (vv. 1-3; 2:10). Christ's coming will be soon (1:1, 3; 3:11; 22:12, 20). However, 'soon' isn't as much a measurement of time as it is a word of certainty and expectation. The faithful find strength at the thought of the Lord's sure return. For the unfaithful, Jesus' coming will be as unexpected as a thief (3:3). Though the time of Christ's return is unknown (Mark 13:32), it should not be unexpected: 'But you, brothers and sisters, are not in darkness so that this day should surprise you like a thief' (1 Thessalonians 5:4).

At Christ's ascension, the angels promised that 'this same Jesus, who has been taken from you into heaven, will come back in the same way you have seen him go into heaven' (Acts 1:11). Revelation 1:7 confirms this truth: 'Look, he is coming with the clouds, and 'every eye will see him." When Jesus comes He will reward 'each person according to what they have done' (22:12). The faithful are described as those who have 'washed their robes and made them white in the blood of the Lamb' (7:14; see 22:14). They will 'have the right to the tree of life and may go through the gates into the city' (22:14). After Adam and Eve sinned, they were denied access to the Garden of Eden (Genesis 3:22-24). When Jesus returns, perfect fellowship with God will be restored. So, with John, we plead: 'Come, Lord Jesus' (Revelation 22:20).

Bible Exploration   Revelation 1:1-3, 7-8; 2:10b; 3:3, 11; 22:12-14, 16, 20-21

SAY: **God prepared for salvation, sent salvation, and now offers salvation to all people. God's story doesn't end. It continues with us!**

Have children turn in their Bibles to Revelation 1:1-2, and have volunteers read the verses aloud. SAY: **The book of Revelation is a book of Prophecy because it points to the return of Jesus. John wrote the book of Revelation while he was exiled, or banished, to the small island of Patmos. While John was there, God sent an angel to John, who gave John a glimpse of Heaven.** Ask a volunteer to stand by the map and point out Patmos. The volunteer can attach the John figure by Patmos. **This is where we pick up God's story.**

Ask children to come up with actions they would like to do for these words: Jesus/Lord; angel; Word of God/words of prophecy; coming; crown; Alpha and Omega/First and Last/Beginning and End. Once decided on, practice the actions together. SAY: **You can follow along as I read from Revelation, or you can just listen. When you hear the words you created actions for, do those actions.** You could have a volunteer stand and lead the children in doing the actions. Read Revelation 1:1-3, 7-8; 2:10b; 3:3, 11; 22:12-14, 16, 20-21 aloud. Be sure to pause slightly after words children will do actions for.

ASK: **When is Jesus coming back?** (soon; we don't know)
How will Jesus return? (with the clouds; like a thief)

Hand out Activity Page *Jesus Will Return!* Read the instructions. Then have volunteers read the first three questions and fill in the blanks. (Answers: 1=John; 2=near; 3=clouds, eye) Then read the instructions for the next section. Tell children they can work on this section by themselves or pair up and work on it with a friend. When children have finished, ask volunteers to read the sentences and tell whether they're true or false. If a sentence is false, children should tell how to change it to make it true. (Answers: 1=F: God will give us life; 2=F: we don't know when He will return; 3=T; 4=T; 5=T; 6=F: He's coming soon!)

SAY: **Look at the picture on the activity page and notice the different expressions people have.**

ASK: **Why do you think some people are smiling and filled with joy, while others are sad?** (Christians are ready for Jesus' return and will be glad when He returns; others don't know Jesus and are not ready for his return.)

SAY: **Though we don't know when, Jesus *is* coming soon! Let's be ready!**

Materials

Bible Map on page 244, reusable adhesive, Bibles, Activity Page *Jesus Will Return* on page 314, pencils

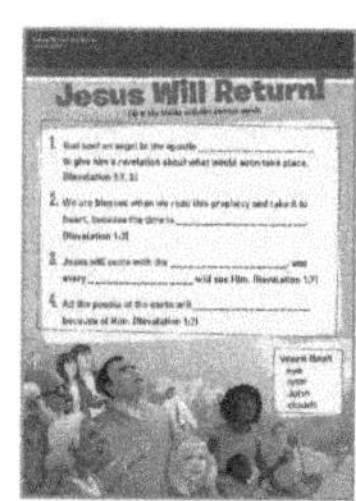
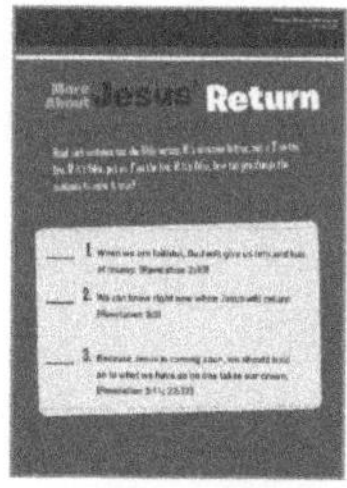
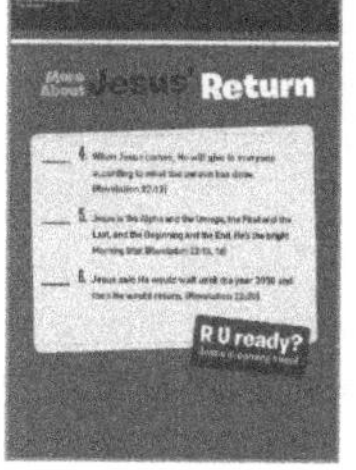

Media Option

Go to www.biblegateway.com or a similar website and play a dramatised reading of the Bible verses.

Jesus Will Return **Session 51**

Make It Real

3 Use this activity to help children **desire to be ready for Jesus' return.**

Materials
none

Game

Teaching Tips
If you have a large session, form more than one circle.

You may have some children interested in learning more about being ready for Jesus' return. See the HeartShaper website: *www.heartshaper.co.uk* for help in discussing this with your children.

I Want to Be Ready

Ask children to form a circle. SAY: **Get one thing in mind that you want to be ready for. It might be something we've already talked about, such as a holiday or joining a sports team, or it can be something else.** Start the game by saying something you want to be ready for. The child on your right should say what you said, then add what she wants to be ready for. Keep going around the circle like this. SAY: **We all have different things we want to be ready for.**

ASK: **Why should we want to be ready for Jesus' return?** Encourage lots of children to offer ideas. (I believe in Jesus and believe He's coming back; I want to live in Heaven with Jesus; Jesus is coming soon, but we don't know when.)

If Jesus comes today or tomorrow or next week, will you be ready? Encourage children to think about this, but not reply out loud.

SAY: **I hope you want to be ready for Jesus' return. It's the most important thing you can ever get ready for. When you desire to be ready for Jesus' return, you'll make Jesus and everything *He's* about what *your* life is about.**

Live It Out

4 Use this activity to help children **plan to be ready for Jesus' return.**

Materials
sunglasses (1 pair per child), index cards, pencils

Discover

Look at Life Differently

SAY: **Think about who Jesus is—the First and the Last, the Alpha and the Omega, the Almighty. There is no one greater than Him. When you understand *who* Jesus is and realise that Jesus is coming soon, you'll want to be ready for His return. Let's plan to live each day as if that's the day Jesus is coming.** Distribute sunglasses to each child, along with an index card and pencil. Tell them to spread out in the room and put on their sunglasses. **Just as sunglasses make things look a little different, sometimes we need to look at our lives differently, seeing things in a new way. Think about this: If you knew that Jesus was coming back today or tomorrow, would you see things a little differently? What would you do today? Write your answer on the card.** Tell children that this is just between them and God; no one will see their answers.

When children have finished, lead them in a time of prayer. Encourage them to silently talk to God about what they've written. After a brief time of silence, close in prayer.

Jesus Will Return!

Fill in the blanks with the correct words.

1. God sent an angel to the apostle _____________________
to give him a revelation about what would soon take place.
(Revelation 1:1, 2)

2. We are blessed when we read this prophecy and take it to
heart, because the time is _____________________.
(Revelation 1:3)

3. Jesus will come with the _____________________, and
every _________________ will see Him. (Revelation 1:7)

4. All the people of the earth will _____________________
because of Him. (Revelation 1:7)

Word Bank
eye
near
John
clouds

More About Jesus' Return

Read each sentence and the Bible verses. If a sentence is true, put a *T* on the line. If it's false, put an *F* on the line. If it's false, how can you change the sentence to make it true?

_____ **1.** When we are faithful, God will give us lots and lots of money. (Revelation 2:10)

_____ **2.** We can know right now when Jesus will return. (Revelation 3:3)

_____ **3.** Because Jesus is coming soon, we should hold on to what we have so no one takes our crown. (Revelation 3:11; 22:12)

More About Jesus' Return

_____ **4.** When Jesus comes, He will give to everyone according to what the person has done. (Revelation 22:12)

_____ **5.** Jesus is the Alpha and the Omega, the First and the Last, and the Beginning and the End. He's the bright Morning Star. (Revelation 22:13, 16)

_____ **6.** Jesus said He would wait until the year 3050 and then He would return. (Revelation 22:20)

R U ready?
Jesus is coming soon!

Worship and Praise

Session 52

Scripture: Revelation 5:9b, 12b; 11:15-19; 12:10-12; 14:6-7, 13; 15:3b-4; 19:1-2a, 5-7a
Focus: God is worthy of our worship and praise.

Heart to Heart Teacher Devotion

Have you ever been in a large gathering where thousands lifted their praise and worship to God? Imagine joining millions and millions of people in Heaven, lifting our praise and worship to Almighty God. What a roar that will be! 'Hallelujah! For our Lord God Almighty reigns' (Revelation 19:6).

Focus
God is worthy of our worship and praise.

Materials
whiteboard, dry-erase markers and erasers

Game

Focus In

**①** Use this activity to help children **examine the concepts of worship and praise.**

Welcome

Welcome each children warmly by name.

Thinking About Praise and Worship

Divide the session into two teams. In the middle of the board, draw a large stick figure. Above the figure write 'Sports Star'. On one side of the figure write 'Praise' and on the other side write 'Worship'. Ask one team to come up with how people might praise a sports star. Tell them to write their ideas under the word 'Praise'. Ask the other team to come up with how people might worship a sports star. Tell them to write their ideas under the word 'Worship'. Tell teams they'll get 10 points for each good answer. After a few minutes, call time. Read through their answers and assign points. If you have time, do another round, labeling the stick figure a movie star or a singing star.

ASK: **What does it mean to praise someone?** (say good things; express love; express thanks; say words of admiration)
What does it mean to worship someone? (express deep love and devotion; show great respect and honour; express reverence)

SAY: **We probably all say words of praise to others. But whom do we worship? Let's dig into God's Word to see what it says about offering praise and worship.**

Explore His Word

② Use these activities to help children **tell why God is worthy of our worship and praise.**

Bible Background for the Teacher

Though often misinterpreted and misunderstood, Revelation is a practical book. By scrutinizing its details, many miss the common themes that recur throughout the book. One such theme is that God will reward the faithful and punish the unfaithful. Don't be confused by the word *reward*. Salvation can't be earned. Reward isn't given for what we've done, it's for what Jesus did for us at Calvary. Christ purchased us with His blood (Revelation 5:9; 12:11). 'He was pierced for our transgressions, he was crushed for our iniquities; the punishment that brought us peace was on him, and by his wounds we are healed' (Isaiah 53:5). Heaven is the reward that we get because Jesus took our sins.

This reward isn't limited to any specific race, sex, social session, or financial status. Jesus 'purchased for God persons from every tribe and language and people and nation' (Revelation 5:9; also 7:9 and 14:6). Galatians 3:28 says the same thing: 'There is neither Jew nor Gentile, neither slave nor free, nor is there male and female, for you are all one in Christ Jesus.' Truly, the dead are blessed 'who die in the Lord from now on' (Revelation 14:13). The flip side of reward is punishment. Judgment will surely come upon those who embrace wickedness instead of Jesus. 'Fear God and give him glory, because the hour of his judgment has come' (v. 7). 'But woe to the earth and the sea, because the devil has gone down to you! He is filled with fury, because he knows that his time is short' (12:12). The natural response of faithful people is to worship God (Revelation 5:9, 12; 11:15-17). 'Worthy is the Lamb, who was slain, to receive power and wealth and wisdom and strength and honour and glory and praise!' (5:12).

Bible Exploration

Revelation 5:9b, 12b; 11:15-19; 12:10-12; 14:6-7, 13; 15:3b-4; 19:1-2a, 5-7a

Ask children to look in their Bibles at the table of contents and find the book of Revelation. Have children turn in their Bibles to Revelation 5:9b.

> ASK: **Who wrote the book of Revelation?** (John)
>
> **Where was John when he wrote this book?** (Patmos)

Have a volunteer point to Patmos on the map and the figure of John.

SAY: **John had been taken to the island of Patmos because he taught about Jesus even when the Roman government didn't want him to. While John was at Patmos, God sent an angel to John, who gave him a revelation of Heaven.** Have a volunteer point to the 'Jesus will return' icon on the Bible time line. **Last week we learned that Jesus is coming soon. After Jesus returns, the final judgment and redemption will take place. This is where we pick up God's story. What we'll read today will give us a glimpse into what will happen during the final judgment and redemption.** Have volunteers read Revelation 5:9b, 12, while everyone follows along.

> ASK: **Who is the Lamb who was slain, or killed?** (Jesus)
>
> **Why is Jesus worthy of our praise and worship?** (He was slain, and with His blood He purchased people for God.)

Distribute the Activity Page *God Is Worthy!* Read the directions, and have volunteers read the sentences and finish them with the correct answers. (Answers: 1=was slain; 2=has great power; 3=made the heavens and the earth; 4=reigns forever as king)

SAY: **Let's imagine we're in Heaven. God is seated on His throne, and the great multitude is worshipping and praising God. Let's worship with them, because God is worthy of our worship and praise.** Tell children to get into a position that helps them worship God. They might want to stand, kneel, bow, have folded hands, and so forth.

Materials

Bible map and Bible time lines on page 244, reusable adhesive, Bibles, Activity page *God is Worthy!* on page 322, pencils

Discover

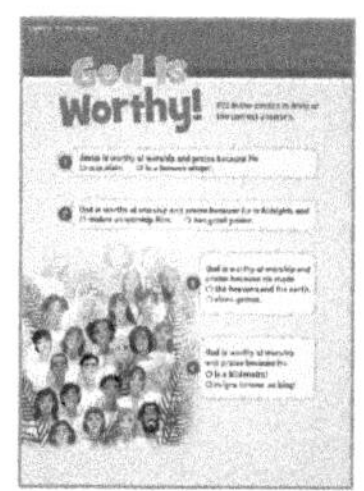

Make It Real

3 Use this activity to help children **discover ways to worship and praise God.**

Materials

Activity page *Worshipping and Praising* on pages 320-321, pencils  Act It Out

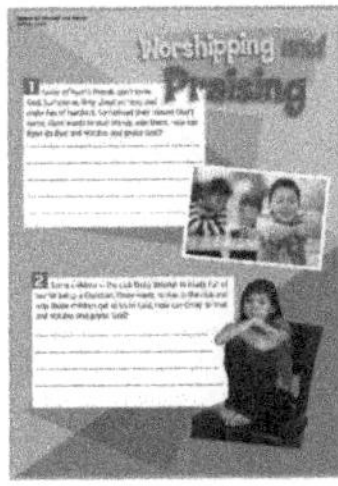 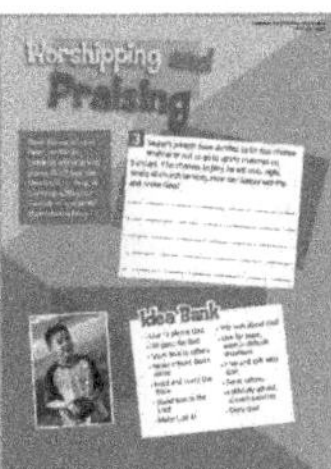

How Can We Worship and Praise?

SAY: **Because we know that God is worthy of our worship and praise, let's discover some ways to do that.** Ask children to look at the Activity Page *Worshipping and Praising*. Read the directions, and have a volunteer read the first situation. Ask volunteers to answer the question. Encourage them to use the Idea Bank for help. (Possible answers: Ryan should stand firm in the Lord, talk well about God, never misuse God's name, do good for God, etc.) Let children work together in pairs or small groups to do the other situations. When children have finished, let volunteers read the situations and tell how they answered the questions.

Ask for volunteers to act out a few of the situations. Let the actors have a few minutes to plan how they will act out their situations. Encourage them to act out how the children decide to give their worship and praise to God. After the children have presented their skits, thank them for their participation. SAY: **When we worship God by talking well about Him and not misusing His name, we're showing great respect, admiration, and reverence for God. When we worship God by loving and serving others, we're expressing our deep love for God. When we worship God by praying and talking with Him, we're saying thanks and showing deep devotion to Him. There are so many ways to worship and praise God. Let's do it because God is worthy of our worship and praise!**

Live It Out

4 Use this activity to help children **worship and praise God.**

Materials

roll paper, markers, Bibles, reusable adhesive  Art

Teaching Tip

If you have a large session, let children work on more than one banner.

 Some children with special needs may prefer working away from the large group. Provide drawing paper and encourage these children to create worship pages that can be added to the room banner.

Worship Banner

Place a long length of roll paper where all the children can work on it. SAY: **One way to worship God is by talking well *about* God. Another way is by talking *with* Him. Let's do both of those things on this paper. Let's make this paper a worship banner.** Tell children to talk well *about* God on the banner by writing words that describe Him, such as 'powerful' and 'awesome'. They can also write about things He has done, such as creating the world. Tell children to talk *with* God on the banner by writing prayers that worship and praise Him. The prayers can be any length they desire. You can also encourage children to look in their Bibles for inspiration about what to write, specifically the Scriptures studied today.

When children have finished with the banner, display it on a wall. Ask everyone to gather around it. Read some of the things children wrote. SAY: **Look at the banner and choose a few things that you want to say to God right now. Let's worship and praise God because only God is worthy of our worship and praise. Please bow your heads and talk to God.** After a brief time of silence, close in prayer.

Worshipping and Praising

1 Some of Ryan's friends don't know God. Sometimes they cheat on tests and make fun of teachers. Sometimes they misuse God's name. Ryan wants to stay friends with them. How can Ryan do that and worship and praise God?

____

____

____

____

____

2 Some children in the club Emily belongs to made fun of her for being a Christian. Emily wants to stay in the club and help those children get to know God. How can Emily do that and worship and praise God?

____

____

____

____

____

Worshipping and Praising

Read the situations. How can these children worship and praise God? See the Idea Bank for help, or come up with your own ideas and write them on the lines.

3 Sanjay's parents have decided to let him choose whether or not to go to sports matches on Sundays. If he chooses to play, he will miss eight weeks of church services. How can Sanjay worship and praise God?

____

____

____

____

____

Idea Bank

- Live to please God
- Do good for God
- Show love to others
- Never misuse God's name
- Read and study the Bible
- Stand firm in the Lord
- Make God #1
- Talk well about God
- Live for Jesus, even in difficult situations
- Pray and talk with God
- Serve others
- Faithfully attend church services
- Obey God

God Is Worthy!

Fill in the circles in front of the correct answers.

1 Jesus is worthy of worship and praise because He
○ was slain.   ○ is a famous singer.

2 God is worthy of worship and praise because He is Almighty and
○ makes us worship Him.   ○ has great power.

3 God is worthy of worship and praise because He made
○ the heavens and the earth.
○ video games.

4 God is worthy of worship and praise because He
○ is a billionaire!
○ reigns forever as king!

Appendix

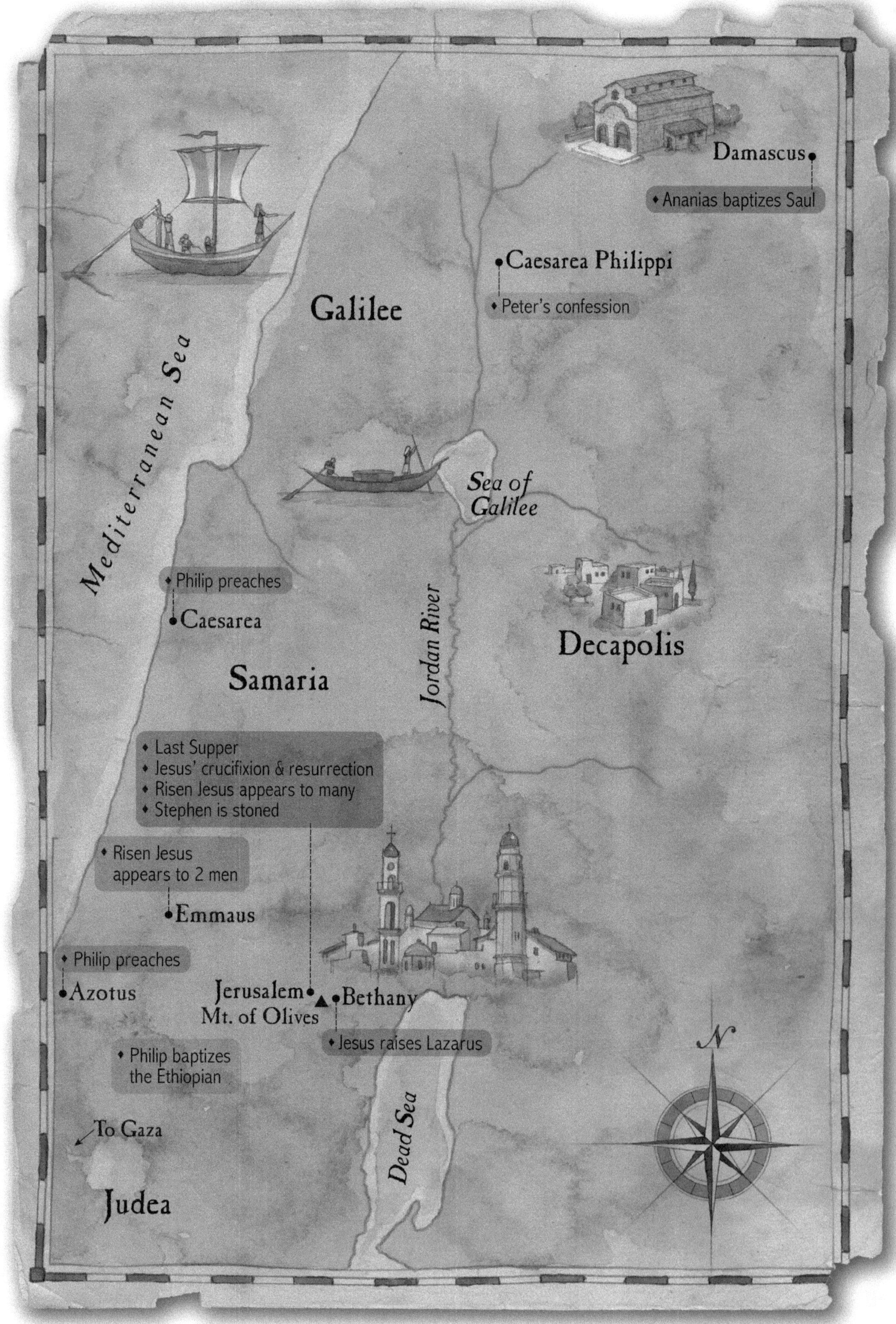
Damascus
♦ Ananias baptizes Saul
♦ Caesarea Philippi
♦ Peter's confession
Galilee
Mediterranean Sea
Sea of Galilee
Jordan River
Decapolis
♦ Philip preaches
Caesarea
Samaria
♦ Last Supper
♦ Jesus' crucifixion & resurrection
♦ Risen Jesus appears to many
♦ Stephen is stoned
♦ Risen Jesus appears to 2 men
Emmaus
♦ Philip preaches
Azotus
Jerusalem
Mt. of Olives
Bethany
♦ Jesus raises Lazarus
♦ Philip baptizes the Ethiopian
To Gaza
Dead Sea
Judea
N

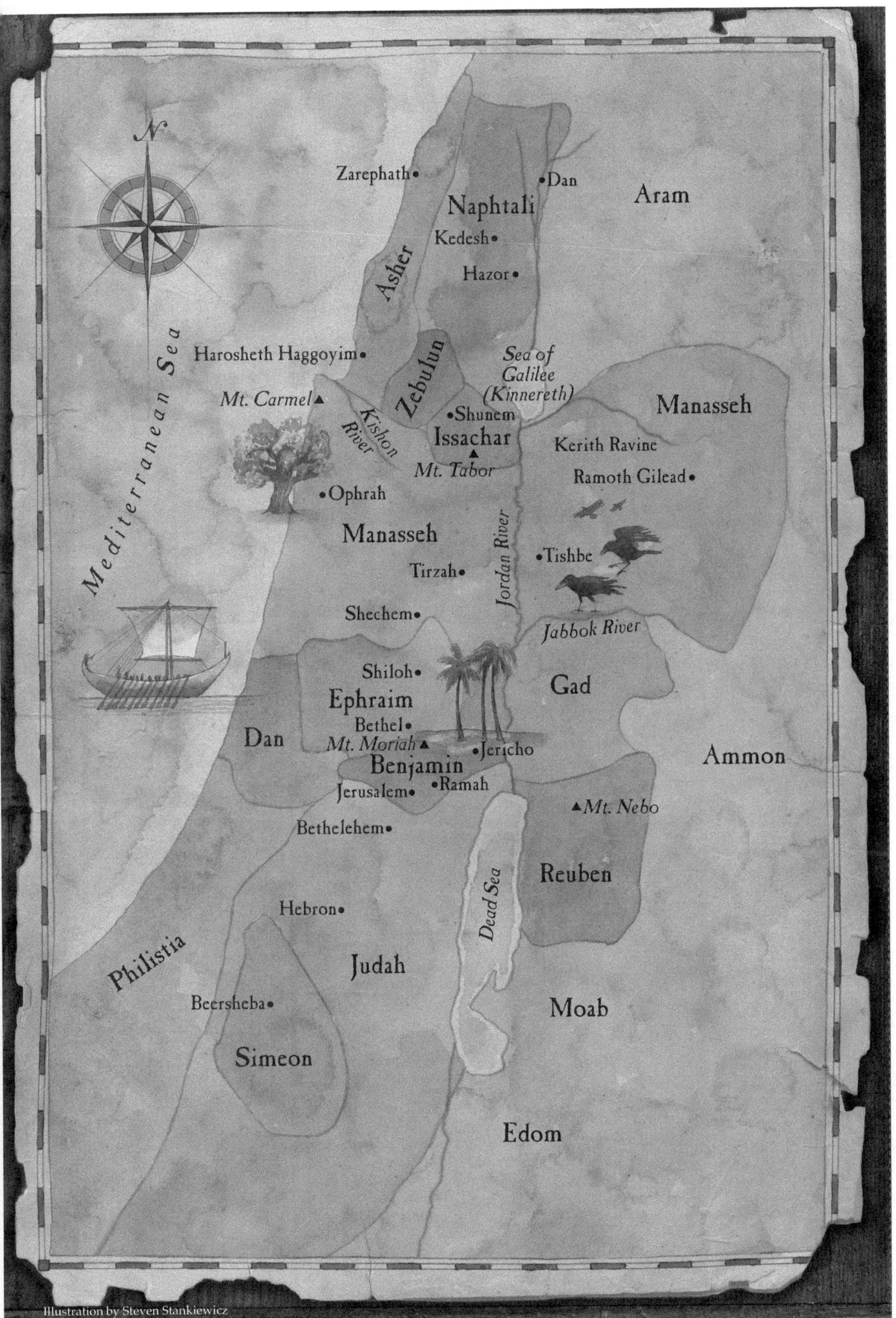

HeartShaper Primary Blue Edition, Activity page
Permission is granted to reproduce this page for ministry purposes only—not for resale.

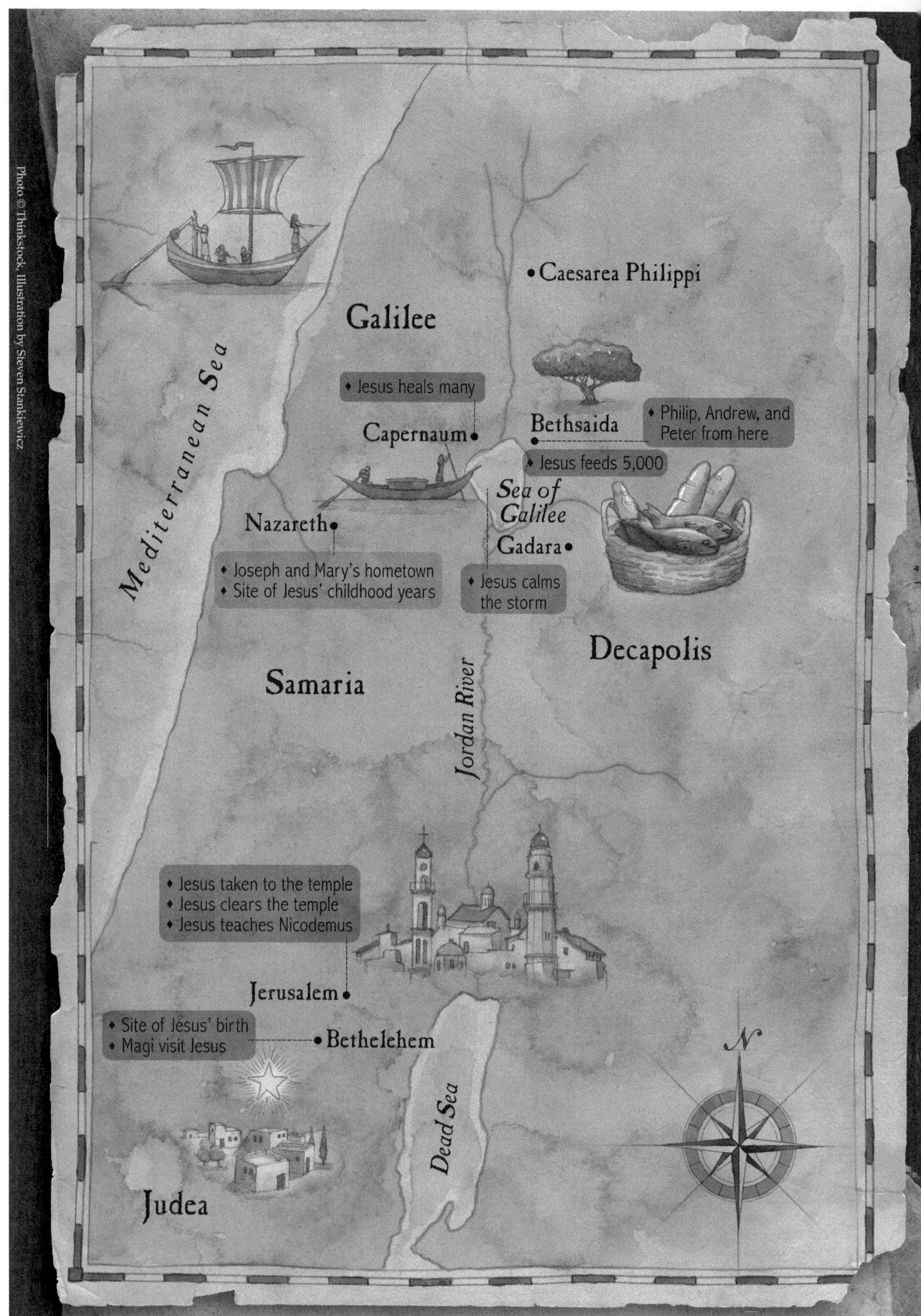
Photo © Thinkstock. Illustration by Steven Stankiewicz
Galilee
Caesarea Philippi
Mediterranean Sea
Jesus heals many
Bethsaida
Philip, Andrew, and Peter from here
Capernaum
Jesus feeds 5,000
Sea of Galilee
Nazareth
Gadara
Joseph and Mary's hometown
Site of Jesus' childhood years
Jesus calms the storm
Decapolis
Samaria
Jordan River
Jesus taken to the temple
Jesus clears the temple
Jesus teaches Nicodemus
Jerusalem
Site of Jesus' birth
Magi visit Jesus
Bethelehem
Dead Sea
N
Judea